AutoCAD Drawing Setup Roadmap

See Chapters 4 and 5 for details of each step.

Ribbon/Application Menu	Classic Menu	Command	Description
Model Space			
1. Application menu⇨New⇨ Drawing	File⇨New	NEW (Ctrl+N)	Specifies a template drawing (DWT file)
2. Application menu⇨ Drawing Utilities⇨Units	Format⇨Units	UNITS	Specifies linear and angular units
3. None	Format⇨ Drawing Limits	LIMITS	Specifies working area
4. View tab⇨Navigate panel⇨ Zoom drop-down flyout⇨All	View⇨Zoom⇨All	ZOOM, All	Zooms to limits
5. None	Tools⇨ Drafting Settings	DSETTINGS	Specifies snap and grid spacings
6. None	None	LTSCALE	Sets linetype scale
7. Home tab⇨Annotation panel⇨ Dimension Style	Format⇨ Dimension Style	DIMSTYLE	Sets dimension scale (on the Fit tab)
8. Application menu⇨Drawing Utilities⇨Drawing Properties	File⇨ Drawing Properties	DWGPROPS	Enters drawing informational properties
Paper Space			
9. None	Tools⇨Wizards⇨ Create Layout	LAYOUTWIZARD	Creates a paper space layout
10. Quick Access toolbar⇨Save	File⇨Save	QSAVE (Ctrl+S)	Saves the drawing

Drawing Scale and Limits Charts: Feet and Inches

Drawing Scale	8-½" x 11"	11" x 17"	24" x 36"	30" x 42"	36" x 48"
1/16" = 1'–0"	136' x 176'	176' x 272'	384' x 576'	480' x 672'	576' x 768'
1/8" = 1'–0"	68' x 88'	88' x 136'	192' x 288'	240' x 336'	288' x 384'
1/4" = 1'–0"	34' x 44'	44' x 68'	96' x 144'	120' x 168'	144' x 192'
1/2" = 1'–0"	17' x 22'	22' x 34'	48' x 72'	60' x 84'	72' x 96'
3/4" = 1'–0"	11'–4" x 14'–8"	14'–8" x 22'–8"	32' x 48'	40' x 56'	48' x 64'
1" = 1'–0"	8'–6" x 11'	11' x 17'	24' x 36'	30' x 42'	36' x 48'
1-1/2" = 1'–0"	5'–8" x 7'–4"	7'–4" x 11'–4"	16' x 24'	20' x 28'	24' x 32'
3" = 1'–0"	2'–10" x 3'–8"	3'–8" x 5'–8"	8' x 12'	10' x 14'	12' x 16'

For Dummies: Bestselling Book Series for Beginners

Ten Top AutoCAD Keyboard Shortcuts

Keyboard Shortcut	Command	Purpose
Ctrl+S	QSAVE	Saves the drawing
Ctrl+O	OPEN	Displays the Select File dialog box
Ctrl+P	PLOT	Displays the Plot dialog box
Ctrl+Tab	None	Switches to the next open drawing
Ctrl+PgUp/Ctrl+PgDn	None	Switches to the previous/next tab in the current drawing
F2	TEXTSCR	Toggles the AutoCAD Text Window on and off
F3	OSNAP	Toggles running object snap mode on and off
F8	ORTHO	Toggles ortho mode on and off
F9	SNAP	Toggles snap mode on and off
F10	POLAR	Toggles polar mode on and off

Drawing Scale and Limits Charts: Millimeters

Drawing Scale	210 x 297 mm	297 x 420 mm	420 x 594 mm	594 x 841 mm	841 x 1,189 mm
1:200	42,000 x 59,400 mm	59,400 x 84,000 mm	84,000 x 118,800 mm	118,800 x 168,200 mm	168,200 x 237,800 mm
1:100	21,000 x 29,700 mm	29,700 x 42,000 mm	42,000 x 59,400 mm	59,400 x 84,100 mm	84,100 x 118,900 mm
1:50	10,500 x 14,850 mm	14,850 x 21,000 mm	21,000 x 29,700 mm	29,700 x 42,050 mm	42,050 x 59,450 mm
1:20	4,200 x 5,940 mm	5,940 x 8,400 mm	8,400 x 11,880 mm	11,880 x 16,820 mm	16,820 x 23,780 mm
1:10	2,100 x 2,970 mm	2,970 x 4,200 mm	4,200 x 5,940 mm	5,940 x 8,410 mm	8,410 x 11,890 mm
1:5	1,050 x 1,485 mm	1,485 x 2,100 mm	2,100 x 2,970 mm	2,970 x 4,205 mm	4,205 x 5,945 mm

For Dummies: Bestselling Book Series for Beginners

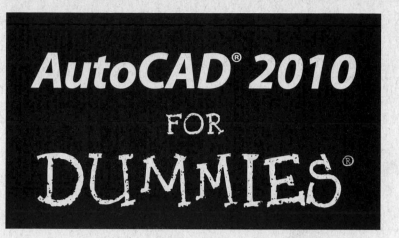

AutoCAD® 2010 FOR DUMMIES®

by David Byrnes

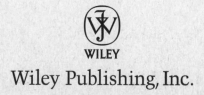

WILEY

Wiley Publishing, Inc.

AutoCAD® 2010 For Dummies®

Published by
Wiley Publishing, Inc.
111 River Street
Hoboken, NJ 07030-5774
www.wiley.com

WILEY

About the Author

David Byrnes is one of those grizzled old-timers you'll find mentioned every so often in *AutoCAD 2010 For Dummies*. He began his drafting career on the boards in 1979 and discovered computer-assisted doodling (you always wondered what CAD stood for, didn't you?) shortly thereafter. He first learned AutoCAD with version 1.4, around the time when personal computers switched from steam to diesel power. Dave is based in Vancouver, British Columbia, and is gainfully employed as a civil/structural technician at a major international consulting engineering company. He has been an AutoCAD consultant and trainer since 1988, since which he has been a contributing author to ten books on AutoCAD. He taught AutoCAD and other computer graphics applications for fifteen years at Emily Carr Institute of Art + Design and British Columbia Institute of Technology in Vancouver. Dave has been with the *AutoCAD For Dummies* series for longer than he cares to remember. He was technical editor for four *AutoCAD For Dummies* and two *AutoCAD LT For Dummies* titles and then coauthor of two more *AutoCAD For Dummies* editions as well as the first edition of the *AutoCAD and AutoCAD LT All-in-One For Dummies*.

Dedication

I left the bohemian lifestyle of the AutoCAD consultant at the beginning of 2009 and rejoined the engineering company I last worked for in 1988 (luckily they'd forgotten all about that chandelier). Working full-time (oh! the horror!) and keeping up with AutoCAD so I can revise this book has made me somewhat inaccessible for 3 months a year, and I'm forever grateful to Annie and Delia, still and always the two women in my life, who remind me there are other things besides keyboards and mice (and sometimes they have to try *really* hard).

Author's Acknowledgments

Thanks, first of all, to Mark Middlebrook for bringing me into the *AutoCAD For Dummies* world. Mark asked me to tech edit both *AutoCAD 2000 For Dummies and AutoCAD LT 2000 For Dummies* and their following four editions, then to join him as co-author, and finally to take over the title altogether. I hope my torch bearing comes close to the high standards that Mark set, and I wish him well in his new career in the world of fine wine (what, *me* jealous?).

Thanks, too, to colleagues and friends at Autodesk: above all Matt Stein, Nate Bartley, Shaan Hurley, and Bud Schroeder, who never seem to mind being asked even the dumbest questions, and Denis Cadu and Jim Quanci, who always come through with software and technical support almost before I ask for it. And speaking of colleagues, thanks to my cubicle-mates at Sandwell for showing me how things are done in the *real* world of engineering.

My thanks also to the good people at Wiley. Acquisitions Editor Kyle Looper was a consistently reliable source of calm but firm direction. It was a pleasure to work with project editor Pat O'Brien and copy editor Jennifer Riggs. And by no means least (but someone has to bring up the rear), thanks to Lee Ambrosius for once again taking on the tech-editing job. Lee's expertise is well known and respected in the AutoCAD community, and I'm delighted to have him along as technical overseer.

Publisher's Acknowledgments

We're proud of this book; please send us your comments through our online registration form located at www.dummies.com/register/.

Some of the people who helped bring this book to market include the following:

Acquisitions, Editorial, and Media Development

Project Editor: Pat O'Brien

Acquisitions Editor: Kyle Looper

Copy Editor: Jennifer Riggs

Technical Reviewer: Lee Ambrosius

Editorial Manager: Kevin Kirschner

Editorial Assistant: Amanda Foxworth

Sr. Editorial Assistant: Cherie Case

Cartoons: Rich Tennant
(www.the5thwave.com)

Composition Services

Project Coordinator: Katherine Key

Layout and Graphics: Carrie A. Cesavice, Reuben W. Davis, Melissa K. Jester, SD Jumper, Christin Swinford, Ronald Terry

Proofreaders: Laura Albert, David Faust, Kathy Simpson

Indexer: Valerie Haynes Perry

Publishing and Editorial for Technology Dummies

Richard Swadley, Vice President and Executive Group Publisher

Andy Cummings, Vice President and Publisher

Mary Bednarek, Executive Acquisitions Director

Mary C. Corder, Editorial Director

Publishing for Consumer Dummies

Diane Graves Steele, Vice President and Publisher

Composition Services

Debbie Stailey, Director of Composition Services

Contents at a Glance

Table of Contents

Introduction

*I*t's amazing to think that AutoCAD came into being more than a quarter of a *century* ago (AutoCAD 2009 was marked by Autodesk as the 25th Anniversary Edition), at a time when most people thought that personal computers weren't capable of industrial-strength tasks like CAD. (The acronym stands for Computer-Aided Drafting, Computer-Aided Design, or both, depending on whom you talk to.) What's equally amazing to the grizzled old-timer writing these words is the fact that many of today's hotshot AutoCAD users weren't even born when the program first hit the street! It's almost as amazing that, 25 years and counting after its birth, AutoCAD remains the king of the microcomputer CAD hill by a tall margin, making it one of the longest-lived PC programs ever. It's conceivable that the long-term future of CAD may belong to special-purpose, 3D-based software such as the Autodesk Inventor and Revit programs, but for the present and the near future anyway, AutoCAD is where the CAD action is.

AutoCAD has grown more complex over the years, in part to keep up with the increasing complexity of the design and drafting processes that AutoCAD is intended to serve. It's not enough just to draw nice-looking lines anymore. If you want to play CAD with the big boys and girls, you need to carefully organize the objects you draw, their properties, and the files in which they reside. You need to coordinate your CAD work with other people in your office who will be working on or making use of the same drawings. You need to be savvy about shipping drawings around via the Internet.

AutoCAD 2010 provides the tools for doing all these things, but it's not always easy to figure out which hammer to pick up or which nail to bang on first. With this book, you have an excellent chance of creating a presentable, usable, printable, and sharable drawing on your first or second try without putting a T square through your computer screen in frustration.

What's Not (And What Is) in This Book

Unlike many other *For Dummies* books, this one *does* sometimes tell you to consult the official software documentation — such as it is. AutoCAD is just too big and complicated for a single book to attempt to describe it completely.

AutoCAD is also too big and complicated for me to cover every feature. I don't address advanced topics like database connectivity, customization, 3D modeling, or programming, in the interest of bringing you a book of a reasonable

size — one that you'll read rather than stick on your shelf with those other thousand-page tomes!

Autodesk likes to keep its users (and us authors!) guessing about new features in future releases of the software. AutoCAD 2009 surprised users and authors alike with a totally revamped user interface, replacing the drop-down menus and toolbars of previous versions with a Microsoft Office 2007-style Ribbon (happily, Autodesk doesn't *force* its users to adopt the new look like Microsoft does — there's still an "AutoCAD Classic" interface available). In AutoCAD 2010, the new interface receives some gentle tweaking, with a much more focused Application Menu replacing 2009's Menu Browser (unfortunately, however, the new Application Menu doesn't make things any easier to find).

Along with a whole bunch of nice tweaks which I highlight in the chapters ahead, AutoCAD 2010 comes with two significant new features — parametric drawing, which I introduce in Chapter 19, and organic (or free-form) 3D modeling which — as I mention in the preceding paragraph — I don't cover at all. My take on AutoCAD's free-form modeling is that it's meant for conceptual design. The objects created are mesh-based and therefore not precise enough for manufacturing, but they're fine for visualizing things. Parametric drawing, on the other hand, is this release's killer feature. Imagine changing a dimension and having your lines and circles redraw themselves! Well, you can do it in AutoCAD 2010 (and, to a limited extent, in AutoCAD LT 2010).

This book focuses on AutoCAD 2010 and addresses its slightly less-capable but much lower-priced sibling, AutoCAD LT 2010. I do occasionally mention differences with previous versions, sometimes going back as far as the highly popular AutoCAD Release 14, so that everyone has some context and upgraders can more readily understand the differences. I also mention the important differences between full AutoCAD and AutoCAD LT so that you'll know what you — or your LT-using colleagues — are missing. This book does *not* cover the discipline-specific features in AutoCAD-based products such as AutoCAD Architecture 2010 or AutoCAD Mechanical 2010, except for some general discussion in Chapter 1, but most of the information in this book applies to the general-purpose AutoCAD features in the AutoCAD 2010–based versions of those programs as well.

Who Do I Think You Are?

AutoCAD has a large, loyal, dedicated group of long-time users. This book is not for the sort of people who have been using AutoCAD for a decade or more, who plan their vacation time around Autodesk University, or who consider 1,000-page-plus technical tomes about AutoCAD to be pleasure reading. This book *is* for people who want to get going quickly with AutoCAD but who also know the importance of developing proper CAD techniques from the beginning.

However, you do need to have some idea of how to use your computer system before tackling AutoCAD — and this book. You need to have a computer system with AutoCAD or AutoCAD LT (preferably the 2010 version). A printer or plotter and a connection to the Internet will be big helps, too.

You also need to know how to use your version of Windows to copy and delete files, create a folder, and find a file. You need to know how to use a mouse to select (highlight) or to choose (activate) commands, how to close a window, and how to minimize and maximize windows. Make sure that you're familiar with the basics of your operating system before you start with AutoCAD.

How This Book Is Organized

Appearances can be deceptive. For example, had you wandered into my office and seen the apparently random piles of stuff that covered my desk while I was writing this book, you might wonder how I could possibly organize a sentence, let alone an entire book. But, given a suitable degree of concerted thought, I know *exactly* where to put my hands on that list of new dimension variables, my bag of 1/2" binder clips, or the rest of that bagel and cream cheese I started at coffee break.

I hope you'll find that the book also reflects some concerted thought about how to present AutoCAD in a way that's both easy-to-dip-into and smoothly-flowing-from-beginning-to-end.

The organization of this book into parts — collections of related chapters — is one of the most important, uh, *parts* of this book. You really can get to know AutoCAD one piece at a time, and each part represents a group of closely related topics. The order of parts also says something about priority; yes, you have my permission to ignore the stuff in later parts until you've mastered most of the stuff in the early ones. This kind of building-block approach can be especially valuable in a program as powerful as AutoCAD.

The following sections describe the parts that the book breaks down into.

Part 1: AutoCAD 101

Need to know your way around the AutoCAD screen? Why does AutoCAD even exist, anyway? What are all the different AutoCAD-based products that Autodesk sells, and should you be using one of them — for example, AutoCAD LT — instead of AutoCAD? Is everything so slooow because it's supposed to be slow, or do you have too wimpy a machine to use this wonder of modern-day computing? And why do you have to do this stuff in the first place?

Part I answers all these questions and more. This part also includes what may seem like a great deal of excruciating detail about setting up a new drawing in AutoCAD. But what's even more excruciating is doing your setup work incorrectly and then feeling as if AutoCAD is fighting you every step of the way. With a little drawing setup work done in advance, it won't.

Part II: Let There Be Lines

In this part, you discover some essential concepts, including object properties and CAD precision techniques. I know that you're raring to make some drawings, but if you don't get a handle on this stuff early on, you'll be terminally confused when you try to draw and edit objects. If you want to make drawings that look good, plot good, and *are* good, read this stuff!

After the concepts preamble, the bulk of this part covers the trio of activities that you'll probably spend most of your time in AutoCAD doing: drawing objects, editing them, and zooming and panning to see them better on the screen. These are the things that you do in order to create the *geometry* — that is, the CAD representations of the objects in the real world that you're designing. By the end of Part II, you should be pretty good at geometry, even if your ninth-grade math teacher told you otherwise.

Part III: If Drawings Could Talk

CAD drawings don't live on lines alone — most of them require quite a bit of text, dimensioning, and hatching in order to make the design intent clear to the poor chump who has to build your amazing creation. (Whoever said "a picture is worth a thousand words" must not have counted up the number of words on the average architectural drawing!) This part shows you how to add these essential features to your drawings.

After you've gussied up your drawing with text, dimensions, and hatching, you'll probably want to create a snapshot of it to show off to your client, contractor, or grandma. Normal people call this process *printing,* but CAD people call it *plotting.* Whatever you decide to call it, I show you how to do it.

Part IV: Advancing with AutoCAD

A good CAD user, like a good kindergartner, plays well with others. AutoCAD encourages this behavior with a host of drawing- and data-sharing features. Blocks, external reference files, and raster images encourage reuse of parts of drawings, entire drawings, and bitmap image files. You can create symbols with changeable text or appearance, and you can apply parametric "rules" to drawing objects so they help maintain design intent. This part of the book

ends by explaining how to use AutoCAD's Internet features to enable sharing of drawings well beyond your hard disk and local network.

The drawing- and data-sharing features in AutoCAD take you way beyond old-style, pencil-and-paper design and drafting. After you've discovered how to apply the techniques in this part, you'll be well on your way to full CAD nerd-hood. (You may want to warn your family beforehand.)

Part V: The Part of Tens

This part contains a concise catalog of differences between AutoCAD and AutoCAD LT, and lists of resources and settings that can make the time you spend in AutoCADland more enjoyable. There's a lot of meat packed into these three chapters — juicy tidbits from years of drafting, experimentation, and fist-shaking at things that don't work right — not to mention years of compulsive list-making. I hope that these lists help you get on the right track quickly and stay there.

Icons Used in This Book

Throughout this book, I point out certain morsels of particularly important or useful information by placing handy little icons in the margin. Naturally, different icons indicate different types of information:

This icon tells you that herein lies a pointed insight that can save you time and trouble as you use AutoCAD. In many cases, Tip paragraphs act as a funnel on AutoCAD's impressive but sometimes overwhelming flexibility: After telling you all the ways that you *can* do something, I tell you the way that you *should* do it in most cases.

The Technical Stuff icon points out places where I delve a little more deeply into AutoCAD's inner workings or point out something that most people don't need to know most of the time. These paragraphs definitely are not required reading the first time through, so if you come to one of them at a time when you've reached your techie detail threshold, feel free to skip over it.

This icon points out text that tells you how to stay out of trouble when living close to the edge. Failure to heed its message may have unpleasant consequences for you or your drawing — or both.

There's a lot to remember when you're using AutoCAD, so I've remembered to remind you not to forget about some of those things that you should remember. These paragraphs usually refer to a crucial point earlier in the chapter or in a previous chapter. So if you're reading sequentially, a Remember paragraph

serves as a friendly reminder. If you're not reading sequentially, this kind of paragraph may help you realize that you need to review a central concept or technique before proceeding.

This icon points to new stuff in AutoCAD 2010 (and sometimes AutoCAD LT 2010). It's mostly designed for people who are somewhat familiar with a previous version of AutoCAD and want to be alerted to what's new in this version. New AutoCAD users starting out their CAD working lives with AutoCAD 2010 will find this stuff interesting, too — especially when they can show off their new book learnin' to the grizzled AutoCAD veterans in the office who don't yet know about all the cool, new features.

This icon highlights text that shows the differences between AutoCAD LT and AutoCAD. If you're using AutoCAD LT, you'll find out what you're missing compared to "full" AutoCAD. If your friend is using LT, you'll know where to look to find stuff in AutoCAD to brag about.

A Few Conventions — Just in Case

You can probably figure out for yourself all the information in this section, but here are the details just in case.

Commanding from the keyboard

Text you type into the program at the command line, in a dialog box, in a text box, and so on appears in **boldface type**. Examples of AutoCAD prompts appear in a `special typeface`, as does any other text in the book that echoes a message, a word, or one or more lines of text that actually appear on-screen. Sequences of prompts that appear in the AutoCAD command line area have a shaded background, like so:

```
Specify lower left corner or [ON/OFF] <0.0000,0.0000>:
```

Many of the figures — especially in Chapters 8 through 11 — also show AutoCAD command line sequences that demonstrate AutoCAD's prompts and example responses.

Many AutoCAD commands have *aliases* — shortcut (fewer-letter) versions for the benefit of those who like to type commands at the AutoCAD command line. In this book, I show command names in uppercase letters. Chapters throughout the book include tables listing, respectively, the most commonly used drawing and editing commands, and in these tables I list both the full command name and its alias in parentheses; for example, LINE (L), ARRAY (AR), and so forth. If you're using the keyboard to enter commands, this means you can type either **LINE** or simply **L** and then press the Enter key

to execute the command. You can view a list of all the command aliases by typing **ALIASEDIT** (not in AutoCAD LT) — *but just look, and be careful not to change anything!*

Tying things up with the Ribbon

As you've noticed if you've skimmed through the book and looked at a few of the figures, AutoCAD 2010 doesn't look like earlier releases you may be familiar with. Throughout the book, I tell you where to find commands on the new Office 2007–style Application Menu and Ribbon interface. (The Ribbon is organized into a series of task-based tabs, and each tab has a number of panels containing specific tool buttons.)

Where to Go from Here

If you read this Introduction, you're like me — you like to read. (The cut-to-the-chase people tend to flip to the index right away and look up what they need to know at that instant.) If you're a total AutoCAD newbie, you can read this book in order, from front to back; it follows a straightforward route from setting up your drawing environment, to outputting your masterworks to hard copy, to sharing your work with others. If you're an experienced user, you'll probably be one of those index flippers looking for the missing information you need to complete a specific task. You can probably find the index on your own, but I encourage you to browse through the book anyway, with highlighter or sticky notes in hand, so you can find those particularly important places when you need them again. If you're competent in most areas of AutoCAD and pretty familiar with the previous version, look for the New In 2010 icons in the margins to find out the latest features you never knew you couldn't live without. Whichever route you choose, I hope you enjoy your time with *AutoCAD 2010 For Dummies*. And . . . *you're off!*

Part I
AutoCAD 101

The 5th Wave By Rich Tennant

"The Arc command? Guy in the next cubicle
seems to know a lot about that."

In this part . . .

AutoCAD 2010 is more than just another drawing program; it's a complete environment for drafting and design. So if you're new to AutoCAD, you need to know several things to get off to a good start – especially how to use the command line area and how to set up your drawing properly. These key techniques are described in this part of the book.

If you've used earlier versions of AutoCAD, you'll be most interested in the high points of the new release, including some newer interface components. The lowdown on what's new is here, too.

Chapter 1

Introducing AutoCAD and AutoCAD LT

Maybe you're one of the few remaining holdouts who continue to practice the ancient art of manual drafting with pencil and vellum. If so, I must tell you, you're a dwindling breed. Or maybe you're completely new to drafting and yearn for the wealth and fame (would I lead you on?) of the drafter's life. Maybe you're an engineer or architect who needs to catch up with the young CAD hotshots in your office. Maybe you tried to use AutoCAD a long time ago, but gave up in frustration or just got rusty. Or maybe you currently use an older release, such as AutoCAD 2006 or even (if you're into antiques) AutoCAD 2000.

Whatever your current situation or motivation, I hope that you enjoy the process of becoming proficient with AutoCAD. Drawing with AutoCAD is challenging at first, but it's a challenge worth meeting. AutoCAD rewards those who think creatively about their work and look for ways to do it better. You can always find out more, discover a new trick, or improve the efficiency and quality of your drawing production.

AutoCAD first hit the bricks in the early 1980s, around the same time as the first IBM PCs. It was offered for a bewildering variety of operating systems, including CP/M (ask your granddad about that one!), various flavors of UNIX, and even Apple's Macintosh. By far the most popular of those early versions was for MS-DOS (your dad can tell you about that one). Eventually, Autodesk settled on Microsoft Windows as the sole operating system for AutoCAD. AutoCAD 2010 is officially supported in all Windows Vista versions (32- and 64-bit) except Home Basic, as well as 32-bit and 64-bit Windows XP Professional and Windows XP Home (32-bit only). Although it's not officially

supported, it can also run in Windows XP Tablet 2005 Edition and make use of the tablet functionality included in Windows Vista (again, except for the Home Basic edition). Trying to do production drafting on a tablet isn't a great idea due to limitations in the graphics system, but I know it works, because I'm running it that way myself!

Because of AutoCAD's MS-DOS heritage and its emphasis on efficiency for production drafters, it's not the easiest program to master, but it *has* gotten easier and more consistent over the past decade or so. AutoCAD is pretty well integrated into the Windows environment now, but you still bump into some vestiges of its MS-DOS legacy — especially the *command line* (that text area lurking at the bottom of the AutoCAD screen — see Chapter 2 for details). But even the command line — oops! command *window* — is kinder and gentler in AutoCAD 2010. This book guides you around the bumps and minimizes the bruises.

Why AutoCAD?

AutoCAD has been around a long time — since 1982, which I suspect, dear readers, is longer than some of you! AutoCAD ushered in the transition from *really expensive* mainframe and minicomputer CAD systems costing tens of thousands of dollars to merely *somewhat expensive* microcomputer CAD programs costing a few thousand dollars.

AutoCAD is, first and foremost, a program for creating *technical drawings:* drawings in which measurements and precision are important because these kinds of drawings often get used to build something. The drawings you create with AutoCAD must adhere to standards established long ago for hand-drafted drawings. The up-front investment to use AutoCAD is certainly more expensive than the investment needed to use pencil and paper, and the learning curve is much steeper, too. So why bother? The key reasons for using AutoCAD rather than pencil and paper are

✔ **Precision:** Creating lines, circles, and other shapes of the exact dimensions is easier with AutoCAD than with pencils.

✔ **Modifiability:** Drawings are much easier to modify on the computer screen than on paper. CAD modifications are a lot cleaner, too.

✔ **Efficiency:** Creating many kinds of drawings is faster with a CAD program — especially drawings that involve repetition, such as floor plans in a multistory building. But that efficiency takes skill and practice. If you're an accomplished pencil-and-paper drafter, don't expect CAD to be faster at first!

Figure 1-1 shows several kinds of drawings in AutoCAD 2010.

Figure 1-1:
Cities,
houses, little
toy trains —
what do you
want to draw
today?

Why choose AutoCAD? AutoCAD is just the starting point of a whole industry of software products designed to work with AutoCAD. Autodesk has helped this process along immensely by designing a series of programming interfaces to AutoCAD (but not, alas, to AutoCAD LT — see the "Seeing the LT" section later in the chapter) that other companies — and Autodesk itself — have used to extend the application. Some of the add-on products have become such winners that Autodesk acquired them and incorporated them into its own products. When you compare all the resources — including the add-ons, extensions, training courses, books, and so on — AutoCAD doesn't have much PC CAD competition.

The Importance of Being DWG

To take full advantage of AutoCAD in your work environment, you need to be aware of the *DWG* file format, the format in which AutoCAD saves drawings. Here are some DWG facts to keep in mind:

✔ In some cases, an older version of AutoCAD can't open a DWG file that's been saved by a newer AutoCAD release.

✔ A newer version of AutoCAD can *always* open files saved by older versions.

✔ *Some* previous AutoCAD releases can open files saved by the subsequent one or two versions. For example, AutoCAD 2007 and AutoCAD 2008 can open DWG files saved by AutoCAD 2009. That's because Autodesk didn't change the DWG file format between those releases. However, the drawing file format *did* change with AutoCAD 2010, so drawings created in the current release must be saved in an older format to be openable in AutoCAD 2009 and earlier.

✔ You can use the Save As option in newer releases to save the file to some older DWG formats. In fact, AutoCAD 2010 can save as far back as AutoCAD Release 14, which dates all the way back to 1997!

Table 1-1 shows which versions (described later in this chapter) use which DWG file formats.

Table 1-1	AutoCAD Versions and DWG File Formats		
AutoCAD Version	*AutoCAD LT Version*	*Release Year*	*DWG File Format*
AutoCAD 2010	AutoCAD LT 2010	2009	Acad 2010
AutoCAD 2009	AutoCAD LT 2009	2008	Acad 2007
AutoCAD 2008	AutoCAD LT 2008	2007	Acad 2007
AutoCAD 2007	AutoCAD LT 2007	2006	Acad 2007
AutoCAD 2006	AutoCAD LT 2006	2005	Acad 2004
AutoCAD 2005	AutoCAD LT 2005	2004	Acad 2004
AutoCAD 2004	AutoCAD LT 2004	2003	Acad 2004
AutoCAD 2002	AutoCAD LT 2002	2001	Acad 2000
AutoCAD 2000i	AutoCAD LT 2000i	2000	Acad 2000
AutoCAD 2000	AutoCAD LT 2000	1999	Acad 2000
AutoCAD Release 14	AutoCAD LT 98 and 97	1997	Acad R14
AutoCAD Release 13	AutoCAD LT 95	1994	Acad R13
AutoCAD Release 12	AutoCAD LT Release 2	1992	Acad R12

The new file format in AutoCAD 2010 was necessary to handle new features — especially parametric drafting. The new format is also more efficient at saving files and can handle much larger objects. Best of all from the user's perspective, it's noticeably faster to work with than AutoCAD 2009.

Working with AutoCAD is easier when your coworkers and colleagues in other companies all use the same release of AutoCAD and AutoCAD-related tools. That way, your DWG files, add-on tools, and even the details of your

CAD knowledge can be mixed and matched among your workgroup and partners. In the real world, you may work with people, probably from other companies, who use AutoCAD releases as old as AutoCAD 2000 — or even older.

Many programs claim to be *DWG compatible* — that is, capable of converting data to and from AutoCAD's DWG format. But achieving this compatibility is a difficult thing to do well. Even a small error in file conversion can have results ranging in severity from annoying to appalling. Every time you open a drawing file, AutoCAD checks its parentage and warns you if the drawing was created by a non-Autodesk program. If you exchange DWG files with people who use other CAD programs, you may have to spend time finding and fixing translation problems.

Seeing the LT

AutoCAD LT is one of the best deals around, a shining example of the old 80/20 rule: roughly 80 percent of the capabilities of AutoCAD for roughly 20 percent of the money. (Actually, with recent price creep, it's now more like a 70/30 rule!) Like AutoCAD, AutoCAD LT runs on mainstream Windows computers and doesn't require any additional hardware devices. With AutoCAD LT, you can be a player in the world of AutoCAD, the world's leading CAD program, for a comparatively low starting cost.

AutoCAD LT is a very close cousin to AutoCAD. Autodesk creates AutoCAD LT by starting with the AutoCAD program, taking out a few features to justify charging a lower price, and adding a couple of features to enhance ease of use versus full AutoCAD. As a result, AutoCAD LT looks and works much like AutoCAD. The drawing areas, Ribbons, and Application Menu of the two programs are nearly identical. (LT is missing a few Ribbon tabs, panels, and commands.)

In fact, the major difference between the programs has nothing to do with the programs themselves. The major difference is that AutoCAD LT lacks support for several customization and programming languages that are used to develop AutoCAD add-ons. So almost none of the add-on programs or utilities offered by Autodesk and others are available to LT users.

AutoCAD LT also has only limited 3D support. You can view and edit 3D objects in AutoCAD LT, so you can work with drawings created in AutoCAD that contain 3D objects. However, you can't create true 3D objects in LT.

The lack of 3D object creation in LT isn't as big a drawback for many users as you may think. Despite a lot of hype from the computer press and CAD vendors (including Autodesk), 3D CAD remains a relatively specialized activity. The majority of people use CAD programs to create 2D drawings.

Although you may hear claims that AutoCAD LT is easier to master and use than AutoCAD, the truth is that they're about equally difficult (or easy, depending on your *NQ* [nerd quotient]). The LT learning curve doesn't differ significantly from that of AutoCAD. AutoCAD was originally designed for maximum power and then modified somewhat to improve ease of use. AutoCAD LT shares this same heritage.

Fortunately, the minimal differences between LT and AutoCAD mean that after you've climbed that learning curve, you'll have the same great view. You'll have almost the full range of the AutoCAD 2D drafting tools, and you'll be able to exchange DWG files with AutoCAD users without data loss.

This book covers AutoCAD 2010, but almost all the information in it applies to AutoCAD LT 2010 as well. The icon that you see to the left of this paragraph highlights significant differences.

Checking system requirements

If you're upgrading from AutoCAD 2009 or another recent release, and you work mostly or entirely in 2D, you're probably already current with system requirements. In fact, if your work is mostly or entirely 2D — and therefore, this applies especially for LT users — AutoCAD 2010 will run fine on pretty well any computer that will run Windows XP or Vista.

AutoCAD's requirements for running in Vista are substantially higher than for running in XP. This section covers the details.

You should know the following before you upgrade from any older AutoCAD release:

- ✔ **Wash those old Windows:** AutoCAD 2010 does *not* support older versions of Windows, such as Windows 2000, NT, 98, or Me. For AutoCAD 2010, you have two choices:

 - • Windows XP (Home or Professional, SP2 or later)

 - • Windows Vista (Enterprise, Business, Ultimate or Home Premium, SP1 or later)

 If you like to be cutting edge, there are 64-bit versions of AutoCAD 2010 and AutoCAD LT 2010 that run in the 64-bit versions of XP and Vista.

- ✔ **DWG file compatibility:** The previous three releases shared a common DWG file format, but AutoCAD 2010 uses a new format. You have to use the Save As option on the Application Menu, or the SAVEAS command, to create DWG files for users of AutoCAD 2006 and earlier versions. You can save as far back as Release 14, and if you need to go even further back, you can save to the Release 12 DXF format. Look up *DXF files* in the online help index for instructions.

✔ **Application compatibility:** If you use third-party applications with a previous AutoCAD release, they may not work with AutoCAD 2010. AutoCAD applications developed with the .NET or the ObjectARX (AutoCAD Runtime eXtension) interfaces will probably need to be recompiled. VBA (Visual Basic for Applications) applications may or may not work with AutoCAD 2010, but many LSP (AutoLISP) programs written for the last several versions of AutoCAD should work without change.

Built-in support for VBA applications has been removed from AutoCAD 2010. You now have to download and install the VBA enabler from Autodesk's Web site. At the time of updating this chapter, the URL has not been finalized; just go to `www.autodesk.com` and enter **VBA enabler** in the Search box.

✔ **Computer system requirements:** For AutoCAD 2010, Autodesk recommends a 1.6 GHz or better Intel or AMD processor with at least 2 GB of RAM if running in Windows XP, and a 3.0 GHz or better chip and 2 GB of RAM if running in Windows Vista. Multiple processors and dual core are supported. You also need a 1024 x 768 or higher display resolution with True Color graphics, 1 to 1.6 GB of available hard disk space, an Internet connection, and Microsoft Internet Explorer 7.0 or later (Internet Explorer 7.0 or later for 64-bit).

✔ **Additional requirements for working in 3D:** AutoCAD recommends a 3 GHz or better processor; 2 GB or more of RAM; a workstation-class, Direct3D-capable graphics card with at least 128 MB of memory; and an additional 2 GB of hard disk space beyond the 1 GB required for installation.

I find even the recommended system requirements on the minimal side. For example, my desktop computer runs at a screen resolution of 1280 x 1024, and my tablet computer runs at 1400 x 1050. The figures in this book were shot at a resolution of 1024 x 768, and as you can see, things can get pretty crowded at that resolution.

Suddenly, It's 2010!

There's been a new release of AutoCAD every spring since AutoCAD 2004 was launched in 2003. That's not much time for even an army of programmers to deliver a compelling new feature set that's going to convince all users that they just have to upgrade. What seems to have been happening is a concentration on particular areas in recent releases. For example, AutoCAD 2007 was the 3D release; the 3D modeling engine was made much easier to use, but there was relatively little to please the 2D crowd. By contrast, AutoCAD 2008 was deemed to be "the drafter's release" because of the number of enhancements to 2D drawing capabilities — above all, the introduction of annotative documentation objects. In AutoCAD 2009, the new Microsoft Office 2007-style

interface got the lion's share of development time; significant new features were limited to some 3D navigation tools.

The interface gets some minor changes this time. There are a few new or renamed tabs, and AutoCAD 2009's Menu Browser is completely remodeled into the new Application Menu, which is even *more* Office 2007-like than it was in AutoCAD 2009. I introduce you to the updated interface in Chapter 2, but here are several truly new features to mention first:

- **Parametric drafting:** The 3D folks don't get all the goodies. If anything, parametric drafting is an even greater benefit to 2D drafters than organic modeling is to the 3D types. Put as simply as possible, parameters are dimensional or geometric *constraints;* changing the value of a parametric dimension, or adding or removing geometric constraints, causes the object geometry itself to change. AutoCAD's parametric features work in 2D only (so far). AutoCAD LT users can edit parameters but can't create any.

 I introduce you to parametric drafting in Chapter 19.

- **New or improved commands:** The new REVERSE command lets you reverse the direction of lines and polylines. You can convert splines to polylines for additional editing options. A new MEASUREGEOM tool set on the Ribbon gathers several inquiry commands into a single home.

 I introduce you to these features in Chapters 8 through 11.

- **Annotation enhancements:** The HATCH command now indicates graphically where gaps in the boundary prevent a hatch object from being created. Dimension text can be placed below the dimension line or positioned so it can be read from right to left *or* left to right.

 I discuss text, dimensions, and hatching in Chapters 13, 14, and 15, respectively.

- **Reference files:** You can now attach PDFs as well as DWFs and MicroStation DGN files as drawing underlays.

 For more about using external reference files, see Chapter 18.

- **Viewport enhancements:** You can now rotate the view of objects within a viewport to better fit your drawing sheet. (I *love* this one!) I cover layouts and viewports in Chapter 5.

- **Organic modeling:** Yes, AutoCAD now offers preservative-free 3D! Okay, what organic modeling *really* means is freeform shape creation. AutoCAD (but not AutoCAD LT) offers a new set of mesh-based primitive objects than you can pull and push to create any shape you like.

 I don't cover 3D modeling in *AutoCAD 2010 For Dummies*, so if you want to find out more, have a look in the online help or visit www.autodesk. com/autocad-tutorials.

Chapter 2

Le Tour de AutoCAD 2010

AutoCAD 2010 is a fully fledged and thoroughly up-to-date member of the Windows world, but if you skipped AutoCAD 2009, or you're using Windows XP, or you've yet to kick the tires of the Microsoft Office 2007 suite, you may not recognize much in AutoCAD's newest release. But the title bar says "AutoCAD 2010," so you must be in the right place!

Like the rest of the book, this chapter is written for someone who has used other Windows programs but has little or no experience with AutoCAD. If you *are* experienced with recent releases of AutoCAD, some of this chapter may be old hat (even if it does *look* different). Here and throughout the rest of the book, I show you how to do things with AutoCAD's implementation of Microsoft's Fluent User Interface (or FUI for short). In the "Going for that classic look" sidebar later in this chapter, I show you how to make the new version look a lot like an old one.

The very first time you launch AutoCAD 2010, a new Initial Setup routine asks you to specify the industry you work in, whether you want to include 3D or drawing management tools (not in AutoCAD LT), and which template you want to use to start new drawings. AutoCAD then creates a new workspace named (what else?) Initial Setup Workspace and a new profile named . . . (I don't need to tell you that, do I?). You can create multiple initial setups (sounds oxymoronic, doesn't it?) through the Options dialog box. By default, AutoCAD 2010 opens in this new Initial Setup Workspace.

A *profile* is a collection of settings including support file paths, drawing window colors, default file format to save to, and a whack of other user preferences. Profiles are handy if more than one person works on your computer, or for different support paths for different clients. You create or modify profiles in the Options dialog box, which you can access from the Application Menu. Note that AutoCAD LT does not support profiles.

Because there are so many possible permutations of the Initial Setup Workspace, for this book I use the 2D Drafting & Annotation workspace instead, and if you want to follow along, I recommend you do the same by following these steps:

1. **Click the Workspace Switching button at the bottom right of the AutoCAD window.**

 AutoCAD 2010 displays the name of the current workspace on the button. Clicking the button displays a menu listing all available workspaces (see Figure 2-1).

2. **Choose 2D Drafting & Annotation from the menu.**

 Depending on what you selected during initial program setup, AutoCAD turns on or off Ribbon panels and, in a few seconds, settles down to the standard 2D Drafting & Annotation workspace.

Figure 2-1:
Switching to the 2D Drafting & Annotation workspace.

If you've been away from AutoCAD for a while, you may be asking, "Where are my toolbars? Where is my menu?" Unlike older Windows programs, AutoCAD 2010 sports just one toolbar — the Quick Access toolbar on the application title bar, right next to the Application button (known informally as the Big Red A) — and doesn't sport a menu bar in this environment. Instead, the 2D Drafting & Annotation workspace sports two major interface items:

✔ **The Application Menu:** Clicking the Application button at the top-left corner of the AutoCAD window opens AutoCAD 2010's Application Menu. Unlike AutoCAD 2009's menu browser, which replicated the entire

pull-down menu system, AutoCAD 2010's Application Menu presents file-related commands only; here you can create new drawings, open existing drawings, save files, or print your masterpieces.

📎 **The Ribbon:** The Ribbon replaces the menus, toolbars, many of the palettes, and the dashboard of earlier releases. Where the Application Menu focuses on file management, the Ribbon is where you find commands to create and modify drawing objects. The Autodesk programmers made a best guess at a task-based approach to drafting and organized the old interface items into panels of related tools.

I discuss both of these items in more detail in the following sections. For the dyed-in-the-wool traditionalists, you can reset the AutoCAD 2010 environment so it looks pretty much like it did in AutoCAD 2008. I show you how a little later in the chapter.

AutoCAD Does Windows (And Office)

Whether you're a total newcomer, an experienced user from a few releases back, or an AutoCAD 2008 or 2009 ace, I can guarantee that finding your way around AutoCAD 2010 is going to be a challenging experience.

If you're already familiar with the Microsoft Office 2007 suite, you may recognize some program features, such as the Ribbon and the Application Menu, which you use for choosing commands or changing system settings. But even if AutoCAD's new look does seem a little familiar in places, many aspects of the program's appearance — and some of the ways in which you work with it — are quite different from other Windows programs. Depending on the workspace you've chosen to use, you can, in many cases, tell the program what to do in at least five ways — pick a toolbar button, pick from a pull-down menu, pick a tool button from a Ribbon panel, type on the keyboard, or pick from a right-click menu — none of which is necessarily the best method to use for every task.

Slick as they are, Ribbon panels and browsing through the Application Menu aren't always the most efficient way of doing things. When you want to get real work done, you need to combine the Ribbon panels with other methods — especially entering options with the keyboard or choosing them from the right-click menus. I show you how throughout this book.

Profiling your display

The illustrations and descriptions in this chapter and throughout the book show the *default* configuration of AutoCAD 2010's 2D Drafting & Annotation workspace — that is, the way the screen looks if you use the standard version of AutoCAD 2010 (not a flavored version, such as AutoCAD Architecture 2010 or AutoCAD Mechanical 2010) and don't change any display settings. You can change workspaces by clicking the Workspace Switching button on the status bar and choosing a workspace from the menu. You can change the appearance of the workspace itself with settings on the Display tab of the Options dialog box (click the Application button and then click Options at the bottom of the Application Menu) and by dragging toolbars and other screen components.

The main change from AutoCAD's default settings that I've made for this book is to configure the drawing area background to be white because the figures show up better that way. The default background color in both AutoCAD 2010 and AutoCAD LT 2010 is off-white, but many longtime users prefer a black background because they believe there's less glare that way. (This is much less of an issue with LCD flat-panel displays.) You may want to set a black or a white background on your own system or stay with the default off-white background — it's your choice, and there's no right or wrong way. Some of AutoCAD's colors show up better on a light background, and some are better on a black one.

You can reset the default AutoCAD 2010 color scheme from the Options dialog box's Display tab. Click Colors to open the Drawing Window Colors dialog box and click the Restore Classic Colors button. AutoCAD 2010 includes a couple of built-in color schemes, also accessible from the Display tab of the Options dialog box. Designed to enhance the look of the new interface and ingeniously named Light and Dark, the differences between them are pretty subtle and apply to Windows elements like the title and taskbar, not to AutoCAD elements like crosshairs or background colors.

And They're Off: AutoCAD's Opening Screens

As I explain at the beginning of this chapter, the first time you start AutoCAD 2010, the program opens by default in the Initial Setup Workspace, but I suggest you switch to the 2D Drafting & Annotation workspace while you read this book.

A *workspace* is a collection of menus, palettes, toolbars, and/or Ribbon panels tailored for specific tasks, such as 3D modeling or 2D drafting.

After that, AutoCAD remembers which workspace you last used and opens in that one. Either three or four standard workspaces are created when you install AutoCAD 2010 (make that either two or three with AutoCAD LT 2010):

✔ **2D Drafting & Annotation:** This workspace (as shown in Figure 2-2) is configured for a 2D drafting environment, with Ribbon tabs and panels optimized for technical drawing in two dimensions.

✔ **3D Modeling:** This Ribbon-based workspace is configured for a 3D modeling environment, with navigation, visualization, and modeling tools suitable for working in 3D. This workspace isn't included in AutoCAD LT because LT doesn't do 3D.

✔ **AutoCAD Classic:** This workspace is configured for a 2D drafting environment, with toolbars and tool palette arrangements similar to those in AutoCAD 2008 and earlier. In AutoCAD LT this workspace is called *AutoCAD LT Classic*.

✔ **Initial Setup Workspace:** This workspace is created if you (or whoever installed your AutoCAD) answer a series of questions about the type of drafting you do during program installation. If you skip this routine, the workspace is not created.

Application button

Quick Access toolbar Title bar InfoCenter Ribbon

Figure 2-2:
Where's my AutoCAD?: The AutoCAD 2010 2D Drafting & Annotation workspace.

Status bar Command prompt

Ribbon panel

Running with Ribbons

Whether you're running AutoCAD 2010 in Windows Vista or XP, most of AutoCAD's default screen (refer to Figure 2-2) is pretty different from traditional Windows fare. Yes, you have title bars and a status bar, but the rest of the interface might look foreign. I cover the familiar stuff first.

A hierarchy of title bars

Like most Windows programs, AutoCAD has a *title bar* at the top of its application window that reminds you which program you're in (not that you'd ever mistake the AutoCAD 2010 window for, say, FreeCell — or even AutoCAD 2008!).

- At the right side of the program title bar is the standard set of three Windows control buttons: Minimize, Maximize/Restore, and Close.

- Each nonmaximized drawing window within the AutoCAD program window has its own title bar, as shown in Figure 2-3. You can use the control buttons on a drawing window's title bar to minimize, maximize/restore, or close that drawing instead of the entire AutoCAD program.

Drawing window title bar Drawing window control buttons

Figure 2-3:
The AutoCAD screen with the drawing window restored.

As in other Windows programs, if you maximize a drawing's window, it expands to fill the entire drawing area. In AutoCAD 2010's 2D Drafting & Annotation workspace, a maximized drawing window's control buttons have migrated south, from the menu bar (which isn't there anymore) to the upper-right corner of the drawing area itself. To unmaximize (restore) the drawing so that you can see any other drawings that you have open, click the lower Restore button.

The program title and drawing name are centered in the title bar instead of being off to the left, beside a program icon. The AutoCAD title bar also has a couple of devices added to it:

- **InfoCenter:** Forced out of its old home in the menu bar to a new location at the right side of the program title bar, this is Information Central for AutoCAD. Type a keyword and click the binoculars for more information, or click the satellite dish to connect to the Communication Center and check for updates.

 You can save InfoCenter topics to a Favorites list, and you can access or sign up for the AutoCAD Subscription Center (alas, not included in the price of admission). Access to the online help is via the question-mark button at the end of the InfoCenter panel.

- **Quick Access toolbar:** This permanent toolbar (the only one common to all workspaces) contains frequently used commands in an easily accessible location. You can add and remove tool buttons by clicking the down arrow at the right end of the Quick Access toolbar and selecting or deselecting the ones you want to add or remove, respectively.

 If you're floundering around looking for the commands you used to be able to find, a life preserver is hiding in the drop-down menu at the right end of the Quick Access toolbar. Click Show Menu Bar, and the old familiar classic menu appears above the Ribbon.

Making choices from the Application Menu

The Application Menu is accessible from all workspaces. Where AutoCAD 2009's Menu Browser (which lived in the same place) basically duplicated the classic pull-down menu structure, AutoCAD 2010's Application Menu follows Microsoft's Fluent User Interface (or FUI — honest!) and places file management commands here, and places all drawing and editing commands on the Ribbon. The Application Menu is divided into ten categories, as follows:

- **New:** Create a new drawing from a list of templates or create a new sheet set (not in AutoCAD LT, and in any case, I don't cover sheet sets in this book).

- **Open:** Open an existing drawing or sheet set for editing, or import data from a MicroStation DGN file into a new AutoCAD drawing.

- **Save:** Save the current drawing in the current location; if the current drawing hasn't been saved, you're prompted for a filename and a location.

✔ **Save As:** Save the current drawing to a new filename and/or location and make the newly named or located file the current drawing. Also save the drawing as a template (DWT) or standards (DWS) file, or export a paper space layout to a new drawing.

✔ **Export:** Save the current drawing to a variety of Design Web Format (DWF) files, or a PDF, a DGN or another file format. I discuss these formats in Chapters 18 and 20.

✔ **Print:** Print a single drawing or multiple drawings, create or modify named page setups, and manage plotters and plot styles (I cover most of these operations in Chapter 16).

✔ **Publish:** Send a 3D model to an outside 3D printing service or create an archived sheet set. AutoCAD LT doesn't support 3D or sheet sets, and neither of these topics is covered in this book.

✔ **Send:** E-mail the current drawing file or create a Zip file containing the current drawing and any associated files needed to display the drawing completely (most often, those associated files are external references, which I introduce in Chapter 18).

✔ **Drawing Utilities:** Set file properties or drawing units; purge unused blocks, layers, and styles from the current drawing; and audit or recover damaged drawings.

✔ **Close:** Close the current drawing or close all drawings. If any drawings have been changed, you're prompted to save before AutoCAD closes the file.

But wait! There's more under the Big Red A

In addition to the Application Menu's actual file menu items, a few other features are worth a mention:

✔ **Recent Documents:** If you choose this option, the right pane displays a list of drawings you've recently edited but that aren't currently open. You can show them in a simple list or as thumbnail images, as shown in Figure 2-4. You can also pin them to stop them from scrolling off the list. Naturally enough, clicking one of the icons opens the drawing.

✔ **Open Documents:** Choose this option to see what's already open, and click an item to switch to it. This is equivalent to pressing Ctrl+Tab to switch between open documents in any Windows program and works the same basic way as the new Quick View Drawings feature, described in the "Looking for Mr. Status Bar" section, later in the chapter.

✔ **Options:** Click this button to open the Options dialog box, where you can make hundreds of system settings. You can also open Options by typing **OP** (the alias for the OPTIONS command).

✔ **Search:** If you're not sure of a command name or you want help on a topic, just start typing in the Application Menu's search bar. AutoCAD 2010 very quickly displays a categorized list, complete with links to start commands or to access the online help (see Figure 2-5).

Figure 2-4:
Find that
drawing you
know you
worked on
yesterday.

Figure 2-5:
If you can't
find it in the
Ribbon or
tool buttons,
just start
typing!

Unraveling the Ribbon

It's a whole new racetrack in AutoCAD 2010. In AutoCAD 2008 and prior releases, you bounced around a bunch of palettes, toolbars, and dashboard panels to find the commands you wanted. Now everything (well . . . almost everything) lives in one place: the Ribbon.

The primary interface element in both the 2D Drafting & Annotation and 3D Modeling workspaces is the *Ribbon,* an adjustable area that contains different collections of tabbed, task-oriented collections of panels. Some panels — those marked with a little black triangle on the panel label — have more tools concealed on a slideout (see Figure 2-6). Click the panel label to open the slideout. You can click the pushpin icon to pin open the slideout — otherwise, it will slide away home after you click a button.

In AutoCAD 2010, you can click-and-drag a Ribbon panel and pull it into the drawing area. So if, for example, you find yourself doing a whack of dimensioning, but you also want to move away from the Annotate tab to other Ribbon tabs, you can drag the Dimensions panel into the drawing, and it will stay put, even as you switch to other panels or tabs. Just be sure to put it back where it came from when you're finished with it (as your mom used to say).

Figure 2-6:
More tools than you can wave a Ribbon at.

No Express service?

If your Ribbon doesn't include the Express menu panel (it's at the far right in Figure 2-2), you should consider installing the Express Tools from your AutoCAD DVD (AutoCAD LT does not include or support the Express Tools).

When you first install AutoCAD 2010, you choose between a Typical and a Custom installation. If you choose Typical, the next screen asks if you want to install the Express Tools. If you choose a Custom installation, in the next screen, make sure to check the Express Tools item in the list of components. If you do not install the Express Tools during initial setup, you'll have to rerun the setup routine from your AutoCAD 2010 DVD. If you haven't installed AutoCAD yet, I strongly recommend that you choose the Typical installation option — or at least make sure the Express Tools box is checked during a Custom installation.

Autodesk's programmers see the Ribbon as an alternative way of interacting with the program. Theoretically, the Ribbon eliminates the need for menus and separate toolbars, although the change-averse may think otherwise. The Ribbon is fully customizable, but I don't get into customizing AutoCAD in this book — if you want to find out more, check out the Customization Guide in the AutoCAD 2010 online help.

By default, the Ribbon is docked at the top of the screen, but it can be docked against any edge, anchored to the left or right side of the AutoCAD window, or floated. To gain some screen space, you can click the little white button to the right of the last tab on the Ribbon's tab bar to minimize the Ribbon, first to tabs and panel labels, and then to tabs only. Click one more time to revert to the full Ribbon.

Instead of menus of grouped commands like Draw, Modify, Insert, and so forth, the tabs are organized by task as follows:

- **Home:** The Home tab contains Draw, Modify, Layers, Annotation, Block, Properties, Utilities, and Clipboard panels. Some panels may be displayed as collapsed depending on your screen resolution (the Annotation Scaling panel at the right end of the Annotate tab in Figure 2-6 is in a collapsed state). I cover most of the commands in these panels in other parts of the book.

- **Insert:** This tab groups Block and Reference panels, as well as Import commands and a series of commands for working with nongraphical information, including fields and data links. I do cover blocks (Chapter 17) and external references (Chapter 18), but importing and data tools are beyond the scope of this book and aren't covered.

- **Annotate:** The Annotate tab expands on the minimalist Annotation panel on the Home tab, with many more options for creating text, dimensions, leaders, and tables, as well as markup functions and a few annotation scaling tools.

✔ **Parametric:** This new tab is home for one of AutoCAD 2010's best new features — parametric drawing. You can apply geometric or dimensional parameters or constraints to drawing objects so that, say, two circles are always concentric or the length of a rectangle is always twice its width. (AutoCAD LT is limited in this department: You can modify or delete existing constraints, but you need the full version to create them.) I introduce parametric drawing in Chapter 19.

✔ **View:** The View tab contains tools and panels for controlling drawing display, working with user coordinate systems and viewports, loading various palettes, and organizing Windows functions such as cascading open files or displaying different parts of the application window. I explain viewports in Chapter 5 but don't address the other functions in this tab. For most 2D drafting, you seldom need to change the user coordinate system, and most functions in the other panels are more conveniently handled in other parts of the program.

✔ **Manage:** This tab contains panels that access the Action Recorder, CAD Standards (neither of which is in AutoCAD LT), and a set of drawing management and customization tools. I don't cover anything on the Manage tab in this book.

✔ **Output:** Panels on this tab let you get those drawings off your hands by printing, publishing, or simply sending them electronically to others. I cover some of these functions in Chapter 16. Autodesk Seek is a replacement for Content Search in AutoCAD 2009; after it's set up, it lets you link to various manufacturers' Web sites and download AutoCAD-compatible files.

The Export to Impression panel on the Output tab is usable only if you're a subscription customer, and then only for the full version of AutoCAD (not AutoCAD LT). So for many people, this panel is a waste of space. You can hide it by right-clicking the panel label and then choosing Panels and deselecting Export to Impression.

✔ **Express Tools:** The Express Tools are an invaluable set of custom commands that will streamline your work procedures in pretty well every aspect of AutoCAD. They're officially unsupported, but they've been an install option for many releases now, and mostly, they work very well. You get this tab only if you have the full version of AutoCAD — the Express Tools are not available in AutoCAD LT.

Going for that classic look

Like it or not, the Ribbon-based interface isn't going to go away any time soon. I didn't care for the 2D Drafting & Annotation workspace when it first showed up in AutoCAD 2007, but thanks to the Ribbon, I'm now sold on it. AutoCAD 2010's 2D Drafting & Annotation workspace is where I spend most of my time, and that's what nearly all the figures in this book show.

Unlike Microsoft's Office 2007 suite, which dragged longtime users kicking and screaming into the new Fluent User Interface, AutoCAD users can stay with the old interface. The easiest way to go back to the future is to switch workspaces using (what else?) the Workspace Switching button on the status bar. Select AutoCAD Classic, and presto — this is (almost) your father's AutoCAD! You end up with a menu bar; some familiar-looking toolbars docked to the top, left, and right sides of the drawing area; and a floating tool palette near the middle of the display.

The new interface lets you add bits of the old one, too. You can display the classic drop-down list by clicking the down arrow at the right end of the Quick Access toolbar and choosing Show Menu Bar. It's slightly trickier displaying classic toolbars, but the most straightforward way — assuming that you know the name of the toolbar you want to open — is to type **-TOOLBAR** (don't omit the hyphen!) and press Enter; then type the name of the toolbar (for example, **LAYERS**) and press Enter again.

Getting with the Program

For the rest of the book I focus on 2D drafting, by far the easiest way of getting your feet wet with AutoCAD. (Just don't be dripping water on your computer.) And if you're not back there already, I suggest that you use the Workspace Switching button to return to the 2D Drafting & Annotation workspace. After you make the switch, AutoCAD displays the interface shown earlier in Figure 2-2.

Like all good Windows programs, AutoCAD has *tooltips,* those short descriptions that appear in little text boxes when you hover the mouse pointer over a button. In AutoCAD 2010, tooltips display two levels of information. When you hover the mouse pointer over a tool button, you first see a quick identification of the command. If you keep hovering, a longer description of the icon's function, often with a graphic image, appears in an extended tooltip. Helpful as they are when you're starting with AutoCAD, you'll probably want to remove these training wheels sooner or later. You can do so in the Options dialog box. (See the online help for more information.)

Looking for Mr. Status Bar

The *application status bar* (see Figure 2-7) appears at the bottom of the AutoCAD screen. The status bar displays and allows you to change several important drawing modes, aids, and settings that affect how you draw and edit in the current drawing. I introduce them in this section.

You can set status bar buttons to display icons or the traditional text labels that will be familiar to users of previous versions. To switch from one style to the other, right-click any of the drawing mode buttons at the left side of the status bar and select or deselect Use Icons.

Status bar buttons showing icons

Figure 2-7: Status (bars) check.

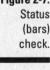

Status bar buttons showing text labels

Some of these status bar settings won't make complete sense until you've used the AutoCAD commands that they influence, but here's a brief description, with references to detailed descriptions of how to use each setting, starting at the left end of the status bar (and note that not all buttons are displayed at all times, so Figure 2-7 doesn't show all the buttons listed):

✔ **Coordinates of the crosshairs:** The coordinates readout displays the current X,Y,Z location of the crosshairs in the drawing area, with respect to the origin point (whose coordinates are 0, 0, 0). Chapter 7 describes AutoCAD's coordinate conventions and how to use this area of the status bar.

If the coordinates in the lower-left corner of the screen are grayed out, coordinate tracking is turned off. Click the coordinates so that they appear in dark numbers that change when you move the crosshairs in the drawing area.

✔ **SNAP, GRID, and ORTHO mode:** These three buttons control three of AutoCAD's tools that help with precision drawing and editing:

- **SNAP** constrains the crosshairs to regularly spaced intervals, enabling you to draw objects a fixed distance apart more easily.

- **GRID** displays a series of regularly spaced dots, which serve as a distance reference.

- **ORTHO** constrains the crosshairs to horizontal and vertical movement, which makes drawing *orthogonal* (straight horizontal and vertical) lines easy.

See Chapter 4 for instructions on how to configure these modes and Chapter 7 for information about why, when, and how to use them in actual drawing operations.

✔ **POLAR tracking mode:** Polar tracking causes the crosshairs to jump to certain angles when you draw and edit objects. The default angle settings are multiples of 90 degrees, but you can specify other angle increments, such as 45 or 30 degrees. See Chapter 7 for instructions on specifying the polar tracking angles that you prefer. Clicking the POLAR button toggles polar tracking on and off. Ortho and polar tracking are mutually exclusive — turning on one mode disables the other.

✔ **Object Snap (OSNAP) and Object Snap Tracking (OTRACK):** *Object snap* is another AutoCAD tool for ensuring precision drawing and editing. You use object snaps to grab points on existing objects — for example, the endpoint of a line or the center of a circle.

- When you turn on *running object snap,* AutoCAD continues to hunt for object snap points. Chapter 7 contains detailed instructions on how to use this feature.

- When you turn on *object snap tracking,* AutoCAD hunts in a more sophisticated way for points that are derived from object snap points. Chapter 7 briefly describes this advanced feature.

✔ **Dynamic User Coordinate System (DUCS):** This one's for 3D object creation (and so is not included in AutoCAD LT). As noted in the introduction, I don't cover 3D modeling in this book.

✔ **Dynamic Input (DYN):** *Dynamic input* displays commands, options, prompts, and user input in a tooltip adjacent to the crosshairs and enables you to keep focused on what you're drawing. In addition, the dynamic input tooltip displays what you type in response to prompts. I describe dynamic input later in this chapter.

✔ **Lineweight (LWT) display mode:** One of the properties that you can assign to objects in AutoCAD is *lineweight* — the thickness that lines appear when you plot the drawing. This button controls whether you see the lineweights on the screen. (This button doesn't control whether lineweights appear on plots; that's a separate setting in the Plot dialog box.) Chapter 6 gives you the skinny (and the wide) on lineweights.

✔ **Quick Properties (QP):** When *Quick Properties* is enabled, selecting an object in the drawing displays a pop-up window that lists the main properties of that object. You can choose which properties you want displayed by right-clicking the QP button and choosing Settings. I fill you in on object properties in Chapter 6.

MODEL

✔ **MODEL/PAPER:** Clicking this button toggles between model space and paper space.

As I describe in the section "Down the main stretch: The drawing area," later in this chapter, AutoCAD's drawing area is composed of two overlapping environments: *Model space* is where you create your model geometry, and *paper space* is where you compose your drawing sheet to document that geometry. Clicking this button when the Model *tab* is active (that is, you're in full-screen model space) switches you to a paper space layout. A completed layout includes *viewports,* which reveal the objects in model space at a particular scale. (I tell you more about viewports and layouts in Chapter 5.) After you switch to a paper space layout, clicking this button toggles between paper space and model space *within the layout.* The button label switches from MODEL to PAPER to show you which space you're in.

✔ **Model and Layout:** (These two buttons disappear if Model and Layout tabs are displayed.) Clicking the Model button switches you out of the layout and back to full-screen model space. (If Model and Layout tabs are displayed, you click the Model *tab* to switch to full-screen model space.) Clicking Layout switches you to whichever paper space layout was active when you switched to model space. (Note that the tooltip for the Layout button displays the name of the layout, which might be changed from the default Layout1 or Layout2.)

✔ **Quick View Layouts:** Clicking this button displays a horizontal row of graphic images of all layouts in the current drawing. Click a layout image to make that layout current. The Quick View toolbar below the layout images contains buttons for pinning the Quick View Layouts bar so it stays open, creating a new layout, publishing the selected layout, and closing Quick View Layouts. I cover layout creation in Chapter 5 and publishing in Chapter 16.

✔ **Quick View Drawings:** Clicking this button displays a row of graphic images of all currently open drawings. Click a drawing image to make it current. (Why, yes, it *is* the same as Ctrl+Tabbing!) Quick View Drawings includes the same Quick View toolbar as Quick View Layouts.

✔ **Pan and Zoom:** These buttons provide access to two commonly used display commands, PAN and ZOOM. These and other display commands are described in Chapter 12.

✔ **SteeringWheel:** You were probably wondering when this motoring metaphor was going to pay off, right? Well, believe it or not, there really is an AutoCAD function called the SteeringWheel! (I'm still looking for the Gas Pedal . . . oops, I mean GasPedal.) A steering wheel is described in the

online help as a tracking menu — the idea here is that you combine a number of display operations into a single input "device." I mention the Steering Wheel in Chapter 12 but point out here that it's of little use in 2D drafting.

 ✔ **ShowMotion:** The ShowMotion command starts a rudimentary animation program. As the online help describes it, you can generate effects similar to those in TV commercials to dress up motion studies of your designs. ShowMotion isn't included in AutoCAD LT and is beyond — *well* beyond — the scope of this book.

 ✔ **Maximize/Minimize Viewport (appears on paper space layouts only):** When you're looking at one of the Layout tabs instead of the Model tab, the status bar displays an additional Maximize Viewport button. Click this button to expand the current paper space viewport so that it fills the entire drawing area. Click the button — now called Minimize Viewport — again to restore the viewport to its normal size. (Chapter 5 describes viewports.)

The next six buttons control the size and appearance of AutoCAD's annotative objects — things like text, dimensions, hatching, and so forth. Annotative objects are complex, so don't worry if you don't understand at this point — remember, in this chapter, I'm just showing you what the buttons do. Because *annotative objects* means text more than anything else, I explain this feature in Chapter 13.

 ✔ **Lock/Unlock Viewport:** After you're satisfied with the display inside your viewport, and you've assigned a viewport scale, use this button to lock the viewport display so you don't accidentally pan or zoom inside it. (See Chapter 5 for more on viewports.)

 ✔ **Annotation Scale (appears in full-screen model space only):** Clicking Annotation Scale displays a list of preset annotation scales; if the Automatically Add Scales button is toggled on, changing a scale here causes all annotative objects to update to the new scale.

 ✔ **Viewport Scale:** This button appears only in a layout, when a model space viewport is activated. If the viewport is locked, this button is inactive. If the viewport is unlocked, clicking the button displays a list of scales; choose the desired scale from the list.

 ✔ **Annotation Scale Is Not Equal To Viewport Scale:** If the scale assigned to annotative objects within the viewport differs from the scale assigned to the viewport itself, clicking this button will synchronize the annotation scale to the viewport scale.

 ✔ **Annotation Visibility:** This button toggles the visibility of annotative objects. When the light bulb is off (gray), only annotative objects of the current annotation scale are visible; when the light bulb is on (yellow), all annotative objects in the drawing, regardless of scale, are visible.

⌂ 2D Drafting & Annotation ▾

✔ **Automatically Add Scales:** When this button is toggled on, additional annotative scales are automatically added to objects inside the viewport when you change the viewport scale.

✔ **Workspace Switching:** Clicking this button displays a list of saved workspaces, including the four default workspaces (three in AutoCAD LT): Initial Setup Workspace, AutoCAD Classic, 2D Drafting & Annotation, and (not in AutoCAD LT) 3D Modeling, plus any user-defined and saved workspaces.

✔ **Lock/Unlock Toolbar Palette Positions:** "Now, where did I leave that Properties palette?" You'll never have to ask yourself again — AutoCAD 2010 lets you lock the Ribbon, toolbars, or palettes (which for some reason it's started calling *windows*) in position, so you'll always know where they are.

The remaining status bar icons, with the exception of Clean Screen at the very end, live in a special area of the status bar called the *tray*. The tray displays icons that represent drawing services, and most do not appear at all times. These tray icons include

✔ **Trusted Autodesk DWG:** A *trusted drawing* is one created by AutoCAD, AutoCAD LT, or any program developed by Autodesk. In recent years, more and more programs have been able to save in DWG format, but in Autodesk's eyes, these files are not to be trusted. If you open such a drawing file, you'll get a warning dialog box and a little yellow danger sign over the trusted DWG icon.

✔ **Associated Standards File:** You see this button if you've enabled CAD standards checking and configured a drawing standards (DWS) file. Clicking this button displays the Check Standards dialog box. AutoCAD's CAD Standards functions are not included in AutoCAD LT. I don't cover standards checking in this book.

✔ **Manage Xrefs:** You won't see this combination button and notification symbol until you open a drawing that contains *xrefs* (external DWG files that are incorporated into the current drawing). Chapter 18 tells you how to use xrefs and what the Manage Xrefs button does.

✔ **Status Bar Menu:** When you click the easy-to-miss, downward-pointing arrow near the right end of the status bar, you open a menu with options for toggling off or on each status bar button. Now you can decorate your status bar to your taste. You can also turn on the *drawing status bar*. Doing so moves the three annotation scaling buttons described above to a separate drawing-specific status bar. (My personal preference is to leave it turned off.)

✔ **Clean Screen:** No, this button doesn't squeegee your monitor. Clicking this button frees up a bit more screen space by first maximizing the AutoCAD window and then turning off the title bar, toolbars, palettes, and the Windows taskbar. Click the button again to restore those elements.

Several status bar buttons, including Snap, Polar Tracking, Object Snap, and Object Snap Tracking, sport right-click menus that offer a speedier way of setting options. With some of the other buttons, such as Grid and Dynamic Input, you right-click the button and choose Settings to open the Drafting Settings dialog box to specify options. Chapters 4 and 6 give you specific guidance about when and how to change these settings.

Let your fingers do the talking: The command window

The infamous command window (or command line, or command prompt, or command area, whatever you want to call it), shown in Figure 2-8, is a throwback to the dark ages of AutoCAD. It puzzles newcomers and delights AutoCAD aficionados. Despite the promise of AutoCAD's heads-up dynamic input, for now at least, the hard truth is that you have to come to like — or at least tolerate — the command window if you want to become at all comfortable using AutoCAD.

Figure 2-8:
Obey the command window.

```
Command: <Polar on>
Command: <Polar off>
Command: LINE
Specify first point:
```

You should cotton on and cozy up to the command window because it's still AutoCAD's primary communications conduit with you. AutoCAD sometimes displays prompts, warnings, and error messages in the command window that dynamic input doesn't show — there simply isn't room in the dynamic input tooltip to show as much information as you get at the command window. True, when using dynamic input, you can press the down-arrow key to see more options. But which is less efficient: moving your eyes down the screen to glance at the command window or taking your eyes right off the screen to find the down-arrow key on your keyboard?

The key (board) to AutoCAD success

Despite (or is it because of?) AutoCAD's long heritage as the most successful CAD software for personal computers, newcomers are still astonished at the amount of typing they have to do. Some more-modern programs have much less dependency on the keyboard than AutoCAD, but as you get used to it, you'll find that no other input method gives you as much flexibility as pounding the ivories . . . oops, wrong keyboard!

Typing at your *computer's* keyboard is an efficient way to run some commands and the *only* way to run a few others. Instead of clicking a button or a menu choice, you can start a command by typing the command name and then pressing Enter. Even better, for most common commands, you can type the keyboard shortcut for a command name and press Enter. Most of the keyboard shortcuts (called *aliases*) for command names are just one or two letters — for example, L for the LINE command and CP for the COPY command. Most people who discover how to use the shortcuts for the commands that they run most frequently find that their AutoCAD productivity improves noticeably. Even if you're not worried about increasing your productivity with this technique, several everyday commands are nowhere to be found on the Ribbon. If you want to run those commands, you have to type them!

Not all command aliases are as obvious as L for LINE (for example, CP for COPY or — believe it or not — T for MTEXT). To see a complete list of command aliases, look in the AutoCAD (or the AutoCAD LT) Program Parameters (PGP) file by going to the Manage tab and clicking Edit Aliases on the Customization panel. Windows Notepad opens with the `acad.pgp` (or `acadlt.pgp`) file loaded. Scroll down to the section headed "Sample aliases for AutoCAD commands." I don't recommend changing anything, but it's a good idea to print this file and pin up the aliases section over your desk.

After you've started a command — whether from a Ribbon panel tool button or by typing — the dynamic input tooltip and the command window are where AutoCAD prompts you with options for that command. You activate one of these options by typing the uppercase letter(s) in the option and pressing Enter.

In many cases, you can activate a command's options by right-clicking in the drawing area and choosing the desired option from the menu that appears, instead of by typing the letter(s) for the option and pressing Enter.

I like dynamic input. Really, I do. But sometimes it fights with normal command input, and that can make things really confusing. In the following chapters, I tell you when to be wary.

The following sequence demonstrates how you use the keyboard to run commands and to view and select options. If you have dynamic input toggled on, your results are going to be different from what I say, so I suggest you click the DYN button to turn it off, temporarily at least. In the following steps, watch the command window, and pay attention to messages from AutoCAD:

1. **Type L and press Enter.**

 AutoCAD starts the LINE command and displays the following prompt in the command window:

   ```
   LINE Specify first point:
   ```

2. **Click a point anywhere in the drawing area.**

 The command window prompt changes to

   ```
   Specify next point or [Undo]:
   ```

3. **Click another point anywhere in the drawing area.**

 AutoCAD draws the first line segment.

4. **Click a third point anywhere in the drawing area.**

 AutoCAD draws the second line segment and prompts

   ```
   Specify next point or [Close/Undo]:
   ```

 The command line now displays two options, Close and Undo, separated by a slash.

 In this case, the Close and Undo options appear in brackets. AutoCAD's command line always displays command options in square brackets. To activate an option, type the letter(s) shown in uppercase and press Enter. You can type the option letter(s) in lowercase or uppercase.

5. **Type** U **and press Enter.**

 AutoCAD undoes the second line segment.

6. **Type** 3,2 **(without any spaces) and press Enter.**

 AutoCAD draws a new line segment to the point whose X coordinate is 3 and Y coordinate is 2.

7. **Click several more points anywhere in the drawing area.**

 AutoCAD draws additional line segments.

8. **Type** X **and press Enter.**

 X isn't a valid option of the LINE command, so AutoCAD displays an error message and prompts you again for another point:

   ```
   Point or option keyword required.
   Specify next point or [Close/Undo]:
   ```

 Option keyword is programmer jargon for the letter(s) shown in upper-case that you type to activate a command option. This error message is AutoCAD's way of saying, "I don't understand what you mean by typing X. Either specify a point or type a letter that I do understand."

9. **Type** C **and press Enter.**

 AutoCAD draws a final line segment, which creates a closed figure and ends the LINE command. A blank command line returns, indicating that AutoCAD is ready for the next command:

   ```
   Command:
   ```

10. Press F2.

AutoCAD displays the AutoCAD Text Window, which is simply an enlarged, scrollable version of the command window, as shown in Figure 2-9.

The normal three-line command window usually shows you what you need to see, but occasionally you want to review a larger chunk of command-line history ("What was AutoCAD trying to tell me a minute ago?!").

Figure 2-9:
My, how you've grown: F2 expands the command line to a command text window.

```
AutoCAD Text Window - Drawing3.dwg
Edit
Command:

Command: L
LINE Specify first point:
Specify next point or [Undo]:
Specify next point or [Undo]:
Specify next point or [Close/Undo]: U

Specify next point or [Undo]: 3,2

Specify next point or [Close/Undo]:
Specify next point or [Close/Undo]:
Specify next point or [Close/Undo]:
Specify next point or [Close/Undo]: X

Point or option keyword required.

Specify next point or [Close/Undo]: C

Command: |
```

11. Press the F2 key again.

AutoCAD closes the AutoCAD Text Window.

Here are a few other tips and tricks for effective keyboarding:

✔ **Use the Esc key to bail out of the current operation.** Sometimes you might get confused about what you're doing in AutoCAD and/or what you're seeing in the command window or the dynamic input tooltip. If you need to bail out of the current operation, just press Esc one or more times until you see a blank command line — Command: at the bottom of the command window, with nothing after it. As in most other Windows programs, Esc is the cancel key. Unlike many other Windows programs, AutoCAD keeps you well informed of whether an operation is in progress. The blank command line indicates that AutoCAD is resting, waiting for your next command.

✔ **Press Enter to accept the default action.** Some command prompts include a default action in angled brackets. For example, the first prompt of the POLYGON command is

```
Enter number of sides <4>:
```

The default here is four sides, and you can accept it simply by pressing Enter. (That is, you don't have to type **4** first.)

AutoCAD uses two kinds of brackets when it prompts.

- Command options appear in regular square brackets: [Close/ Undo].

 To activate a command option, type the letter(s) that appear in uppercase and then press Enter. The dynamic input tooltip doesn't display options in brackets; instead, you press the down-arrow key to display additional command options in rows next to the crosshairs.

- A default value or option appears in angled brackets: <4>.

 To choose the default value or option, simply press Enter. Default values in angled brackets appear in both the dynamic input tooltip and the command-line prompts.

You don't always have to press the Enter key to forward your input to AutoCAD. Depending on what you're doing, you can often right-click and pick Enter from the top of the shortcut menu. And most efficient of all, even for the most inept typists, you can use the spacebar as an Enter key — as long as you're not entering text.

✔ **Watch the command line.** You can discover a lot about how to use the command line simply by watching it after each action that you take. When you click a toolbar button or menu choice, AutoCAD types the name of the command automatically and displays it in the dynamic input tooltip and at the command line. If you're watching the command line, you'll absorb the command names more or less naturally.

When AutoCAD echoes commands automatically in response to your toolbar and menu clicks, it usually adds one or two extra characters to the front of the command name:.

- AutoCAD usually puts an underscore in front of the command name (for example, _LINE instead of LINE). The underscore is an Autodesk programmers' trick that enables non-English versions of AutoCAD to understand the English command names that are embedded in the menus.

- AutoCAD sometimes puts an apostrophe in front of the command name and any underscore (for example, '_ZOOM instead of ZOOM). The apostrophe indicates a *transparent* command; you can run the command in the middle of another command without canceling the first command. For example, you can start the LINE command, run the ZOOM command transparently, and then pick up where you left off with the LINE command.

✔ **Leave the command line in the default configuration.** The command window, like most other parts of the AutoCAD screen, is resizable and

movable. The default location (docked at the bottom of the AutoCAD screen) and size (three lines deep) work well for most people. Resist the temptation to mess with the command window's appearance — at least until you're comfortable with using the command line.

- ✔ **Right-click in the command window for options.** If you right-click in the command window, you see a menu with some useful choices, including Recent Commands — the last six commands that you ran.

- ✔ **Press the up- and down-arrow keys to cycle through the stack of commands that you've used recently.** This is another handy way to recall and rerun a command. Press the left- and right-arrow keys to edit the command line text that you've typed or recalled.

Most Windows users are familiar with Alt-key shortcuts. Press the Alt key in traditional Windows programs, and your menu bar lights up with one character of each menu item underlined. You type the underlined letter to open the menu or execute the command. AutoCAD 2010's implementation of the Fluent User Interface has an equivalent, called *KeyTips,* and they work in much the same way. In Figure 2-10, I've just pressed the Alt key. If I tap the A key now, the Annotate tab will open with a new set of KeyTips, and I can keep tapping the keys to execute a specific command.

Figure 2-10:
Hold down the Alt key to display a kazillion KeyTips.

Keeping tabs on palettes

Palettes are refined (well-mannered) versions of dialog boxes. Unlike regular dialog boxes, which insist on your undivided attention as long as they're open, palettes stay discreetly in the background as you carry on with other tasks. AutoCAD still has many dialog boxes, but over the past several releases, quite a few former dialog boxes have been replaced by palettes.

AutoCAD 2010 contains more than a dozen palettes (more than a half-dozen in AutoCAD LT). Unless noted otherwise, you can open any of these palettes from the Palettes panel of the View tab. The more commonly used palettes are

✔ **Properties and DesignCenter:** These two palettes are used to control object properties and named objects (layers, blocks, and so on), respectively. Chapter 6 shows you how.

✔ **Tool Palettes:** Each tool palette holds *content* (drawing symbols and hatch patterns) and/or *commands* (not regular AutoCAD commands — what would be the point? — but macros that make commands do specific things) instead of paints. You can create your own tool palettes, but the ones that come with AutoCAD contain dozens of symbols you can drag into your drawing — check 'em out!

✔ **Sheet Set Manager:** Provides tools for managing all of a project's drawings as a *sheet set.* Chapter 5 gives you some brief theory on why you might want to use sheet sets and how to do so. (AutoCAD LT does not support sheet sets.)

✔ **External References:** Used to attach external files to the current drawing; file types include raster images, Drawing Web Format (DWF, or DWFx) files, PDF files, MicroStation DGN files, and other drawing files. I discuss attaching external reference files in Chapter 18.

✔ **Markup Set Manager:** Displays design and drafting review comments from users of Autodesk Design Review. For more information on markup sets, see the online help.

✔ **QuickCalc:** A handy pushbutton scientific calculator that hides out on the Home tab's Utilities panel. You'll know if you need this.

✔ **Layer Properties Manager:** The main control center for managing the layers on your drawing had been basically unchanged for the past 15 years. AutoCAD 2009 palettized the Layer Properties Manager so it not only stays open while you're doing other things, but also applies any changes you make *instantly* in the drawing. The Layer Properties Manager can be found on the Layers panel of the Home tab.

Using the View and Home tabs is one way of opening palettes. Alternatively, several palettes have keyboard shortcuts. You can toggle these by pressing Ctrl+1 (Properties), Ctrl+2 (DesignCenter), Ctrl+3 (Tool Palettes), Ctrl+4 (Sheet Set Manager), Ctrl+7 (Markup Set Manager), or Ctrl+8 (QuickCalc).

Down the main stretch: The drawing area

After all these warmup laps, you're probably itching for the main event — the AutoCAD drawing area. This is where you do your drawing, of course. In the course of creating drawings, you click points to specify locations and distances, click objects to select them for editing, and zoom and pan to get a better view of what you're working on.

Most of this book shows you how to interact with the drawing area, but you should know a few things up front.

Model space and paper space layouts

One of the initially disorienting things about AutoCAD is that finished drawings can be composed of objects drawn in different *spaces,* which AutoCAD indicates with either two status bar buttons, or two or more tabs at the bottom left of the drawing area:

- ✔ **Model space** is where you create and modify the objects that represent things in the real world — walls, widgets, waterways, or whatever.

- ✔ **Paper space** is where you create particular views of these objects for plotting, usually with a title block around them. Paper space comprises one or more *layouts,* each of which can contain a different arrangement of model space views and different title block information.

When you click the Model button on the status bar, or the Model tab, you see pure, unadulterated model space, as shown in Figure 2-11. When you click the Layout button, you see a paper space layout, as shown in Figure 2-12. A completed layout usually includes one or more *viewports,* which are windows that display all or part of model space at a particular scale. A layout also usually includes a title block or other objects that exist only in the layout and don't appear when you click the Model tab. (Think of the viewport as a window looking into model space and the title block as a frame around the window.) Thus, a layout displays model space and paper space objects together, and AutoCAD lets you draw and edit objects in either space. See Chapter 5 for information about creating paper space layouts and Chapter 16 for the lowdown on plotting them.

When a layout is current, you can move the crosshairs back and forth between model space and paper space while remaining in the layout. You can't be in both spaces at the same time, however; if paper space is current, you can click directly over a model space object, but it won't be selected. Similarly, if model space is current, you can't select anything in paper space. To move between the two spaces, double-click inside a viewport to switch to model space or outside a viewport to switch to paper space.

This back-and-forth double-clicking is necessary only when you're drawing things while viewing one of the paper space layouts or adjusting the view of the drawing objects within the viewport. In practice, you probably won't draw very much using this method. Instead, you'll do most of your drawing on the Model tab, and after you've set up a paper space layout, click its layout tab only when you want to plot.

Figure 2-11:
A building model ready for editing in model space.

Figure 2-12:
Freshly laid out in paper space.

Drawing on the drawing area

Here are a few other things to know about the AutoCAD drawing area:

- ✔ Efficient, confident use of AutoCAD requires that you continually glance from the drawing area to the command window (to see those all-important prompts!) and then back up to the drawing area. This sequence is not a natural reflex for most people, and that's why the dynamic input tooltip at the crosshairs was introduced. But you still get information from the command line that you don't get anywhere else. Get in the habit of looking at the command line after each action that you take.

- ✔ Clicking at random in the drawing area is not quite as harmless in AutoCAD as it is in many other Windows programs. When you click in the AutoCAD drawing area, you're almost always performing some action — usually specifying a point or selecting objects for editing. Feel free to experiment, but look at the command line after each click. If you get confused, press Esc a couple of times to clear the current operation and return to the naked command prompt.

- ✔ In most cases, you can right-click in the drawing area to display a menu with some options for the current situation.

Fun with F1

The full AutoCAD 2010 Help menu is accessible only as a drop-down list on the program title bar (as always, pressing F1 at any time opens the online help window). Click the down arrow beside the question mark to open the menu (see Figure 2-13) to see what's available. I describe most of the help options here:

Figure 2-13:
Lots of
AutoCAD
help.

- ✔ **Help:** The main AutoCAD 2010 online help system, as shown in Figure 2-14, uses the same help engine as the Microsoft Office programs, Internet Explorer, and other modern Windows applications. As with these other programs, AutoCAD's help is context-sensitive; for example, if you start

the LINE command and just don't know what to do next, Help will . . . er, help. Click the Contents tab to browse through the various online reference manuals, click the Index tab to look up commands and concepts, and click the Search tab to look for specific words. In this book, I sometimes direct you to the AutoCAD online help system for information about advanced topics.

✔ **New Features Workshop:** This describes the new and enhanced features in AutoCAD 2010. It's especially useful for people who are upgrading from a previous AutoCAD release.

✔ **Additional Resources:** Most of the choices in the Additional Resources submenu connect you to various parts of Autodesk's Web site. The most useful is probably the Support Knowledge Base. From this link, you can search the Autodesk Knowledge Base, download software updates, and get help from Web- and newsgroup-based discussion groups.

Figure 2-14:
Help is at your F1 fingertip.

AutoCAD is one program with which you really need to take advantage of the online help resources. AutoCAD contains many commands, options, and quirks. (Alas, the quirks aren't listed in the online help.) Everyone from the greenest beginner to the most seasoned expert can find out something by using the AutoCAD online help. Take a moment to peruse the Contents tab of the main help system so that you know what's available. Throughout this book, I direct you to pages in the help system that I think are particularly useful, but don't be afraid to explore on your own when you get stuck or feel curious.

Chapter 3

A Lap around the CAD Track

In This Chapter

▶ Setting up a simple drawing

▶ Drawing some objects

▶ Zooming and panning in your drawing

▶ Editing some objects

▶ Plotting your drawing

The previous two chapters introduce you to the AutoCAD world and the AutoCAD 2010 interface. The chapters that follow present the techniques that underlie good drafting practice. By now, you're probably eager to start moving the crosshairs around and draw something! This chapter takes you on a gentle tour of the most common CAD drafting functions:

✔ **Setting up a new drawing**

✔ **Drawing some objects**

✔ **Editing those objects**

✔ **Zooming and panning so that you can view those objects better**

✔ **Plotting (printing) the drawing**

Much of the stuff in this chapter may be mysterious to you. Don't worry — I tell you where to look for more information on specific topics. In this chapter, you're simply taking AutoCAD for a test drive to get a feel for what it can do. Go ahead and kick the tires — and don't worry about putting a dent in the fender!

In this chapter, you create a drawing of an architectural detail — a base plate and column, as shown in Figure 3-1. Even if you don't work in architecture or building construction, this exercise gives you some simple shapes to work with and demonstrates commands you can use in most drafting disciplines.

Throughout this book, I show AutoCAD running in the Ribbon-based 2D Drafting & Annotation workspace introduced in AutoCAD 2009 and present in both AutoCAD 2010 and AutoCAD LT 2010. Likewise, I tell you where to find commands and what to select using the Ribbon.

If you're familiar with earlier versions of AutoCAD and the new user interface looks just too weird, you can strap on some training wheels while you're getting used to it. Just type **MENUBAR**, press Enter, type **1**, and press Enter to display the traditional AutoCAD pull-down menus above the Ribbon. If you're really and truly a Luddite where the Ribbon is concerned, you can revert to the 'classic' way of doing things by selecting the Workspace Switching button on the status bar and choosing AutoCAD Classic (AutoCAD LT Classic in that version). *Presto change-o* — suddenly it's 2008!

Although the drafting example in this chapter is simple, the procedures that it demonstrates are real, honest-to-CADness, proper drafting practice. I emphasize from the beginning the importance of proper drawing setup, putting objects on appropriate layers, and drawing and editing with due concern for precision. Some of the steps in this chapter may seem a bit complicated at first, but they reflect the way that experienced AutoCAD users work. My goal is to help you develop good CAD habits and do things the right way from the very start.

The step-by-step procedures in this chapter, unlike those in most chapters of this book, form a sequence. You must do the steps in order. It's like learning to drive, except that here you're free to stop in the middle of the street and take a break.

Figure 3-1:
How base is
my plate.

If you find that object selection or editing functions work differently from how I describe them in this chapter, you or someone else probably changed the configuration settings on the Option dialog box's Selection tab. Chapter 10 describes these settings and how to restore the AutoCAD defaults.

A Simple Setup

In this chapter, I walk you through creating, editing, viewing, and plotting a new drawing — refer to Figure 3-1 if you want to get an idea of what the finished product looks like. You can follow these steps using either imperial or metric units; I show metric values in brackets after the imperial ones, like this: Type **1.5 [38]** and press Enter.

Pay attention to AutoCAD's feedback. Glance at the messages AutoCAD sends after each step via the command window at the bottom of the screen or the dynamic input tooltip near the crosshairs, so that you begin to get familiar with the names of commands and their options. (If you don't see any messages next to the crosshairs as you use the program, click the DYN button on the status bar.)

In this first set of steps, you create a new drawing from a template, change some settings to establish a 1:10 (that is, 1 inch or 1 millimeter on the drawing is equivalent to 10 inches or 10 millimeters on the real object) scale, and save the drawing. As I describe in Chapter 4, drawing setup is not a simple task in AutoCAD. Nonetheless, drawing setup is an important part of the job, and if you don't get in the habit of doing it right, you run into endless problems later on — especially when you try to plot. (See Chapter 16 for the lowdown on plotting your drawings.)

1. **Start AutoCAD by double-clicking its shortcut on the Windows desktop.**

 If you don't have an AutoCAD shortcut on your desktop, choose Start⇨ All Programs⇨Autodesk⇨AutoCAD 2010⇨AutoCAD 2010. (The last two will be AutoCAD LT 2010, if that's your version.)

 The workspaces in AutoCAD 2010 look very similar to one another. To make sure you're in the same workspace that I am, look at the Workspace Switching button at the right side of the status bar. If it *doesn't* say 2D Drafting & Annotation, click the little black arrow on the button and then choose 2D Drafting & Annotation from the menu.

2. **Click the Application button to display the Application Menu. Click New, or pause the mouse pointer over New and select Drawing.**

 Don't click the New button on the Quick Access toolbar — use the menu. I explain why in Chapter 4, but just humor me for now. The Select Template dialog box appears with a list of drawing templates (DWT files), which you can use as the starting point for new drawings. Chapter 4 describes how to create and use drawing templates.

3. **Select acad.dwt [acadiso.dwt], as shown in Figure 3-2, and click Open. (For AutoCAD LT, select acadlt.dwt [acadltiso.dwt].)**

 AutoCAD creates a new, blank drawing with the settings in acad.dwt or acadiso.dwt. The acad.dwt template (acadlt.dwt in AutoCAD LT) is AutoCAD's default, plain-Jane template for drawings in *imperial units* (that is, units expressed in inches and/or feet). The acadiso.dwt (acadltiso.dwt in AutoCAD LT) template is the corresponding version for drawings created in metric units. Chapter 4 contains additional information about these and other templates.

Figure 3-2: Starting a new drawing from a template.

4. **Click all the buttons on the left side of the status bar except DYN until they look like they're turned off. If your status bar displays button icons rather than text labels, right-click the button with the tooltip that reads 'Dynamic Input'.**

 Some of these settings can make selecting points difficult. It's best to start with them all turned off and then toggle them on and off as needed. I tell you which ones to use in the steps that follow. I start you off with dynamic input enabled, but you'll turn it off before you actually draw anything.

 If your status bar buttons show icons instead of text, right-click *any* button, click Use Icons to *de*select the option, and display text labels. You can leave them that way or right-click and select Use Icons again to toggle the icon display back on.

5. **Type LIMITS and press Enter.**

 Drawing limits define your working area. AutoCAD prompts you to reset the model space limits. For now, ignore the dynamic input tooltip next to the crosshairs and look at the command window. The command line reads:

```
Specify lower left corner or [ON/OFF] <0.0000,0.0000>:
```

6. **Press Enter to keep 0,0 as the lower-left corner value.**

AutoCAD prompts for the upper-right corner. The command line reads:

```
Specify upper right corner <12.0000,9.0000>
        [<420.0000,297.0000>]:
```

7. **Type** 100,75 [2750,1850] **(no spaces) and press Enter.**

AutoCAD echoes the values you enter at the command line.

100 x 75 corresponds to 10 inches by 7.5 inches (a little smaller than an 8.5-x-11-inch piece of paper turned on its long side) times a drawing scale factor of 10 (because you're eventually going to plot at 1:10 scale). If you're a metric maven, 2750 x 1850 corresponds to 275 mm by 185 mm (slightly smaller than an ISO A4 sheet turned lengthways) times a drawing scale factor of 10 (because you, too, will eventually plot at 1:10 scale). See Chapter 4 for more information about drawing scales.

8. **Right-click the SNAP button on the AutoCAD status bar and choose Settings. If your status bar displays button icons rather than text labels, right-click the button with the Snap Mode tooltip.**

The Snap and Grid tab of the Drafting Settings dialog box appears, as shown in Figure 3-3. (In AutoCAD LT's dialog box there is no Follow Dynamic UCS option.)

Figure 3-3:
Snap and
Grid
settings.

9. **Change the values in the dialog box, as shown in Figure 3-3:**

 • *Snap On:* Selected

 Snap constrains your crosshairs to moving in an invisible grid of equally spaced points (0.5 [10] units apart in this case).

 • *Grid On:* Selected

 Grid displays a visible grid of little dots on the screen (5 [100] units apart in this case), which you can use as reference points. The grid doesn't appear on printed drawings.

 • *Snap X Spacing:* 0.5 [10]

 • *Snap Y Spacing:* 0.5 [10]

 • *Grid X Spacing:* 5 [100]

 • *Grid Y Spacing:* 5 [100]

10. **Click OK.**

 You see some grid dots, 5 [100] units apart, in the drawing area. If you move your mouse around and watch the coordinate display area at the left side of the status bar, you notice that the values change in 0.5-unit [10-unit] increments.

11. **Click Zoom (the gray button with the magnifying glass) on the status bar (near the middle).**

 AutoCAD prompts at both the command window and the dynamic input tooltip near the crosshairs:

    ```
    Specify corner of window, enter a scale factor (nX or
           nXP), or
    ```

12. **Press the down arrow on your keyboard to unroll the dynamic input tooltip's list of command options and then use your mouse to choose All.**

 AutoCAD zooms out so that the entire area defined by the limits — as indicated by the grid dots — is visible.

13. **Click the Save button on the Quick Access Toolbar or press Ctrl+S.**

 Because you haven't saved the drawing yet, AutoCAD opens the Save Drawing As dialog box.

14. **Navigate to a suitable folder by choosing from the Save In drop-down list and/or double-clicking folders in the list of folders below it.**

 Remember where you save the file so you can go back to it later.

15. **Type a name in the File Name box and click Save.**

 For example, type **Detail** or **My Plate is Base**.

Depending on your Windows Explorer settings, you may or may not see the .dwg extension in the File Name edit box. In any case, you don't need to type it. AutoCAD adds it for you.

AutoCAD saves the new DWG file to the folder you specified.

Whew — that was more work than digging a post hole — and all just to set up a simple drawing! Chapter 4 goes into more detail about drawing setup and describes why all these gyrations are necessary.

Drawing a (Base) Plate

With a properly setup drawing, you're ready to draw some objects. In this example, you use the RECTANG command to draw a steel base plate and column, the CIRCLE command to draw an anchor bolt, and the POLYGON command to draw a hexagonal nut. (Both the RECTANG and POLYGON commands create *polylines* — objects that contain a series of straight-line segments and/or arc segments.) I describe these drawing commands in more detail in Chapters 8 and 9.

AutoCAD, like most CAD programs, uses *layers* as an organizing principle for all the objects that you draw. Chapter 6 describes layers and other object properties in detail. In this example, you create separate layers for the base plate, column, anchor bolts, and nuts. This might seem like layer madness, but when you're doing complex drawings, you need to use a lot of layers just to keep things organized.

Drawing rectangles on the right layers

The following steps demonstrate how to create and use layers, as well as how to draw rectangles. You also see how to apply fillets to objects and offset them. (Chapter 6 describes layers in detail, and Chapter 8 covers the RECTANG command. Chapter 11 explains the FILLET and OFFSET commands.) Start by creating a Column layer and a Plate layer and then drawing a rectangular column on the Column layer and a square base plate on the Plate layer:

1. **Make sure that you complete the drawing setup in the previous section of this chapter and have the drawing open in AutoCAD.**

2. **Click the Home tab on the Ribbon.**

 You'll find the most frequently used commands for 2D drafting tasks on the Ribbon's Home tab. (For a refresher on the contents of the other tabs, refer to the "Unraveling the Ribbon" section in Chapter 2.) Unless I direct you otherwise, look on the Home tab for the panels and buttons I specify in the following steps.

3. **On the Layers panel, click the Layer Properties button.**

 The Layer Properties button is at the upper-left corner of the Layers panel. The LAYER command starts, and AutoCAD displays the Layer Properties Manager palette.

4. **Click the New Layer button.**

 AutoCAD adds a new layer to the list and gives it the default name Layer1 (see Figure 3-4).

Figure 3-4:
Creating a
new layer.

5. **Type a more suitable name for the layer on which you'll draw the column and press Enter.**

 For this example, type **Column**.

6. **Click the color swatch or name (white) in the Column layer row.**

 The Select Color dialog box appears (see Figure 3-5).

Figure 3-5:
Blue is the
color —
select it
from the
standard
color tiles.

7. **Click color 5 (blue) in the single, separate row to the left of the ByLayer and ByBlock buttons and click OK.**

 The Select Color dialog box closes, and AutoCAD changes the color of the Column layer to blue.

8. **Repeat Steps 3 through 6 to create a new layer named Plate and set its color to 4 (cyan).**

9. **With layer Plate still highlighted, click the Set Current button (the green check mark).**

 Plate becomes the current layer, and everything you draw is placed on that layer until you set a different layer current.

10. **Click Close (the 'X' at the top-left corner of the palette) to close the Layer Properties Manager palette.**

 The Layer drop-down list on the Home tab's Layers panel displays Plate as the current layer. Now you can draw a rectangular plate on the Plate layer.

 You probably already know that the RECTANG command will draw a rectangular plate for you, but for the next step, pretend you don't.

11. **Click the Application button, click inside the Search edit box at the top of the Application Menu, and start typing** RECT. . .

 As you type into the Search box, AutoCAD guesses what you might be looking for. When you've typed enough letters, the command you're probably looking for appears at or near the top of the Application Menu.

12. **When "Rectangle" appears in the Search results, simply click the command item.**

 The RECTANG command starts, and AutoCAD prompts you to specify the first corner point. The command line shows:

    ```
    Specify first corner point or [Chamfer/Elevation/
          Fillet/Thickness/Width]:
    ```

13. **Click in the drawing area at the point 20,20 [500,500].**

 By watching the coordinate display on the dynamic input tooltip, you can see the coordinates of the current crosshairs location. Because snap is set to 0.5 [10] units, you can land right on the point 20,20 [500,500]. Picking the first corner in this location gives you enough room to work.

 AutoCAD prompts at the command line:

    ```
    Specify other corner point or [Area/Dimensions/
          Rotation]:
    ```

14. **Type** 36,36 [900,900] **(without any spaces) and press Enter.**

 Make sure that the DYN button is on for this step. If it's not, AutoCAD treats an input of 36,36 as absolute coordinates — that is, 36 units above and 36 units to the right *of the origin*. When DYN is on, an input of 36,36 is treated as 36 units above and 36 units to the right *of the last point* — in

other words, as *relative* to the last point. See Chapter 7 for more information about typing absolute and relative coordinates.

AutoCAD draws the 36 x 36 [900 x 900] rectangle, as shown in Figure 3-6. It's on the Plate layer and inherits that layer's cyan color.

You draw the column next, but first you have to change layers.

15. **On the Layers panel of the Home tab, click the Layer drop-down list to display the list of layers. Click Column to set it as the current layer.**

Using the Layer drop-down list saves you from having to open the Layer Properties Manager, selecting the layer, clicking the Set Current button, and clicking Close. Becoming an AutoCAD master is *all* about efficiency!

16. **Press Enter to repeat the RECTANG command.**

You can repeat the last command at any time by pressing Enter.

In the next steps, you create a hollow steel column.

17. **At the Specify First Corner Point prompt, type** 32,29 [800,725] **and press Enter.**

18. **At the Specify Other Corner Point prompt, type** 12,18 [300,450] **and press Enter.**

A second rectangle is drawn in the middle of the base plate.

Next, you round the corners of the column with the FILLET command and then use OFFSET to give it some thickness.

Figure 3-6:
Your (base) plate is empty.

19. **On the Home tab's Modify panel, click the Fillet button.**

 The FILLET command starts, and AutoCAD prompts you to select the first object. Look at the command line to see the options for this command. In the next step, you specify a 2-inch [50 mm] radius fillet to all four corners.

20. **Type R and press Enter to set a new fillet radius. Type 2 [50] and press Enter.**

 AutoCAD again prompts you to select the first object. You could pick each of the eight lines that need to be filleted, but because the column is a continuous polyline, in this case a more efficient method is to use the FILLET command's Polyline option to fillet all four corners in one fell swoop.

21. **Type P to choose the Polyline option and then press Enter.**

 AutoCAD prompts you to select a 2D polyline.

22. **Select the rectangle you drew in Steps 14 to 16.**

 All four corners of the column are rounded with a 2-inch [50 mm] radius fillet.

 Next, offset the polyline to create a 3/4-inch [19 mm] thick steel column.

23. **On the Modify panel, click the Offset button.**

24. **At the Specify Offset Distance prompt, type .75 [19] and press Enter.**

25. **At the Select Object to Offset prompt, click the rounded rectangle. At the Specify Point on Side to Offset prompt, click anywhere *inside* the rounded rectangle. Press Enter to complete the command.**

 AutoCAD offsets the selected object toward the inside of the rounded rectangle (see Figure 3-7).

26. **Click the Dynamic Input button on the status bar so the button looks turned off.**

 Now that you've given dynamic input a test drive, turn it off for the rest of this chapter. You know how to turn it off and on now, and if you like it, by all means turn it on again for the remainder of the book. My opinion is that it gets in the way too much to be truly useful, so I rarely use it.

27. **Press Ctrl+S to save the drawing.**

 AutoCAD saves the drawing and renames the previously saved version *drawingname*.bak — for example, My Plate is Base.bak. .bak is AutoCAD's extension for a backup file.

Select the object here.

Figure 3-7:
Give it
some thick-
ness with
OFFSET.

Pick here to show offset directions.

Circling your plate

You can use the CIRCLE command to draw a 1 1/2-inch diameter anchor bolt on an Anchor Bolts layer by following these steps:

1. **Repeat Steps 2 through 6 in the previous section to create a new layer for the anchor bolts. Give the layer the name Anchor Bolts, assign it the color 3 (green), set it as the current layer, and then close the Layer Properties Manager.**

 The Layer drop-down on the Layers panel displays Anchor Bolts as the current layer.

2. **On the Home tab's Draw panel, click the Circle button.**

 The CIRCLE command starts, and AutoCAD prompts you to specify the center point. The command line shows:

   ```
   Specify center point for circle or [3P/2P/Ttr (tan tan
   radius)]:
   ```

3. **Click in the drawing area at point 26,26 [650,650].**

 AutoCAD asks you to specify the size of the circle. The command line shows:

```
Specify radius of circle or [Diameter]:
```

You decide that you want 1 1/2-inch [38 mm] diameter anchor bolts. AutoCAD is asking for a radius. Although you can probably figure out the radius of a 1 1/2-inch [38 mm] diameter circle, specify the Diameter option and let AutoCAD do the hard work.

4. Type D **and press Enter to select the Diameter option.**

AutoCAD prompts:

```
Specify diameter of circle:
```

5. Type 1.5 [38] **and press Enter.**

AutoCAD draws the 1 1/2-inch [38 mm] diameter circle. It's on the Anchor Bolts layer and inherits that layer's green color (see Figure 3-8).

6. Press Ctrl+S to save the drawing.

Figure 3-8:
Anchor it
with CIRCLE.

Placing your polygon

Every good bolt deserves a nut. Use the POLYGON command to draw a hexagonal shape on a Nuts layer (well, what else would you call it?). Besides showing you how to draw polygons, these steps introduce you to a couple of AutoCAD's more useful precision techniques: object snaps and ortho mode.

1. **Repeat Steps 2 through 6 in the "Drawing rectangles on the right layers" section to create a new layer for the nuts and set it as the current layer. Give the layer the name Nuts and assign it the color 1 (red).**

 The Layer drop-down list displays Nuts as the current layer.

 You don't have to create a separate layer for every type of object that you draw. For example, you could draw both the anchor bolts and nuts on a layer called Hardware. Layer names and usage depend on industry and office practices in addition to a certain amount of individual judgment. Having too many layers is better than having too few because lumping two or more layers together is much easier than dividing the objects on one layer into two or more layers.

 The Ribbon's standard panels aren't big enough to contain a button for every command, so AutoCAD hides the ones that don't fit in slideout panels that you open by clicking the panel label. A small down-pointing triangle beside the panel name means there's a slideout with more commands available.

2. **Click the Draw panel's label to open the panel slideout. On the Draw panel slideout, click the Polygon button — the one that looks like a plan of the Pentagon.**

 The POLYGON command starts, and AutoCAD prompts you to:

   ```
   Enter number of sides <4>:
   ```

 Peek ahead to Figure 3-9 in order to get an idea of how the nut will look after you draw it. Four-sided nuts can be a little difficult to adjust in the real world, so I stick with the conventional hexagonal sort.

3. **Type 6 and press Enter.**

 AutoCAD next prompts you for the center of the polygon:

   ```
   Specify center of polygon or [Edge]:
   ```

 In the next steps, you use one of AutoCAD's precision drafting modes: object snap. I explain object snap mode in detail in Chapter 7, but for now, just follow along here.

4. **Click the OSNAP button on the status bar to turn on object snap mode. When object snap is enabled, the command prompt shows `<Osnap on>`.**

 As you move the crosshairs around near the anchor bolt, notice that AutoCAD tends to pull the crosshairs to certain points on existing objects.

5. **Move the crosshairs over the anchor bolt you just drew.**

 A tooltip should show Center and pull the crosshairs to the center of the anchor bolt circle. If you don't see a Center osnap marker or tooltip, then right-click the OSNAP button and click Center. You may also see tracking vectors across the screen from this point — you can ignore those.

6. **Click when the tooltip reads Center — not Center-Intersection or something similar — just Center.**

 The POLYGON command draws regular closed polygons based on an imaginary circle; the center of this imaginary circle is the point you just picked.

 AutoCAD prompts:

   ```
   Enter an option [Inscribed in circle/Circumscribed
   about circle] <I>:
   ```

7. **Press Enter to accept the default Inscribed in Circle option.**

 The *Inscribed* option draws a polygon whose corners touch the circumference of the imaginary circle. The *Circumscribed* option draws a polygon whose sides are tangent to the circumference of the circle.

 AutoCAD then asks you to:

   ```
   Specify radius of circle:
   ```

8. **Turn on ortho mode by clicking the ORTHO button on the status bar until you see <Ortho on> on the command line.**

 Ortho mode forces the crosshairs to move *orthogonally* — that is in a precise horizontal or vertical direction. I describe ortho mode more fully in Chapter 7.

9. **Click and drag the mouse to the right so the top and bottom sides of the polygon are horizontal, *but don't click yet*.**

10. **Type** 1.5 [38] **and press Enter.**

 AutoCAD draws the nut, as shown in Figure 3-9. It's on the Nuts layer and inherits that layer's red color.

 If your nut-and-bolt looks just like Figure 3-9, way to go — you did it right! If, by chance, your bolt is completely inside the circle, you probably missed Step 4 of the "Circling your plate" section where I tell you to use the CIRCLE command's Diameter option.

11. **Turn off ortho mode and running object snaps by clicking the ORTHO and OSNAP buttons on the status bar until they look dimmed and you see <Ortho off> and <Osnap off> on the command line.**

 Occasionally, ortho and running object snaps interfere with drafting in AutoCAD. Disabling them as you do in this step keeps them from being a problem.

12. **Press Ctrl+S to save the drawing.**

Not much of a base plate yet, is it? But don't worry — I cover creating more nuts and bolts with editing commands later in this chapter. If your brain is feeling full, now is a good time to take a break and go look out the window. If you exit AutoCAD, just restart the program and reopen your drawing when you're ready to continue.

Figure 3-9:
Bolts and
nuts . . .
ready to
anchor.

Getting a Closer Look with Zoom and Pan

The example drawing in this chapter is pretty uncluttered and small, but most real CAD drawings are neither of those. Technical drawings are usually jam-packed with lines, text, and dimensions. CAD drawings often get plotted on sheets of paper that measure two to three feet on a side — that's in the hundreds of millimeters, if you're a metric maven. Anyone who owns a monitor that large probably can afford to hire a whole room of drafters and, therefore, isn't reading this book. You need to zoom and pan in your drawings — a lot. I cover zooming and panning in detail in Chapter 12. Quick definitions should suffice for now:

- **Zoom** means changing the magnification of the display. When you zoom in, you move closer to the drawing objects so you can see detail, and when you zoom out, you move farther away so you can see more of the drawing area.

- **Pan** means moving from one area to another without changing the magnification. If you've used the scroll bars in any application, you've panned the display.

Zooming and panning frequently lets you see the details better, draw more confidently (because you can see what you're doing), and edit more quickly (because object selection is easier when a zillion objects aren't on the screen).

Fortunately, zooming and panning in AutoCAD is as simple as it is necessary. The following steps describe how to use AutoCAD's Zoom and Pan Realtime feature, which is pretty easy to operate and provides a lot of flexibility. Chapter 12 covers additional zoom and pan options.

To zoom and pan in your drawing, follow these steps:

1. **Right-click in a blank area of the drawing and choose Zoom from the shortcut (right-click) menu.**

 The Realtime option of the ZOOM command starts. The crosshairs change to a magnifying glass, and AutoCAD prompts you at the command line:

   ```
   Press ESC or ENTER to exit, or right-click to display
   shortcut menu.
   ```

2. **Move the crosshairs near the middle of the screen, press and hold the left mouse button, and drag the crosshairs up and down until the base plate almost fills the screen.**

 As you can see, dragging up increases the zoom magnification, and dragging down decreases it.

3. **Right-click in the drawing area to display the Zoom/Pan Realtime menu, as shown in Figure 3-10, and choose Pan from the menu.**

Figure 3-10: The Zoom/ Pan Realtime shortcut menu.

The magnifying glass mouse pointer changes to a hand.

4. **Click and drag to pan the drawing until the plate is more or less centered in the drawing area.**

 You're not moving the plate, although it may look like it. You're moving your viewing position while the plate stays put. Never move drawing objects if you just want to view them from a different position.

 You can use the right-click menu to toggle back and forth between Zoom and Pan as many times as you like. If you get lost, choose Zoom Original or Zoom Extents to return to a recognizable view.

5. **Right-click in the drawing area and choose Exit from the Zoom/Pan Realtime menu.**

 The hand pointer returns to the normal AutoCAD crosshairs.

Modifying to Make It Merrier

When you have a better view of your base plate, you can edit the objects on it more easily. In the following sections, you use the ARRAY command to add more anchor bolts, the STRETCH command to change the shape of the plate, and the HATCH command to add crosshatching to the column. As always, I cover these commands in detail later in the book.

Hooray for array

Using the ARRAY command is a great way to generate a bunch of new objects from existing objects at regular angles or spacing. The array pattern can be either *rectangular* (that is, columns and rows of objects) or *polar* (in a circle around a center point, like the spokes of a wheel around its hub). In this example, you use a rectangular array to create three additional anchor bolts:

1. **On the Home tab's Modify panel, click the Array button — the one with four squares.**

 The ARRAY command starts, and AutoCAD displays the Array dialog box.

2. **Select the Rectangular Array radio button.**

3. **Click the Select Objects button.**

 The Array dialog box temporarily disappears, and AutoCAD prompts you to select objects.

4. **Turn off Snap mode by clicking the SNAP button on the status bar until it looks dimmed and you see <Snap off> on the command line.**

 Turning off Snap mode temporarily makes selecting objects easier.

5. **Click the anchor bolt and then click the nut.**

 If you encounter any problems while trying to select objects, press the Esc key a couple of times to cancel the command; then restart the ARRAY command and try again.

 AutoCAD continues to prompt you at the command line:

   ```
   Select objects: 1 found, 2 total
   ```

6. **Press Enter or right-click to end object selection.**

 The Array dialog box reappears.

7. **Click inside the Rows text box and set the value to 2. Press Tab to move to the Columns text box and set the value to 2.**

The source object is included in AutoCAD arrays. The preview shows that you've set up a rectangular array of four evenly spaced objects (see Figure 3-11).

Figure 3-11: The Array dialog box, ready to bolt your base plate.

8. **In the Row Offset text box, type** 24 [600]. **Click inside the Column Offset text box and type** 24 [600].

 A rectangular array creates regularly spaced rows and columns. The Row Offset is the vertical distance separating the rows; Column Offset is the horizontal distance separating columns.

9. **Click the Preview button.**

 AutoCAD shows you what the array will look like if you accept the current settings. You can pan or zoom within preview mode if you need a bigger or a more detailed view.

10. **If anything looks wrong, click the Esc key, make changes, and preview again. When everything looks good, right-click to accept the array.**

 AutoCAD adds the additional objects to the drawing, as shown in Figure 3-12.

11. **Press Ctrl+S to save the drawing.**

Perfect! Except that nutbar engineer has decided the column needs to be 18 x 18 inches [450 x 450 mm] instead of 12 x 18 inches [300 x 450 mm — unfortunately, there are just as many metric nutbars as imperial ones]. And that means the base plate is too small, and the anchor bolts are in the wrong place, too. If you were working on the drawing board, you'd be getting out an eraser and rubbing out all your efforts. AutoCAD to the rescue!

Figure 3-12:
Buttoned-
down base
plate.

Stretching out

The STRETCH command is powerful but a little complicated — it can stretch or move objects, depending on how you select them. The key to using STRETCH is specifying a *crossing selection box* properly. (Chapter 10 gives you more details about crossing boxes and how to use them with the STRETCH command.)

Follow these steps to stretch the column and base plate:

1. **On the Modify panel, click the Stretch button — the one with the corner of a rectangle being stretched.**

 The STRETCH command starts, and AutoCAD prompts you to select objects. This is one of those times (and one of those commands) that really does require you to look at the command line:

   ```
   Select objects to stretch by crossing-window or
           crossing-polygon...
   Select objects:
   ```

2. **Click a point above and to the right of the upper-right corner of the plate (Point 1 in Figure 3-13).**

Point 1

Figure 3-13:
Specifying
a crossing
box for the
STRETCH
command.

Point 2

3. **Move the crosshairs to the left.**

 The pointer changes to a dashed rectangle enclosing a rectangular green area, which indicates that you're specifying a crossing box. AutoCAD prompts you at the command line:

   ```
   Select objects: Specify opposite corner:
   ```

4. **Click a point below the plate, roughly under the center of the column (Point 2 in Figure 3-13).**

 The crossing box must cut through the plate and column in order for the STRETCH command to work (refer to Figure 3-13).

 AutoCAD prompts you at the command line:

   ```
   Select objects: Specify opposite corner: 7 found
   Select objects:
   ```

5. **Press Enter to end object selection.**

 AutoCAD prompts you to specify the base point.

6. **If they're not already on, turn on Snap mode, ortho mode, and running object snap mode by clicking the SNAP, ORTHO, and OSNAP buttons on the status bar until they appear highlighted.**

7. **Click the lower-right corner of the plate.**

 This point serves as the base point for the stretch operation. Chapter 11 describes base points and displacements in greater detail.

 AutoCAD prompts you at the command line:

   ```
   Specify second point or <use first point as
   displacement>:
   ```

8. **Move the crosshairs to the right until the tooltip shows a displacement of 6 [150] units to the right and then click in the drawing space (see Figure 3-14).**

 AutoCAD *stretches* the column and plate by the distance that you indicate and *moves* the anchor bolts that were completely inside the crossing window rectangle, as shown in Figure 3-14.

 If your first stretch didn't work right, hold down the Ctrl key, type **Z**, and try again. STRETCH is an immensely useful command — one that makes you wonder how drafters used to do it all with erasers and pencils — but it does take some practice to get the hang of those crossing boxes.

9. **Press Ctrl+S to save the drawing.**

Figure 3-14:
Stretching the base plate.

Crossing your hatches

Your final editing task is to add some crosshatching to the space between the inside and outside edges of the column to indicate that the drawing shows a section of the column. To do so, follow these steps:

1. **Turn off Snap, ortho, and running object snaps by clicking the SNAP, ORTHO, and OSNAP buttons on the status bar until they look dimmed.**

2. **Repeat Steps 2 through 6 from the "Drawing rectangles on the right layers" section to create a new layer named Hatch. Set its color to 2 (yellow) and make it the current layer.**

3. **On the Home tab's Draw panel, click the Hatch button — the one that shows the fine crosshatching inside a square.**

 The Hatch and Gradient dialog box appears. (If you're using AutoCAD LT, the dialog box title is simply Hatch.) For more information on this dialog box, and hatching in general, see Chapter 15.

4. **In the Hatch tab's Hatch and Pattern area, click the Pattern drop-down list and select ANSI31.**

 The ANSI31 pattern fills the selected area with an arrangement of parallel angled lines.

5. **On the right side of the dialog box, click Add: Pick Points.**

 The dialog box temporarily closes.

6. **At the Pick Internal Point prompt, pick a point between the inside and outside edges of the column. Zoom in if you need to get closer.**

 AutoCAD selects the two filleted polylines.

7. **Press Enter to end object selection.**

 The Hatch and Gradient dialog box reappears. To check if the hatch parameters are correct, click the Preview button. It looks like the hatch pattern may be too fine.

8. **Press Esc to return to the Hatch and Gradient dialog box.**

9. **In the Scale box, set the value to 5 and click Preview again. If it looks okay, right-click to accept the hatch pattern.**

 Your finished column and base plate looks like Figure 3-15.

10. **Click the Zoom button on the status bar, right-click in empty space in the drawing area, and choose All from the menu.**

 AutoCAD zooms out so that the entire area defined by the limits is visible.

11. **Press Ctrl+S to save the drawing.**

Figure 3-15:
Your column is hatched.

After some drawing and editing, you may wonder how you're supposed to know when to turn off or on the various status bar modes (Snap, Grid, Ortho, Osnap, and so on). You'll start to get an instinctive sense of when each mode is useful and when it gets in the way. In subsequent chapters of this book, I give you some more specific guidelines.

Following the Plot

Looking at drawings on a computer screen and exchanging them with others via e-mail or Web sites is all well and good. But sooner or later, someone — maybe you! — will want to see a printed version. Printing drawings — or *plotting,* as CAD geeks like to call it — is much more complicated than printing a word processing document or a spreadsheet. That's because you have to worry about things, such as drawing scale, lineweights, title blocks, and weird paper sizes. I go deeper into plotting in Chapter 16, but here's an abbreviated procedure that helps you generate a recognizable printed drawing.

The following steps show you how to plot the *model space* portion of the drawing. As Chapter 5 describes, AutoCAD includes a sophisticated feature — *paper space layouts* — for creating arrangements of your drawing that you plot. These arrangements usually include a title block. Because I promised you a gentle

tour of AutoCAD drafting functions, I left the paper space layout and title block issues until a bit later. When you're ready for the whole plotting enchilada, turn to Chapter 5 for information about how to set up paper space layouts and see Chapter 16 for full plotting instructions.

Follow these steps to plot a drawing:

1. **Click the Plot button on the Quick Access Toolbar.**

 The Quick Access Toolbar is at the left end of the program's title bar, just to the right of the Application button. The Plot icon looks like an ordinary desktop printer.

 AutoCAD opens the Plot-Model dialog box, with the title bar showing what you're plotting (model space in this case).

2. **Click the More Options button (in the bottom-right corner of the dialog box, next to the Help button).**

 The Plot dialog box reveals additional settings, as shown in Figure 3-16.

Figure 3-16: The Plot dialog box with the More Options area visible.

3. **In the Printer/Plotter area, select a printer from the Name list.**

4. **In the Paper Size area, use the drop-down list to select a paper size that's loaded in your printer or plotter.**

 Anything Letter size (8 1/2 x 11 inches) [A4 (210 x 297 mm)] or larger works for this example.

5. **In the Plot Area, select Limits from the drop-down list.**

 This is the entire drawing area, which you specified when you set up the drawing earlier in this chapter.

6. **In the Plot Offset area, select the Center the Plot check box.**

 Alternatively, you can specify offsets of 0 or other amounts in order to position the plot at a specific location on the paper.

7. **In the Plot Scale area, deselect the Fit to Paper check box and choose 1:10 from the Scale drop-down list.**

 1:10 is the scale used to set up the drawing (in the earlier section, "A Simple Setup"). No prizes for guessing the metric equivalent of 1:10!

8. **In the Plot Style Table (Pen Assignments) area, click the drop-down list and choose** `monochrome.ctb`.

 The `monochrome.ctb` plot style table ensures that all your lines appear solid black, rather than as different colors or weird shades of gray. See Chapter 16 for information about plot style tables and monochrome and color plotting.

9. **Click Yes when a question dialog box appears, asking Assign This Plot Style Table to All Layouts?**

 You can leave the remaining settings at their default values (refer to Figure 3-16).

 Some printers let you print closer to the edges of the sheet than others. To find out the actual printable area of your own printer, move the mouse pointer to the postage stamp-sized partial preview in the middle of the Plot dialog box and pause. A tooltip appears, listing the Paper Size and Printable Area for the printer and paper size that you selected.

10. **Click the Preview button.**

 If the plot scale you entered in the Plot dialog box is out of sync with the drawing's annotation scale, a Plot Scale Confirm dialog box appears, advising you that the annotation scale is not equal to the plot scale. This drawing doesn't contain any text or dimensions, and I didn't bother making the hatch annotative, so it's fine to click Continue and generate the plot.

 Annotative scaling controls the printed size of text, dimensions, hatching, and other types of annotation object at plot time — as long as the drawing's annotation scale matches the plot scale. I explain annotative objects in Chapter 13.

 The Plot dialog box disappears temporarily, and AutoCAD shows how the plot will look on paper. In addition, AutoCAD prompts you on the status bar:

```
Press pick button and drag vertically to zoom, ESC or
ENTER to exit, or right-click to display shortcut
menu.
```

11. **Right-click in the preview area and choose Exit.**

12. **If the preview doesn't look right, adjust the settings in the Plot dialog box and look at the preview again until it looks right.**

13. **Click OK.**

 The Plot Scale Confirm dialog box pops up again. You may be tempted to click Always Continue Under These Conditions, but I recommend against that until you've gained a little familiarity with annotative objects.

 The Plot dialog box closes. AutoCAD generates the plot and sends it to the printer. After generating the plot, AutoCAD displays a Plot and Publish Job Complete balloon notification from the right end of the status bar. (A Click to View Plot and Publish Details link displays more information about the plot job.)

14. **Click the X (close) button in the Plot and Publish Job Complete balloon notification.**

 The balloon notification disappears.

 If you're not happy with the lineweights of the lines on your plot at this point, fear not. You can use the lineweights feature (Chapter 6) or plot styles (Chapter 16) to control plotted lineweights.

15. **Press Ctrl+S to save the drawing.**

Congratulations! You successfully executed your first plot in AutoCAD. Chapter 16 tells you more — much more — about AutoCAD's highly flexible but occasionally perplexing plotting system.

Chapter 4

Setup for Success

In This Chapter

▶ Developing a setup strategy

▶ Starting a new drawing

▶ Setting up model space

▶ Creating and using drawing templates

Surprisingly, drawing setup is one of the trickier aspects of using AutoCAD. It's an easy thing to do incompletely or incorrectly, and AutoCAD 2010 doesn't provide a simple, one-click tool to help you do all of it right. And yet, drawing setup is a crucial thing to get right. Setup steps that you omit or don't do right may come back to bite you later.

Sloppy setup really becomes apparent when you try to *plot* (print) your drawing. Things that seemed more or less okay as you zoomed around on the screen are suddenly the wrong size or scale on paper. And nothing brands someone as a naive AutoCAD wannabe as quickly as the inability to plot a drawing at the right size and scale. Chapter 5 covers plotting procedures, but the information in this chapter is a necessary prerequisite to successful plotting and sheet setup. If you don't get this stuff right, there's a good chance you'll find that . . . the plot sickens.

This chapter describes the decisions you need to make before you set up a new drawing, shows the steps for doing a complete and correct setup, and demonstrates how to save setup settings for reuse.

Don't assume that you can just create a new blank DWG file and start drawing things. *Do* read this chapter before you get too deep into the later chapters in this book. Many AutoCAD drawing commands and concepts depend on proper drawing setup, so you'll have a much easier time drawing and editing things if you've done your setup homework. A few minutes invested in setting up a drawing well can save hours of thrashing around later on.

After you've digested the detailed drawing setup procedures described in this and the following chapter, use the AutoCAD Drawing Setup Roadmap on the Cheat Sheet at the front of this book as a quick reference to guide you through the process.

A Setup Roadmap

You have to set up AutoCAD correctly, partly because AutoCAD is so flexible and partly because, well, you're doing *CAD* — computer-aided drafting (or design). The computer can't aid your drafting (or design) if you don't clue it in on things like system of measure, drawing scale, paper size, and units. In this context, the following facts help explain why AutoCAD drawing setup is important:

- **Electronic paper:** The most important thing you can do to make using AutoCAD fun is to work on a correctly set up drawing so that your screen acts like paper, only smarter. When drawing on real paper, you constantly have to translate between units on the paper and the real-life units of the object you're drawing. But when drawing in AutoCAD's smarter paper, you draw directly in real-life units — feet and inches, millimeters, or whatever you typically use on your projects. AutoCAD can then calculate distances and dimensions for you and add them to the drawing. You can make the mouse pointer jump directly to preset intervals on-screen, and a visible, resizable grid gives you a better sense of the scale of your drawing. However, this smart paper function works well only if you tell AutoCAD some crucial parameters for your specific drawing. AutoCAD can't really do its job until you tell it how to work.

- **Dead-trees paper:** Creating a great drawing on-screen that doesn't fit well on paper is all too easy. After you finish creating your drawing on the smart paper AutoCAD provides on-screen, you then usually have to plot it on the good, old-fashioned paper that people have used for thousands of years. At that point, you must deal with the fact that people like to use certain standard paper sizes and drawing scales. (Most people also like everything to fit neatly on one sheet of paper.) If you set up AutoCAD correctly, good plotting results automatically; if not, plotting time can become one colossal hassle.

- **It ain't easy:** AutoCAD provides templates and Setup Wizards for you, but the templates don't work well unless you understand them, and some of the wizards don't work well even if you do understand them. This deficiency is one of the major weaknesses in AutoCAD. You must figure out on your own (with the help of this book, of course) how to make the program work right. If you just plunge in without carefully setting up, your drawing and printing efforts are likely to wind up a real mess.

Fortunately, setting up AutoCAD correctly is a bit like following a roadmap to a new destination. Although the directions for performing your setup are complex, you can master them with attention and practice. Even more fortunately, this chapter provides a detailed and field-tested route. And soon, you'll know the route like the back of your hand.

While you're working in AutoCAD, always keep in mind what your final output should look like on real paper. Even your first printed drawings should look just like hand-drawn ones — only without all those eraser smudges.

Before you start the drawing setup process, you need to make decisions about your new drawing. The following four questions are absolutely critical; if you don't answer them or your answers are wrong, you'll probably need to rework the drawing later:

- ✔ **What system of measure — metric or imperial — will you use?**
- ✔ **What drawing units will you use?**
- ✔ **At what scale — or scales — will you plot it?**
- ✔ **On what size paper does it need to fit?**

In some cases, you can defer answering one additional question, but it's usually better to deal with it up front: What kind of border or title block does your drawing require?

If you're in a hurry, it's tempting to find an existing drawing that was set up for the drawing scale and paper size that you want to use, make a copy of that DWG file, erase the objects, and start drawing. Use this approach with care, though. When you start from another drawing, you inherit any setup mistakes in that drawing. Also, drawings that were created in much older versions of AutoCAD may not take advantage of current program features and CAD practices. If you can find a suitable drawing that was set up in a recent version of AutoCAD by an experienced person who is conscientious about doing setup right, consider using it. Otherwise, you're better off setting up a new drawing from scratch.

Choosing your units

AutoCAD is extremely flexible about drawing units; it lets you have them *your* way. Usually, you choose the type of units that you normally use to talk about whatever you're drawing: feet and inches for a building in the United States, millimeters for a metric screw, and so on.

Speaking of millimeters, there's another choice you have to make even before you choose your *units* of measure, and that's your *system* of measure.

Most of the world abandoned local systems of measure generations ago. Even widely adopted ones like the imperial system have mostly fallen by the wayside, just like their driving force, the British Empire. Except, of course, in the United States, where feet, inches, pounds, gallons, and degrees Fahrenheit still rule.

Enter the metric system

. . . or, "Let's forget everything we learned about measuring stuff and start over again!" All (well, nearly all) the world is metric. Instead of a system of linear measure based on twelves, of volume measure based on sixteens, and of temperature measure based on who knows *what*, metric bases all types of measure on tens. (Of course, *For Dummies* books are in the metric vanguard because every single *For Dummies* title includes a Part of *Tens*.)

The metric system first gained a toehold (ten toes, of course) in France during the Revolution. Over time, it became apparent that some standardization was called for, and a mere century and a half later, SI Metric became that standard. SI is short for *Systeme International d'Unites*. (That's International System of Units in English. Isn't it great to speak more than one language?)

The United States may be late coming to the party, but the U.S. federal government *has* made a commitment to adopt SI Metric. For more information, point your browser to the National Institute of Standards and Technology's Special Publication 814 (`http://ts.nist.gov/ WeightsAndMeasures/Metric/ pub814.cfm`).

During drawing setup, you choose settings for *Length* units (for measuring linear objects and distances) and *Angle* units (for measuring angles between nonparallel objects or points on arcs or circles) in the Drawing Units dialog box, as shown in Figure 4-1. (I show you how later in this chapter.) The Length unit types are as follows:

- **Architectural** units are based in feet and inches and use *fractions* to represent partial inches.

- **Decimal** units are *unitless* — that is, they're not based on any particular real-world unit. With decimal units, each unit in the drawing could represent an inch, a millimeter, a cubit (if you're into building arks in case that rainy day should come), or any other unit of measure you deem suitable.

- **Engineering** units are based in feet and inches and use *decimals* to represent partial inches.

- **Fractional** units, like decimal units, are unitless and show values as fractions rather than decimal numbers.

- **Scientific** units are also unitless and show values as exponents, used for drawing really tiny or really large things. If you design molecules or galaxies, this is the unit type for you.

The Angle unit types are as follows:

- **Decimal Degrees** show angles as decimal numbers and are by far the easiest to work with — if your type of work allows it!

✔ **Deg/Min/Sec** units are based on the old style of dividing a degree into minutes and minutes into seconds. But seconds aren't fine enough to display AutoCAD's precision capabilities, so seconds can be further divided into decimals.

✔ **Grads** and **Radians** are mathematically beautiful (so I'm told) but are not widely used in drafting. Apparently the French artillery uses grads, but as long as we're friends with them, we shouldn't have to worry.

✔ **Surveyor's Units** are similar to Degrees/Minutes/Seconds, but instead of using a whole circle, where an angle in Deg/Min/Sec might measure 300°0'0.00", the same angle in Surveyor's Units would be represented as S 30°0'0.00" E.

For the great majority of AutoCAD users, the unit types to know and use are *Decimal, Architectural,* and *Decimal Degree.* You'll know or be told if you need to use one of the other types!

Figure 4-1:
The Drawing Units dialog box.

After you specify a type of unit, you draw things on-screen at full size in those units just as though you were laying them out on the construction site or in the machine shop. You draw an 8-foot-high line, for example, to indicate the height of a wall and an 8-inch-high line to indicate the cutout for a doggie door (for a dachshund, naturally). The on-screen line may actually be only 2 inches long at a particular zoom resolution, but AutoCAD stores the length as 8 feet. This way of working is easy and natural for most people for whom CAD is their first drafting experience, but it seems weird to people who've done a lot of manual drafting. If you're in the latter category, don't worry; you'll soon get the hang of it.

When you use dash-dot linetypes (Chapter 6) and hatching (Chapter 15) in a drawing, it matters to AutoCAD whether the drawing uses an imperial (inches, feet, miles, and so on) or metric (millimeters, meters, kilometers, and so on) system of measure. The MEASUREMENT system variable controls whether the linetype and hatch patterns that AutoCAD lists for you to choose from are scaled with inches or millimeters in mind as the plotting units. MEASUREMENT=0 means inches (that is, an imperial-units drawing), whereas MEASUREMENT=1 means millimeters (that is, a metric-units drawing). If you start from an appropriate template drawing, as described later in this chapter, the MEASUREMENT system variable will be set correctly, and you won't ever have to think about it. (For an explanation of system variables and how to set them, see Chapter 23.)

Weighing up your scales

The next decision you should make before setting up a new drawing is choosing the scale at which you'll eventually plot the drawing. This decision gives you the *drawing scale* and *drawing scale factor* — two ways of expressing the same relationship between the objects in the real world and the objects plotted on paper.

The scale factor factor

"Okay," you're saying, "I understand I need to print my drawings at a *scale* acceptable to the discipline I work in. But if I'm drawing stuff full size, why do I need to worry about the *scale factor?*" Grab yourself a nice mug of cocoa and settle down 'round the fire, because I'm going to tell you. By now you know (because I've told you so) that you draw real things full size, but drawings contain other things that are *not* real, such as text, dimensions, hatch patterns, title blocks, dash-dot linetypes, and so forth. And those nonreal things need to be legible on your plotted drawing.

Say, for example, you want to draw a plan of your garage. You need it to fit on an 11- x 17-inch sheet of paper, and you want to add a title like (if you're really original like me) "My Garage." Typically, text annotations are 3/32" or 1/8" high. Now, if you draw your 6"-wide wall full size, put a 1/8"-high title beside it, and then print the drawing at a scale of, say, 1:24 (that's 1 drawing inch equals 24 real inches, usually expressed as 1/2" = 1'-0"), the 6" wall itself will measure 1/4" on the sheet, and the note will be an illegible little speck beside it. You fix it with the help of the drawing scale factor; the "Drawing scale versus drawing scale factor" sidebar explains how you arrive at the scale factor, and Table 4-1, in the following section, presents a list of acceptable standard scales with their corresponding scale factors for both imperial and metric systems of measure.

Drawing scale versus drawing scale factor

CAD users employ two different ways of talking about a drawing's intended plot scale: drawing scale and drawing scale factor.

Drawing scale is the traditional way of describing a scale — traditional in that it existed long before CAD came to be. Drawing scales are expressed with an equal sign or colon; for example, 1/8" = 1'–0", 1:20, or 2:1. You can translate the equal sign or colon as "corresponds to." In all cases, the measurement to the left of the equal sign or colon indicates a paper measurement, and the number to the right indicates a real-world measurement. In other words, the imperial drawing scale 1/8" = 1'–0" means

that 1/8" on the plotted drawing corresponds to 1'–0" in the CAD drawing and in the real world, assuming that the plot was made at the proper scale. A metric drawing scale is usually expressed without units, as a simple ratio. Thus, a scale of 1:20 means 1 unit on the plotted drawing corresponds to 20 units in the real world. In architectural and engineering drawings, the numbers usually refer to millimeters.

Drawing scale factor is a single number that represents a multiplier, such as 96, 20, or 0.5. The drawing scale factor for a drawing is the conversion factor between a measurement on the plot and a measurement in the real world.

Thinking annotatively

AutoCAD 2008 introduced a new way of setting some types of annotation object to the appropriate plotted size. *Annotative objects* possess a special property so that when you change the annotation scale of a layout's viewport or of the model tab, all the annotative objects — including text, dimensions, dash-dot linetypes, hatch patterns, and symbol blocks — change automatically to their correct size for the chosen scale. I take a closer look at annotative objects in Chapter 13, but in the meantime, it's still worthwhile getting familiar with using drawing scale factors because they're useful in a few other ways.

You shouldn't just invent some arbitrary scale based on what looks okay on whatever size paper you happen to have handy. Most industries work with a small set of approved drawing scales that are related to one another by factors of 2 or 10. If you use other scales, you'll at best be branded a clueless newbie — and, at worst, have to redo all your drawings at an accepted scale.

Table 4-1 lists some common architectural drawing scales, using both imperial and metric systems of measure. The table also lists the drawing scale factor corresponding to each drawing scale and the common uses for each scale. If you work in industries other than those listed here, ask drafters or coworkers what the common drawing scales are and for what kinds of drawings they're used.

Table 4-1	Common Architectural Drawing Scales	
Drawing Scale	*Drawing Scale Factor*	*Common Uses*
1/16" = 1'–0"	192	Large building plans
1/8" = 1'–0"	96	Medium-size building plans
1/4" = 1'–0"	48	House plans
1/2" = 1'–0"	24	Small building plans
1" = 1'–0"	12	Details
1:200	200	Large building plans
1:100	100	Medium-size building plans
1:50	50	House plans
1:20	20	Small building plans
1:10	10	Details

After you choose a drawing scale, engrave the corresponding drawing scale factor on your desk, write it on your hand (don't mix those two up, okay?), and put it on a sticky note on your monitor. You need to know the drawing scale factor for many drawing tasks and for some plotting. You should be able to recite the drawing scale factor of any drawing you're working on in AutoCAD without even thinking about it.

Even if you're going to use the Plot dialog box's Fit to Paper option (rather than a specific scale factor) to plot the drawing, you still need to choose a scale to make the nonreal things (such as text, hatch patterns, and so on) appear at a useful size. Choose a scale that's in the neighborhood of the Fit to Paper plotting factor, which AutoCAD displays in the Plot Scale area of the Plot dialog box. For example, if you determine that you need to squeeze your drawing down about 90 times to fit on the desired sheet size, choose a drawing scale of 1/8 inch = 1'–0" (drawing scale factor = 96) if you're using architectural units or 1:100 (drawing scale factor = 100) for other kinds of units.

Thinking about paper

With knowledge of your industry's common drawing scales, you can choose a provisional scale based on what you're depicting. But you won't know for sure whether that scale works until you compare it with the size of the paper that you want to use for plotting your drawing. Here again, most industries use a small range of standard sheet sizes. Three common sets of sizes exist, as shown in Figure 4-2 and Table 4-2:

▸ ANSI (American National Standards Institute)

▸ Architectural

▸ ISO (International Organization for Standardization)

ANSI sizes Architectural sizes ISO sizes

Figure 4-2:
Relation-
ships among
standard
paper sizes.

Table 4-2	Common Plot Sheet Sizes	
Sheet Size	*Dimensions*	*Comment*
ANSI *E*	34 x 44"	
ANSI *D*	22 x 34"	*E* sheet folded in half
ANSI *C*	17 x 22"	*D* sheet folded in half
ANSI *B*	11 x 17"	*C* sheet folded in half
ANSI *A*	8 1/2 x 11"	*B* sheet folded in half
Architectural Large *E*	36 x 48"	
Architectural *E*	30 x 42"	
Architectural *D*	24 x 36"	Large *E* sheet folded in half
Architectural *C*	18 x 24"	*D* sheet folded in half
Architectural *B*	12 x 18"	*C* sheet folded in half
Architectural *A*	9 x 12"	*B* sheet folded in half
ISO *A0*	841 x 1189 mm	
ISO *A1*	594 x 841 mm	*A0* sheet folded in half
ISO *A2*	420 x 594 mm	*A1* sheet folded in half
ISO *A3*	297 x 420 mm	*A2* sheet folded in half
ISO A4	210 x 297 mm	A3 sheet folded in half

You select a particular set of sheet sizes based on the common practices in your industry. You then narrow down your choice based on the area required by what you're going to draw. For example, most imperial-units architectural plans are plotted on Architectural D- or E-size sheets, and most metric architectural plans go on ISO A1 or A0 sheets.

If you know the desired sheet size and drawing scale factor, you can calculate the available drawing area easily. Simply multiply each of the sheet's dimensions by the drawing scale factor. For example, if you choose an 11- x 17-inch sheet and a drawing scale factor of 96 (corresponding to a plot scale of 1/8" = 1'–0"), you multiply 17 times 96 and 11 times 96 to get an available drawing area of 1,632 inches x 1,056 inches (or 136 feet x 88 feet). If your sheet size is in inches but your drawing scale is in millimeters, you need to multiply by an additional 25.4 to convert from inches to millimeters. For example, with an 11- x 17-inch sheet and a scale of 1:200 (drawing scale factor = 200), you multiply 17 times 200 times 25.4 and 11 times 200 times 25.4 to get 86,360 x 55,880 mm or 86.36 x 55.88 m — not quite big enough for a football field (American *or* European football).

Conversely, if you know the sheet size that you're going to use and the real-world size of what you're going to draw, and you want to find out the largest plot scale you can use, you have to divide, not multiply. Divide the needed real-world drawing area's length and width by the sheet's dimensions. Take the larger number — either the length result or the width result — and round up to the nearest real drawing scale factor (that is, one that's commonly used in your industry). For example, suppose you want to draw a 60- x 40-foot (or 720- x 480-inch) floor plan and print it on 11- x 17-inch paper. You divide 720 by 17 and 480 by 11 to get 42.35 and 43.64, respectively. The larger number, 43.64, corresponds in this example to the short dimension of the house and the paper. The nearest larger common architectural drawing scale factor is 48 (corresponding to 1/4" = 1'–0"), which leaves a little room for the plotting margin and title block.

The Cheat Sheet at the front of this book includes two tables that list the available drawing areas for a range of sheet sizes and drawing scales. Those tables can help you decide on an appropriate paper size and drawing scale; revert to the calculation method for situations that the tables don't cover. If you don't keep a favorite old calculator on your physical desktop, don't despair: AutoCAD 2010 has one lurking on the Ribbon. You'll find it on the Home tab's Utilities panel (hint: It looks like a calculator). You speed demons can toggle QuickCalc off and on with the Ctrl+8 key combo!

When you select a sheet size and drawing scale, always leave some extra room for the following two reasons:

- ✔ **Margin allowance:** Most plotters and printers can't print all the way to the edge of the sheet — they require a small margin. For example, my trusty old Hewlett-Packard LaserJet 4050 has a printable area of about 8.0 x 10.7 inches on an 8.5- x 11-inch ANSI A-size (letter-size) sheet. (You can find this information in the Plot dialog box, as described in Chapter 16.) If you're a stickler for precision, you can use the printable area instead of the physical sheet area in the calculations described earlier in this section.

- ✔ **Annotations:** Most drawings require some annotations — text, dimensions, grid bubbles, and so on — outside the objects you're drawing, plus a title block surrounding the objects and annotations. If you don't leave some room for the annotations and title block, you'll end up having to cram things together too much or change to a different sheet size. Either way, you'll be slowed down later in the project, when you can least afford it.

Some industries deal with the sheet-is-too-small/drawing-scale-is-too-large problem by breaking up drawings onto multiple plotted sheets. You might consider doing the same.

Don't be afraid to start with *real* paper. Experienced drafters often make a quick, throwaway pencil-and-paper sketch indicating the dimensions of the sheet of paper they intend to plot on, a sketch of the title block, and a very rough, schematic sketch of the thing they're going to draw. By sketching on paper first, you'll often catch scale or sheet size problems before you set up a drawing, when repairs take only a few minutes — not after you've created the drawing, when fixing the problem can take hours.

Defending your border

The next decision to make is what kind of border your drawing needs. The options include a full-blown title block, a simple rectangle, or nothing at all around your drawing. If you need a title block, do you have one, can you borrow an existing one, or will you need to draw one from scratch? Although you can draw title block geometry in an individual drawing, you'll save time by reusing the same title block for multiple drawings. Your company may already have a standard title block drawing ready to use, or someone else who's working on your project may have created one for the project.

The most efficient way of creating a title block is as a separate DWG file, drawn at its normal plotted size (for example, 36 inches long by 24 inches high for an architectural D-size title block, or 841 mm long by 594 mm high for an ISO A1-size version). You then insert or xref the title block drawing into each sheet drawing. Chapters 17 and 18 describe how to insert or xref separate DWG files.

A Template for Success

When you start in either the 2D Drafting & Annotation workspace (as I do throughout this book) or the old AutoCAD Classic workspace, AutoCAD creates a new, blank drawing configured for 2D drafting. Depending on where you live (your country, not your street address!) and the dominant system of measure used there, AutoCAD will base this new drawing on one of two default drawing templates: acad.dwt for the imperial system of measure, as used in the United States, or acadiso.dwt for the metric system, used throughout the rest of the galaxy. (In AutoCAD LT, the two default templates are acadlt.dwt and acadltiso.dwt.) When you explicitly create a new drawing from within AutoCAD, the Select Template dialog box, as shown in Figure 4-3, appears by default so that you can choose a template on which to base your new drawing.

Figure 4-3:
A toolbox of templates.

You may be familiar with Microsoft Word or Excel template files, and AutoCAD drawing templates work pretty much the same way — because Autodesk stole the idea from them (encouraged, of course, by Microsoft).

A *template* is simply a drawing whose name ends in the letters *DWT,* which you use as the starting point for another drawing. When you create a new drawing from a template, AutoCAD makes a copy of the template file and opens the copy in a new drawing editor window. The first time you save the file, you're prompted for a new filename to save to; the original template file stays unchanged.

Using a suitable template can save you time and worry because many of the setup options are already set correctly for you. You know the drawing will

print correctly; you just have to worry about getting the geometry and text right. Of course, all this optimism assumes that the person who set up the template knew what she was doing.

The stock templates that come with AutoCAD are okay as a starting point, but you'll need to modify them to suit your purposes or create your own from scratch. In particular, the stock AutoCAD templates are probably not set up for the scales that you'll want to use. The instructions in the rest of this chapter tell you how to specify scale-dependent setup information.

So the only problems with templates are creating good ones and then later finding the right one to use when you need it. Later in this chapter, in the "Making Templates Your Own" section, I show you how to create templates from your own setup drawings. Here, I show you how to use an already created template, such as one of the templates that comes with AutoCAD 2010 or from one of your CAD-savvy colleagues. If you're lucky, someone in your office has created suitable templates that you can use to get going quickly.

Follow these steps to create a new drawing from a template drawing:

1. **Run the NEW command by pressing Ctrl+N or clicking the Application button and choosing New.**

 The Select Template dialog box appears.

 The first button on the Quick Access Toolbar runs the QNEW (Quick NEW) command instead of the ordinary NEW command. If you or someone else has changed the Default Template File Name for QNEW in the Options dialog box, QNEW will *not* open the Select template dialog box but will instead simply present you with a new, blank drawing — possibly not the one you wanted. You *can* take advantage of QNEW though — for information about how, see the "Making Templates Your Own" section at the end of this chapter.

2. **Click the name of the template that you want to use as the starting point for your new drawing and click the Open button.**

 A new drawing window with a temporary name, such as `Drawing2.dwg`, appears. (The template you opened remains unchanged on your hard disk.)

 Depending on which template you choose, your new drawing may open in a paper space layout, not in model space. If that's the case, click the Model button on the status bar before changing the settings described in the next section, "Making the Most of Model Space." I describe how to set up and take advantage of paper space layouts in Chapter 5.

3. **Press Ctrl+S or click the Application button and choose Save to save the file under a new name.**

 Take the time to save the drawing to the appropriate name and location now.

4. **Make needed changes.**

 With most of the templates that come with AutoCAD, consider changing the units, limits, grid and snap settings, linetype scale, and dimension scale. See the next section, "Making the Most of Model Space," for instructions.

5. **Save the drawing again.**

 If you'll need other drawings in the future similar to the current one, consider saving your modified template as a template in its own right. See the section "Making Templates Your Own," later in this chapter.

A few of the remaining templates that come with AutoCAD include title blocks for various sizes of sheets. In addition, most templates come in two versions — one for people who use color-dependent plot styles and one for people who use named plot styles. You probably want the color-dependent versions. (Chapter 16 describes the two kinds of plot styles and why you probably want the color-dependent variety.) I warned you that this drawing setup stuff would be complicated!

Making the Most of Model Space

After you've decided on drawing scale and sheet size, you're ready to set up your drawing. Most drawings require a two-part setup:

1. Set up model space, where you'll create most of your drawing.

2. Create one or more paper space layouts for plotting.

As I explain in Chapter 2, model space is the infinitely large, three-dimensional environment in which you create the "real" objects you're drawing. You can perform model space setup as described in this section. Chapter 5 introduces you to setting up your paper space layouts.

Setting your units

First, set the linear and angular units that you want to use in your new drawing. The following procedure describes how:

1. **Click the Application button and then choose Units from the Drawing Utilities group.**

 The Drawing Units dialog box appears, as shown in Figure 4-4.

Figure 4-4:
Set your
units here.

2. **Choose a linear unit type from the Length Type drop-down list.**

 Choose the type of unit representation that's appropriate for your work. Engineering and Architectural units are displayed in feet and inches; the other types of units aren't tied to any particular unit of measurement. You decide whether each unit represents a millimeter, centimeter, meter, inch, foot, or something else. Your choice is much simpler if you're working in metric: Choose Decimal units.

 AutoCAD can think in inches! If you're using Engineering or Architectural units (feet and inches), AutoCAD understands any distance or coordinate you enter as that many inches. You use the ' (apostrophe) character on your keyboard to indicate a number in feet instead of inches.

3. **From the Length Precision drop-down list, choose the level of precision you want when AutoCAD displays coordinates and linear measurements.**

 The precision setting controls how precisely AutoCAD displays coordinates, distances, and prompts in some dialog boxes. For example, the Coordinates section of the status bar displays the current coordinates of the crosshairs using the current precision.

 The linear and angular precision settings affect only AutoCAD's *display* of coordinates, distances, and angles on the status bar, in dialog boxes, and in the command window and dynamic input tooltip areas. For drawings stored as DWG files, AutoCAD *always* uses maximum precision to store the locations and sizes of all objects that you draw regardless of how many decimal places you choose to display in the Drawing Units dialog box. In addition, AutoCAD provides separate settings for controlling the precision of dimension text — see Chapter 14 for details.

4. **Choose an angular unit type from the Angle Type drop-down list.**

 Decimal Degrees and Deg/Min/Sec are the most common choices.

The Clockwise check box and the Direction button provide additional angle measurement options, but you'll rarely need to change the default settings: Measure angles counterclockwise and use east as the 0 degree direction.

5. **From the Angle Precision drop-down list, choose the degree of precision you want when AutoCAD displays angular measurements.**

6. **In the Insertion Scale area, choose the units of measurement for this drawing.**

 Choose your base unit for this drawing — that is, the real-world distance represented by one AutoCAD unit.

 The AutoCAD (but not the AutoCAD LT) Drawing Units dialog box includes a Lighting area where you specify the unit type to be used to measure the intensity of photometric lights. That's a fairly advanced 3D feature that I don't cover in this book.

7. **Click OK to exit the dialog box and save your settings.**

Telling your drawing its limits

The next model space setup task is to set your drawing's *limits*. Well, you wouldn't want it staying out all night and hanging out with just anybody, would you? The limits represent the rectangular working area that you'll draw on, which usually corresponds to the paper size. Setting limits correctly gives you the following advantages:

✔ **Showing the grid:** If you use default settings, when you turn on the grid (described in the following section), the grid appears within the rectangular limits area. With the grid on, the grid settings at their defaults, and the limits set correctly, you see the working area that corresponds to what you'll eventually be plotting, so you won't accidentally sail off the edge of your paper.

✔ **Using ZOOM All:** The ZOOM command's All option zooms to the greater of the limits or the drawing extents. (The *extents* of a drawing consist of a rectangular area just large enough to include all the objects in the drawing.) When you set limits properly and color within the lines, ZOOM All gives you a quick way to zoom to your working area.

✔ **Plotting:** If you plot from model space, you can choose to plot the area defined by the drawing limits. This option gives you a quick, reliable way to plot your drawing, but only if you've set limits correctly!

Many CAD drafters don't set limits properly in their drawings. After you read this section, you can tell them — in a nice way, of course — why they should and how.

Despite the importance of setting correct limits, no dialog box, Application Menu selection, or Ribbon button gets you started. LIMITS is a keyboard-input-only command, and all subsequent action takes place in the command window or the dynamic input tooltip.

The following procedure shows you how to set your drawing limits:

1. **Type** LIMITS **and press Enter to start setting your drawing limits.**

 AutoCAD prompts you, with a dynamic input tooltip if DYN mode is enabled and in the command window, to reset the model space limits:

   ```
   Command: '_limits
   Reset Model space limits:
   Specify lower left corner or [ON/OFF] <0.0000,0.0000>:
   ```

 The value at the end of the last line of the command prompt is the default value for the lower-left corner of the drawing limits. It appears according to the units and precision that you selected in the Drawing Units dialog box — for example, 0'–0" if you selected Architectural units with precision to the nearest inch.

2. **Type the coordinates of the lower-left corner of the limits you want to use and press Enter.**

 The usual value to enter at this point is **0,0**. (Type a zero, a comma, and then another zero, with no spaces.) You can just press Enter to accept the default value.

 Regardless of what you see in the dynamic input tooltip, when you press Enter to accept a default value, the value that will be accepted is the one that shows at the command prompt. Make sure you know where you're entering your values, or you could end up with some pretty weird errors.

 AutoCAD now prompts you for the upper-right corner of the limits:

   ```
   Specify upper right corner <12.0000,9.0000>:
   ```

 The initial units offered by AutoCAD correspond to an Architectural A-size sheet of paper in landscape orientation. (Almost no one uses Architectural A-size paper; here's a classic example of a programmer choosing a silly default that no one has bothered to change in 25 years!)

 If you live in a metric-dominant location, the second prompt will read

   ```
   Specify upper right corner <420.0000,297.0000>:
   ```

 These numbers correspond to an ISO A3-size sheet (much more up to date than those silly, old-fashioned imperial settings!).

3. **Type the coordinates of the upper-right corner of the limits you want to use and press Enter.**

 You calculate the usual setting for the limit's upper-right corner by multiplying the paper dimensions by the drawing scale factor. For example,

if you're setting up a 1/8" = 1'–0" drawing (drawing scale factor = 96) to be plotted on a 24- x 36-inch sheet in landscape orientation, the upper-right corner of the limits should be 36 inches times 96, 24 inches times 96. Okay, pencils down. The correct answer is 3456,2304 (or 288 feet, 192 feet).

Alternatively, you can cheat when specifying limits and read the limits from the tables on the Cheat Sheet in the front of this book.

If you have the grid turned on, AutoCAD by default redisplays it in the new limits area after you press Enter.

If you're using Architectural or Engineering units, and you want to enter measurements in feet and not inches, you must add the foot designator after the number, such as **6'**; otherwise, AutoCAD assumes that you mean inches. If you're using Decimal units or one of the other "unitless" types, AutoCAD won't accept the foot mark as input.

4. **On the Navigate panel of the Ribbon's View tab, choose All from the drop-down or type Z, press Enter, type A, and press Enter again.**

 AutoCAD zooms to the new limits.

Making the drawing area snap-py (and grid-dy)

AutoCAD's *grid* is a set of evenly spaced dots that serve as a visual distance reference. (As I describe in the preceding section, "Telling your drawing its limits," the grid also indicates how far the drawing limits extend.) AutoCAD's *snap* feature creates a set of evenly spaced, invisible *hot spots,* which make the crosshairs move in nice, even increments. Both grid and snap are like the intersection points of the lines on a piece of grid paper, but the grid is simply a visual reference, whereas snap constrains the points that you can pick with the mouse. You can — and usually will — set the grid and snap spacing to different values.

Set the grid and the snap intervals in the Drafting Settings dialog box by following these steps:

1. **Right-click the Snap or Grid button on the status bar and choose Settings.**

 The Drafting Settings dialog box appears with the Snap and Grid tab selected, as shown in Figure 4-5.

 The Snap and Grid tab has five sections, but the Snap and Grid areas within that tab are all you need to worry about for most 2D drafting work.

2. Select the Snap On check box to turn on snap.

This action enables default snaps half a unit apart.

AutoCAD usually has several ways of doing things. You can also click the Snap Mode button on the status bar to toggle snap on and off; the same goes for the Grid Display button and the grid setting. Or you could use the function keys: F7 toggles the grid off and on, and F9 does the same for Snap.

3. Enter the snap interval you want in the Snap X Spacing box.

Use the information in the sections preceding this procedure to decide on a reasonable snap spacing.

If the Equal X and Y Spacing check box is selected, the Y spacing automatically changes to equal the X spacing, which is almost always what you want.

4. Select the Grid On check box to turn on the grid.

5. Enter the desired grid spacing in the Grid X Spacing box.

Use the information in the sections preceding this procedure to decide on reasonable grid spacing.

Just like with snap spacing, if the Equal X and Y Spacing check box is selected, the Y spacing automatically changes to equal the X spacing. Again, you usually want to leave it that way.

X measures horizontal distance; Y measures vertical distance. The AutoCAD drawing area normally shows an X and Y icon in case you forget.

6. Specify additional grid display options in the Grid Behavior area.

If you select the Adaptive Grid check box, AutoCAD changes the density or spacing of the grid dots as you zoom in and out. If you also select Allow Subdivision Below Grid Spacing, the spacing can go lower than what you've set, and it may go higher if you're zoomed a long way out of your drawing. (If it didn't, you couldn't see your drawing for the grid dots!)

Selecting Display Grid Beyond Limits allows the grid to display over the entire drawing area, no matter how far you're zoomed out. Clearing this check box makes AutoCAD behave the way it's always behaved — that is, the grid is displayed only in the area defined by the drawing limits.

I recommend you leave this box deselected as an effective way to tell whether you're drawing beyond your drawing limits. What's the point of setting limits if you don't know where they are?

The Follow Dynamic UCS option (not available in AutoCAD LT) is a 3D-specific feature that changes your drawing plane as you mouse over 3D objects. I don't cover Dynamic UCS or 3D modeling in this book.

7. Click OK to close the Drafting Settings dialog box.

Entering drawing properties

Do one last bit of bookkeeping before you're finished with model space drawing setup: Enter summary information in the Drawing Properties dialog box, as shown in Figure 4-6. Click the Application button; in the Drawing Utilities section, choose Drawing Properties to open the Drawing Properties dialog box; then click the Summary tab. Enter the drawing scale and the drawing scale factor you're using in the Comments area, plus any other information you think useful.

Don't confuse *drawing* properties (which are really file properties) with your drawing's *object* properties — they're different things. The properties you enter here can help you or someone you love when she opens your drawing and wonders how you set it up. *Object* properties are a big enough topic to merit their own chapter — see Chapter 6.

Figure 4-6:
Surveying
your
drawing's
properties.

Making Templates Your Own

You can create a template from any DWG file by using the Save Drawing As dialog box. Follow these steps to save your drawing as a template:

1. Click the Application button and choose Save As.

The Save Drawing As dialog box appears, as shown in Figure 4-7.

Figure 4-7:
Saving a
drawing as
a template
and apply-
ing options.

2. **From the Files of Type drop-down list, choose AutoCAD Drawing Template (*.dwt) or AutoCAD LT Drawing Template (*.dwt).**

3. **Navigate to the folder where you want to store the drawing.**

 The AutoCAD 2010 default folder for template drawings is Template and is buried deep in the bowels of your Windows user profile. Save your templates there if you want them to appear in AutoCAD's Select Template list. You can save your templates in another folder, but if you want to use them later, you have to navigate to that folder each time to use them. See the Technical Stuff paragraph that follows this procedure for additional suggestions.

4. **Enter a name for the drawing template in the File Name text box and click Save.**

 A dialog box for the template description and units appears.

5. **Specify the template's measurement units (English or Metric) in the drop-down list.**

 Enter the key info now — you can't do it later unless you save the template to a different name. Don't bother filling in the Description field; AutoCAD doesn't display it in the Select Template dialog box.

6. **Click OK to save the file.**

7. **To save your drawing as a regular drawing, click the Application button and choose Save As.**

 The Save Drawing As dialog box appears again.

8. **From the Files of Type drop-down list, choose AutoCAD 2010 Drawing (*.dwg).**

 Choose the AutoCAD LT equivalent, if that's your version. AutoCAD 2010 uses a new DWG file format. Choose an earlier version if you want to be able to open your drawing in AutoCAD 2009 or earlier.

9. **Navigate to the folder where you want to store the drawing.**

 Use a different folder from the one with your template drawings.

10. **Enter the name of the drawing in the File Name text box and click Save.**

 The file is saved. Now, when you save it in the future, the regular file, not the template file, gets updated.

The AutoCAD QNEW (Quick NEW) command, when properly configured, can bypass the Select Template dialog box and create a new drawing from your favorite template. The first button on the Quick Access Toolbar — the button with the plain white sheet of paper — runs the newer QNEW command instead of the older NEW command.

To put the Quick into QNEW, though, you have to tell AutoCAD which default template to use: Click the Application button and then click the Options button at the lower-right corner of the Application Menu. On the Files tab, choose Template Settings⇨Default Template File Name for QNEW. The QNEW default file name setting is None, which causes QNEW to act just like NEW (that is, QNEW opens the Select Template dialog box). Specify the name of your favorite template here, and you get a new drawing file based on it every time you click QNEW.

AutoCAD 2010 stores template drawings and many other support files under your Windows user folder. To discover where your template folder is hiding, open the Options dialog box. On the Files tab, choose Template Settings⇨Drawing Template File Location, as shown in Figure 4-8.

Figure 4-8:
Seek and you shall find your template folder.

You don't have to keep your template files where that nice Mister Gates tells you. Create a folder that you can find easily (for example, `C:\Acad-templates` or `F:\Acad-custom\templates` on a network drive), put the templates that you actually use there, and change the Drawing Template File Location setting so that it points to your new template folder.

Chapter 5

Planning for Paper

In This Chapter
- ▶ Setting up paper space layouts
- ▶ Buttons or tabs for layout fashionistas
- ▶ Looking into viewports
- ▶ Working in paper space

Most of what the earlier chapters look at revolves around setting up the model space environment — that infinitely large, three-dimensional realm wherein you create your gleaming towers, your wondrous electronic gadgetry . . . or your garden shed or your angle bracket. However, you may have picked up a hint here or there that AutoCAD has a whole different environment known as *paper space.*

The final product of all this setup, remember, is a printed drawing on a piece of paper. Unless you're prepared to send your computer out to the work site, you're going to have to get those designs off the screen and onto paper. The first part of that process is configuring the sheet layout in paper space, which I explain in this chapter. For the actual process of outputting either model space or layouts to printer or plotter, see Chapter 16.

Chapter 2 introduces you to the two spaces — model and paper — and Chapter 4 explains how to configure model space for efficient drawing. Before you plunge into paper space, a quick recap of model space is in order.

Model space is the drawing environment that's current when the Model tab (not the Model button) on the status bar is active. Model space is where you create the "real" objects that you're drawing, so these objects are referred to as *model geometry* whether they're 2D or 3D entities. When the Model tab is active, you see objects in model space only — anything in paper space is invisible.

In AutoCAD 2010, it's still possible to ignore paper space layouts entirely and do all your drawing *and* plotting in model space. But you owe it to yourself to give layouts a try. You'll probably find that they make plotting more consistent and predictable. They'll give you more plotting flexibility when you need it. And you'll certainly encounter drawings from other people that make extensive use of paper space, so you need to understand it if you plan to exchange drawings with anyone else.

Setting Up a Layout in Paper Space

A *paper space layout* is a representation of a drawing sheet. Although the model geometry — the real stuff — goes in model space, the "not-real" drawing objects (for example, a drawing border, title block, general notes, perhaps view labels, and symbols like North arrows) all go in paper space on the layout. Where model space is like the world, infinitely large and three-dimensional, paper space is finite — the size of a drawing sheet, in fact — and two-dimensional, just like a drawing sheet.

Aside from just an arrangement of your drawing sheet, layouts also store plot information. AutoCAD saves separate plot settings with each layout as well as model space so that you can plot each one differently. In practice, you'll probably need to use only one of the paper space layout tabs, especially when you're getting started with AutoCAD.

Rather than just reading about it, you may also want to open a few of the AutoCAD 2010 sample drawings and click the Model and Layout buttons or tabs to witness the variety of ways in which paper space is used.

The AutoCAD and AutoCAD LT sample drawings are no longer installed with the program, but they're still available — online. Download them from www.autodesk.com/autocad-samples or www.autodesk.com/autocad lt-samples. The upside of the change is that users of either program now have access to the other's sample files.

Will that be tabs or buttons?

The Autodesk documentation sometimes refers to the *Model tab,* or to *layout tabs,* and sometimes (like just a second ago) I do here as well. If you're working in the AutoCAD Classic workspace, you do see actual, selectable tabs at the lower-left edge of the drawing window, clearly labeled Model, Layout1, and Layout 2 (refer to Figure 2-2 in Chapter 2). The 2D Drafting & Annotation workspace — the workspace I favor in this book — replaces those tabs with the Model and Layout buttons near the middle of the status bar.

If you want to see the actual tabs, and you're in the 2D Drafting & Annotation workspace — or if you're staying in AutoCAD Classic and want the buttons — the following steps explain how to switch between the two systems and view the drawing layouts in each. If you see Model and Layout tabs at the lower-left edge of the drawing area, go to Step 4.

1. **If your status bar shows the Model and Layout buttons, right-click either button and choose Display Layout and Model Tabs.**

 At least one labeled tab will appear at the lower-left edge of the drawing window. Depending on the drawing you're viewing, you may need to

click the little black left-pointing arrow until you see the first tab, labeled Model.

2. **Without clicking anything, move the mouse pointer over the Model and Layout tabs.**

 A preview image of the layout or model space appears near the tab. As you move across the tabs, the preview changes, letting you visually identify the layout you want.

3. **Click a layout tab to make that layout current.**

 The selected layout fills the drawing window.

 You can rename layout tabs — but not the Model tab — by double-clicking the layout name twice to open an edit box.

 To switch from tabs to buttons, proceed as follows:

4. **Right-click the Model tab or any layout tab and choose Hide Layout and Model Tabs.**

 The tabs disappear, and the Model and Layout buttons appear on the status bar.

5. **Click the Model button.**

 Selecting Model sets AutoCAD's full-screen model space environment current, hiding any paper space layout objects.

6. **Click the Layout button.**

 Note that the Layout button's tooltip doesn't say *Layout* but instead lists the actual layout name. (The default layout names are Layout1 and Layout 2.) Whichever layout was activated last appears in the drawing window.

7. **Click the Quick View Layouts button on the status bar.**

 Where hovering over Model and Layout tabs displays an image of their contents, you have to launch a new command — Quick View Layouts — to preview the drawing's layouts. I describe the new Quick View Layouts feature more fully in the following section.

8. **Click a layout's preview image to make the layout current.**

 The selected layout is activated and fills the drawing window.

Of course, you can work in any configuration you please — for example, you may like the AutoCAD Classic workspace but prefer Model/Layout buttons instead of tabs. However, if you switch workspaces and then go back to AutoCAD Classic, the change you made from tabs to buttons will not be retained. For information on saving your own custom workspace, look up *workspace* in the online help system.

View Layouts Quick (view) ly

Quick View Layouts is the second of two AutoCAD 2010 features that use the Quick View image strip to display preview images of drawings or layouts. I introduce Quick View Drawings — which previews all your open drawings in the Quick View strip — in Chapter 2.

In earlier versions of AutoCAD, with buttons enabled rather than tabs, you would right-click the Layout button to open a shortcut menu listing the drawing's layouts. But mere words in a menu are *so* previous release! The following steps explain how to change between model space and a layout or switch between layouts:

1. **Click the Quick View Layouts button on the status bar.**

 The Quick View Layouts button is present on both the AutoCAD Classic and 2D Drafting & Annotation status bars. The Quick View image strip appears over the status bar and displays resizable image panels for model space and all layouts. Right below the row of images is the Quick View toolbar. Figure 5-1 shows a typical arrangement in a multilayout drawing.

Quick View Layouts preview images

Figure 5-1:
View those layouts, and make it Quick!

Quick View toolbar — Model or Paper space toggle — Quick View Layouts button

Model button — Layout button

Don't confuse the Quick *View* toolbar with the Quick *Access* toolbar that lives up top, next to the Application button. AutoCAD is getting so quick, it's hard to keep up with it!

The Quick View toolbar contains four buttons that perform the following tasks (buttons listed from left to right):

- **Pin Quick View Layouts:** Normally the images disappear as soon as you select a layout or click outside it. Clicking this button reorients the side view of the pushpin so it looks like it's poking a hole in your screen (don't worry — I promise it won't leave a mark!) and forces the image panels to remain open.

- **New Layout:** Click this button to create a new layout with a single viewport. The new layout appears as a new image at the end of the strip.

- **Publish:** Click this button to open the Publish dialog box. You use the PUBLISH command if you have a whole set of drawings you want to output and package at one time. I explain the AutoCAD version of publishing in Chapter 20.

- **Close:** Use this button to close the Quick View Layouts image strip if you pinned it open. Simply clicking outside the image strip closes the image strip if it's unpinned.

2. **Move your mouse pointer over each image in the Quick View panel.**

 The image background highlights to indicate the layout the pointer focus is on.

 When a panel is highlighted, two icons appear at the top right and top left of the panel. The Publish button at top right does the same thing as Batch Plot on the Application Menu. If you want to print the individual layout without going through all the Publish rigmarole, click the Plot icon at the top left.

 If you have a wheel mouse, you can resize the previews by mousing over an image and then pressing the Ctrl key and scrolling the wheel back and forth.

3. **Click the preview image of model space or the layout you want to make current.**

 The selected layout is activated and fills the drawing window, and the preview image strip closes.

Creating a layout

Creating a simple paper space layout is straightforward, thanks to the Create Layout Wizard, as shown in Figure 5-2. (Yes! Finally, a useful AutoCAD wizard.) The command name is LAYOUTWIZARD, and it's missing in action from AutoCAD 2010's new user interface; to get to it, enter LAYOUTWIZARD at the keyboard.

Figure 5-2:
The Create
Layout
Wizard.

Although the Create Layout Wizard guides you step by step through the process of creating a paper space layout from scratch, it doesn't eliminate the necessity of coming up with a sensible set of layout parameters. The sheet size and plot scale that you choose provide a certain amount of space for showing your model (see the information earlier in this chapter), and wizards aren't allowed to bend the laws of arithmetic to escape that fact. For example, a map of Australia at a scale of 1 inch = 1 foot won't fit on an 8 1/2- x 11-inch sheet, no way, no how. In other words, garbage in, garbage (lay)out. Fortunately, the Create Layout Wizard lends itself to experimentation, and you can easily delete layouts that don't work.

Follow these steps to create a layout:

1. **Type** LAYOUTWIZARD **and press Enter.**

 The Create Layout Wizard displays its first page and prompts you to enter a name for the new layout.

2. **Give the new layout a name and click Next.**

 In place of the default name, Layout3, I recommend something more descriptive — for example, *D-Size Sheet.* Or you can call it *A1-Size Sheet* if you're of the metric persuasion.

3. **Choose a printer or plotter to use when plotting this layout and click Next.**

 Think of your choice as the *default* plotter for this layout. You can change to a different plotter later or create page setups that plot the same layout on different plotters. (I explain page setups in Chapter 16.)

 Many of the names in the configured plotter list should look familiar because they're your Windows printers (*system printers* in AutoCAD lingo). Names with a .pc3 extension represent nonsystem printer drivers. See Chapter 16 for details.

4. **Choose a paper size, specify whether to use inches or millimeters to represent paper units, and click Next.**

 The available paper sizes depend on the printer or plotter that you selected in Step 3.

5. **Specify the orientation of the drawing on the paper and click Next.**

 The icon displaying the letter *A* on the piece of paper shows you which orientation is which.

6. **On the Create Layout – Title Block page, select None and click Next.**

 I don't recommend selecting one of the two available title blocks, as the odds are slim that either will fit on the paper size you selected earlier.

 Earlier AutoCAD releases included a handy set of predrawn title blocks for a range of both imperial and metric paper sizes. All but two of them have disappeared, and those two are still the only ones in AutoCAD 2010. Unfortunately, neither of them is likely to work out for you. If in Step 4 you chose inches as your units and any paper size *other than* ARCH D (36.00 x 24.00 inches), or millimeters as your units and *any paper size at all,* the title block will not fit the sheet.

 When you know your way around the program a bit, you can always draw, insert, or xref a title block later. See Chapters 17 and 18 for information about inserting or xrefing a title block. You can also add custom title block drawings to your AutoCAD Template folder. If you want to know where to put them, see the section on making templates in Chapter 4.

7. **Define the arrangement of viewports that AutoCAD should create and select the viewport scale for them all from the drop-down list. Then click Next.**

 A *viewport* is a window from paper space into model space. You must create at least one viewport to display the model in your new layout. I tell you more about viewports later in this chapter.

 The default Viewport scale, Scaled to Fit, ensures that all of your model drawing objects appear in the viewport, but it results in an arbitrary scale factor. Most technical drawings require a specific scale, such as 1:100 or 1/8" = 1'–0".

8. **Click Select Location to specify the location of the viewport(s) on the layout; then pick the viewport's corners. When the wizard returns, click Next.**

 After you click the Select Location button, the Create Layout Wizard displays the preliminary layout with any title block that you've chosen. Pick two points to define a rectangle that falls within the drawing area of your title block (or within the plottable area of the sheet, if you chose no title block in Step 6).

AutoCAD represents the plottable area of the sheet with a dashed rectangle near the edge of the sheet. If you don't select a location for the viewport(s), the Create Layout Wizard creates a viewport that fills the plottable area of the sheet.

9. Click Finish.

AutoCAD creates the new layout.

Like the other wizards, the Create Layout Wizard is aimed at new users, or old-timers who have somehow overlooked the introduction of paper space layouts. You won't need to run this wizard every time you start a new drawing, but you may well run it once and then save the resulting file as a template for future drawings (see Chapter 4 for more about templates).

Copying and changing layouts

After you create a layout, you can delete, copy, rename, and otherwise manipulate it by clicking Quick View Layouts on the status bar and right-clicking a preview image. If you're using layout tabs rather than buttons, right-click its tab to display the menu or simply drag the tab to a new position. Figure 5-3 shows the right-click menu options in Quick View Layouts.

New layout
From template...
Delete
Rename
Move or Copy...
Select All Layouts

Activate Previous Layout
Activate Model Tab

Page Setup Manager...
Plot...

Import Layout as Sheet...
Export Layout to Model...

Figure 5-3:
The Quick View Layouts right-click menu.

The From Template option refers to layout templates. After you create layouts in a template (DWT) or a drawing (DWG) file, you can use the From Template option to import these layouts into the current drawing. For details, see the LAYOUT command's Template option in the Command Reference section of online help.

Many drawings require only one paper space layout. If you always plot the same view of the model and always plot to the same device and on the same size paper, a single paper space layout should suffice. If you want to plot

your model in different ways (for example, at different scales, with different layers visible, with different areas visible, or with different plotted line characteristics), you may want to create additional paper space layouts.

Lost in paper space

After you create a paper space layout, you suddenly have two views of the same drawing geometry: the view in your original model space and the new layout's view (perhaps decorated with a handsome title block and other accoutrements of plotting nobility). It's important to realize that both views are of the *same*·geometry. If you change the model geometry on one view, you're changing it everywhere because all layouts display the same model space objects.

When you make a layout current, you can switch the active space between paper space (that is, drawing and zooming on the sheet of paper) and model space (drawing and zooming on the model, inside the viewport) in several ways, including the following:

- ✔ In the drawing area, double-click inside a viewport boundary to move the crosshairs into model space in that viewport. Alternatively, you can double-click outside all viewports (for example, in the gray area outside the sheet) to move the crosshairs into paper space.

- ✔ Click the Maximize/Minimize Viewport button on the status bar. (For more information, see Chapter 2.)

- ✔ Enter **MSPACE** (the command alias is **MS**) or **PSPACE** (**PS**) at the keyboard.

- ✔ Click the MODEL/PAPER button on the status bar.

When the crosshairs are in model space, anything you draw or edit changes the model in model space and therefore, through the viewports, on all paper space layouts. When the crosshairs are in paper space, anything you draw appears only on that one layout. It's as though you were drawing on an acetate sheet over the top of that sheet of plotter paper — the model beneath remains unaffected.

This behavior can make your brain hurt until you get used to it. To avoid confusion, stick with the following approach (at least until you're more familiar with paper space):

- ✔ **If you want to edit the model,** do so in full-screen model space. Click the Model tab if tabs are displayed, or click the Model button if tabs are hidden. (The Model button is the one with the little black icon; don't confuse it with the MODEL/PAPER button, which switches between

model and paper space within the same layout.) Don't try to edit the model in a paper space viewport — it's a very inefficient use of your screen space.

✔ **If you want to edit a particular layout without affecting the model,** use one of the methods I've described to make that layout current, and make sure that the crosshairs are in paper space.

What space am I in?

When you start working in layouts, it may not always be crystal clear whether you're in model space or paper space. The status bar button will help — it will say PAPER if you're in paper space or MODEL if you're in the other place. Here are a few other ways to tell your spaces apart:

✔ **Check the crosshairs.** If you're in paper space, you can move the crosshairs over the entire drawing area. If you're in model space, you can move the crosshairs only within the currently active viewport; if you try to move the crosshairs outside the viewport, they turn into a Windows selection arrow.

✔ **Select some model geometry.** Try clicking some objects you know are in model space. If you can select them and they highlight, you're in model space. If nothing happens when you click them, they're inaccessible because you're in paper space.

✔ **Check the UCS icon.** The UCS icon is that . . . er, iconic symbol at the lower-left corner of the drawing area. The model space icon takes the shape of two arrows at right angles to each other, with the arrows pointing away from their intersection. The paper space icon is triangular, and the closed, three-sided shape represents a flat plane. If you don't see such a symbol, click the View tab on the Ribbon, and on the Coordinates panel, click the Show UCS Icon flyout; then choose either Show UCS Icon or Show UCS Icon at Origin, as shown in Figure 5-4.

Figure 5-4:
Displaying
the UCS
icon.

A view (port) for drawing in

A *viewport* is a rectangular paper space object — a window into your drawing sheet — through which you view model space objects from paper space. By default, when you create a new layout, a large single viewport is created.

The viewports I talk about in this chapter are paper space viewports. You can also create viewports in model space, but they're completely different animals. Model space viewports are also known as *tiled* viewports because they can't have any space between them, like bathroom tiles. You can use tiled viewports to look up close at widely separated areas of your screen. What's potentially confusing is that AutoCAD uses the same command name, and even the same dialog box, for creating the two different types. For this chapter, make sure that you're in paper space when you create layouts.

Paper space viewports are assigned drawing scales, and you can have multiple viewports with different scales on the same layout. For example, one viewport can show the floor plan of an exhibit space at 1/4" to one foot, and another viewport can show an enlarged view of a display cabinet at 1"=1'. Because the individual viewports are scaled, the entire layout can be plotted at 1:1.

The Create Layout Wizard is fine when you're starting out, but most real drawings have unique, *non*-standardized arrangements of viewports. When creating layouts, it's often easiest to create viewports from scratch. The following procedure explains how:

1. **Using one of the techniques described in the "Creating a layout" section earlier in this chapter, create a new layout in your drawing.**

 For example, click Quick View Layouts to display the preview images and then right-click any of the images and choose New Layout. A new layout is added to the end of the image strip.

2. **Click the image for the new layout to open it.**

 A new layout appears in the drawing window, showing the default sheet area and a single rectangular viewport centered on the sheet. You aren't going to use this viewport.

3. **Move the crosshairs over the viewport boundary and click to select it. Press the Delete key.**

 Although they don't behave like other drawing objects, viewports are objects, just like lines or circles. And like any other drawing objects, they can be selected and moved, copied, arrayed — or deleted.

4. **On the Ribbon, click the View tab; then, in the Viewports panel, choose New. In the Viewports dialog box, click Single in the list of standard viewports at the left and then click OK.**

 AutoCAD prompts you to pick the first corner for the new viewport.

You must be in paper space for these steps to work as described. If you opened the Viewports dialog box, clicked Single, and clicked OK, and nothing happened, you're still in model space, where you already have a single viewport.

5. **Pick a point somewhere on the blank page to locate the first corner of the new viewport.**

 AutoCAD prompts you to pick the second corner.

6. **Pick another point to place the second corner of the new viewport.**

 AutoCAD draws the viewport, and the model space geometry appears inside it. Next, specify a drawing scale for your viewport(s).

 Specifying the correct viewport scale sooner rather than later bestows a couple of important benefits:

 - Correctly scaling viewports allows you to use annotative documentation objects, such as text, dimensions, hatch patterns, blocks, and noncontinuous (dash-dot) linetypes. I introduce you to annotative objects in Chapter 13.

 - Correctly scaling all your viewports allows you to easily plot the completed layout at a scale of 1:1 while retaining individual, true-to-scale viewports.

7. **Double-click inside the viewport you want to apply a scale to.**

 Model space becomes active, as it must, because that's the space you have to scale. The Viewport Scale button appears toward the right side of the status bar when model space is activated in a layout.

8. **Click the Viewport Scale button on the status bar.**

 Clicking the Viewport Scale button opens a pop-up list of every drawing scale registered in the scales list — including metric scales even if you're working in an English-units drawing, and vice versa.

 Most of the time, for most people, there are way too many scales in the lists you see in the Viewport Scale button and the Plot dialog box. AutoCAD has a handy dandy Edit Scale List dialog box that lets you remove those imperial scales if you never work in feet and inches and vice versa, if you work only in metric. To run through your scales, choose Scale List from the Annotation Scaling panel on the Annotate tab, or type **SCALELISTEDIT** and press Enter to open the Edit Scale List dialog box. If you make a mistake, the Reset button in the Edit Scale List dialog box will restore all the default scales.

9. **Find the scale you want to apply to the active viewport and select it from the list.**

 The display zooms in or out to adjust to the chosen viewport scale.

Reread that last sentence and then think about how often you have to pan and zoom in your drawing. If you zoom inside a viewport whose scale you've set — *kaboom!* — you just blew the scale off the map. Luckily, you can prevent yourself or anyone else from inadvertently destroying your beautifully arranged and scaled viewport by completing the final steps of viewport setup:

10. **Make sure you're in paper space (check the UCS icon or move the crosshairs).**

11. **Select the boundary of the viewport whose arrangement you want to protect.**

 If you have Quick Properties turned on at the status bar, a window appears listing the main object properties of the viewport (see Chapter 6 for more about Quick Properties and object properties in general). If Quick Properties is disabled, you can right-click after selecting the viewport.

12. **Select Display Locked and then select Yes.**

 Locking the display sets AutoCAD up for some nifty zooming . . . if you're in paper space, a normal zoom is executed. If you're in model space inside a viewport, a normal zoom would wreck the scale, so when you try to zoom, AutoCAD near-instantaneously switches to paper space, zooms you in, and then switches back to model space. Sheer prestidigitation!

Sometimes the perfect viewport arrangement requires that a smaller viewport be completely surrounded by a larger one. Easy enough to create, yes, and easy to select — as long as you're in paper space. However, if you're in model space and you want to click from one viewport to the next to make it current, it's impossible to make model space current in a completely surrounded viewport by clicking inside it. Let your fingers come to the rescue: The Ctrl+R key combination cycles through model space in all drawing viewports, even if they're completely surrounded by other viewports.

And there you have your 12-step program to layout bliss! All that setup had a purpose, of course: to enable you to print perfect paper plots (or plot perfect paper prints. if you prefer to see it that way). I cover plotting in depth in Chapter 16, but a short introductory word here might be useful.

What happens when you want to rotate a viewport? Perhaps you're drawing an elevator shaft, and the view would fit better on the sheet lengthwise than in its "correct" vertical orientation. A logical person might think that rotating a viewport, say, 90° would rotate the view as well. Until now, AutoCAD hasn't worked like that; you might rotate the viewport object, but the contents remained firmly fixed in model space. AutoCAD 2010 introduces a welcome enhancement to viewports: You can now rotate the displayed viewport content and the viewport itself:

✔ When the new system variable VPROTATEASSOC is set to 1, the displayed viewport content rotates with the viewport.

✔ When the variable is set to 0, the content doesn't rotate, as in earlier AutoCAD releases.

About paper space layouts and plotting

As this chapter describes, you can use AutoCAD's paper space feature to compose one or more *layouts* for plotting your drawing in particular ways. Each layout lives on a separate tab, which you click at the bottom of the drawing area — or in a secret hiding place if you've hidden the Model and Layout tabs. AutoCAD saves plot settings (plot device, paper size, plot scale, and so on) separately for each of the layouts as well as model space.

Whether to plot model space or a layout in a drawing depends entirely on how the drawing was set up. If you or someone else went through a layout setup procedure similar to the one in this chapter, you probably should plot the layout. If not, plot model space.

Viewport boundaries will print if you don't pay attention to where you create them. What that means is that each drawing view has a nice rectangular border around it. Nice, but a definite no-no in every drafting office. In Chapter 6, I introduce you to object properties, including probably the most important one, *layers*. You can define a layer so that objects on it do not plot, and that's where you should create your viewports.

One thing that might tip the scales in favor of hiding the layout tabs and going with status bar buttons is the teensy bit of drawing space along the bottom of the drawing area you can regain by turning off the layout tabs. Just right-click the Model tab or a layout tab and select Hide Layout and Model Tabs. The tabs vanish, and the Model and Layout buttons appear on the status bar. To put things back the way they were, right-click one of the new status bar buttons and choose Display Layout and Model Tabs.

If you don't have any paper space drawings handy, you can use one of the AutoCAD sample drawings. Refer to the New in AutoCAD 2010 paragraph in the "Setting Up a Layout in Paper Space" section earlier in the chapter.

Some different ways of plotting the same model can be handled in a single paper space layout with different page setups. See Chapter 16 for more details. If your projects require lots of drawings, you can parlay layouts into *sheet sets* — a feature that makes for more sophisticated creation, management, plotting, and electronic transfer of multisheet drawing sets. (Sorry, LT users — AutoCAD LT doesn't support sheet sets.) Again, see Chapter 16 for more information.

Part II
Let There Be Lines

The 5th Wave By Rich Tennant

UBER-USER DWAYNE GRANTZ CHALKS UP BEFORE PUTTING AutoCAD 2010 THROUGH ITS PACES.

In this part . . .

Lines, circles, and other elements of geometry make up the heart of your drawing. AutoCAD offers many different drawing commands, many ways to use them to draw objects precisely, and many properties for controlling the on-screen and plotted appearance of objects. After you draw your geometry, you'll probably spend at least as much time editing it as your design and drawings evolve. And in the process, you'll need to zoom in and out and pan all around to see how the entire drawing is coming together.

Drawing geometry, editing it, and changing the displayed view are the foundation of the drawing process; this part shows you how to make that foundation solid.

Chapter 6

Manage Your Properties

C AD programs are different from other drawing programs. You have to pay attention to little details like object properties and the precision of the points that you specify when you draw and edit objects. If you ignore these details and just start drawing, you'll end up with a mess of sloppy geometry that's hard to edit, view, and plot.

This chapter introduces you to *object properties,* one set of AutoCAD tools and techniques that help you prevent CAD messes. Chapter 7 explains the most important precision drawing techniques that you need to observe in order to create usable AutoCAD drawings. The information in these two chapters is essential to know before you start drawing and editing objects, procedures that I describe in Chapters 8, 9, 10, and 11.

When you first start using AutoCAD, one of its most overwhelming features is the number of property settings and precision controls that you need to pay attention to — even when you draw a simple line. Unlike many other programs, it's not enough to draw a line in a more-or-less adequate location and then slap some color on it. But all those settings and controls can inspire the feeling that you have to find out how to drive a Formula 1 car to make a trip down the street. (The advantage is that after you *are* comfortable in the driver's seat, AutoCAD will take you on the long-haul trips and get you there faster.)

Following are the three keys to good CAD drawing practice:

✔ Pay attention to and manage the *properties* of every drawing object that you create — especially the layer that each drawing object is on. I explain layers and other object properties in the next section.

✔ Pay attention to and use the *named objects* in every drawing — the layers, text styles, block definitions, and other *non-graphical* objects that serve to define the look of all the *graphical* objects in the drawing. I enlighten you in the "Using Named Objects" section later in this chapter.

✔ Pay attention to and control the *precision* of every point and distance that you use to draw and edit each object. I fill you in on AutoCAD's precision drawing techniques in Chapter 7.

These can seem like daunting tasks at first, but the following sections help you cut them down to size.

Managing Your Properties

All the objects that you draw in AutoCAD are like good Monopoly players: They own *properties*. In AutoCAD, these properties aren't physical things; they're an object's characteristics, such as layer, color, linetype, lineweight, and plot style. You use properties to communicate information about the characteristics of the objects you draw, such as the kinds of real-world objects they represent, their materials, their relative location in space, or their relative importance. In AutoCAD, you also use properties to organize objects for editing and plotting purposes.

You can view — and change — *all* properties of an object in the Properties palette and many of them in Quick Properties. In Figure 6-1, the Properties palette at the left and the Quick Properties panel at the right show properties for the selected line object.

The Properties palette was joined in AutoCAD 2009 by its more streamlined little sibling, *Quick Properties*. When Quick Properties is toggled on in the status bar, selecting an object opens a floating panel that displays a customizable selection of that object's properties. (If your status bar buttons show text rather than icons, look for the QP button.)

Figure 6-1:
Compre-
hensive
or quick?
Sometimes
you need
lots of infor-
mation, and
sometimes
you don't.

To toggle the full Properties palette on and off, click the Properties button on the View tab of the Ribbon or use the Ctrl+1 key combination. Before you select an object, the Properties palette displays the *current properties* — properties that AutoCAD applies to new objects when you draw them. After you select an object, the Properties palette displays the properties for that object. If you select more than one object, the Properties palette displays the properties that they have in common.

If the Quick Properties button is turned *off* in the status bar, you can double-click most object types, and the Properties palette will open, displaying information about that object. If Quick Properties is turned *on,* single- or double-clicking an object opens the Quick Properties panel.

Putting it on a layer

Every object has a layer as one of its properties. You may be familiar with *layers* — independent drawing spaces that stack on top of each other to create an overall image — from using drawing programs. AutoCAD, like most CAD programs, uses layers as the primary organizing principle for all the objects that you draw. You use layers to organize objects into logical groups of things that belong together; for example, walls, furniture, and text notes usually belong on three separate layers, for a couple of reasons:

✔ Layers give you a way to turn groups of objects on and off — both on the screen and on the plot.

✔ Layers provide the most efficient way of controlling object color, linetype, lineweight, and plot style.

So, to work efficiently in AutoCAD, you create some layers, assigning them names and properties, such as color and linetype. Then you draw objects on those layers. When you draw an object, AutoCAD automatically puts it on the *current* layer — the layer that you see in the Layer drop-down list on the Home tab's Layer panel when no objects are selected. If a layer already exists in your drawing, you can make it the current layer by choosing it in the Layer drop-down list, as shown in Figure 6-2.

It's not absolutely necessary to create *all* your layers before you draw anything, but it will save you some time if you start with a few basic layers and then add new layers as needed. Many experienced AutoCAD users draw things first and then create appropriate layers and change the objects to the new layers. You can easily change an object's layer by selecting it and then choosing the desired new layer name from the Layer drop-down list.

Figure 6-2:
Setting an existing layer current.

Make sure that no objects are selected before you use the Layer drop-down list to change the current layer. (Press the Esc key twice to be sure.) If objects are selected, the Layer drop-down list displays (and lets you change) those objects' layers. When no objects are selected, the Layer drop-down list displays (and lets you change) the current layer.

Stacking up your layers

How do you decide what to call your layers and which objects to put on them? Some industries have developed layer guidelines, and many offices have created documented layer standards. Some projects even impose specific layer requirements. (But be careful; if someone says, "You need a brick layer for this project," that can mean a couple of different things.) Ask experienced CAD drafters in your office or industry how they use layers in AutoCAD. If you can't find any definitive answer, create a chart of layers for yourself. Each row in the chart should list the layer name, default color, default linetype, default lineweight, and what kinds of objects belong on that layer. If you use named plot styles to control your plotted output, add default plot style to the list — that's not necessary for traditional color-based plotting.

Accumulating properties

Besides layers, the remaining object properties that you're likely to want to use often are color, linetype, lineweight, and possibly plot style. Table 6-1 summarizes these four properties.

Table 6-1	Useful Object Properties
Property	*Controls*
Color	Displayed color and plotted color or line width
Linetype	Displayed and plotted dash-dot line pattern
Lineweight	Displayed and plotted line width
Plot style	Plotted characteristics (see Chapter 16)

Long before AutoCAD could display lineweights on the screen and print those same lineweights on paper, object *colors* controlled the printed lineweight of objects. AutoCAD 2000 introduced a more logical system, where you could assign an actual plotted thickness to *objects*. As logical as that method seems, the older method, in which the color of objects determines their plotted lineweight, continues to dominate. You may find yourself working this way even in AutoCAD 2010, for compatibility with drawings (and coworkers) that use the old way.

AutoCAD gives you two different ways of controlling object properties:

✔ **By Layer:** Each layer has a default color, linetype, lineweight, and plot style property. Unless you tell AutoCAD otherwise, objects inherit the properties of the layers on which they're created. When objects are selected in a drawing created using this system, the object properties are listed as *ByLayer*.

✔ **By Object:** AutoCAD also enables you to override an object's layer's property setting and give the object a specific color, linetype, lineweight, or plot style that differs from the layer's.

If you've worked with other graphics programs, you may be used to assigning properties, such as color, to specific objects. If so, you may be tempted to do the same in AutoCAD. Resist the temptation. Did you catch that? One more time: *Resist the temptation.*

In almost all cases, it's better to create layers, assign properties to each layer, and let the objects on each layer inherit that layer's properties. Here are some benefits of using the ByLayer approach:

✔ You can easily change the properties of a group of related objects that you put on one layer. You simply change the property for the layer, not for a bunch of separate objects.

✔ Experienced drafters use the ByLayer approach, so if you work with drawings from other people, you'll be much more compatible with them if you do it the same way. You'll also avoid getting yelled at by irate CAD managers, whose job duties include haranguing any hapless newbie who assigns properties to individual objects.

If you take my advice and assign properties ByLayer, all you have to do is set layer properties in the Layer Properties Manager palette (I tell you how in this section), as shown in Figure 6-3. Before you draw any objects, make sure the Color Control, Linetype Control, and Lineweight Control drop-down lists on the Ribbon Home tab's Properties panel are set to ByLayer, as shown in Figure 6-4 (remember that the configuration of panels and drop-down lists may vary according to the resolution of your display). If the drawing is set to use color-based plot styles instead of named plot styles (see Chapter 16), the Plot Style Control drop-down list will be inactive and will display ByColor.

AutoCAD 2009 replaced the old-style Layer Properties Manager *dialog box* with the Layer Properties Manager *palette*. Like all palettes in AutoCAD, you can leave the Layer Properties Manager open while you do other things in the drawing — unlike the dialog box method of stopping what you're doing, opening the dialog box, making adjustments, closing the dialog box, and then resuming what you were doing. Also like other palettes, the Layer Properties Manager can be set to auto-hide itself to its title bar, to be either floating or docked, or to be anchored (do you get the sense that there are some nautical types amongst the AutoCAD programmers?) to either side of the screen.

Figure 6-3:
Use layer properties to control object properties.

Lineweight control

Color control

Figure 6-4:
ByLayer
(nearly) all
the way.

Linetype control Plot Style control

If the drawing is set to use named plot styles instead of color-based plot styles (see Chapter 16), the Plot Style control drop-down list should also display ByLayer.

If you want to avoid doing things the wrong way and getting yelled at by CAD managers, don't assign properties to objects in either of these ways:

✔ Don't make the *very* common beginner's mistake of choosing a specific color, linetype, lineweight, or plot style from the appropriate drop-down list on the Properties panel of the Ribbon's Home tab, or from the Properties palette, and then drawing the objects.

✔ Don't make the also-very-common beginner's mistake of drawing the objects, selecting them, and then choosing a property from the same drop-down lists.

If you prefer to do things the right way (that is, *my* way!), assign these properties ByLayer, as I describe in this section.

AutoCAD's SETBYLAYER command lets you correct those non-ByLayer properties — on the Ribbon's Home tab, click the Modify panel label to open its slideout menu and then click Set to ByLayer. Answer the prompts at the command line to finish modifying objects. For more information, refer to SETBYLAYER in the online help.

Creating new layers

If a suitable layer doesn't exist, you need to create one in the Layer Properties Manager palette. Follow these steps:

1. **Click the Layer Properties button on the Layers panel of the Ribbon's Home tab, or type** LAYER **(or** LA**) at the command line and press Enter.**

 The Layer Properties Manager palette appears. A new drawing has only one layer: Layer 0. You need to add the layers necessary for your drawing.

2. **Click the New Layer button (it looks like the sun setting on a sheet of paper) to create a new layer.**

 A new layer appears. AutoCAD names it Layer1 but highlights the name in an edit box so you can type a new name to replace it easily, as shown in Figure 6-5.

Figure 6-5:
Adding a
new layer
in the Layer
Properties
Manager
palette.

3. **Type a name for the new layer.**

 Type the layer name with *initial caps* (only the first letters of words in uppercase). Layer names written completely in uppercase are much wider, which means that they often get truncated in the Layer Control drop-down list.

4. **On the same line as the new layer, click the color block or color name (White by default) of the new layer.**

 The Select Color dialog box appears, as shown in Figure 6-6.

 The normal AutoCAD color scheme — AutoCAD Color Index (ACI) — provides 255 colors. So many choices are overkill for ordinary drafting.

 For now, stick with the first nine colors — the ones that appear in a single, separate row to the left of the ByLayer and ByBlock buttons on the Index Color tab of the Select Color dialog box — for the following reasons:

 • These colors are easy to distinguish from one another.

 • Using a small number of colors makes configuring your plot parameters easier. (I describe the procedure in Chapter 16.)

Figure 6-6:
The Select
Color dia-
log box.
Magenta
is selected
from the
Standard
Colors list.

In the Select Color dialog box, the True Color tab offers a choice of more than 16 million colors, which you can specify by using *HSL* (Hue Saturation Luminance) or *RGB* (Red Green Blue) numbers. The Color Books tab enables you to use PANTONE and RAL color schemes, which are popular in publishing. If your work requires tons of colors or close color matching between the computer screen and printed output, you're probably familiar with the relevant color palette and how to use it. If you're using AutoCAD for ordinary drafting or design, stick with the AutoCAD Color Index palette.

5. Click a color to select it as the color for this layer and click OK.

The Layer Properties Manager palette reappears. In the Color column, the new layer color changes to either the name or the number of the color that you selected.

AutoCAD's first seven colors have both numbers and standard names: 1 = red, 2 = yellow, 3 = green, 4 = cyan, 5 = blue, 6 = magenta, and 7 = white (which appears black when displayed on a white background). The remaining 248 colors have numbers only.

6. On the same line as the new layer, click the Linetype name of the new layer.

The Select Linetype dialog box appears, as shown in Figure 6-7.

The default AutoCAD linetype is *Continuous,* which means no gaps in the line.

If you already loaded the linetypes you need for your drawing, or if the template file you started from has some linetypes loaded, the Select Linetype dialog box displays them in the Loaded Linetypes list. If not, click the Load button to open the Load or Reload Linetypes dialog box. By default, AutoCAD displays linetypes from the standard AutoCAD or AutoCAD LT linetype definition file — `acad.lin` for imperial-units

drawings or `acadiso.lin` for metric-units drawings (`acadlt.lin` and `acadltiso.lin` in AutoCAD LT). Load the desired linetype by selecting its name and clicking OK.

Figure 6-7:
The Select
Linetype
dialog box.

Unless you have a really good reason (for example, your boss tells you so), avoid loading or using any linetypes labeled ACAD_ISO. These linetypes are normally used only in metric drawings and rarely even then. They overrule everything I'm trying to show you about printed lineweight in what follows, so if at all possible, just say NO to ACAD_ISO. I promise you'll find it easier to use the linetypes with the more descriptive names: CENTER, DASHED, and so on.

7. **Click the desired linetype in the Loaded Linetypes list to select it as the linetype for the layer; say that really fast five times and then click OK.**

 The Select Linetype dialog box disappears, returning you to the Layer Properties Manager palette. In the Name list, the linetype for the selected layer changes to the linetype you just chose.

8. **On the same line as the new layer, click the new layer's lineweight.**

 The Lineweight dialog box appears, as shown in Figure 6-8.

Figure 6-8:
The
Lineweight
dialog box.

9. **Select the lineweight you want from the scrolling list and click OK.**

The lineweight 0.00 mm tells AutoCAD to use the thinnest possible lineweight on the screen and on the plot. I recommend that for now, you leave lineweight set to Default and instead map screen color to plotted lineweight, as described in greater detail in Chapter 16.

The Plot Style column's contents depend on whether the drawing uses named plot styles or the traditional color-based plotting. Drawings set up to use color-based plotting display an unchangeable plot style name based on the layer's color property. The grayed-out style name changes only when the layer color changes. If, on the other hand, your drawing uses named plot styles, you can assign a named plot style to the layer in this column. (Chapter 16 explains why you might not want to.)

The setting in the Plot column controls whether the layer's objects appear on plots. Click the little printer icon to toggle this setting off (the little printer gets a red bar through it) for any layer whose objects you want to see on the screen but hide on plots.

10. **(Optional) If you want to add a description to the layer, scroll the layer list to the right to see the Description column, click in the Description box corresponding to your new layer, and type a description.**

My advice is to name your layers so you can tell what's on them. If you do choose to use layer descriptions, stretch the Layer Properties Manager palette to the right so that you can see the descriptions without having to scroll the layer list.

11. **Repeat Steps 2 through 10 to create any other layers that you want.**

12. **Select the new layer that you want to make current and click the Set Current button (the green check mark).**

Changes you make in the Layer Properties Manager palette are instantaneous, unlike a dialog box in which you have to click OK to close the dialog box and apply the change.

The Layer drop-down list now displays your new layer as the current layer — the one on which AutoCAD places new objects that you draw.

If you're one of those new-trick-hating old dogs who are really attached to doing things in the time-honored fashion, you can enter **CLASSICLAYER** at the command line to open the . . . er, classic Layer Properties Manager dialog box.

After you create layers, you can set any one of them to be the current layer. Make sure that no objects are selected and then choose the layer name from the Layer Control drop-down list on the Layers panel in the Ribbon or the Layers toolbar.

A load of linetypes

When you load a linetype, AutoCAD copies its *linetype definition* — a formula for how to create the dashes, dots, and gaps in that particular linetype — from the `acad.lin` (imperial units) or `acadiso.lin` (metric units) file into the drawing. (The files are `acadlt.lin` and `acadltiso.lin`, respectively, in AutoCAD LT.) The definition doesn't automatically appear in other drawings; you have to load each linetype that you want to use into each drawing in which you want to use it. If you find yourself loading the same linetypes repeatedly into different drawings, consider adding them to your template drawings instead. (See Chapter 4 for information about templates and how to create them.) After you add linetypes to a template drawing, all new drawings that you create from that template will start with those linetypes loaded automatically.

Don't go overboard on loading linetypes. For example, you don't need to load *all* the linetypes in the `acad.lin` file on the off chance that you might use them all someday. The resulting linetype list would be long and unwieldy. Most drawings require only a few linetypes, and most industries and companies settle on a half dozen or so linetypes for common use. Your industry, office, or project may have guidelines about which linetypes to use for which purposes.

If you're the techno-dweeb type and don't mind editing a text file that contains linetype definitions, you can define your own linetypes or weed out the ones you'll never use. Press F1 to open the main online help window. Then choose Contents⇨Customization Guide⇨Custom Linetypes.

Manipulating layers

After you create layers and draw objects on them, you can turn a layer off or on to hide or show the objects on that layer. In the Layer Properties Manager palette, the first three icons to the right of the layer name control AutoCAD's layer visibility modes:

- **Off/On:** Click the light-bulb icon to toggle visibility of all objects on the selected layer. AutoCAD does not regenerate the drawing when you turn layers back on. (I give you the lowdown on regenerations in Chapter 12.)

- **Freeze/Thaw:** Click the sun icon to toggle off visibility of all objects on the selected layer. Click the snowflake icon to toggle visibility on. AutoCAD regenerates the drawing when you thaw layers.

- **Lock/Unlock:** Click the padlock icon to lock and unlock layers. When a layer is locked, you can see but not edit objects on that layer.

You can rearrange column order by simply dragging and dropping the column label to a new place. And you can right-click any column label to display a menu from which you can turn columns off and on.

Off/On and Freeze/Thaw do almost the same thing — both settings let you make objects visible or invisible by layer. In the old days, turning layers off and on was often a faster process than thawing frozen layers because thawing layers always required regenerating the drawing. But modern computers, modern operating systems, and recent AutoCAD releases make regenerations much less of an issue on all but the largest drawings. You'll probably find it makes no appreciable difference whether you freeze and thaw layers or turn them off and on.

You can turn layers off and on, freeze and thaw them, and lock and unlock them by clicking the appropriate icons in the Layer Control drop-down list on the Ribbon.

The state of your layers

Say you have a floor plan of a house that includes a layer showing the framing and another layer showing the wiring. You'd probably never show both of those elements on the same drawing, so you'd need to do some layer management when you showed your drawing to the framers or the electricians. Rather than turning a dozen layers off and a different dozen layers on when you want a different view into your drawing, you can save groups of layer settings as a named *layer state*. You can manage your layer states in the appropriately named Layer States Manager dialog box by clicking the Layer States Manager button in the Layer Properties Manager. You can also access the Layer States Manager directly by entering **LAYERSTATES** at the command line or choosing Manage Layer States from the Layer State drop-down list in the Layers panel.

AutoCAD fades locked layers, giving you a really effective visual reference without confusing you about which layers might be locked or not. You can control the amount of fading by setting a nonzero value for the system variable LAYLOCKFADECTL. (See Chapter 23 for an explanation of system variables, and check out the online help for specific info on this one.) Turn off the fading altogether by setting this value to 0.

If you find yourself using lots of layers, you can create *layer filters* to make viewing and managing the layer list easier. A *group filter* is simply a subset of layers that you choose (by dragging layer names into the group filter name or by selecting objects in the drawing). A *property filter* is a subset of layers that AutoCAD creates and updates automatically based on layer property criteria that you define (for example, all layers whose names contain *Wall* or whose color is green). To find out more, move your mouse pointer into the Layer Properties Manager palette, press F1, and click the New Property Filter hyperlink.

In both AutoCAD and AutoCAD LT, you can access a set of layer tools through the Layers panel of the Ribbon's Home tab (you have to open the panel slide-out to see them all — see Figure 6-9). Layer Isolate and Layer Off are especially useful — you simply click an object to specify the layer to isolate (that is, fade

all layers except the chosen one) or turn off altogether. For more information, open the online help system and choose User's Guide⇨Create and Modify Objects⇨Control the Properties of Objects⇨Work with Layers⇨Use Layers to Manage Complexity.

Figure 6-9:
Tooling
through the
layer tools.

The LAYISO command incorporates the same layer fading feature described previously for locked layers — and it locks the layers as well. Set it up the way you want by typing **S** (for Settings) and pressing Enter; then type the option letter for the specific settings you want. Look up LAYISO in the online help Index for more information.

Using Named Objects

One of the things that can make AutoCAD a tough nut to crack is the somewhat cavalier naming conventions used in the program's documentation. For years, things like lines, arcs, and other *graphical* items were called *entities,* but more recently, they started being called *objects.* Fair enough, but *object* has also long been used to define certain *non-graphical* components of a drawing — things that you'd hardly consider to be objects at all — and those are the kind of named objects I describe in what follows.

Hidden in the innards of every AutoCAD drawing file is a set of *named objects.* Named objects are organized into *symbol tables,* and the properties that are common to all AutoCAD objects are defined in these tables. For example, all the line objects in a drawing are stored on one or more layers, so a layer property is common to all lines and is defined in the layer table. But the coordinates that define the start and end points of a given line are unique to that line (or they should be!) — so the coordinate properties are *not* common to all lines.

Layers are one example of a named object. The layer table in a given drawing contains a list of the layers in the current drawing, along with the settings for each layer (color, linetype, on/off setting, and so on).

Named objects don't appear as graphical objects in your drawing. They're like the hard-working pit crew that keeps the race cars running smoothly behind the scenes. The named objects include

- Layers (covered in this chapter)
- Linetypes (covered in this chapter)
- Text styles (see Chapter 13)
- Table styles (see Chapter 13)
- Multileader styles (see Chapter 13)
- Multiline styles (not covered; see the online help)
- Dimension styles (see Chapter 14)
- Block definitions and xrefs (see Chapters 17 and 18)
- Layouts (see Chapter 5)

When you use commands, such as LAYER, LINETYPE, and DIMSTYLE, you're creating and editing named objects. After you've created named objects in a drawing, AutoCAD DesignCenter gives you the tools to copy them to other drawings.

Donald Trump might think otherwise, but you can have too many properties (at least in AutoCAD). You may have created layers or loaded linetypes, text, or dimension styles that you end up not using. If you think you may have some of these superfluously named objects in your drawing, the PURGE command can help you get rid of them. Click the Application button to display the Application Menu. Choose Drawing Utilities, and then Purge to open the Purge dialog box. You can click the plus sign beside each category and purge individual items, or you can click Purge All and get rid of tons of stuff at once. Visit the online help for more about purging.

Using AutoCAD DesignCenter

DesignCenter is a dumb name for a useful, if somewhat busy, palette. (At least they didn't call it DesignCenter Manager!) The DesignCenter palette is handy for borrowing data from all kinds of drawings. Whereas the Properties palette, described earlier in this chapter, is concerned with properties of graphical objects, the DesignCenter palette deals primarily with named objects: layers, linetypes, block definitions, text styles, and other organizational objects in your drawings.

The DesignCenter palette (as shown in Figure 6-10) consists of a toolbar at the top, a set of three tabs below that, a tree view pane on the left, and a content pane on the right. The tree view pane displays a Windows Explorer–like navigation panel, showing drawing files and the symbol tables contained in each drawing. The content pane usually displays the contents of the selected drawing or symbol table.

Tabs

Tool bar

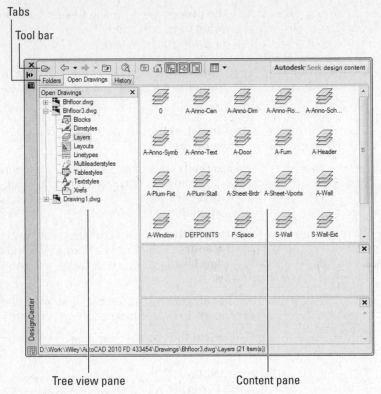

Figure 6-10:
The
AutoCAD
Design-
Center
palette.

Tree view pane Content pane

The three tabs just below the DesignCenter toolbar control what you see in the tree view and content panes:

- **Folders:** This tab shows the folders on your local and network drives, just like the Windows Explorer Folders pane does. Use this tab if the drawing you want to copy from isn't currently open in AutoCAD.

- **Open Drawings:** This tab (current in Figure 6-10) shows the drawings that are currently open in AutoCAD. Use this tab to copy named objects between open drawings.

- **History:** This tab shows drawings that you've recently browsed in DesignCenter. Use this tab to jump quickly to drawings that you've used recently on the Folders tab.

The Autodesk Seek button on DesignCenter's toolbar links to parts libraries that are available on Autodesk's Web sites. Autodesk Seek is essentially an online catalog of building products. Browse the offerings to see whether any of the online libraries can be useful in your work.

The toolbar buttons further refine what you see in the tree view and content panes. A few of these buttons toggle different parts of the panes.

The following steps outline the procedure for using DesignCenter to copy named objects from one drawing to another. See the next section, "Copying layers between drawings," for a specific example.

1. **If it isn't already open, switch to the Ribbon's View tab, find the Palettes panel, and click DesignCenter to open the DesignCenter palette.**

 You can also press Ctrl+2.

2. **Select or load the drawing(s) whose content you want to view or use into the navigation pane on the left.**

 If the source drawing is already open, you can access its content from the Open Drawings tab. If the source drawing isn't open but is stored on your hard drive or network, click Load on the DesignCenter toolbar and navigate to the file's location in the Folders tab.

3. **In the Open Drawings tab (if the source drawing is currently open) or the Folders tab (if the source drawing is not open) of the tree view pane, click the + sign beside the source file to expand the list of named object categories.**

 The list of named object categories appears in a list in the tree view pane on the left and as icons in the content pane on the right.

4. **In the tree view pane, select the category of named object you want to copy.**

 The content pane now displays the individual named objects within the named object category. For example, in Figure 6-10 (shown previously), the Layers category is selected in the tree view pane, and icons for each named layer are shown in the content pane.

5. **In the content pane, select the items you want to copy. Right-click and choose Add [Symbol] (or Insert Block if you're copying block definitions) or simply drag and drop them into the drawing area.**

 Use Shift or Ctrl to select multiple named objects.

Copying layers between drawings

The previous set of steps outlines the general procedure for copying named objects from one drawing to another by using DesignCenter. The following steps show a specific example: copying layers from one drawing to another. You can use the same technique to copy dimension styles, layouts, linetypes, table styles, and text styles.

1. **Open the drawing that contains the layers you want to copy (the *source* drawing).**

2. **Open the drawing to which you want to copy the layers (the *destination* drawing).**

If you already had both drawings open, make sure that you can see the destination drawing. If you can't, click Switch Windows in the View tab's Windows panel and choose the destination drawing in order to bring it to the foreground, or tile the windows, as shown in Figure 6-11, by clicking Tile Vertically in the same Windows panel.

3. **Click the DesignCenter button on the Palettes panel of the Ribbon's View tab or press Ctrl+2.**

4. **In the DesignCenter palette, click the Open Drawings tab.**

 The DesignCenter tree view pane on the left side of the palette displays a list of drawings that you currently have open in AutoCAD.

TIP

 You can also use the Folders tab, the Load button, or the Search button to load a drawing into DesignCenter without opening it in AutoCAD.

5. **In the tree view pane of the DesignCenter palette, click the plus sign (+) next to the name of the source drawing that you opened in Step 1.**

 A list of symbol categories that you can copy, including layers, appears in the tree view pane.

Figure 6-11:
Copying a
layer from
one drawing
to another.

Layer named object being dragged to new drawing

6. **Click Layers in the list in the tree view pane.**

 The display in the content pane at the right changes to show the individual layers that are stored in the source drawing.

7. **Click and drag the desired layer or layers from the content pane of the DesignCenter palette into the window containing the destination drawing that you opened in Step 2, as shown in Figure 6-11.**

If the current drawing contains a layer whose name matches the name of one of the layers you're copying, AutoCAD doesn't change the current drawing's layer definition. For example, if you add a Doors layer whose color is red into a drawing that already includes a Doors layer whose color is green, the destination drawing's Doors layer remains green. Named objects from DesignCenter never overwrite objects with the same name in the destination drawing. AutoCAD always displays the message `Duplicate definitions will be ignored` even if there aren't any duplicates.

If you're repeatedly copying named objects from the same drawings or folders, add them to your DesignCenter favorites list. On the Folders tab, right-click the drawing or folder and choose Add to Favorites from the menu. This procedure adds another shortcut to your list of favorites.

 ✔ To see your favorites, click the DesignCenter toolbar's Favorites button.

 ✔ To return to a favorite, double-click its shortcut in the content pane.

Chapter 7

Preciseliness Is Next to CADliness

In This Chapter

▶ Typing coordinates at the keyboard

▶ Snapping to object features

▶ Using other precision drawing and editing techniques

Drawing precision is vital to good CAD drafting practice, even more than for manual drafting. (Accuracy, of course, is vital to both types of drafting — if you're sketchy on the difference between accuracy and precision, look ahead to the "CAD precision versus accuracy" sidebar later in this chapter.) If you think CAD managers get a little tense when you assign properties directly to objects instead of *ByLayer*, wait until you see them lay into someone (I sincerely hope it's not you!) who doesn't use precision techniques when creating drawings in AutoCAD.

Controlling Your Precision

In AutoCAD, lack of precision makes later editing, hatching, and dimensioning tasks much more difficult and time consuming. Keep these facts in mind:

✔ Small errors in precision in the early stages of creating or editing a drawing often have a big effect on productivity and precision later.

✔ Drawings may guide manufacturing and construction projects; drawing data may drive automatic manufacturing machinery. Huge amounts of money and even lives can ride on a drawing's precision.

In recognition of these facts, a passion for precision permeates the profession. Precision is one of the characteristics that separates CAD from ordinary illustration-type drawing work. The sooner you get fussy about precision in AutoCAD, the happier everyone is.

When I talk about drawing things precisely, I mean using precision techniques and tools to specify points and distances with as much exactness as the program allows. Luckily, AutoCAD provides a comprehensive package of

tools for doing just that. Table 7-1 lists the more important AutoCAD precision techniques, along with visual cues to the status bar buttons that you click to toggle some of the features.

As I describe in Chapter 2, you can switch the display on status bar buttons between text and icons by right-clicking any of those buttons and selecting or unselecting Use Icons. Table 7-1 shows the icons and lists the text for both alternatives.

AutoCAD 2010 introduces another P-for-precision technique with *parametric* drawing. In AutoCAD you've always been able to indicate that, for example, two circles are concentric by adding dimensions from their center points to another point in the drawing. With parametrics, you can add geometric *relations* which might say that these two circles are *always* concentric, even if they end up being dimensioned from different points in the drawing. Parametrics, as you might imagine, is a complex technology, into which I delve more deeply in Chapter 19.

Precision is especially important when you're drawing or editing *geometry* — the lines, arcs, and so on that make up whatever you're representing in the CAD drawing. Precision placement usually is less important with notes, leaders, and other *annotations* that describe, not show.

CAD precision versus accuracy

You often hear *precision* and *accuracy* used interchangeably, but it's useful to understand the difference. In this book, when I use *precision,* I mean controlling the placement of objects so they lie exactly where you want them to lie in the drawing. For example, lines whose endpoints meet must meet *exactly,* and a circle that's supposed to be centered on the coordinates 0,0 must be drawn with its center *exactly* at 0,0. I use *accuracy* to refer to the degree to which your drawing matches its real-world counterpart. An accurate floor plan is one in which the dimensions of the CAD objects equal the dimensions of the as-built house. In

a sense, then, it's not the drawing that should be accurate — it's the house!

CAD precision usually helps produce accurate drawings, but that's not always the case. You can produce a precise CAD drawing that's inaccurate because you started from inaccurate information (for example, the contractor gave you a wrong field measurement). Or you might deliberately exaggerate certain distances to convey the relationship between objects more clearly on the plotted drawing. Even where you must sacrifice accuracy, aim for precision.

Table 7-1	Precision Tools and Techniques		
Technique	*Status Bar Button Label*	*Status Bar Button Icon*	*Description*
Snap mode	SNAP		Forces the crosshairs to move on an imaginary grid of equally spaced *hot spots*.
PolarSnap	—	—	Forces the crosshairs to move specific distances along polar tracking angles.
Grid display	GRID		Displays a non-printing reference grid of dots arranged in rows or columns.
Ortho mode	ORTHO		Forces the crosshairs to move horizontally or vertically from the previous point.
Polar tracking	POLAR		Causes the crosshairs to jump to specified angles.
Object snap	OSNAP		Enables picking specific points on existing drawing objects multiple times.
Object snap tracking	OTRACK		Causes the crosshairs to locate new points based on multiple object snap points.
Object snap overrides	—	—	Enables picking specific points on existing drawing objects one time only.
Coordinate input	—	—	Enables you to type exact X,Y or polar coordinates.
Direct distance entry	—	—	Enables you to locate a point by typing a distance and moving the crosshairs to show the direction.

Before you draw objects, always check the status bar's SNAP, ORTHO, POLAR, OSNAP, and OTRACK buttons and set the buttons according to your precision needs.

- ✔ A button that looks lit (that is, just a little brighter than its neighbors) indicates that the feature is *on*.
- ✔ A button that looks dimmed indicates that the feature is *off*.

Keyboard capers: Coordinate input

The most direct way to enter points precisely is to type numbers at the keyboard. AutoCAD uses these keyboard coordinate entry formats:

- ✔ Absolute Cartesian (X,Y) coordinates in the form *X,Y* (for example, 7,4)
- ✔ Relative X,Y coordinates in the form @*X,Y* (for example, @3,2)
- ✔ Relative polar coordinates in the form @*distance<angle* (for example, @6<45)

Cartesian coordinates are named for French philosopher René Descartes (who reasoned, "I think, therefore I am"). In his *Discourse on Method,* Descartes came up with the idea of locating any point on a planar surface by measuring its distance from a pair of axes (that's *axes* as in more than one axis, not the tool for chopping wood). In this book, I refer to Cartesian coordinates as X,Y coordinates.

AutoCAD locates *absolute X,Y coordinates* with respect to the 0,0 point (otherwise known as the *origin*) of the drawing — usually its lower-left corner. AutoCAD locates *relative X,Y coordinates* and *relative polar coordinates* with respect to the previous point that you picked or typed. Figure 7-1 demonstrates how to use all three coordinate formats to draw a pair of line segments that start at absolute coordinates 2,1; then go 3 units to the right and 2 units up relative to the first point; then relative to *that* point go 4 units at an angle of 60 degrees.

In case you're wondering, AutoCAD also understands *absolute polar coordinates* in the form *distance<angle,* but this format is almost never useful.

You can find out the X,Y location of your crosshairs by moving them around in the drawing area and reading the coordinate values at the left end of the status bar. The X,Y coordinates should change while you move the crosshairs. If the coordinates don't change, click the drawing coordinates area until you see <Coords on> in the command window.

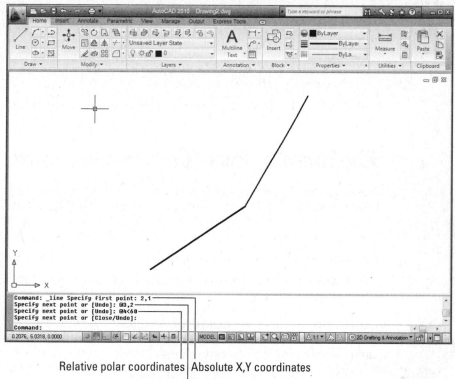

Relative polar coordinates | Absolute X,Y coordinates

Relative X,Y coordinates

Astute observers of the full version of AutoCAD will have noticed that there are *three* numbers at the left end of the status bar (AutoCAD LT is numerically deprived). AutoCAD is actually showing you the X,Y,Z coordinates of the crosshairs. However, in 2D drafting, the Z value is (or should be) 0, so you can continue calling them X,Y coordinates.

Although it's not apparent at first, there are, in fact, three coordinate display modes. Clicking the coordinates readout cycles through:

- ✓ **Off `<coords off>`:** The status bar coordinates readout is dimmed, and the coordinate values don't update until you pick a point.

- ✓ **On, showing X,Y coordinates `<coords on>`:** The coordinates readout appears black, and the absolute X,Y coordinates update continuously as you move the crosshairs. If no command is active, clicking the coordinates readout alternates between this mode and `<coords off>`.

- ✓ **On, showing polar coordinates `<coords on>`:** This mode, which displays distance and angle relative to the last point picked rather than absolute X,Y values, appears if a command is active and AutoCAD is waiting for you to pick a point.

If you start a command, such as LINE, pick a point, and then click the Coordinates area a few times; the display changes from coordinates off to live absolute coordinates (X,Y position) to live polar coordinates (distance and angle from the previous point). The live polar coordinates display mode is the most informative most of the time.

When you type coordinates at the command line, do *not* add any spaces because AutoCAD interprets a space as though you've pressed Enter. This "Spacebar = Enter" weirdness is a productivity feature that's been in AutoCAD forever. It's easier to find the spacebar than the Enter key when you're entering lots of commands and coordinates in a hurry — and it's especially handy for touch typists who are all thumbs.

If you're working in AutoCAD's Architectural or Engineering units, the default unit of entry is *inche s,* not feet. Here are some things to consider about entering numeric values when you work in feet and inches:

- To specify feet, you must enter the symbol for feet after the number. For example:

 6' for 6 feet

- You can enter a dash to separate feet from inches, as architects often do:

 6'–6" is 6 feet, 6 inches.

- Both the dash and the inch mark are optional when you're entering coordinates and distances.

 AutoCAD understands **6'6"** and **6'6** as the same as **6'–6"**.

- If you're typing a coordinate or distance that contains fractional inches, you *must* enter a dash — not a space — between the whole number of inches and the fraction.

 6'6–1/2 (or **6'–6–1/2**) represents 6 feet, 6 1/2 inches.

- If all this dashing about confuses you, enter partial inches by using decimals instead.

 6'6.5 is the same as **6'6–1/2"** to AutoCAD, whether you're working in Architectural or Engineering units.

Have you ever wanted to check the accuracy (or precision!) of something that's already drawn? AutoCAD 2010's new MEASUREGEOM command is a one-stop shop where you can query drawing objects for distances, angles, areas, and other geometric or locational information about drawing objects. You can find it on the Utilities panel of the Home tab — look for an icon with a yellow ruler.

Grab an object and make it snappy

After you've drawn a few objects precisely in a new drawing, the most efficient way to draw more objects with equal precision is to grab specific, geometrically precise points, such as endpoints, midpoints, or quadrants, on the existing objects. Every object type in AutoCAD has at least one of these points, and you can "snap" to them precisely as you draw by using *object snaps* (*osnaps* for short by those in the know).

AutoCAD provides two ways of using object snaps:

- ✔ **Object snap *overrides:*** An object snap override is active for a single pick.
- ✔ ***Running* object snaps:** A running object snap stays in effect until you turn it off.

Grabbing points with object snap overrides

Here's how you draw precise lines by using object snap overrides:

1. **Open a drawing containing some geometry.**

2. **Turn off running osnap mode by clicking the OSNAP button on the status bar until the button appears to be dimmed and `<Osnap off>` appears in the command window.**

 Although you can use object snap overrides while running object snap mode is turned on, you should turn off running osnap mode while you're getting familiar with object snap overrides. After you have the hang of each feature separately, you can use them together.

3. **Start the LINE command by clicking the Line button on the Ribbon's Draw panel or typing LINE (or L) and pressing Enter.**

 AutoCAD prompts you to select the starting point of the line:

   ```
   Specify first point:
   ```

4. **Hold down the Shift key, right-click anywhere in the drawing area, and release the Shift key.**

 The object snap menu appears, as shown in Figure 7-2.

5. **Choose an object snap mode, such as Endpoint, from the object snap menu.**

 The object snap menu disappears, and the command window displays an additional prompt indicating that you've directed AutoCAD to seek out, for example, endpoints of existing objects:

   ```
   _endp of:
   ```

6. **Move the crosshairs slowly around the drawing, pausing over various lines and other objects without clicking yet.**

 When you move the crosshairs near an object with an endpoint, a colored square icon appears at the endpoint, indicating that AutoCAD can snap to that point. If you stop moving the crosshairs for a moment, a tooltip displaying the object snap mode (for example, Endpoint) appears to reinforce the idea.

7. **Click when the Endpoint object snap square appears on the point you want to snap to.**

 AutoCAD snaps to the endpoint, which becomes the first point of the new line segment that you're about to draw. The command line prompts you to select the other endpoint of the new line segment:

   ```
   Specify next point or [Undo]:
   ```

 When you move the crosshairs around the drawing, AutoCAD no longer seeks out endpoints because object snap overrides last for only a single pick. You can use the object snap right-click menu again to snap the other end of your new line segment to another point on an existing object.

8. **Use the Shift+right-click sequence described in Step 4 to display the object snap menu again. Then choose another object snap mode, such as Midpoint, from the object snap menu.**

 The command line displays an additional prompt indicating that you've directed AutoCAD to seek, for example, midpoints of existing objects:

   ```
   _mid of:
   ```

 When you move the crosshairs near the midpoint of an object, a colored triangle appears at the snap point. Each object snap type (endpoint, midpoint, intersection, and so on) displays a different symbol. If you stop

moving the crosshairs, the tooltip text reminds you what the symbol means. Figure 7-3 shows what the screen looks like during this step.

9. **Draw additional line segments by picking additional points. Use the object snap right-click menu to specify a single object snap type before you pick each point.**

 Try the Intersection, Perpendicular, and Nearest object snaps. If your drawing contains arcs or circles, try Center and Quadrant.

10. **When you're finished experimenting with object snap overrides, right-click anywhere in the drawing area and choose Enter from the menu to end the LINE command.**

 There's a difference between right-clicking and Shift+right-clicking in the drawing area:

 • *Right-clicking* displays menu options for the current command (or common commands and settings when no command is active).

 • *Shift+right-clicking* always displays the same object snap menu.

Already object-snapped to endpoint — New line segment

Figure 7-3:
A snappy
line.

About to object-snap to midpoint

Running with object snaps

Often, you use an object snap mode (such as Endpoint) repeatedly. Use running object snaps to address this need.

The following steps set a running object snap:

1. **Right-click the OSNAP button on the status bar.**

 The object snap menu appears, as shown in Figure 7-4.

 In AutoCAD 2010, the Object Snaps button, together with the Snap Mode, Polar Tracking, and Object Snap Tracking buttons, display a shortcut menu when you right-click, as shown in Figure 7-4. (Object Snaps and Object Snap Tracking both display the menu of running object snaps.) Many settings, including all running object snap modes, can be set by clicking a menu item — you no longer need to open the Drafting Settings dialog box, make your settings, and then click OK to close the dialog box.

Active object snap mode

Figure 7-4:
Grabbing
multiple
object fea-
tures is an
osnap.

Inactive object snap mode

2. **Click in the list to select one or more object snap modes.**

 Active running object snap modes show a highlighted square around the icon (see Figure 7-4).

You click the Object Snaps button on the status bar to toggle running object snap mode. After you turn on running object snap, AutoCAD hunts for points that correspond to the object snap modes you checked on the Object Snaps button's shortcut menu. As with object snap overrides, AutoCAD displays a special symbol — such as a square for an endpoint object snap — to indicate

that it has found an object snap point. If you keep the crosshairs still, AutoCAD also displays a tooltip that lists the kind of object snap point.

Use object snap overrides or running object snaps to enforce precision by making sure that new points you pick coincide *exactly* with points on existing objects. In AutoCAD, it's not good enough for points to *almost* coincide or to look like they coincide. You lose points, both figuratively and literally, if you don't use object snaps or one of the other precision techniques covered in this chapter to enforce precision.

Most, but not all, object snap overrides have running object snap equivalents. For example, Endpoint, Midpoint, and Center work as either overrides or running object snaps, but Mid Between 2 Points works only in override mode.

Other practical precision procedures

The following are some other AutoCAD precision techniques (refer to Table 7-1, earlier in this chapter):

 ✔ **Snap:** If you turn on snap mode, AutoCAD constrains the crosshairs to an imaginary rectangular grid of points at the spacing that you've specified. Follow these steps to turn on snap mode:

 1. *Right-click the SNAP button on the status bar.*

 2. *Choose Settings.*

 The Snap and Grid tab on the Drafting Settings dialog box appears.

 3. *Enter a snap spacing in the Snap X Spacing field and click OK.*

 Click the Snap Mode button on the status bar (labeled SNAP if your status bar buttons show text) or press F9 to toggle snap mode off and on. To use snap effectively, change the snap spacing frequently — changing to a smaller spacing as you zoom in and work on smaller areas. You often need to toggle snap off and on because selecting objects and doing some editing tasks are easier with snap off.

 In AutoCAD 2010, you can switch between Grid Snap (that is, snap points in rows and columns) and PolarSnap (snap points based on distances and angles) using the Snap Mode button's shortcut menu. See the PolarSnap item later in this list for more info.

 ✔ **Ortho:** Ortho mode forces the crosshairs to move horizontally or vertically. Click the Ortho Mode button (ORTHO for text buttons) on the status bar or press F8 to toggle ortho mode. Because technical drawings often include lots of orthogonal lines, you may use ortho mode a lot, although take a close look at polar tracking as well.

✔ **Direct distance entry (DDE):** This point-and-type technique is an easy and efficient way to draw with precision. You simply point the crosshairs in a particular direction, type a distance at the command line, and press Enter. You can use DDE any time the crosshairs are anchored to a point, and the command line or dynamic input tooltip prompts you for another point or a distance.

You'll usually use DDE with polar tracking turned on to specify distances in particular directions (for example, in angle increments of 45 degrees). You can also combine DDE with ortho mode to specify a distance in an orthogonal direction (0, 90, 180, or 270 degrees).

✔ **Object snap tracking:** This feature extends running object snaps so that you can locate points based on more than one object snap point. For example, you can pick a point at the center of a square by tracking to the midpoints of two perpendicular sides. Click Object Snap Tracking on the status bar (if you're showing text instead of icons, this button is labeled OTRACK — which has nothing at all to do with the Irish railway system) or press F11 to toggle object snap tracking.

✔ **Polar tracking:** When you turn on polar tracking, the crosshairs jump to increments of the angle you specified in the Drafting Settings dialog box or chose on the right-click menu. When the crosshairs jump, a tooltip label starting with `Polar:` appears. Right-click the Polar Tracking button on the status bar (POLAR on buttons that show text labels) and choose the Settings option to display the Polar Tracking tab on the Drafting Settings dialog box. Select an angle from the Increment Angle drop-down list and then click OK. Click the Polar Tracking button on the status bar or press F10 to toggle polar tracking mode.

Remember, you can set a predefined polar tracking angle by right-clicking the Polar Tracking button and choosing it from the menu. If you want to add an angle that's not on the list, you have to click Settings to open the Drafting Settings dialog box.

✔ **PolarSnap:** You can force polar tracking to jump to specific incremental distances along the tracking angles by changing the snap type from grid snap to polar snap. For example, if you turn on *polar tracking* and set it to 45 degrees, then turn on *polar snap* and set it to 2 units, polar tracking jumps to points that are at angle increments of 45 degrees and distance increments of 2 units from the previous point. Polar snap has a similar effect on object snap tracking.

To activate polar snap, right-click the Snap Mode button and choose PolarSnap from the menu. To specify a polar snap distance follow these steps:

1. *Right-click the SNAP button on the status bar.*

2. *Choose Settings.*

 The Snap and Grid tab on the Drafting Settings dialog box appears.

3. *Click the PolarSnap radio button, type a distance in the Polar Distance text box, and then click OK.*

When you want to return to ordinary rectangular snap, as described at the beginning of this list, right-click the Snap Mode button and choose Grid Snap from the menu.

✔ **Temporary overrides:** Settings, such as SNAP, ORTHO, and POLAR remain on until you turn them off. You can also use *temporary overrides,* which last only as long as you hold down their key or key combination. For example, with ortho turned off, holding down the Shift key puts AutoCAD into a temporary ortho mode for as long as you press Shift. For additional information, look up *temporary override keys* in the online help system.

If you're new to AutoCAD, its wide range of precision tools probably seems overwhelming at this point. Rest assured that there's more than one way to skin a cat precisely (with cats, accuracy is unimportant), and not everyone needs to understand all the ways. You can make perfectly precise drawings without using every single implement in AutoCAD's precision toolkit. I recommend these steps:

1. Get comfortable with typing coordinates, ortho mode, direct distance entry, and object snap overrides.

2. Become familiar with running object snaps and try snap mode.

3. After you have all these precision features under your belt, feel free to experiment with polar tracking, polar snap, and object snap tracking.

It's easy to confuse the names of the snap and object snap (osnap) features. Remember that *snap* limits the crosshairs to locations whose coordinates are multiples of the current snap spacing. Snap works whether or not there are objects in the drawing. *Object snap (osnap)* enables you to grab points on existing objects, whether or not those points happen to correspond with the snap spacing.

Chapter 8

Down the Straightaway

In This Chapter

▶ Drawing linear things with the AutoCAD drawing commands

▶ Lining up for lines and polylines

▶ Closing up with rectangles and polygons

As you probably remember from your crayon and coloring book days, drawing stuff is *fun*. CAD imposes a little more discipline, but drawing stuff with AutoCAD is still fun (trust me on this one). In computer-aided drafting, you usually start by drawing *geometry* — shapes such as lines, circles, rectangles, and so on — that represents the real-world object that you're documenting. This chapter shows you how to draw *linear* geometry objects that proceed in a straightforward manner from one point to the next. In Chapter 9, I throw some curves at you.

After you've created some straight or curvy geometry, you'll probably need to add some dimensions, text, and hatching, but those elements come later (in Part III of this book). Your first task is to get the geometry right; then you can worry about labeling things.

Drawing geometry properly in AutoCAD depends on paying attention to object properties and the precision of the points that you specify to create the objects. I cover these matters in Chapters 6 and 7, so if you eagerly jumped to this chapter to get right to the fun stuff, take a moment to review those chapters first.

Introducing the AutoCAD Drawing Commands

For descriptive purposes, I'm dividing the drawing commands into three groups:

✔ Straight lines and objects composed of straight lines (covered in this chapter)

✔ Curves (which I explain in Chapter 9)

✔ Points (see Chapter 9 if you're wondering what the point is)

Table 8-1 presents the most important commands for drawing 2D linear objects in AutoCAD. It lists each command by name, with the shortcut keys, or *alias* (when one exists), in parentheses. The table also displays each command's graphical icon, as found on the Draw panel of the Ribbon's Home tab, and in identical form on toolbar buttons and pull-down menus in the AutoCAD Classic workspace.

Table 8-1 AutoCAD Drawing Commands for Linear Objects

Button	Command	Draw Panel Button	Draw Toolbar Button	Draw Menu
	LINE	Line (L)	Line	Line
	RAY	Ray (on slideout)	None	Ray
	XLINE (XL)	Construction line (on slideout)	Construction line	Construction line
	PLINE (PL)	Polyline	Polyline	Polyline
	Polygon (on slide-out)	Polygon	Polygon	Polygon
	RECTANG (REC)	Rectangle	Rectangle	Rectangle

If you're coming from an earlier version, AutoCAD 2010's Ribbon is obviously very different from what you're used to; it's even a little different from the Ribbon in AutoCAD 2009. Like many Ribbon panels, the Draw panel has additional tool buttons on a slideout you can use once or pin so it stays open — refer to Chapter 2 for a refresher on Ribbon panels and slideouts. Similarly, many of the choices on the AutoCAD Draw menu open submenus containing several variations on each drawing command.

AutoCAD's drawing commands are highly interactive. You need to read and respond to the prompts in the command window (or at the dynamic input tooltip next to the crosshairs if Dynamic Input mode is turned on). You can also access many of the command options that you see in command window prompts by pressing the up- and down-arrow keys to display the options at the dynamic input tooltip. You can even right-click and select command options from the context-specific shortcut menu.

AutoCAD's Dynamic Input system displays a lot of the information that you used to have to look down to the command window to see. To use Dynamic Input, make sure the Dynamic Input button on the status bar is turned on (that is, it looks highlighted). You can also press the F12 function key to toggle Dynamic Input on and off. Don't turn the command window off just yet, though, especially if you're new to AutoCAD. I recommend that you keep the command window open and docked at all times.

So what's the best course: to enter drawing commands from the command line, which you can do in any workspace? Or to choose commands from the Ribbon in the 2D Drafting & Annotation workspace, or the AutoCAD Classic workspace's menus or toolbars? Well . . . it all depends:

✔ **If you've never used AutoCAD in your life,** use the Ribbon (that is, the default 2D Drafting & Annotation workspace) rather than the toolbars and menus of the traditional AutoCAD Classic workspace. As much as I've wished otherwise, I don't think the Ribbon is going away. I suspect more and more programs are going to adopt its look, if for no other reason than to avoid looking old-fashioned. At this early stage of the game, it also looks like Windows 7 might incorporate the Ribbon into the operating system itself — so you might as well get used to it!

✔ **If you're an experienced AutoCAD user who's been away for a release or two,** give the Ribbon a decent test drive before you switch to the AutoCAD Classic workspace. To ease your transition, you can display the classic menu bar above the Ribbon. Type **MENUBAR**, press Enter, type **1**, and press Enter.

Whichever kind of user you are and regardless of the workspace you choose, it's a truth universally acknowledged that the most efficient way of working with AutoCAD is to use the keyboard to enter command aliases or open and close palettes. No matter how many times the graphical user interface changes, just remember that you can *always* use the system that's been part of AutoCAD since version 1.0 in 1982: Use the keyboard and let your fingers do the talking.

The Straight and Narrow: Lines, Polylines, and Polygons

As I harp on a bunch of times elsewhere in this book, CAD programs are for precision drawing, so you'll spend a lot of your AutoCAD time drawing objects composed of straight-line segments. This rest of the chapter covers these commands:

- ✔ **LINE (L):** Draws a series of straight line segments; each segment is a separate object.

- ✔ **PLINE (PL):** Draws a *polyline* — a series of straight and/or curved line segments. (Yes, I'm cheating a bit here — curvy things are covered in Chapter 9 — but I didn't want you to have to read about one command in two different places!) All the segments remain connected to each other as a single object.

- ✔ **RECTANG (REC):** Draws a polyline in the shape of a rectangle.

- ✔ **POLYGON (POL):** Draws a polyline in the shape of a *regular* polygon (that is, a closed shape with all sides equal and all angles equal).

The following additional straight-line drawing commands are also available in AutoCAD:

- ✔ **RAY:** Draws a line that starts at a point and just keeps on going; a ray therefore is a line that extends infinitely in one direction.

- ✔ **XLINE (XL):** Draws a line that passes through a point and extends infinitely in both directions.

The RAY and XLINE commands are used to draw *construction lines* that guide the construction of additional geometry. Drawing construction lines is less common in AutoCAD than in some other CAD programs. AutoCAD's many precision techniques often provide more efficient methods for creating new geometry than adding construction lines to your drawing does.

Toeing the line

The LINE command in AutoCAD draws a series of one or more connected line segments. Well, it *appears* to draw a series of connected segments. In fact, each *segment,* or piece of a line with endpoints, is a separate object. This construction doesn't seem like a big deal until you try to move or otherwise edit a series of segments that you drew with the LINE command; you must select every piece separately. To avoid such a hassle, use polylines (described later in this chapter), not lines (or lines and arcs), when you want the connected segments to act as a single object.

If you're used to drawing lines in other programs, you may find it confusing at first that AutoCAD's LINE command doesn't stop after you draw a single segment. AutoCAD keeps prompting you to specify additional points so that you can draw a series of (apparently) connected segments. When you're finished drawing segments, just press Enter to finish the LINE command.

Unlike a lot of the AutoCAD drawing commands, LINE doesn't offer a bunch of potentially confusing options. It has a Close option to create a closed polygonal shape and an Undo option to remove the most recent segment that you drew.

Like all drawing commands, LINE puts the line segments that it draws on the current layer and uses the current color, linetype, lineweight, and plot style properties. When you're doing real drafting, as opposed to just experimenting, make sure of the following:

✔ Think about setting these properties before you start drawing. Although you can easily change an object's layer or other object properties, it's often more efficient to set properties first. (I recommend that you set color, linetype, lineweight, and, if you're using named plot styles, plot style to ByLayer.) See Chapter 6 for information on setting the current properties with the Properties toolbar.

✔ Make sure that you use one of AutoCAD's precision tools, such as object snaps, typed coordinates, and tracking, to ensure that you specify each object point precisely. Chapter 7 describes these tools.

Follow these steps to draw a series of line segments by using the LINE command:

1. **Set an appropriate layer current and set other object properties that you want applied to the line segments that you'll draw.**

2. **Click the Home tab on the Ribbon.**

 The panels on the Home tab contain the most commonly used commands in AutoCAD.

3. **Click the Line button on the Draw panel of the Ribbon's Home tab, or type L and press Enter.**

 AutoCAD starts the LINE command and prompts you to select the first point.

4. **Specify the starting point by clicking a point or typing coordinates.**

 Remember to use one of the precision techniques I describe in Chapters 6 and 7 if you're doing real drafting. For the first point, object snap, snap, and typing coordinates all work well.

 AutoCAD prompts you to specify the other endpoint of the first line segment. The command window prompt shows

   ```
   Specify next point or [Undo]:
   ```

 You can also see command prompts at the dynamic input tooltip beside the crosshairs by pressing the down-arrow key (press F12 or click the Dynamic Input status bar button to enable Dynamic Input mode). The arrow icon on the dynamic input tooltip is your indicator that there are options available.

5. **Specify additional points by clicking or typing.**

 Again, use one of the AutoCAD precision techniques if you're doing real drafting. For the second and subsequent points, all the techniques

mentioned in the previous step work well, as do ortho, polar, object snap tracking, and direct distance entry.

After you specify the third point, AutoCAD adds the Close option. The command prompt shows

```
Specify next point or [Close/Undo]:
```

6. **When you're finished drawing segments, end with one of these steps:**

 • Either press Enter or right-click anywhere in the drawing area and choose Enter from the right-click menu to leave the figure open.

 • Type **C** and press Enter or press the down arrow on your keyboard and choose Close from the menu (as shown in Figure 8-1) to close the figure.

 In either case, the blank command prompt indicates that the LINE command is finished:

```
Command:
```

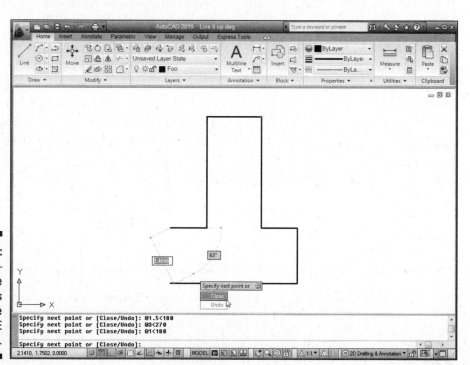

Figure 8-1:
Line it up —
drawing line
segments
with the
LINE
command.

Connecting the lines with polyline

The LINE command is fine for some drawing tasks, but the PLINE command is a better, more flexible choice in many situations. The PLINE command draws a special kind of object — a *polyline*. You may hear CAD drafters refer to a polyline as a *pline* (rhymes with *beeline)* because of the command name.

The most important differences between the LINE and PLINE commands are these:

✔ **The LINE command draws a series of separate line segments.** Even though they appear to be connected on the screen, each segment is a separate object. If you move one line segment, the other segments that you drew at the same time don't move with it.

✔ **The PLINE command draws a single, connected, multisegment object.** If you select any segment for editing, your changes affect the entire polyline. Figure 8-2 shows how the same sketch drawn with the LINE and the PLINE commands responds when you select one of the objects.

Figure 8-2:
Results of drawing with the LINE and PLINE commands.

Each segment is a separate object All segments form one object

TIP

Use PLINE instead of LINE in most cases where you need to draw a series of connected line segments. If you're drawing a series of end-to-end segments, there's a good chance that those segments are logically connected — for example, they might represent the outline of a single object or a continuous pathway. If the segments are connected logically, it makes sense to keep them connected in AutoCAD. The most obvious practical benefit of grouping segments together into a polyline is that many editing operations are more efficient when you use polylines.

When you select any segment in a polyline for editing, the entire polyline is affected.

✔ **The PLINE command can draw curved segments as well as straight ones.** If you want a combination of separate linear and curved segments you must switch back and forth between the LINE and ARC commands (I cover arcs in Chapter 9). With PLINE you can switch between linear or circular-curve sections by choosing the command options described in the steps that come after this list.

✔ **Polylines can have width.** Polyline segment width is visually similar to AutoCAD's lineweight object property, except that polyline segment width can be uniform or tapered. The ability to create polyline segments with line widths was more important in the old days, before AutoCAD had lineweight as an object property. People used to draw polylines with a small amount of width to show the segments as just slightly bolder than regular lines, which are always displayed as a single pixel wide. Nowadays, it's easier and more efficient to achieve this effect with object lineweights (as described in Chapter 6) or plot styles (as described in Chapter 16).

After you create a polyline, you can adjust its segments by grip editing any of the vertex points. (The little squares on the vertices in Figure 8-2 are *grips;* see Chapter 10 for details on grip editing.) For more complicated polyline editing tasks, you can use the PEDIT command to edit the polyline, or you can convert the polyline to a collection of line and arc segments by using the EXPLODE command — although you lose any width defined for each segment when you explode a polyline. For more information on these two commands, look them up in the index of the online help.

Drawing polylines composed of straight segments is pretty much like drawing with the LINE command, as demonstrated in the following procedure. The PLINE command has lots of options, so watch the prompts! If Dynamic Input is on, use the down-arrow key to see the options listed at the crosshairs, or right-click to display the PLINE right-click menu, or simply read the command line.

To draw a polyline composed of straight segments, follow these steps:

1. **Set an appropriate layer current and set other object properties that you want applied to the line segments that you'll draw.**

2. **Click the Polyline button on the Ribbon's Draw panel or type** PL **and press Enter.**

 AutoCAD starts the PLINE command and prompts you to specify a start point.

3. **Specify the starting point by clicking a point or typing coordinates.**

 AutoCAD displays the current polyline segment line width at the command line and prompts you to specify the other endpoint of the first polyline segment:

```
Current line-width is 0.0000
Specify next point or [Arc/Halfwidth/Length/Undo/
       Width]:
```

4. **If the current line width isn't zero, change it to zero by typing** W
 to select the Width option, and then entering 0 **as the starting and**
 ending widths as shown in the following command line sequence:

```
Specify next point or [Arc/Halfwidth/Length/Undo/
       Width]: W
Enter Specify starting width <0.0000>: 0
Enter Specify ending width <0.0000>: 0
Enter Specify next point or [Arc/Halfwidth/Length/
       Undo/Width]:
```

Despite what you may think, a zero-width polyline segment isn't the
AutoCAD equivalent of writing with invisible ink. *Zero width* means "dis-
play this segment using the normal, single-pixel width on the screen."

5. **Specify additional points by clicking or typing.**

 After you specify the second point, AutoCAD adds the Close option to
 the prompt. The command line shows

```
Specify next point or [Arc/Close/Halfwidth/Length/
       Undo/Width]:
```

 In addition, you can view and choose options from the dynamic input
 options list, as shown in Figure 8-3, by pressing the down arrow on your
 keyboard.

Figure 8-3:
Making a
PLINE.

6. **After you finish drawing segments, either press Enter (to leave the figure open) or type C and press Enter (to close it).**

 AutoCAD draws the final segment. The blank command line indicates that the PLINE command is finished.

In the following procedure, I spice things up a bit and give you a preview of coming (curvy) attractions by adding an arc segment to a polyline.

Just so you know, curved segments in polylines are *circular arcs* — pieces of circles with center points that you can draw with AutoCAD's ARC command. AutoCAD can draw other kinds of curves, including ellipses and splines, but not within the PLINE command.

To draw a polyline that includes curved segments, follow these steps:

1. **Repeat Steps 1 though 6 of the previous procedure.**

2. **When you're ready to add one or more arc segments, type A and press Enter to select the Arc option.**

 The prompt changes to show arc segment options. Most of these options correspond to the many ways of drawing circular arcs in AutoCAD; see the section on arcs in Chapter 9. The command line shows

   ```
   Specify endpoint of arc or [Angle/CEnter/CLose/
       Direction/Halfwidth/Line/Radius/Second
       pt/Undo/Width]:
   ```

3. **Specify the endpoint of the arc by clicking a point or typing coordinates.**

 AutoCAD draws the curved segment of the polyline. The prompts continue to show arc segment options.

 Your options at this point include

 - Specifying additional points to draw more arc segments.

 - Choosing another arc-drawing method (such as Center or Second pt).

 - Returning to drawing straight-line segments with the Line option.

 In this example, you return to drawing straight-line segments.

Perhaps the most useful of the alternative arc-drawing methods is Second pt. That gives you more control over the direction of the arc, but at the cost of losing tangency of adjacent segments. Sometimes it's best not to go off on a tangent, anyway.

4. **Type L and press Enter to select the Line option.**

   ```
   Specify endpoint of arc or [Angle/CEnter/CLose/
           Direction/Halfwidth/Line/Radius/Second pt/
           Undo/Width]: L
   ```

The prompt changes back to showing straight-line segment options.

```
Specify next point or [Arc/Close/Halfwidth/Length/
         Undo/Width]:
```

5. **Specify additional points by clicking or typing.**

6. **After you're finished drawing segments, either press Enter or type** C **and press Enter.**

Figure 8-4 shows some of the things that you can draw with the PLINE command by using straight segments, arc segments, or a combination of both.

Figure 8-4:
A plethora
of polylines.

The LINE and PLINE commands work well for drawing a series of end-to-end single lines, but what if you want to draw a series of double lines to represent, for example, the edges of a wall or roadway? Here are some options:

- Use the AutoCAD MLINE command to draw *multilines* — series of two or more parallel straight lines. The AutoCAD multiline feature was full of limitations when it debuted way back in 1994 (in the notorious Release 13), and despite some minor tweaks in AutoCAD 2006, it hasn't improved significantly since then. Look up the MLINE and MLSTYLE commands in AutoCAD's online help system if you want to tangle with this feature, but be prepared to spend time experimenting and struggling.

- In AutoCAD LT only, use the DLINE (DL), or Double Line, command to draw pairs of parallel line and/or arc segments. AutoCAD LT doesn't include the MLINE command, which, given MLINE's problems, is more of a blessing than a limitation. AutoCAD, on the other hand, doesn't include the DLINE command. (Score one for the little brother!)

- Use the PLINE command to draw a single set of connected line and/or arc segments, and then use the OFFSET command to create one or more sets of parallel segments. Chapter 11 covers the OFFSET command.

Squaring off with rectangles

You can use the PLINE or LINE command to draw a rectangle segment by segment. In most cases, though, you'll find it easier to use the special-purpose RECTANG command. The following procedure demonstrates how:

1. **Set an appropriate layer current and set other object properties that you want applied to the line segments that you'll draw.**

2. **Click the Rectangle button on the Home tab's Draw panel or type** REC **and press Enter.**

 AutoCAD starts the RECTANG command and prompts you to specify a point for one corner of the rectangle. The command line shows

    ```
    Specify first corner point or [Chamfer/Elevation/
            Fillet/Thickness/Width]:
    ```

 You can add fancy effects with the additional command options. The default options work best for most purposes. Look up RECTANG in the AutoCAD help system if you want to know more about the options.

3. **Specify the first corner by clicking a point or typing coordinates.**

 AutoCAD prompts you to specify the other corner of the rectangle — the one that's diagonally opposite from the first corner.

    ```
    Specify other corner point or [Area/Dimensions/
            Rotation]:
    ```

4. **Specify the other corner by clicking a point or typing coordinates.**

 If you know the size of the rectangle that you want to draw (for example, 100 units long by 75 units high), type relative coordinates to specify the dimensions (for example, **@100,75**). (Chapter 7 describes how to type coordinates.)

 AutoCAD draws the rectangle.

Unlike the neglected MLINE command, the RECTANG command has improved considerably since its debut. You can specify a rotation angle and — very handy for space planners — you can provide one dimension and an area. RECTANG will calculate the length of the other side and draw the rectangle.

Choosing your sides with polygon

Rectangles and other closed polylines are types of *polygons,* or closed figures with three or more sides. The AutoCAD POLYGON command provides a quick way of drawing *regular polygons* — polygons in which all sides and angles are equal.

The following procedure demonstrates the POLYGON command:

1. **Set an appropriate layer current and set other object properties that you want applied to the line segments that you'll draw.**

2. **Click the Polygon button on the Home tab's Draw panel or type** POL **and press Enter.**

 AutoCAD starts the POLYGON command and prompts you to enter the number of sides for the polygon.

    ```
    Enter number of sides <4>:
    ```

3. **Type the number of sides for the polygon that you want to draw and press Enter.**

 AutoCAD prompts you to specify the center point of the polygon.

    ```
    Specify center of polygon or [Edge]:
    ```

 You can use the Edge option to draw a polygon by specifying one side instead of the center and radius of an imaginary inscribed or circumscribed circle. The imaginary circle method is much more common.

4. **Specify the center point by clicking a point or typing coordinates.**

 AutoCAD prompts you to specify whether the polygon will be *inscribed in* (that is, the corners touch the circumference of the circle) or *circumscribed about* (that is, the sides are tangent to the circle) an imaginary circle whose radius you will specify in the following step:

    ```
    Enter an option [Inscribed in circle/Circumscribed
             about circle] <I>:
    ```

5. **Type** I **or** C **and press Enter.**

 The command line prompts you to specify the radius of an imaginary circle.

    ```
    Specify radius of circle:
    ```

6. **Specify the radius by typing a distance or clicking a point.**

 AutoCAD draws the polygon.

 If you type a distance or you click a point with ortho turned on, the polygon will be aligned orthogonally, as shown in Figure 8-5.

Figure 8-5 shows the results of drawing plenty of polygons — a practice known as *polygony,* which, as far as I know, is legal nearly everywhere.

Figure 8-5:
A polygonal
party.

Chapter 9

Dangerous Curves Ahead

A lthough straight-line segments predominate in many CAD drawings, even the most humdrum, rectilinear design is likely to have a few curves. And if you're drawing Audi car bodies or Gaudí buildings, your drawings are going to contain a *lot* of curves! Your drawings should also have a point; in fact, they may have several points, so at the end of this chapter, I fill you in on creating point objects in AutoCAD. But to begin, I show you how to use the following AutoCAD curve-drawing commands:

- ✔ **CIRCLE:** Draws circles. (You were expecting hyperbolic paraboloids, maybe?)

- ✔ **ARC:** Draws *circular* arcs — arcs with center points and fixed radii, not arcs cut from ellipses, parabolas, or some other complex curve.

- ✔ **ELLIPSE:** Draws ellipses and elliptical arcs.

- ✔ **SPLINE:** Draws smoothly flowing curves of a variety of shapes.

- ✔ **DONUT:** Draws filled-in rings and circles.

- ✔ **REVCLOUD:** Draws freeform "clouds," the most common application of which is to indicate revised areas in the drawing.

(Throwing) Curves

Table 9-1 lists the AutoCAD commands for drawing curvy things. It shows you the tool icons found on the Ribbon, toolbars, and menus, and gives the command name with alias (where one exists) if you like to type. It also tells you where to find or how to enter the commands using both the Ribbon in the 2D Drafting & Annotation workspace and the Draw toolbar and Draw menu in the AutoCAD Classic environment.

Button	Command	Draw Panel Button	Draw Toolbar Button	Draw Menu
	ARC (A)	Arc	Arc	Arc + submenu
	CIRCLE (C)	Circle	Circle	Circle + sub-menu
	REVCLOUD	Revision Cloud	Revision Cloud	Revision C
	DONUT (DO)	Donut (on slideout panel)	None	Donut
	SPLINE (SPL)	Spline (on slideout panel)	Spline	Spline
	ELLIPSE (EL)	Ellipse	Ellipse	Ellipse + sub-menu
	ELLIPSE (EL), A	Ellipse Arc (on flyout button)	Ellipse Arc	Ellipse + sub-menu

Table 9-1 AutoCAD Drawing Commands for Curved Objects

REMEMBER

Slideout panels are part of the Ribbon interface in AutoCAD 2010's 2D Drafting & Annotation and 3D Modeling workspaces. Slideouts are present in panels that show a small down-pointing triangle next to the panel title. To open a slideout, click the panel title bar (for example, Draw on the Home tab). The panel expands downward, and a pushpin icon appears at the left end of the panel title bar. After you click a tool button, the slideout panel closes. Click the pushpin in the title bar to *pin* the panel — that is, force it to stay open.

If you're familiar with an earlier version of AutoCAD, you may suspect that the Draw panel in AutoCAD 2010's new Ribbon interface is also missing some commands. Well, as they used to say in the '90s, the paradigm has shifted! Those commands are still there, they've just shifted around to reflect the new task-based Ribbon layout. For example, block creation and insertion lived on the classic Draw menu and Draw toolbar, but in the new user inter-face, those tools have moved to the Blocks panel, which can be found on both the Insert and Home tabs. Similarly, the text commands (whose classic interface home was also on the Draw menu and Draw toolbar) are on the Ribbon's Annotate and Home tabs.

Going full circle

AutoCAD offers an easy and intuitive way to draw circles, and it also offers . . . *other* ways. The easy way is to define the center point of the circle and then to specify the radius (the default option) or the diameter. You can also define a circle by choosing one of the following options of the command (for those other ways):

- **2-Point (2P):** Draws a circle where the distance between two specified points is equal to the diameter of the circle. If you're keyboarding, enter **2P** at the command prompt to choose this option; it's spelled out as 2-Point on tooltips.

- **3-Point (3P):** Draws a circle through any three specified points.

- **Tangent-Tangent-Radius (Ttr):** Draws a circle tangent to two existing drawing objects and a specified radius.

- **Tangent-Tangent-Tangent:** Draws a circle tangent to three *valid* existing drawing objects. (By *valid,* I mean it's mathematically possible to construct a circle tangent to the three selected objects.) Note that you can't create this kind of circle by typing a command option at the command line because there's no such option. This method is actually a macro and must be chosen from the Ribbon panel's tool button.

Figure 9-1 illustrates these six different ways of drawing circles. Whether these additional methods are useful depends on the kinds of drawings that you make and how geometry is defined in your industry. Get familiar with the default center point/radius method and then try the other methods to see whether they may be helpful to you. If you find yourself going around in circles, you can always draw them the default way and move them into position with other geometry.

Figure 9-1: Pi R squared; circles R round.

Center, Radius Center, Diameter Tan, Tan, Radius

2 Point 3 Point Tan, Tan, Tan

Follow these steps to use the CIRCLE command:

1. **Click the Home tab on the Ribbon.**

 The most frequently used commands in AutoCAD are found on the Ribbon's Home tab.

2. **Set an appropriate layer current and set other object properties that you want applied to the circles that you'll draw.**

3. **Click the Circle button on the Ribbon's Draw panel or type C and press Enter.**

 AutoCAD starts the CIRCLE command and prompts you to specify the center point of the circle. If dynamic input is toggled on, press the down arrow on your keyboard to see the options at the crosshairs. The command line shows

   ```
   Specify center point for circle or [3P/2P/Ttr (tan tan
           radius)]:
   ```

 The prompts show the methods other than "center point plus radius" that you can use to draw circles in AutoCAD. (No, tan tan radius is not a mathematician's dance.) Look up *CIRCLE command* in the online help if you think you may have a use for these less common circle-drawing techniques.

4. **Specify the center point by clicking a point or typing coordinates.**

 Use one of the precision techniques described in Chapter 7 if you're doing real drafting. Object snap, snap, and typing coordinates all work well for specifying the center point.

 AutoCAD then prompts you to specify the circle's radius.

   ```
   Specify radius of circle or [Diameter]:
   ```

 Type **D** and press Enter if you prefer to enter the diameter rather than the radius and you've forgotten your two-times tables — or, more seriously, if the diameter is easier to type exactly than the radius is.

5. **Specify the radius by typing a distance or clicking a point.**

 AutoCAD draws your circle and returns to a blank command prompt. The first point you picked is the center. The command prompt doesn't tell you so, but if you pick a second point instead of entering a number (or typing **D** to invoke the Diameter option), AutoCAD interprets the distance between the first and second points as the radius value.

Arc-y-ology

Arcs in AutoCAD are, quite simply, pieces of circles. As with circles, AutoCAD offers you an easy way to define arcs. Just specify three points on-screen to

define the arc, easy as one-two-three. These points tell AutoCAD where to start the arc, how much to curve it, and where to end it.

Sounds pretty easy, right? So where's the problem? The trouble is that you nearly always have to specify arcs more exactly than is possible by using this method. AutoCAD helps you specify such arcs, too, but the procedure ain't easy.

You can start your arc by specifying the center of the arc or the start point. If you choose the Center option, AutoCAD prompts you for the center point first and the start point second. AutoCAD defines arcs counterclockwise, so pick a start point in a clockwise direction from the endpoint. After you specify the center and start point, AutoCAD presents several options you can choose, including the following:

✔ **Angle:** This option specifies the included angle that the arc sweeps out. A 180-degree angle, for example, is a semicircle.

✔ **Length of chord:** This option specifies the length of an imaginary straight line connecting the endpoints of the arc. Most people seldom or never use this option.

✔ **End point:** This option specifies where the arc ends. It's the default option and is often the easiest to use.

If you specify the start point as the first option, you can choose among the following three command options as well:

✔ **Center:** This option prompts you for the arc's center point and then finishes with the three options listed previously.

✔ **End:** This option specifies the endpoint of the arc. You then need to define the angle that the arc covers, its direction, its radius, or its center point.

✔ **Second point:** This is the default option. The second point you choose isn't the endpoint; instead, it's a point on the arc that, along with the start and end points, defines how much the arc curves. After you enter the second point, you must enter an endpoint to complete the arc.

To get a feel for how these permutations can be strung together to create different arc-drawing methods, press the down arrow beside the Arc tool button on the Ribbon's Draw panel and look at the impressive flyout that unfurls, as shown in Figure 9-2. Using the Ribbon is also the most direct way of actually using any of these options — at least until you're really familiar with the program and are adept at entering keyboard shortcuts.

Figure 9-2:
A deluge of
Arc options,
with the
results of
using some
of those
options.

The following example shows how you draw an arc with the default start point/second point/endpoint method:

1. **Set an appropriate layer current and set other object properties that you want applied to the arcs that you'll draw.**

2. **Click the Arc button on the Home tab's Draw panel or type** A **and press Enter.**

 AutoCAD starts the ARC command and prompts you to specify the first endpoint of the arc. The command line shows

   ```
   Specify start point of arc or [Center]:
   ```

3. **Specify the start point by clicking a point or typing coordinates.**

 AutoCAD prompts you to specify a second point on the arc.

4. **Specify a second point on the arc by clicking a point or typing coordinates.**

 The second point lies somewhere along the curve of the arc. AutoCAD determines the exact curvature of the arc after you choose the final endpoint in the following step. To align the second point with an existing object, use an object snap mode.

 AutoCAD prompts you to specify the other endpoint of the arc; as you move the crosshairs around, AutoCAD shows how the arc will look.

5. **Specify the other endpoint of the arc by clicking a point or typing coordinates.**

 AutoCAD draws the arc, as shown previously in Figure 9-2.

As you may recall, pressing Enter repeats the last command. What often throws new AutoCAD users is that Enter doesn't repeat the *options* of the last command. If you draw an arc using the Center, Start, End option, for example, pressing Enter isn't going to repeat that method — it's going to repeat the ARC command in its default form, and the three points you pick probably won't give you the arc you meant to draw. Bottom line: Watch the command line!

Solar ellipses

In case you've forgotten your ninth-grade math, an *ellipse* is like a squished circle (please excuse the technical jargon). Mathematically, an ellipse is defined by a *major* (long) axis and a *minor* (short) axis. These axes determine the ellipse's length, width, and degree of curvature. An *elliptical arc* is an arc cut from an ellipse.

The AutoCAD ELLIPSE command provides a straightforward way of drawing an ellipse: You specify the two endpoints of one of its axes and then specify an endpoint on the other axis. But like the ARC command, the ELLIPSE command offers a bunch of other options:

- ✔ **Arc:** This option generates an elliptical arc, not a full ellipse. You define an elliptical arc just as you do a full ellipse. The following methods for creating an ellipse apply to either.

- ✔ **Center:** This option requires that you define the center of the ellipse and then the endpoint of an axis. You can then either enter the distance of the other axis or specify that a rotation around the major axis defines the ellipse. If you choose the latter, you can enter (or drag the ellipse to) a specific rotation for the second axis that, in turn, completely defines the ellipse.

- ✔ **Rotation:** With this option, you specify an angle which defines the curvature of the ellipse — small angles make fat ellipses (0 degrees creates a circle, in fact), and large angles make skinny ellipses. The name of the option, Rotation, has something to do with rotating an imaginary circle around the first axis. If you can figure out the imaginary circle business, you have a better imagination than I do.

The following command line example creates an ellipse by using the default endpoints of the axes method. Figure 9-3 shows an ellipse and an elliptical arc.

```
Command: ELLIPSE
Specify axis endpoint of ellipse or [Arc/Center]: pick or
       type the first endpoint of one axis
Specify other endpoint of axis: pick or type the other
       endpoint of one axis
Specify distance to other axis or [Rotation]: pick or type
       the endpoint of the other axis
```

You can create elliptical arcs (as opposed to the circular arcs that the AutoCAD ARC command draws) by using the Arc option of the ELLIPSE command; it's perfect for drawing those cannonball trajectories! Alternatively, you can draw a full ellipse and use the TRIM or BREAK command to cut a piece out of it.

Figure 9-3:
To make
an omelet,
you have to
break a few
ellipses.

Splines: The sketchy, sinuous curves

Most people use CAD programs for precision drawing tasks: straight lines, carefully defined curves, precisely specified points, and so on. AutoCAD is not the program to free your inner artist — unless your inner artist is Mondrian. Nonetheless, even meticulously created CAD drawings sometimes need freeform curves. The AutoCAD *spline object* is just the thing for the job.

You can use AutoCAD splines in two ways:

- Eyeball the location and shape of the curve and don't worry too much about getting it just so. That's the freeform, sketchy, not-too-precise approach that I describe here.

- Specify their control points and curvature characteristics precisely.

Beneath their easygoing, informal exterior, AutoCAD splines are really highly precise, mathematically-defined entities called *NURBS curves* (NonUniform Rational B-Spline curves). Mathematicians and some mechanical and industrial designers care a lot about the precise characteristics of the curves they work with. For those people, the AutoCAD SPLINE and SPLINEDIT commands

include a number of advanced options. Look up *spline curves* in the AutoCAD online help if you need precision in your splines.

Drawing splines is straightforward, if you ignore the advanced options. The following procedure draws a freeform curve with the SPLINE command:

1. **Set an appropriate layer current and set other object properties that you want applied to the spline segments that you'll draw.**

2. **Click the Spline button on the Home tab's Draw panel or type** SPL **and press Enter.**

 AutoCAD starts the SPLINE command and prompts you to specify the first endpoint of the spline. The command line shows:

Specify first point or [Object]:

3. **Specify the start point by clicking a point or typing coordinates.**

 AutoCAD prompts you to specify additional points:

Specify next point:

4. **Specify additional points by clicking or typing coordinates.**

 After you pick the second point, press the down-arrow key to display additional options at the dynamic input tooltip. (Enable dynamic input at the status bar if you need to.) The command line shows

Specify next point or [Close/Fit tolerance] <start tangent>:

 Because you're drawing a freeform curve, you usually don't need to use object snaps or other precision techniques when picking spline points.

5. **Press Enter after you've chosen the final endpoint of your spline.**

 AutoCAD prompts you to specify tangent lines for each end of the spline:

   ```
   Specify start tangent:
   ```

Specify end tangent:

 The Specify start tangent and Specify end tangent prompts can control the curvature of the start points and endpoints of the spline. In most cases, just pressing Enter at both prompts to accept the default tangents works fine.

6. **Press Enter twice to accept the default tangent directions.**

 AutoCAD draws the spline.

Figure 9-4 shows some examples of splines.

Figure 9-4:
A slew of
splines.

After you've drawn a spline, you can grip edit it to adjust its shape. See Chapter 10 for information about grip editing. If you need finer control over spline editing, look up the SPLINEDIT command in the AutoCAD online help.

Donuts: The circles with a difference

A *donut* in AutoCAD is another special type of polyline object that you create with (what else?) the DONUT command. (The rectangles and regular polygons I show you in Chapter 8 are also polyline objects.) Creating a *donut* is a simple way to define a single object that consists of two concentric circles with the space between them filled.

When you start the DONUT command, AutoCAD prompts you for the inside diameter and the outside diameter — the size of the hole and the size of the donut — as measured across their widest points. After you've entered these values, AutoCAD prompts you for the center point of the donut. But one donut is rarely enough, so AutoCAD keeps prompting you for additional center points until you press Enter (the AutoCAD equivalent of saying, "no, really, I'm full now!").

 The following example draws a regulation-size donut, with a 1.5-inch hole and 3.5-inch outside diameter.

```
Command: DONUT
Specify inside diameter of donut <0.5000>: 1.5
Specify outside diameter of donut <1.0000>: 3.5
Specify center of donut or <exit>: pick or type the center
            point of one or more donuts
```

 You can use the DONUT command to create a filled circle — also known as a jelly-filled donut. Just specify an inside diameter of 0. Figure 9-5 shows both kinds of donuts.

Figure 9-5:
Donuts,
plain and
jelly-filled.

Inside Diameter = 1.5
Outside Diameter = 3.5

Inside Diameter = 0
Outside Diameter = 3.5

Revision clouds on the horizon

It's customary in many industries to submit a set of drawings at different project milestones or stages of completion and then submit them again later with *revisions* — corrections, clarifications, and requested changes. Usually, the recipients like to locate changed stuff easily, and a common drafting convention is to call attention to revised items by drawing freeform clouds around them. The REVCLOUD command makes quick work of drawing such clouds.

Drawing revision clouds is easy, after you understand that you click only once in the drawing area. That one click defines the starting point for the cloud's perimeter. After that, you simply move the crosshairs around, and the cloud takes shape. When you return to near the point that you clicked in the beginning, AutoCAD automatically closes the cloud.

The following command line example shows you how to draw a revision cloud. Figure 9-6 shows what revision clouds look like.

```
Command: REVCLOUD
Minimum arc length: 0.5000 Maximum arc length: 0.5000
        Style: Normal
Specify start point or [Arc length/Object/Style] <Object>:
        pick a point along the perimeter of your future
        cloud
Guide crosshairs along cloud path... sweep the crosshairs
        around to define the cloud's perimeter
```

You don't need to click again. Simply move the crosshairs around without clicking. AutoCAD draws the next arc segment of the cloud when your crosshairs reach the minimum arc length distance from the end of the previous arc segment.

Continue moving the crosshairs around until you return to the point where you clicked first.

Min. arc length = 0.5
Max. arc length = 0.5

Min. arc length = 0.5
Max. arc length = 1.0

Min. arc length = 1.0
Max. arc length = 1.0

Here are a few tips for using revision clouds:

✔ It's a good idea to put revision clouds on their own layer so that you can choose to plot with or without the clouds visible.

✔ You'll probably find it easier to control the shape of revision clouds if you turn off ortho mode before you start the command.

✔ You may need to add a triangle and number, as shown in Figure 9-6, to indicate the revision number. A block with an attribute is a good way to handle this requirement: Chapter 17 covers blocks and attributes.

If the revision cloud's arcs are too small or too large, erase the cloud, restart the REVCLOUD command, and use the command's Arc Length option to change the minimum and maximum arc lengths. The default minimum and maximum lengths are 0.5 (or 15 in metric drawings) multiplied by the DIMSCALE (DIMension SCALE) system variable setting. If you make the minimum and maximum lengths equal (which is the default), the lobes will be approximately equal in size. If you make them unequal, there will be more variation in lobe size — you'll get fluffier clouds. Fortunately, all these options are more than most non-meteorologists will need. If you set DIMSCALE equal to the drawing scale factor (see Chapter 4), REVCLOUD should do a pretty good job of guessing reasonable default arc lengths.

Scoring Points

I thought about not covering points in this book, but I didn't want you complaining that *AutoCAD 2010 For Dummies* is pointless.

The word *point* describes two different things in AutoCAD:

✔ A *location* in the drawing that you specify (by typing coordinates or clicking with the mouse)

✔ An *object* that you draw with the POINT command

Throughout this chapter and most of the book, I tell you to specify points — that's the location meaning. This section tells you how to draw point objects.

A *point object* in AutoCAD can serve two purposes:

✔ **Points often identify specific locations in your drawing to other people who look at the drawing.** A point can be something that displays on the screen, either as a tiny dot or as another symbol, such as a cross with a circle around it.

✔ **You can use points as precise object snap locations.** Think of them as construction points. For example, when you're laying out a new building, you might draw point objects at some of the engineering survey points and then snap to those points as you sketch the building's shape with the PLINE command. You use the *Node* object snap mode to snap to AutoCAD point objects.

What makes AutoCAD point objects complicated is their almost limitless range of display options, provided to accommodate the two different kinds of purposes just described (and possibly some others that I haven't figured out yet). You use the Point Style dialog box, as shown in Figure 9-7, to specify how points should look in the current drawing.

Figure 9-7:
The Point Style dialog box controls the way point objects appear on-screen.

The Point Style dialog box can be found on the Home tab's Utilities panel slideout, or by typing its command name — which happens to be about the least intuitive command name in all of AutoCAD: **DDPTYPE** (pronounced *ddptype*). The top portion of the dialog box shows the available point display styles. Most of the choices do pretty much the same thing. Just click one of the squares that says, "Hey, that's a good point!" to you.

The first choice, a single-pixel dot, is hard to see on the screen, and the second choice, invisible (a stealth point?), is impossible to see. Avoid these choices if you want your point objects to show up on the screen and on plots. The single-pixel dot, which is the default display style, works well if you use point objects as object snap locations and don't want obtrusive points on plots.

The remaining settings in the Point Style dialog box control the size at which points appear on the screen at different zoom resolutions. The default settings often work fine, but if you're not satisfied with them, click the Help button in the dialog box to find out how to change them.

After you specify the point style, placing points on-screen is easy. The following example shows you how; just type **POINT** and press Enter.

```
Command: POINT
Current point modes: PDMODE=0 PDSIZE=0.0000
Specify a point: pick or type the coordinates of a
            location in the drawing
```

The PDMODE and PDSIZE items listed in the command window are system variables that correspond to the point display mode and display size options in the Point Style dialog box. If you want to know exactly how the system variables correspond to the dialog box choices, you have all the makings of a successful CAD nerd. Click the Help button in the Point Style dialog box to find out more (about the system variables — not about yourself).

How many points you make depends on how you start the command. If you type **POINT** (or its alias **PO**) and press Enter, AutoCAD creates a single point object and returns to the command prompt. Choosing Point from the Home tab's Draw panel (it's hiding on the slideout) keeps drawing points everywhere you pick on-screen; you must press Esc to stop. The same Draw panel slideout presents two additional commands that do their work by creating point objects: DIVIDE and MEASURE. Those two useful commands can help you in laying out drawing objects — look them up in the index of the online help for more information.

Chapter 10

Get a Grip on Object Selection

In This Chapter

▶ Using command-first editing

▶ Selecting objects with maximum flexibility

▶ Editing with grips

*E*diting objects is the flip side of creating them, and in AutoCAD, you spend a lot of time editing — far more than drawing objects from scratch. That's partly because the design and drafting process is by its nature repetitive and also because AutoCAD makes it easy to edit objects cleanly.

When you edit objects in AutoCAD, you need to be just as concerned about specifying precise locations and distances as you are when you originally create the objects. Make sure that you're familiar with the precision techniques described in Chapter 7 before you apply the editing techniques from this chapter to real drawings.

Commanding and Selecting

AutoCAD offers three styles of editing:

✓ Command-first editing

✓ Selection-first editing

✓ Direct object manipulation (grip editing)

AutoCAD refers to command-first editing as *verb-noun editing* and to selection-first editing as *noun-verb editing*. When you see this terminology — for example, in the Options dialog box or the online help system — don't worry, you haven't dropped back into your fifth-grade English class!

Command-first editing

With *command-first editing,* you start a command and then select the objects on which the command works. This style of editing may seem backward to you at first unless you're a longtime AutoCAD user. Command-first editing works well for power users who are in a hurry and who are willing to memorize most of the commands they need to do their work. It's also the *only* way to use some of the editing commands (such as FILLET and BREAK). It's no surprise that command-first editing is the classic editing style in AutoCAD, and the one method with which you need to be most comfortable.

Selection-first editing

In *selection-first editing,* you perform the same steps — in the same order — as in most Windows applications: Select the object first and then choose the command. Selection-first editing tends to be easier to master and makes AutoCAD more approachable for new and occasional users.

Direct object manipulation

With *direct object manipulation,* you perform common editing operations by using the mouse to grab the selected object and perform an action on it, such as moving all or part of it to a different place in the drawing. No named command is involved; the act of moving the mouse and clicking the mouse buttons in certain ways causes the editing changes to happen. AutoCAD supports direct object manipulation through a powerful but somewhat complicated technique called *grip editing. Grips* are the little square handles that appear on an object when you select it. You can use the grips to stretch, move, copy, rotate, scale, or otherwise edit the object.

Choosing an editing style

This book emphasizes command-first editing, but I also discuss grip editing at the end of this chapter. AutoCAD in its heart of hearts is a command-first program. In fact, it started out offering *only* command-first editing and later added selection-first methods; AutoCAD 2010 inherits this ancestral trait. I stress command-first editing for the following reasons:

- ✔ It's the editing style that's been in AutoCAD the longest and the one with which experienced AutoCAD users are most familiar.
- ✔ It works consistently with *all* editing commands — some editing commands remain command-first only.
- ✔ It provides added object selection flexibility, which is useful when you work on complicated, busy drawings.

After you know how to do command-first editing, you can simply reverse the order of many editing operations to do them selection-first style instead. But if you don't get familiar with command-first editing in the beginning, you'll be bewildered by a few useful AutoCAD commands that work only in the command-first style; commands such as these ignore any already selected objects and prompt you to select objects before you can continue.

Much of the information in the rest of this book assumes that you're using the default AutoCAD selection settings. If object selection or grip editing works differently than I describe in this chapter, click the Application button, choose Options from the bottom of the Application Menu to open the Options dialog box, and then check the settings on the Selection tab. The seven check box settings listed next should be selected, as shown in Figure 10-1. (All other check box settings should be deselected.)

- ✔ Selection Preview When a Command is Active
- ✔ Selection Preview When No Command is Active
- ✔ Noun/Verb Selection
- ✔ Implied Windowing
- ✔ Object Grouping
- ✔ Enable Grips
- ✔ Enable Grip Tips

Figure 10-1: Setting selection options in the Options dialog box.

For information on what these options do, hover the mouse pointer over an option to display a tooltip with information from the online help.

Grab It

Part of AutoCAD's editing flexibility comes from its object selection flexibility. For example, command-first editing offers 16 selection modes! (I describe the most useful ones in this chapter.) Don't worry, though; you can get by most of the time with three selection modes, each of which I describe in this section:

✔ Selecting a single object by picking it

✔ Selecting multiple objects by enclosing them in a *window* selection box

✔ Selecting multiple objects by enclosing them in a *crossing* selection box

One-by-one selection

The most obvious way to select objects is to pick (by clicking) them one at a time. One or more objects that are selected and ready for editing are called a *selection set*. You can build a selection set cumulatively with this pick-one-object-at-a-time selection mode, but this cumulative convention may be different from what you're used to. In most Windows programs, if you select one object and then another, the first object is *de*selected, and the second one selected; only the object you select last remains selected. In AutoCAD, *all* the objects you select, one at a time, remain selected and are added to the selection set, no matter how many objects you pick. (You can change this behavior to make AutoCAD work like other Windows programs by turning on the Use Shift to Add to Selection option on the Option dialog box's Selection tab, but I suggest that you don't change it.) Most editing commands affect the entire group of selected objects.

Selection boxes left and right

Selecting objects one at a time works great when you want to edit a small number of objects, but many CAD editing tasks involve editing lots of objects. Do you really want to pick 132 lines, arcs, and circles, one at a time?

Like most Windows graphics programs, AutoCAD provides a selection window feature for grabbing a bunch of objects in a rectangular area. As you may guess by now, the AutoCAD version of this feature is a bit more powerful than the similar feature in other Windows graphics programs and, therefore, is slightly confusing at first. AutoCAD calls its version *implied windowing*. Here's how you use it.

If you click a blank area of the drawing — that is, not on an object — you're *implying* to AutoCAD that you want to specify a selection window, or box. If you move the crosshairs to the right before picking the other corner of the selection box, you're further implying that you want to select all objects that

reside *completely* within the selection box. If you move the crosshairs to the left before picking the other corner of the selection box, you're implying that you want to select all objects that reside completely *or partially* within the selection box.

The AutoCAD terminology for these two kinds of selection boxes gets a little confusing:

✔ *Window* object selection is the move-to-the-right, only-select-objects-completely-within-the-box mode.

✔ *Crossing* object selection is the move-to-the-left, select-objects-completely-or-partially-within-the-box mode.

Fortunately, AutoCAD gives you visual cues that there's a difference. As you move to the right, the window box appears as a rectangle with a blue fill and a solid border. As you move to the left, the crossing box appears as a rectangle with green fill and a dashed border.

Figures 10-2 and 10-3 show a window box and a crossing box in action.

Pick point 2

Figure 10-2:
A window selection box, drawn left to right, selects only objects completely within the box.

Pick point 1 Selection box

Pick point 2

Figure 10-3:
A crossing selection box, drawn right to left, selects objects that are completely or partially within the box.

Selection box Pick point 1

You can mix and match selecting individual objects, specifying a window box, and specifying a crossing box. Each selection adds to the current selection set, allowing you to build an enormously complicated selection of objects and then operate on them with one or more editing commands.

You can press the Shift key in combination with any of the three standard selection modes — single object, window box, and crossing box — to *remove* already-selected objects from the selection set. This feature is especially useful when you're building a selection set in a crowded drawing; you can select a big batch of objects by using Window or Crossing and then hold down the Shift key while selecting to remove the objects that you want to exclude from the editing operation.

Perfecting Selecting

When you edit in command-first mode, you have all the selection options described in the previous section — single object, window box, and crossing

box — plus a slew of others. If you type **?** and press Enter at any `Select objects` prompt, AutoCAD lists all the selection options at the command line:

```
Window/Last/Crossing/BOX/ALL/Fence/WPolygon/CPolygon/
    Group/Add/Remove/Multiple/Previous/Undo/AUto/
    SIngle/SUbobject/Object
```

Subobject and Object apply specifically to 3D solids and therefore are not available in AutoCAD LT. In any event, this book doesn't cover 3D construction.

Table 10-1 summarizes the most useful command-first selection options.

Table 10-1	Some Useful Command-First Selection Options
Option	*Description*
Window	All objects completely within a rectangle that you specify by picking two points
Crossing	All objects within or crossing a rectangle that you specify by picking two points
WPolygon	All objects completely within a polygonal area whose corners you specify by picking points
CPolygon	All objects within or crossing a polygonal area whose corners you specify by picking points
Fence	All objects touching an imaginary polyline whose vertices you specify by picking points
Last	The last object you drew (whether or not it's visible in the display)
Previous	The previous selection set that you specified
ALL	All objects on layers that aren't frozen or locked and that are in the current space (model space or paper space)

To use any of the command-first selection options at the `Select objects` prompt, type the uppercase letters indicated in Table 10-1 that correspond to the desired option and press Enter. After you're finished selecting objects, you must press Enter again to tell AutoCAD that you've finished selecting objects and want to start the editing operation.

After you're finished selecting objects, you must press Enter again to tell AutoCAD that you've finished selecting objects and want to start the editing operation. Say . . . is there an echo in here? As a matter of fact, I *am* repeating myself. One of the things that most new AutoCAD users find hardest to remember is the necessity of pressing Enter after you finish selecting objects.

AutoCAD's *Selection preview* features remove any doubt about which objects you're selecting. *Rollover highlighting* displays individual objects with a thick, dashed lineweight as you move the crosshairs over them. *Area selection* displays a transparent, colored highlight over multiple selections when you use Window and Crossing options. You can enable and disable both features on the Selection tab of the Options dialog box (refer to Figure 10-1).

The following example demonstrates how to use the ERASE command in command-first mode with several different selection options. The selection techniques used in this example apply to most AutoCAD editing commands.

1. **Open a drawing that contains some objects, or start a new drawing and create some lines, arcs, or circles.**

 You needn't be too particular drawing these because you're going to blow them away in the following steps.

2. **Press Esc to make sure that no command is active and no objects are selected.**

 If any objects are selected when you start an editing command, the command, in most cases, will operate on those objects (selection-first editing) instead of prompting you to select objects (command-first editing). For the reasons that I describe earlier in this chapter, I recommend that you use command-first editing style until you're thoroughly familiar with it. Later, you can experiment with selection-first editing if you like. (Just reverse the sequence of commanding and selecting that I describe in this chapter.)

3. **Click the Erase button on the Home tab's Modify panel.**

 AutoCAD displays the Select objects prompt at the command line and, if Dynamic Input is enabled on the status bar, the dynamic input tooltip.

4. **Select two or three individual objects by clicking each one.**

 AutoCAD adds each object to the selection set. All the objects you select remain highlighted, and AutoCAD continues to display the Select objects prompt.

5. **Specify a window selection box that completely encloses several objects.**

 Move the crosshairs to a point below and to the left of the objects, click, release the mouse button, move the crosshairs above and to the right of the objects, and click again.

 All objects that are completely within the box are selected.

6. **Specify a crossing selection box that completely encloses a few objects and cuts through several others.**

Move the crosshairs to a point below and to the right of some of the objects, click, release the mouse button, move the crosshairs above and to the left of some of the objects, and click and release again.

All objects that are completely within or cross through the box are selected. AutoCAD continues to display the `Select objects` prompt.

7. **Type WP and press Enter to activate the WPolygon selection option.**

 AutoCAD prompts you to pick points that define the selection polygon.

8. **Pick a series of points and press Enter.**

 Figure 10-4 shows an example. After you press Enter, AutoCAD selects all objects that are completely within the polygon. AutoCAD continues to display the `Select objects` prompt until you press Enter.

9. **Press Enter to end object selection.**

 AutoCAD erases all the selected objects and returns to an empty command prompt.

Notice how you could use a combination of object selection methods to build a selection set and then press Enter to execute the command on the selected objects. Most AutoCAD editing commands work this way in command-first mode.

Figure 10-4:
Lassoing objects with a WPolygon.

If, after erasing a selection set, you immediately realize that you didn't really mean to do away with so many objects, you can use the Undo button on the Quick Access Toolbar to restore them all. But AutoCAD has one additional unerase trick up its sleeve — the aptly named OOPS command. When you type **OOPS** and press Enter, AutoCAD restores the last selection set that you erased — even if you've run other commands after ERASE.

The ERASE command isn't the only way to remove unwanted objects from your drawing. Easiest of all in any workspace is to simply select an item and press the Del key.

Get a Grip

Although command-first editing is the most flexible and widespread editing style in AutoCAD, it's not the only way. Grip editing is a useful adjunct to command-first editing, especially when you want to modify just one or two objects. You may have encountered grip editing when using other kinds of graphics programs. But even if you're an experienced user of other graphics programs, you've never seen grips used in quite the way that AutoCAD uses them.

Anything that you can do with grip editing can be done with command-first editing as well. In some situations, grip editing is a little more efficient or convenient than command-first editing, but command-first editing always gets the job done. If you master only one style of editing, make it command-first style. In other words, feel free to skip this section — at least until you're comfortable with command-first editing.

About grips

Grips are those little square or triangular handles that appear on an object after you select it.

In their simplest guise, AutoCAD grips work similarly to the little squares on graphical objects in other Windows programs. But in AutoCAD, instead of clicking and dragging a grip, you must click, release the mouse button, move the crosshairs, and click again at the new location. (By separating the selection of beginning and ending points into two different operations, AutoCAD allows you to use different techniques — such as different object snap modes — to select each point.)

AutoCAD grips are, for sophisticated users, better than the grips found in most other programs because you can do so much more with them. You can, for example, use AutoCAD grips to move, stretch, or copy an object. You also can use them to rotate an object, scale it to a different size, or mirror an object — that is, create one or more reversed copies. Grips also act as *visible object snaps,* or little magnets that attract the crosshairs.

A gripping example

The following sections cover in detail the five grip-editing modes: STRETCH, MOVE, ROTATE, SCALE, and MIRROR. Follow these steps to explore the grip-editing modes:

1. **Draw some simple geometry, such as the object shown in Figure 10-5.**

 Here's a great place to practice some of the straight-line object creation tools I describe in Chapter 8!

2. **Press Esc to make sure that no command is active and no objects are selected, and then click Quick Properties on the status bar to turn off the Quick Properties panel.**

 The Quick Properties panel is pretty useful for editing the properties of objects, but more often than not, it gets in the way when you want to edit the objects themselves.

 AutoCAD displays a blank command prompt — that is, no command is currently active.

3. **Click an object on-screen to select it and display its grips.**

 Grips — solid blue squares on the selected object — appear at various points on the object. Note that the AutoCAD command prompt remains blank; you haven't started a command or grip-editing operation yet.

4. **Click another object.**

 Both the newly selected object and the previously selected object display grips.

5. **Click one of the grips on either object.**

 The blue square turns to a dark red square. This grip is now *hot,* or selected and ready for a grip-editing operation. Grip-editing options now appear on the command line. The first option to appear is STRETCH.

6. **Press the spacebar repeatedly to cycle through the five grip-editing options on the command line.**

```
** STRETCH **
Specify stretch point or [Base point/Copy/Undo/eXit]:
** MOVE **
Specify move point or [Base point/Copy/Undo/eXit]:
** ROTATE **
Specify rotation angle or [Base point/Copy/Undo/
      Reference/eXit]:
** SCALE **
Specify scale factor or [Base point/Copy/Undo/
      Reference/eXit]:
** MIRROR **
Specify second point or [Base point/Copy/Undo/eXit]:
```

The grip-editing option displayed on the command line and the dynamic input tooltip (if Dynamic Input is enabled) changes as you press the spacebar. If you move the crosshairs (without picking) in between each press of the spacebar, the appearance of your selected object changes as you display each option. Choosing STRETCH, for example, causes a stretched version of the object to appear on-screen.

Pressing the spacebar a bunch of times is a good way to become familiar with the grip-editing modes, but there's a more direct way to choose a particular mode. After you click a grip to make it hot, right-click to display the grip-editing menu. That menu contains all the grip-editing options plus some other choices, as shown in Figure 10-5.

Figure 10-5:
The grip-editing crosshairs menu.

If Dynamic Input is enabled, pressing the down-arrow key while cycling through the grip-editing options displays a dynamic menu at the crosshairs from which you can choose options specific to the current grip-editing function.

7. **Press the spacebar until STRETCH (or the option you want) reappears as the grip-editing option.**

8. **Move the hot grip in the direction in which you want to stretch (or otherwise manipulate) your object.**

 AutoCAD dynamically updates the image of the object to show you what the modified object will look like before you click the final location.

9. **Click again to finish the grip-editing operation.**

 The selected object with the hot grip updates.

10. **Click the same grip that you chose in Step 5 (now in a different location) to make it hot.**

11. **This time, move the crosshairs near one of the grips on the other object. When you see the magnetic pull of the grip on the other object, click again to connect the hot grip with the other grip.**

 The object point represented by the hot grip now coincides exactly with the grip on the other object.

12. **Press Esc to deselect all objects and remove all grips.**

Figure 10-6 shows a hot endpoint grip of a line being connected to the end-point grip of another line (it appears dark red on your screen). The angled line shows the original position of the line being edited, and the thin vertical line shows the new position. Using a grip in this way as a visible object snap offers the same advantage as using object snap overrides, as described in Chapter 7: It ensures precision by making sure that objects meet exactly.

Red (hot) grip

Figure 10-6:
Using grips
to connect
two objects.

You can experiment with all the grip-editing options to find out how they affect a selected object. Because MOVE and STRETCH are the most useful grip-editing modes, I cover them in more detail.

Move it!

Back in the days of manual drafting, moving objects was a big pain in the eraser. You had to erase the stuff you wanted to move and redraw the objects in their new location. In the process, you usually ended up erasing parts of other stuff that you didn't want to move and left smudged lines and piles of eraser dust everywhere. CAD does away with all the fuss and muss of moving objects, and AutoCAD grip editing is a great way to make it happen. The following steps describe how to move objects:

1. **Select one or more objects.**

 Use any combination of the three editing modes — single object, window box, and crossing box — described in the "Grab It" section, earlier in this chapter.

2. **Click one of the grips to make it hot.**

 At this point in your editing career, it doesn't matter which grip you click. As you become more familiar with grip editing, you'll discover that certain grips serve as better reference points than others for particular editing operations.

3. **Right-click anywhere in the drawing area and choose Move from the crosshairs menu.**

4. **Move the crosshairs to a different location and click.**

 As you move the crosshairs around, AutoCAD displays the tentative new positions for all the objects, just as it does for the regular Move command, as shown previously in Figure 10-6. After you click, the objects assume their new positions.

5. **Press Esc to deselect all objects and remove all grips.**

Copy, or a kinder, gentler Move

If you were paying attention during the section "A gripping example," earlier in the chapter, you may have noticed while pressing the spacebar that *copy* was not among the five grip-editing modes. Why not? Because *every* grip mode includes a copy option (as the command-line prompts show in the "A gripping example" section). In other words, you can STRETCH with copy, MOVE with copy, ROTATE with copy, SCALE with copy, and MIRROR with copy.

The copy option leaves the selected objects in place and does the editing operation on a new copy of the objects.

By far the most common use for the copy option is with the MOVE grip-editing mode. If you think about "MOVE with copy" for about two seconds, you'll realize that it's just a complicated way of saying "copy." The following steps show how to copy objects quickly by using grip editing:

1. **Select one or more objects.**

2. **Click any one of the grips to make it hot.**

3. **Right-click anywhere in the drawing area and choose Move from the menu.**

4. **Right-click again and choose Copy from the menu.**

5. **Move the crosshairs to a different location and click.**

 After you click, new objects appear in the new location.

6. **Move the crosshairs to additional locations and click there if you want to make additional copies.**

7. **Press Esc twice — once to end the copying operation and once to deselect all objects and remove all grips.**

A warm-up Stretch

The STRETCH grip-editing mode works differently from the other modes. By default, it affects only the object with the hot grip on it, not all objects with grips on them. You can override this default behavior by using the Shift key to pick multiple grips and make them hot. Follow these steps to get acquainted with using the STRETCH grip-editing mode to stretch one or more objects:

1. **Make sure that Ortho mode is toggled off on the status bar by clicking the Ortho Mode button until <Ortho off> appears on the command line.**

 Ortho mode forces stretch displacements to be *orthogonal* — that is, parallel to lines running at 0 and 90 degrees. During real editing tasks, you'll often want to turn on Ortho mode, but while you get acquainted with stretching, leaving ortho mode off makes things clearer.

2. **Select several objects, including at least one line.**

3. **On one of the lines, click one of the endpoint grips to make it hot.**

 All the objects remain selected, but as you move the crosshairs, only the line with the hot grip changes. Figure 10-7 shows an example.

4. **Click a new point for the hot endpoint grip.**

 The line stretches to accommodate the new endpoint location.

5. **On the same line, click the midpoint grip to make it hot.**

 As you move the crosshairs, the entire line moves. Using the STRETCH grip-editing mode with a line's midpoint "stretches" the entire line to a new location.

Displacement vector

Original location

Figure 10-7:
Dragging
a line's
endpoint in
the middle
of the
STRETCH
grip-editing
operation.

Drag endpoint to new location

6. **Click a new point for the hot midpoint grip.**

 The line moves to the new midpoint location.

7. **Hold down the Shift key. On one of the lines, click one of the endpoint grips to make it hot.**

8. **Still holding down the Shift key, click one of the endpoint grips on a different line to make it hot.**

 Two grips on two different lines are now hot because you held down the Shift key and then clicked both grips.

 You can create more hot grips by holding down the Shift key and clicking more grips.

9. **Release the Shift key and re-pick any one of the hot grips.**

 Releasing the Shift key signals that you're finished making grips hot. Re-picking one of the hot grips establishes it as the base point for the stretch operation.

10. **Click a new point for the grip.**

 All the objects with hot grips stretch based on the displacement of the grip that you clicked in Step 9 (see Figure 10-8).

11. **Turn on Ortho mode by clicking its status bar button until `<Ortho on>` appears on the command line. Repeat Steps 2 through 10 to see the effect of Ortho mode on stretching.**

Multiple hot grips The hot grip
used as a
base point

Figure 10-8:
Stretching
multiple
objects with
multiple hot
grips.

Chapter 11

Edit for Credit

In This Chapter

▶ Moving, copying, and stretching objects

▶ Manipulating whole objects

▶ Changing pieces of objects

▶ Editing object properties

*I*n Chapter 10, you read that AutoCAD has several different methods of modifying drawing objects. You also read how to select those objects in the first place, so you can edit them. Now it's time to roll up your sleeves and get dirty — in this chapter, I introduce the primary edit commands in AutoCAD.

The following sections cover the most important AutoCAD editing commands, using command-first editing mode.

As explained in Chapter 10, command-first — or *verb-noun* editing in AutoCAD-ese — is one of three different approaches to modifying objects in AutoCAD. I concentrate on this method, where you start a command and then you pick the objects on which the command will act, because it's the only method that works for all editing commands in AutoCAD.

Your AutoCAD Tool Kit

Table 11-1 lists AutoCAD's most frequently used editing commands. It shows the tool icons found on the Ribbon, the classic toolbar, and the classic menu, and it gives the official command name with corresponding alias (where one exists) for the typists in the room. Ribbon buttons are on the Home tab's Modify panel in the 2D Drafting & Annotation workspace. In the AutoCAD Classic workspace, look for these commands on the Modify toolbar and Modify menu.

Table 11-1		AutoCAD's Modify Commands		
Button	**Command**	**Modify Panel Button**	**Modify Toolbar Button**	**Modify Menu**
	ERASE (E)	Erase	Erase	Modify, Erase Edit, Clear
	COPY (CO or CP)	Copy	Copy	Modify, Copy (not Edit, Copy)
	MIRROR (MI)	Mirror	Mirror	Mirror
	OFFSET (O)	Offset	Offset	Offset
	ARRAY (AR)	Array	Array	Array
	MOVE (M)	Move	Move	Move
	ROTATE (R)	Rotate	Rotate	Rotate
	SCALE (SC)	Scale	Scale	Scale
	STRETCH (S)	Stretch	Stretch	Stretch
	LENGTHEN (LEN)	Lengthen (on slideout panel)	None	Lengthen
	TRIM (TR)	Trim (on flyout button)	Trim	Trim
	EXTEND (EX)	Extend (on flyout button)	Extend	Extend
	BREAK (BR); two points	Break (on slideout panel)	Break	Break

Button	Command	Modify Panel Button	Modify Toolbar Button	Modify Menu
	BREAK (BR); 1 point	Break at point (on slideout panel)	Break at point	Break at point
	JOIN (J)	Join (on slideout panel)	Join	Join
	CHAMFER (CH)	Chamfer (on flyout button)	Chamfer	Chamfer
	FILLET (F)	Fillet (on flyout button)	Fillet	Fillet
	EXPLODE (X)	Explode	Explode	Explode
	REVERSE (?)	Reverse (on slideout panel)	None	None

Whether you start an AutoCAD editing command by clicking a Ribbon button or typing a command name or alias, in almost all cases AutoCAD prompts you for points, distances, and options in the command window. Read the prompts during every step of the command, especially when you're figuring out how to use a new editing command. Otherwise, you're unlikely to complete the command successfully.

AutoCAD's dynamic input system displays command options at the crosshairs. When you see a dynamic input tooltip with a down-arrow icon, press the down-arrow key on the keyboard to display the command options. You then can use the mouse to select an option (see Figure 11-1). Pressing the up-arrow key displays previous input.

As I describe in Chapter 7, maintaining precision when you draw and edit is crucial to good CAD work. If you've used a drawing program and are accustomed to moving, stretching, and otherwise editing objects by eye, you'll need to suppress that habit when you edit in AutoCAD. Nothing ruins a drawing faster than eyeball-editing, in which you shove objects around until they look okay, without worrying about precise distances and points.

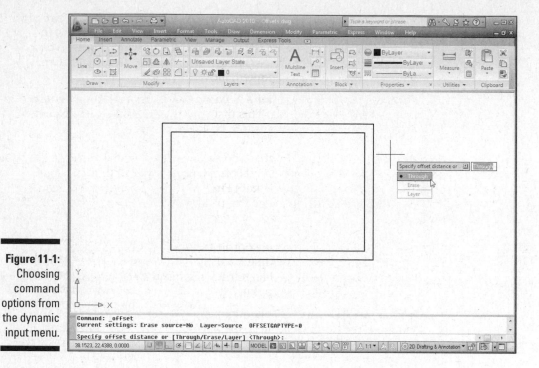

Figure 11-1:
Choosing
command
options from
the dynamic
input menu.

The Big Three: Move, Copy, and Stretch

Moving, copying, and stretching are, for many drafters, the three most common editing operations. AutoCAD obliges this need with the MOVE, COPY, and STRETCH commands.

Base points and displacements

The MOVE, COPY, and STRETCH commands all require that you specify how far and in what direction you want the objects moved, copied, or stretched. After you've started the command and selected the objects to be edited, AutoCAD prompts you for two pieces of information:

```
Specify base point or [Displacement] <Displacement>:
Specify second point or <use first point as displacement>:
```

In a not-so-clear way, these prompts say that two possible methods exist for you to specify how far and in what direction you want the objects copied, moved, or stretched:

✔ **The most common way is to pick or type the coordinates of two points that define a displacement vector.** AutoCAD calls these points the *base point* and the *second point.* Imagine an arrow pointing from the base point to the second point — that arrow defines how far and in what direction the objects get copied, moved, or stretched.

✔ **The other way is to type an X,Y pair of numbers that represents a distance rather than a point.** This distance is the absolute displacement that you want to copy, move, or stretch the objects.

How does AutoCAD know whether your response to the first prompt is a base point or a displacement? It depends on how you respond to the second prompt. (Is that confusing, or what?) First, you pick a point on-screen or enter coordinates at the `Base point` prompt. Next, there are a couple of possibilities:

✔ If you then pick or type the coordinates of a point at the second point prompt, AutoCAD says to itself, "Aha — displacement vector!" and moves the objects according to the imaginary arrow pointing from the base point to the second point.

✔ If you press Enter at the second prompt (without having typed anything), AutoCAD says, "Aha — displacement distance," and uses the X,Y pair of numbers that you typed at the first prompt as an absolute displacement distance.

What makes this displacement business even more confusing is that AutoCAD lets you pick a point at the first prompt and press Enter at the second prompt. AutoCAD still says, "Aha — displacement distance," but now it treats the coordinates *of the point you picked* as an absolute distance. If the point you picked has relatively large coordinates, the objects can get moved way outside the normal drawing area as defined by the limits. The objects fly off into space, and you probably won't see where they've gone because you're zoomed into part of your normal drawing area; it just looks to you like the objects have vanished! In short, be careful when you press Enter during the MOVE, COPY, and STRETCH commands. Press Enter in response to the second prompt only if you want AutoCAD to use your response to the first prompt as an absolute displacement. If you make a mistake, click the Undo button to back up and try again. You can use Zoom Extents (described in Chapter 12) to look for objects that have flown off into space.

Move

The following steps demonstrate command-first editing with the MOVE command, using the base point method of indicating how far and in what direction to move the selected objects. This procedure also gives detailed recommendations on how to use precision techniques when you edit.

1. **Press Esc to make sure that no command is active and no objects are selected.**

 Click the Move button on the Modify panel of the Ribbon.

 The command line displays the `Select objects` prompt.

3. **Select one or more objects.**

 You can use any of the object selection techniques described in the "Perfecting Selecting" section in Chapter 10.

4. **Press Enter when you're finished selecting objects.**

 AutoCAD displays the following prompt:

   ```
   Specify base point or [Displacement] <Displacement>:
   ```

5. **Specify a base point by clicking a point or typing coordinates.**

 This point serves as the tail end of your imaginary arrow indicating how far and in what direction you want the objects moved. After you pick a base point, it's fairly easy to see what's going on because AutoCAD displays a temporary image of the object that moves around as you move the crosshairs. Figure 11-2 shows what the screen looks like.

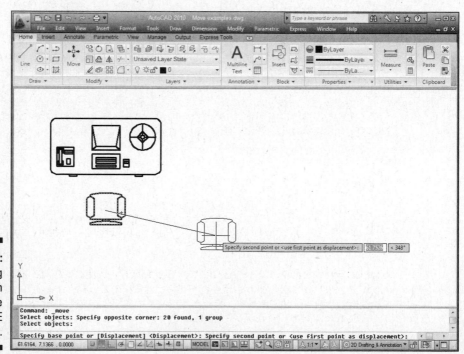

Figure 11-2: Dragging objects in the middle of the MOVE command.

Specify a base point somewhere on or near the object(s) that you're moving. You can use an object snap mode to choose a point exactly on one of the objects.

AutoCAD displays the following prompt:

```
Specify second point or <use first point as
       displacement>:
```

6. **Specify the second point by clicking a point or typing coordinates.**

The second point serves as the arrow end of your imaginary displacement arrow. After you specify the second point, AutoCAD moves the objects.

Don't press Enter alone at this prompt! If you do, AutoCAD treats the X,Y coordinates of the first point you picked as an absolute displacement, and the objects fly off unpredictably. *I repeat: Don't press Enter alone at this prompt!* Pressing Enter without picking a point or typing coordinates at this prompt is one of the most common errors new AutoCAD users make, and it can really pollute your drawing with unwanted objects.

These are common precision techniques for specifying the second point:

✔ Use an object snap mode to pick a second point exactly on another object in the drawing.

✔ Type a relative or polar coordinate, as described in Chapter 7. For example, if you type **@6,2**, AutoCAD moves the objects 6 units to the right and 2 units up. If you type **@3<45**, AutoCAD moves the objects 3 units at an angle of 45 degrees.

Use direct distance entry to move objects in an orthogonal or polar tracking direction. See Chapter 7 for instructions.

Copy

The COPY command works almost identically to the MOVE command, except that AutoCAD leaves the selected objects in place and makes new copies of them in the new location.

The COPY command creates multiple copies by default. If you want only one copy, press Enter after placing it in the drawing. Choosing mOde at the command prompt or the dynamic input options list lets you switch between making a single copy and multiple copies. If you mostly make multiple copies or mostly make single copies, you'll appreciate being able to change the default setting.

The COPY command includes an Undo option with which you can roll back multiple copies within a single COPY operation.

Copy between drawings

You can't copy objects from one drawing to another with the COPY command. Instead, you use the COPYCLIP command together with its companion command, PASTECLIP.

COPYCLIP and PASTECLIP use the Windows Clipboard to temporarily store drawing objects from one file so they can be pasted into another file. The Clipboard panel on the Ribbon contains Cut, Copy, and Paste tools, the three standard Clipboard buttons you find in every Windows program.

As you're figuring out where things are hiding in the AutoCAD 2010 Ribbon, remember that the standard Windows keyboard shortcuts — Ctrl+X (cut), Ctrl+C (copy), and Ctrl+V (paste) — are still available and are often the most efficient way of using the Windows Clipboard — even *after* you've found the Clipboard panel!

Table 11-2 summarizes AutoCAD's most important Clipboard-related commands, along with the equivalent choices on the right-click menu and Ribbon's Clipboard panel. (The classic Standard toolbar buttons' tooltips display the same names.)

Table 11-2	AutoCAD Clipboard Commands		
Command Name	*Right-Click Menu*	*Clipboard Panel Button*	*Classic Standard Toolbar Button*
CUTCLIP	Cut	Cut	Cut (Ctrl+X)
COPYCLIP	Copy	Copy Clip	Copy (Ctrl+C)
COPYBASE	Copy with Base Point	None	None (Ctrl+Shift+C)
COPYLINK	None	None	None
PASTECLIP	Paste	Paste	Paste (Ctrl+V)
PASTEBLOCK	Paste as Block	Paste as Block (on Paste flyout)	None (Ctrl+Shift+V)

Command Name	Right-Click Menu	Clipboard Panel Button	Classic Standard Toolbar Button
PASTEASHYPERLINK	None	Paste as Hyperlink (on Paste flyout)	None
PASTEORIG	Paste to Original Coordinates	Paste to Original Coordinates (on Paste flyout)	None
PASTESPEC	None	Paste Special (on Paste flyout)	None

Stretch

The STRETCH command is superficially similar to COPY and MOVE; it has the same inscrutable base point and displacement prompts, and it shifts objects — or parts of objects — to other locations in the drawing. But it also has important differences that often confound new AutoCAD users to the point that they give up trying to figure out how to use STRETCH. That's a mistake because STRETCH is a valuable command. With it, you can perform editing operations in seconds, whereas other commands would take many minutes to use. Here are the things you need to know to make STRETCH your friend:

✔ **Selecting objects to stretch:** To use STRETCH, you must select objects by using a crossing selection box (or crossing polygon), as described in the section on selecting in Chapter 10. See Figure 11-3 for a visual explanation.

Before Stretch After Stretch

Figure 11-3:
Use a crossing selection box to select objects for stretching.

Pick pt. 1

Pick pt. 2

Crossing window

Displacement

✔ **Defining points:** STRETCH operates on the defining points of objects — endpoints of a line, vertices of a polyline, the center of a circle, and so on — according to the following rule: If a defining point is within the crossing selection box that you specify, AutoCAD moves the defining point and updates the object accordingly.

For example, if your crossing selection box surrounds one endpoint of a line but not the other endpoint, STRETCH moves the first endpoint and redraws the line in the new position dictated by the first endpoint's new location. It's as though you have a rubber band tacked to the wall with two pins, and you move one of the pins.

✔ **Compressing and stretching:** STRETCH can make lines longer or shorter, depending on your crossing selection box and displacement vector. In other words, the STRETCH command really combines stretching and compressing.

✔ **Getting in the mode:** It's a good idea to turn on ortho or polar tracking mode before stretching. Otherwise, you'll end up stretching objects in strange directions, as shown in Figure 11-4.

Figure 11-4: The hazards of stretching without ortho or polar tracking turned on.

The following steps describe how to stretch lines:

1. **Draw some lines in an arrangement similar to the dark lines shown in Figure 11-5.**

 Start your stretching with simple objects. You can work up to more complicated objects — polylines, arcs, and so on — after you've limbered up with lines.

2. **Press Esc to make sure that no command is active and no objects are selected.**

Unselected lines don't move Selected lines being dragged to new location

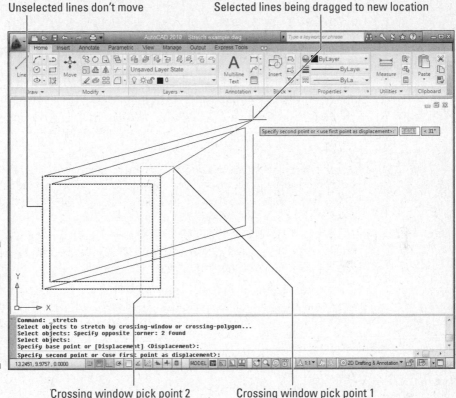

Figure 11-5:
Dragging
objects in
the middle
of the
STRETCH
command.

Crossing window pick point 2 Crossing window pick point 1

3. **Click the Stretch button on the Modify panel of the Ribbon's Home tab.**

 The command line displays the `Select objects` prompt with a warning to use the Crossing or CPolygon object selection mode:

   ```
   Select objects to stretch by crossing-window or
           crossing-polygon...
   Select objects:
   ```

4. **Pick points to specify a crossing selection box that encloses some, but not all, endpoints of the lines.**

 Figure 11-5 shows a sample crossing selection box that completely encloses the two vertical lines on the right side of the figure. This crossing selection box cuts through the four horizontal lines, enclosing only one endpoint of each.

 You specify a crossing selection box by picking a point, moving your mouse to the *left,* and picking a second point.

5. **Press Enter to end object selection.**

 AutoCAD displays the following prompt:

   ```
   Specify base point or [Displacement] <Displacement>:
   ```

6. **Specify a base point by object snapping to a point on an existing object or by typing absolute X,Y coordinates.**

 AutoCAD displays the following prompt:

   ```
   Specify second point or <use first point as
            displacement>:
   ```

Toggle ortho mode on and then off by clicking the Ortho Mode button on the status bar; try moving the crosshairs around first with ortho on and then with it off to see the difference.

Figure 11-5 shows what the screen looks like as you move the crosshairs around without benefit of ortho or polar tracking.

7. **Toggle ortho mode on (if it isn't already) and then specify the second point — usually by using direct distance entry.**

 You can also specify the second point by object snapping to a point on an existing object or by typing relative X,Y coordinates.

 After you pick the second point, AutoCAD stretches the objects. Notice that the STRETCH command *moved* the two vertical lines because the crossing selection box contained both endpoints of both lines. STRETCH lengthened or shortened the four horizontal lines because the crossing selection box enclosed only one endpoint of each.

The STRETCH command takes some practice, but it's worth the effort. Draw some additional kinds of objects and practice stretching with different crossing selection box locations as well as different base points and second points.

The STRETCH command prompt says `Select objects to stretch by crossing-window or crossing-polygon` but picking points as in Step 4 doesn't give you the crossing-polygon option. (See Chapter 10 if you need a refresher on crossing-polygon selection.) To use a polygonal crossing selection, type **CP** at the `Select objects` prompt and press Enter.

More Manipulations

The commands in this section — ROTATE, SCALE, ARRAY, and OFFSET — provide other ways (in addition to MOVE, COPY, and STRETCH) of manipulating objects or creating new versions of them. The procedures for each command assume that you're familiar with the object selection and editing precision techniques presented in the MOVE, COPY, and STRETCH procedures (see Chapter 10 and the previous sections in this chapter).

Rotate

The ROTATE command pivots one or more objects around a point that you specify. Follow these steps to use the ROTATE command:

1. **Press Esc to make sure that no command is active and no objects are selected.**

2. **Click the Rotate button on the Home tab's Modify panel.**

3. **Select one or more objects and then press Enter to end object selection.**

 AutoCAD prompts you for the base point for rotating the selected objects:

   ```
   Specify base point:
   ```

4. **Specify a base point by clicking a point or typing coordinates.**

 The base point becomes the point around which AutoCAD rotates the objects. You also have to specify a rotation angle:

   ```
   Specify rotation angle or [Copy/Reference] <0>:
   ```

5. **Specify a rotation angle by typing an angle measurement and pressing Enter, or just press Enter to accept the default value shown in angle brackets.**

 Alternatively, you can indicate an angle on the screen by moving the crosshairs until the Coordinates section of the status bar indicates the desired angle and then clicking. If you choose this alternative, you will need to use ortho mode or polar tracking to indicate a precise angle (for example, 90 or 45 degrees) or an object snap to rotate an object so that it aligns precisely with other objects.

 After you specify the rotation angle by typing or picking, AutoCAD rotates the objects into their new position. The ROTATE command's Copy option makes a rotated copy while leaving the source object in place.

Scale

If you read all my harping about drawing scales and scale factors in Chapter 4, you may think that the SCALE command performs some magical scale transformation on your entire drawing. No such luck. It merely uniformly scales one or more objects up or down by a factor that you specify. Here's how it works:

1. **Press Esc to make sure that no command is active and no objects are selected.**

2. **Click the Scale button on the Home tab's Modify panel.**

3. **Select one or more objects and then press Enter to end object selection.**

 AutoCAD prompts you for the base point about which it will scale all the selected objects:

   ```
   Specify base point:
   ```

4. **Specify a base point by picking a point or typing coordinates.**

 The base point becomes the point about which the objects are scaled. AutoCAD prompts you for the scale factor:

   ```
   Specify scale factor or [Copy/Reference] <1.0000>:
   ```

 Don't assume that AutoCAD will scale the objects but leave them more or less where they are in the drawing. AutoCAD scales the distance between objects as well as the objects themselves. For example, if you select a circle to scale, pick a point outside the circle as the base point and then specify a scale factor of 2. AutoCAD not only makes the circle twice as big, but also moves the circle twice as far away from the base point that you specified. If you want to make a circle bigger but leave it where it's currently located, make sure to select its center point as the base point for the scale operation.

5. **Type a scale factor and press Enter.**

 AutoCAD then scales the objects by the factor that you type, using the base point that you specified. Numbers greater than 1 increase the objects' sizes. Numbers smaller than 1 decrease the objects' sizes.

Just like the ROTATE command, SCALE also has a copy option with which you can make enlarged or reduced duplicates of selected objects without altering the source objects. And both SCALE and ROTATE remember the last scale factor or rotation angle entered throughout the drawing session.

Array

The ARRAY command is like a supercharged COPY: You use it to create a rectangular grid of objects at regular X and Y spacings or a radial arrangement of objects around a center point at a regular angular spacing. For example, you can use rectangular arrays to populate an auditorium with chairs or a polar array to populate a bicycle wheel with spokes.

The following steps describe how to create a rectangular array, which you'll probably do more often than creating a polar array:

1. **Press Esc to make sure that no command is active and no objects are selected.**

2. **Click the Array button on the Home tab's Modify panel.**

 The Array dialog box appears, as shown in Figure 11-6. When you start the command, "0 objects selected" appears at the upper right.

3. **Make sure that Rectangular Array is selected and then click the Select Objects button.**

 The Array dialog box closes temporarily, allowing you to select items to array using any object selection method.

4. **Select one or more objects; then press Enter.**

 The Array dialog box reappears, and the message below the Select Objects button tells you that objects are selected.

5. **Fill in the five text boxes: Rows, Columns, Row Offset, Column Offset, and Angle of Array.**

 If you see text boxes labeled Center point and a circular image in the preview, you're doing a polar array. Click the Rectangular Array radio button at the top of the dialog box and carry on.

 The Rows and Columns numbers include the row and column of the original objects themselves. In other words, entries of 1 don't create any new objects in that direction. The Row Offset and Column Offset measurements are the distances between adjacent rows and columns. You can use the three buttons to the right of the Row Offset and Column Offset edit boxes to eyeball offset distances, but usually you should specify precise values in the edit boxes. The Angle of Array is the rotation angle of the rectangular array; when the angle is 0 degrees, the array is aligned with the crosshairs.

Figure 11-6:
Configure
rectangular
or polar
(circular)
arrays in
the Array
dialog box.

6. **Click the Preview button.**

Once again the Array dialog box disappears, and you see a preview of what the array will look like with your current settings. You can pan and zoom in the drawing if you need to in order to see the full results.

AutoCAD prompts:

```
Pick or press Esc to return to dialog or <Right-click
      to accept array>:
```

7. **Right-click if you're satisfied with the array or press Esc if you want to change the array parameters.**

Offset

You use OFFSET to create parallel or concentric copies of lines, polylines, circles, arcs, or splines. Follow these steps to use OFFSET:

1. **Click the Offset button on the Home tab's Modify panel.**

AutoCAD displays the current command settings and prompts you for the *offset distance* — the distance from the original object to the copy you're creating:

```
Current settings: Erase source=No Layer=Source
      OFFSETGAPTYPE=0
Specify offset distance or [Through/Erase/Layer]
      <Through>:
```

2. **Type an offset distance and press Enter.**

Alternatively, you can indicate an offset distance by picking two points on the screen. If you choose this method, you should normally use object snaps to specify a precise distance from one existing object to another.

AutoCAD prompts you to select the object from which you want to create an offset copy:

```
Select object to offset or [Exit/Undo] <Exit>:
```

3. **Select a single object, such as a line, a polyline, or an arc.**

Note that you can select only one object at a time with the OFFSET command. AutoCAD asks where you want the offset object.

```
Specify point on side to offset or [Exit/Multiple/
      Undo] <Exit>:
```

4. **Point to one side or the other of the object and then click.**

It doesn't matter how far away from the object the crosshairs are when you click. You're simply indicating a direction.

AutoCAD repeats the `Select object` prompt, in case you want to offset other objects by the same distance:

```
Select object to offset or [Exit/Undo] <Exit>:
```

5. **Go back to Step 3 if you want to offset another object or press Enter if you're finished offsetting objects for now.**

Figure 11-7 shows the OFFSET command in progress. For information on the command options — and Multiple, Erase, and Layer are all useful options — look up *OFFSET* in the online help's Command Reference section.

If you want to offset a series of connected lines (for example, a rectangular house plan outline or one side of a pathway on a map), make sure that you either draw it as a polyline or convert the individual line and/or arc segments into a polyline with the PEDIT command. (Look up *PEDIT* in the online help to find out how.) If you draw a series of line segments with the LINE command and then try to offset it, you have to pick each segment and offset it individually. Even worse, the corners usually aren't finished off in the way that you'd expect because AutoCAD doesn't treat the segments as connected. You avoid all these problems by offsetting a polyline, which AutoCAD does treat as a single object. Figure 11-7 shows an offset polyline. See Chapter 8 for more information about the differences between lines and polylines.

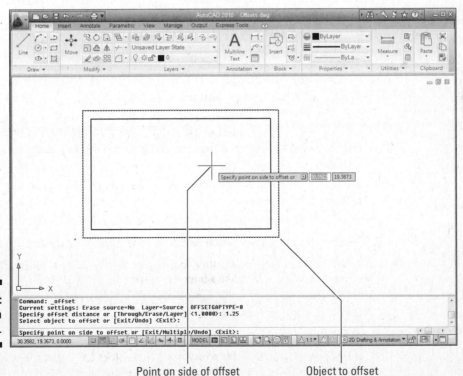

Figure 11-7:
Offsetting a polyline.

Point on side of offset Object to offset

Slicing, Dicing, and Splicing

The commands in this section — TRIM, EXTEND, BREAK, FILLET, CHAMFER, and JOIN — are useful for shortening and lengthening objects, for breaking them in two, and for putting them back together again.

Trim and Extend

TRIM and EXTEND are the twin commands for making lines, polylines, and arcs shorter and longer. They're the yin and yang, the Laurel and Hardy, the Jack Sprat and his wife of the AutoCAD editing world. The two commands and their prompts are almost identical, so the following steps cover both. I show the prompts for the TRIM command; the EXTEND prompts are similar:

1. **Click the Trim or Extend button on the Home tab's Modify panel.**

 AutoCAD prompts you to select cutting edges that will do the trimming (or, if you choose the EXTEND command, boundary edges for extending to):

   ```
   Current settings: Projection=UCS, Edge=None
   Select cutting edges ...
   Select objects or <select all>:
   ```

2. **Press Enter to accept the default option to select all drawing objects, or select individual objects by picking them. Press Enter to end object selection.**

 The objects you select in this step become the cutting edge of the TRIM command or the boundary to which objects will be extended by the EXTEND command.

 Figure 11-8 shows a cutting edge (for TRIM) and a boundary edge (for EXTEND).

 AutoCAD prompts you to select objects that you want to trim or extend (EXTEND doesn't have the eRase option):

   ```
   Select object to trim or shift-select to extend or
           [Fence/Crossing/Project/Edge/eRase/Undo]:
   ```

3. **Select a single object to trim or extend. Choose the portion of the object that you want AutoCAD to trim away or the end of the object that's closer to the extend-to boundary.**

 AutoCAD trims or extends the object to one of the objects that you selected in Step 2. If AutoCAD can't trim or extend the object — for example, if the trimming object and the object to be trimmed are parallel — the command line displays an error message such as `Object does not intersect an edge`.

Cutting edge
(for trim)

Boundary edge
(for extend)

Figure 11-8:
Anatomy of
the TRIM
and EXTEND
operations.

You can select multiple objects to trim and extend by typing **F** and pressing Enter to use the Fence object selection mode or by entering **C** to use Crossing selection. Even better, you can use implied windowing and drag a selection box to select multiple objects. Refer to the section on selection boxes Chapter 10 for more on multiple object selection.

The command line continues to prompt you to select other objects to trim or extend:

```
Select object to trim or shift-select to extend or
         [Fence/Crossing/Project/Edge/eRase/Undo]:
```

4. **Choose additional objects or press Enter when you're finished trimming or extending.**

Here's a triple-threat tip: If you accidentally trim or extend the wrong object and you're still in the TRIM or EXTEND command, type **U** and press Enter to undo the most recent trim or extend. You can switch between TRIM and EXTEND without exiting the command by holding down the Shift key for the other tool. And finally, if you find yourself with a remnant that won't trim because it doesn't cross the cutting edge, type **R** (for eRase) and press Enter to erase it without leaving the TRIM command.

The example in Figure 11-8 shows trimming to a single cutting edge, in which the end of each trimmed line gets lopped off. Another common use of the TRIM command is for trimming out a piece of a line between two cutting edges. In the two-cutting-edges scenario, TRIM cuts a piece out of the middle of the trimmed line. The default option for selecting cutting edges or boundaries is ALL, which works well in this scenario. Pressing Enter to accept the default option selects all objects in the drawing as a cutting edge if you're in the TRIM command, or a boundary if you're in the EXTEND command.

The LENGTHEN (LEN) command provides other useful ways to make lines, arcs, and polylines longer (or shorter). You can specify an absolute distance (or *delta*) to lengthen or shorten by, a percentage to lengthen or shorten by, or a new total length. Look up the *LENGTHEN* command in AutoCAD's help system for more information.

Break

The BREAK command isn't what you use before heading out for coffee. (AutoCAD doesn't have a command for that yet, but I keep hoping.) It's for creating gaps in lines, polylines, circles, arcs, or splines. BREAK also comes in handy if you need to split one object into two without actually removing any visible material.

The following example shows how you BREAK an object (don't worry — in AutoCAD, you won't have to pay for it):

1. **On the Ribbon's Home tab, click the label of the Modify panel to open its slideout and then click the Break button.**

 AutoCAD prompts you to select a single object that you want to break.

2. **Select a single object, such as a line, a polyline, or an arc.**

 The point you pick when selecting the object serves double duty: It selects the object, of course, but it also becomes the *default first break point* (that is, it defines one side of the gap that you'll create). Thus, you should either use one of the AutoCAD precision techniques, such as an object snap, to pick the object at a precise point or use the First point option (described in the next step) to repick the first break point.

 AutoCAD prompts you to specify the second break point or to type **F** and press Enter if you want to respecify the first break point:

   ```
   Specify second break point or [First point]:
   ```

3. **If the point that you picked in the preceding step doesn't also correspond to a break point (see the previous tip), type F and press Enter to respecify the first break point. Then pick the point with an object snap or other precision technique.**

If you do type **F** and press Enter and then respecify the first break point, AutoCAD prompts you to select the second break point:

```
Specify second break point:
```

4. **Specify the second break point by picking a point or typing coordinates.**

 AutoCAD cuts a section out of the object, using the first and second break points to define the length of the gap.

 If you want to cut an object into two pieces without removing anything, click the Break at Point button on the Modify panel's slideout. You first select the object and then choose a point that defines where AutoCAD breaks the object in two. You can then move, copy, or otherwise manipulate each section of the original object as a separate object.

Fillet and chamfer

Whereas TRIM, EXTEND, and BREAK alter one object at a time, the FILLET and CHAMFER commands modify a pair of objects. As Figure 11-9 shows, FILLET creates a curved corner between two lines, whereas CHAMFER creates a beveled corner. (In case you wondered, it's pronounced *FILL-et,* not *fill-AY.* Saying that you know how to *fill-AY* may get you a job in a butcher shop, but it will get you strange looks in a design office.)

Figure 11-9: Cleaning up those corners with FILLET and CHAMFER.

Original lines **Filleted lines** **Chamfered lines** **Lines filleted with zero radius**

The following steps describe how to use the FILLET command. The CHAMFER command works similarly except that, instead of specifying a fillet radius, you specify either two chamfer distances or a chamfer length and angle.

 1. **Click the Fillet button on the Home tab panel of the Ribbon.**

 FILLET and CHAMFER share a flyout button; if you see a straight-line corner instead of a rounded one, click the flyout arrow to select FILLET.

AutoCAD displays the current fillet settings and prompts you to select the first object for filleting or specify one of three options:

```
Current settings: Mode = TRIM, Radius = 0.0000
Select first object or [Undo/Polyline/Radius/Trim/
     Multiple]:
```

2. **Type** R **and press Enter to set the fillet radius.**

AutoCAD prompts you to specify the fillet radius that it uses for future fillet operations:

```
Specify fillet radius <0.0000>:
```

3. **Type a fillet radius and press Enter.**

The number you type will be the radius of the arc that joins the two lines.

AutoCAD then asks you to select the first object:

```
Select first object or [Undo/Polyline/Radius/Trim/
     Multiple]:
```

4. **Select the first line of the pair that you want to fillet.**

AutoCAD prompts you to select the second object for filleting:

```
Select second object or shift-select to apply corner:
```

5. **Select the second line of the pair that you want to fillet.**

AutoCAD fillets the two objects, drawing an arc of the radius that you specified in Step 3.

You can fillet two lines and specify a radius of zero to make them meet at a point. If you have lots of lines to fillet, whether with a zero or the same nonzero radius, use the FILLET command's Multiple option to speed the process.

Holding down the Shift key before picking the second line automatically gives you a clean intersection, the same as if you'd set the fillet radius to 0. The CHAMFER command has the same Shift-select option.

Join

Use the JOIN command to fill gaps in lines, arcs, elliptical arcs, splines, and polylines. If the lines are *collinear* (that is, they lie in the same straight line), or the arcs, splines, polylines, or elliptical arcs are on a similarly curved path, JOIN will create a single new entity to replace the existing separate pieces, as shown in Figure 11-10.

Figure 11-10:
Joining
sundered
pieces.

The following steps describe how to use the JOIN command:

1. **Click the Modify panel title at the bottom edge of the Ribbon's Home tab to open the Modify panel's slideout and then click the Join button.**

 If you foresee doing a lot of joinery, you can pin the slideout open, as shown in Figure 11-10. AutoCAD prompts you to select the source object.

2. **Select the source object — that is, the object you want to join other objects to.**

 AutoCAD prompts according to the object type selected. If you select a line, the command prompt or dynamic input tooltip shows

   ```
   Select lines to join to source:
   ```

3. **Select valid objects to join to the original source object.**

 For example, if you selected a line as your source object, AutoCAD continues prompting for additional collinear lines until you press Enter to end object selection.

4. **Press Enter to end the command.**

 AutoCAD joins the selected objects into a single object. The new object will inherit relevant properties such as layer or linetype of the source object.

Polishing those properties

When you think of editing objects, you probably think first about editing their *geometry:* moving, stretching, making new copies, and so on. That's the kind of editing I cover in this chapter.

Another kind of editing is changing objects' *properties.* As I describe in Chapter 6, every object in an AutoCAD drawing has a set of nongeometrical properties, including layer, color, linetype, lineweight, and maybe plot style. Sometimes, you need to edit those properties — when you accidentally draw something on the wrong layer, for example. A handful of ways of editing an object's properties in AutoCAD are

✔ **The Properties palette:** This is the most flexible way to edit properties. Select any object (or objects), right-click in the drawing area, and choose Properties from the menu. The Properties palette displays the names and values of all properties. Click in the appropriate value cell to change a particular property.

✔ **The Quick Properties panel:** If Quick Properties is enabled by clicking its status bar button, a panel pops up near the crosshairs when you select an object. Like the Properties palette, the Quick Properties panel contains value cells that you can click to change the specific property. You can choose how many lines of information you want Quick Properties to display by right-clicking the Quick Properties status bar button and choosing Settings.

✔ **Layers and Properties control lists:** Another way to change properties is to select objects and then choose from the drop-down lists (Layer, Color, and so on) on the Properties panel. It's fine to change layers this way, but don't be slap-dash about changing the other properties — see Chapter 6 for more information.

✔ **Match Properties:** You can use Match Properties to copy the properties from a source object to one or more other objects. You can find the Match Properties button on the Clipboard panel of the AutoCAD 2010 Ribbon's Home tab. Match Properties works similarly to the Format Painter button in Microsoft applications. Match Properties works even when the objects reside in different drawings.

✔ **Change Space:** I introduce the concepts of model space and paper space in Chapters 4 and 5. Sometimes you add some geometry to paper space and then realize it should have been in model space, or vice versa. The former CHSPACE Express tool is now part of core AutoCAD and AutoCAD LT — you'll find it on the Modify panel on the Ribbon's Home tab. For more information, look up *CHSPACE* in the Command Reference of the online help.

You can turn an arc into a circle or an elliptical arc into a full ellipse with JOIN's cLose option.

 AutoCAD 2010's new REVERSE command provides an easy way of reversing the direction of lines and polylines. Why does that matter? Well, most of the time it doesn't, but if you happen to be using a complex linetype that uses text or a directional arrow block, you probably want the text to read right-way-up and the arrow to point in the right direction. Lines, polylines, and other entity types have start points and end points, and therefore, a direction that runs from the former to the latter. Instead of redrawing linework so your text or symbols appear the right way up, use the REVERSE command to flip the start and end points.

Chapter 12

A Zoom with a View

One of AutoCAD's advantages over manual drawing is its ability to show you different views of your drawing. You can zoom in close, zoom out to a great distance, and pan around. In fact, not only *can* you zoom and pan in your drawing, but in most kinds of drawings, you *must* do it frequently to be able to draw and edit effectively.

Technical drawings are jam-packed with lines, text, and dimensions. Zooming and panning frequently enables you to see the details better, draw more confidently (because you can see what you're doing), and edit more quickly (because object selection is easier when there aren't a zillion objects on the screen). This chapter covers AutoCAD's most useful display control features.

Zoom and Pan with Glass and Hand

Moving your viewpoint in to get a closer view of your drawing data is *zooming in;* moving your viewpoint back to get a more expansive view is called *zooming out*. Moving your viewpoint to another part of your drawing without zooming in or out is called *panning*.

Changing your viewing position lets you do detailed work on tiny objects and then zoom out and move around rooms, houses, or neighborhoods from an Olympian perspective. Early versions of AutoCAD included a sample drawing of our solar system, drawn to scale with kilometers as units, that proved this. If you zoomed all the way out, you could see Pluto's orbit, and you could zoom in close enough to Earth's moon to read the inscription on the plaque left by the Apollo 11 astronauts!

Panning means changing your viewing position without changing the magnification of the view. If you zoom in enough that some of your drawing no longer shows up on-screen, you're going to want to *pan* around — move left, right, up, and down in your drawing — without zooming in and out. AutoCAD makes panning easy with scroll bars and *realtime* panning. And in case you're wondering what realtime panning might be (as opposed to *pretendtime* panning, maybe?), it simply means you can see the objects moving around the screen as you drag the mouse up and down or back and forth. (Of course, it's your viewpoint that's moving, not the objects!)

Both panning and zooming change the *view* — the current location and magnification of the AutoCAD depiction of your drawing. Each time you zoom or pan, you establish a new view. You can give a name to a specific view to make returning to that view easy, as I demonstrate later in this chapter.

You'll get a better sense of panning and zooming around a drawing if you actually have a drawing to look at. Draw some objects on the screen, open one of your own existing drawings, or launch one of AutoCAD's sample drawings. (If you haven't done so already, you can download the sample files from www. autodesk.com/autocad-samples; the AutoCAD LT sample files are also online now, at www.autodesk.com/autocadlt-samples.)

Command access has shifted around in AutoCAD 2010, and the impact naturally shows up most in the most frequently used commands — like PAN and ZOOM. Both PAN and the standard ZOOM command have status bar buttons. In addition, the Navigate panel of the Ribbon's View tab contains a Pan button and a flyout set of Zoom tool buttons (in my opinion, not a very convenient location for such frequently used commands!).

The following steps describe how to use AutoCAD's Zoom and Pan Realtime feature, which is easy to operate and provides a lot of flexibility:

1. **Click the Zoom button on the status bar.**

 The command line version of the ZOOM command starts, and AutoCAD prompts:

   ```
   Specify corner of window, enter a scale factor (nX or
           nXP), or [All/Center/Dynamic/Extents/Previous/
           Scale/Window/Object] <real time>:
   ```

2. **Press Enter to accept Realtime, the default option.**

 The Realtime option of the ZOOM command starts. The crosshairs change to a magnifying glass, and AutoCAD prompts you at the command line:

   ```
   Press ESC or ENTER to exit, or right-click to display
           shortcut menu.
   ```

3. **Move the magnifying glass cursor near the middle of the screen, press and hold down the left mouse button, and drag the cursor up and down until the objects you want to see almost fill the screen.**

 Dragging up increases the zoom magnification, and dragging down decreases it.

4. **Right-click in the drawing area and choose Pan from the menu that appears (as shown in Figure 12-1).**

Figure 12-1:
The Zoom/
Pan
Realtime
right-click
menu.

Because AutoCAD LT doesn't do 3D, there's no 3D Orbit choice on LT's right-click menu. The magnifying glass cursor changes to a hand.

5. **Click and drag to pan the drawing in any direction.**

 You can use the right-click menu to toggle between Zoom and Pan as many times as you like. If you get lost in your drawing, choose Zoom Original or Zoom Extents to return to a more familiar view.

6. **Right-click in the drawing area and choose Exit.**

 The Zoom or Pan Realtime cursor returns to the normal AutoCAD crosshairs.

In the preceding example, you started with zooming and ended with panning. You also have the option of doing the reverse: Click the Pan button on the status bar, and after you've panned, use the right-click menu to switch to zooming. However you start it, the important thing to realize is that Zoom and Pan Realtime is a single AutoCAD function. At any time, you can switch between panning and zooming (or switch to a related function, such as Zoom Window) by using the right-click menu.

You also can pan and zoom by using your mouse's scroll wheel (if it has one) or the middle button of a three-button mouse:

✔ **To pan,** hold down the scroll wheel or the middle button as you move the mouse.

✔ **To zoom in and out,** roll the scroll wheel forward and backward.

✔ **To zoom to the extents of your drawing,** double-click the scroll wheel or the middle button.

The scroll wheel or middle mouse button zoom and pan operations described in the preceding list depend on an obscure AutoCAD system variable named MBUTTONPAN. When MBUTTONPAN is set to 1 — the default value — you can use the middle button to pan and zoom as I describe in the preceding list. Unless your system has been customized by someone, if you change MBUTTONPAN to 0, clicking the middle mouse button displays an object snap menu at the crosshairs, as it did in older AutoCAD versions. If you can't zoom or pan with your middle mouse button, set MBUTTONPAN back to 1. (With MBUTTONPAN set to 1, you use Shift+right-click to display the object snap menu at the crosshairs.)

Realtime zooming and panning is the easiest, most interactive way to get around in your drawings. In some situations, though, this method is less efficient or precise than the old-fashioned methods, the most important of which are described in the next section.

Another way to pan in AutoCAD should be familiar from other Windows programs — the scroll bars in the drawing area. Scrolling is the same in AutoCAD as in any other Windows program; click the arrows in the right and bottom scroll bars on the borders of the drawing window to scroll, or pan, a step at a time; or click and drag the little scroll boxes to pan as little or as much as you want to. By default, scroll bars are turned on in the AutoCAD Classic and AutoCAD LT Classic workspaces, but turned off in the 2D Drafting and Annotation workspaces. To turn them off or on, choose Options in the Application Menu (or type **OPTIONS** or **OP**) to display the Options dialog box. On the Display tab, select or deselect the Display Scroll Bars in Drawing Window check box. My own preference is not to use scroll bars and regain the space, so that's why you don't see them in most figures in this book.

Time to zoom

Realtime zooming is good as far as it goes, but you get much more control over the display if you use some of ZOOM's alternative methods. Because zooming is such a frequent activity in AutoCAD, it's worth knowing some of those alternative ways of doing it.

In the new Ribbon-based workspaces, you'll find tool buttons for all the following ZOOM options on the View tab's Navigate panel. The magnifying-glass button has a menu — click the down arrow beside the magnifying glass, and a menu with the other options opens (see Figure 12-2). There is also a ZOOM button on the status bar; click once, then right click to see a menu with all the ZOOM options.

Figure 12-2:
A menu for
magnifying.

The ZOOM command has several different options, the most important of
which are the following:

✔ **All and Extents:** Zoom Extents (the button with the four-headed arrow
in the magnifying glass) zooms out just far enough to show all the
objects in the current drawing. Zoom All (the button showing the sheet
with the folded-over corner) does the same thing, unless the drawing's
limits are larger than the extents, in which case Zoom All zooms to show
the entire rectangular area defined by the limits. If you've defined your
limits the way I recommend in Chapter 4, Zoom All is a good way to see
your whole drawing area. These two options are especially useful when
you zoom in too small or pan off into empty space and want to see your
entire drawing again.

It's a good idea to Zoom All or Zoom Extents and then save the drawing
before you close it. By performing these steps, you ensure the following:

• The next person who opens the drawing — whether it's you or
someone else — can see the full drawing as soon as they start
working.

• If you've accidentally copied some objects way beyond where they
should be, Zoom All or Extents will make them show up so you can
delete them.

- The drawing preview that appears in the Select File dialog box displays the full drawing, instead of just a tiny, unidentifiable corner of it.

✔ **Window:** This option is great for zooming in quickly and precisely. It zooms to a section of your drawing that you specify by clicking two points. The two points define the diagonal of a window around the area you want to look at.

Note that the ZOOM command's Window option is not a click-and-drag operation — unlike in some other Windows programs and, confusingly, unlike in the Zoom/Pan Realtime Zoom Window option. With the ZOOM command's Window option, you click one corner, release the mouse button, and then click the other corner.

✔ **Scale (X/XP):** The X option zooms by a percentage of the current display; values less than 1 cause you to zoom in, values greater than 1 cause you to zoom out. You can also think of the value as a scaling factor: 0.5X causes the screen image to shrink to half its apparent size, and 2X causes the screen image to double its apparent size. (The XP option after a number is for zooming model space objects in a viewport relative to paper space; see Chapter 5 for information about paper space.)

✔ **Realtime:** Realtime zooming, the technique described previously, enables you to zoom in and out by starting a realtime zoom and then moving the crosshairs up (to zoom in) or down (to zoom out).

✔ **Previous:** This option undoes the last zoom and/or pan sequence, taking you back to where you started.

✔ **Object:** This option zooms in close enough to show selected objects as large as they can be displayed on-screen. Using ZOOM Object is like putting the selected objects under AutoCAD's microscope.

AutoCAD provides *smooth view transitions* whenever you use the non-realtime pan and zoom commands. Sometimes you can get lost if you do a ZOOM All from a small, highly magnified area. It's a bad idea to leave a trail of breadcrumbs across your screen, so these slow-motion pans and zooms may be fine, at least until you do know your way out of the forest . . . or your drawing. If, like me, you find that this feature gets old fast, there's a View Transitions dialog box (type **VTOPTIONS** to open it) in which you can turn it off. Just uncheck the Enable Animation for Pan & Zoom option.

Some of the zoom options take some getting used to. I recommend that you use realtime zoom and pan for most of your zooming and panning. Supplement it with Zoom Window to move quickly into a precise area, Zoom Previous to back up in zoom/pan time, and Zoom All or Zoom Extents to view your whole drawing.

Steering a new course

AutoCAD's ZOOM and PAN partnership have been around since the get-go, and little has changed — apart from the addition of realtime panning and zooming several releases back — in the basics of navigating around in the drawing.

Last time around (AutoCAD 2009, that is) added a couple of new viewing devices. One of them (the Navigation Cube) works exclusively in 3D, and the other (the SteeringWheel) has a 2D configuration that's much less useful than the regular PAN and ZOOM commands. If you want to learn about 3D in general, or the new viewing commands in particular, the best place to start is the User Guide in the online help system. For modeling, check out Work with 3D Models, and for viewing AutoCAD 3D models, see Control the Drawing Views⇨Use Viewing Tools.

A View by Any Other Name . . .

If you find yourself repeatedly zooming and panning to the same area, you can probably get there faster with a named view. After you name and save a view of a particular area of your drawing, you can return to that area quickly by restoring the view. You use the VIEW command, which displays the View Manager dialog box, to create and restore named views.

The View Manager now manages *shots* as well as views. Views have been a part of AutoCAD from very early days, but shots are a recent addition. While views are static, shots are motion based. (If you're using the full version [that is, not AutoCAD LT], you may have noticed the ShowMotion button on the status bar.) And not only can you create animated scenes, you can even add fancy transitions like jump cuts and fades. However, because this kind of pro- duction is associated with 3D and because I don't cover 3D in this book, you should visit the online help. For an especially good take on shots and showing motion, open the Help drop-down list, select New Features Workshop, select AutoCAD 2009 (these features were added to AutoCAD 2009, so technically, they're not *brand*-new features any more), and finally select Viewing Tools.

Follow these steps to create a named view:

1. **Zoom and pan until you find the area of the drawing that you want to assign a name to.**

2. **On the Ribbon's View tab, choose Named Views from the View panel.**

 The View Manager dialog box appears.

3. **Click the New button.**

 The New View / Shot Properties dialog box appears, as shown in Figure 12-3.

4. **Type a name in the View Name text box.**

5. **(Optional) Type a new category in the View Category box or select an existing one from the drop-down list.**

 You create your own View Categories to organize views and certain display characteristics of views. This is mainly used in sheet sets. If you aren't using the sheet sets feature, you can leave this box blank.

6. **Make sure the View Type drop-down is set to Still.**

 Visit the New Features Workshop and the online help if you want to know more about the Cinematic and Recorded Walk options.

 AutoCAD LT doesn't support view categories or types. The New View dialog box in LT is missing the View Category and View Type list boxes as well as the Background area shown in Figure 12-3.

7. **In the Boundary area, select the Current Display radio button, if it's not selected already.**

Figure 12-3:
Save a view into your drawing.

If you want to save a different view boundary, select the Define Window radio button instead, click the Define View Window button to the right of it, and pick two corners of the region's boundary (as if you were zooming windows).

8. **Confirm or change the choices in the Settings area.**

If you select the Save Layer Snapshot with View check box, when you later restore the view, AutoCAD also will restore the layer visibility settings (on/off and freeze/thaw) that were in effect when you created the view. (Chapter 6 describes the layer visibility settings.) The UCS, Live Section, and Visual Style settings are primarily for 3D drawings; the latter two settings are not included in AutoCAD LT.

9. **Click OK.**

The New View/Shot Properties (New View in AutoCAD LT) dialog box disappears, and you see your new named view in the list in the View Manager dialog box.

10. **Click OK.**

The View Manager dialog box disappears.

To restore a named view, proceed as follows:

1. **Go back to the Ribbon's View tab and choose Named Views from the View panel.**

Alternatively, type **VIEW** (or **V**) and press Enter. The View Manager dialog box appears.

2. **In the Views list, expand either Model Views or Layout Views (depending on where you saved your view).**

3. **Click the name of the view that you want to restore, click the Set Current button, and then click OK to close the dialog box.**

You also can plot the area defined by a named view. See Chapter 16 for instructions on plotting views.

Looking Around in Layout Land

All the zoom, pan, and view operations I describe in this chapter work in paper space layouts as well as in model space. (Chapters 4 and 5 describe the differences between model space and paper space and how to navigate between the two.) One little complication exists, though: In a *paper space layout* — that is, any drawing area tab except for the Model

tab — it's possible for the crosshairs to be in either paper space or in model space inside a viewport. Zooming and panning have a different effect depending on which space your crosshairs are in at the moment. You switch between the two spaces using the MSPACE (alias MS) and PSPACE (PS) commands.

Experiment with the different effects by following these steps:

1. **Open a drawing that contains at least one paper space layout with a title block and one or more viewports.**

 If you don't have any such drawings handy, try using one of the AutoCAD sample drawings that you can download from www. autodesk.com/autocad-samples. For example, have a look at architectural_-_annotation_scaling_and_multi leaders.dwg.

2. **Click Quick View Layouts on the status bar and then click one of the layout preview images — that is, any image other than the Model preview image.**

 AutoCAD displays the paper space layout, including any title block and viewports. Click somewhere away from an image to dismiss the Quick View image bar.

3. **Type PSPACE (or its alias PS) and press Enter.**

 AutoCAD will either switch to paper space or tell you that you're already there.

 Alternatively, you can double-click in the gray part of the drawing area outside the layout.

 You should see the triangular paper space UCS icon at the lower-left corner of the display. If you don't see an icon, click the View tab on the Ribbon and then click Show UCS Icon or Show UCS Icon at Origin on the Show UCS Icon flyout. The crosshairs are now in paper space, so zooming and panning changes the appearance of all the objects in the layout, including the title block.

4. **Type Z, press Enter, then type A, then press Enter.**

 AutoCAD displays the entire layout, as shown in Figure 12-4.

 As an alternative to typing — or to navigating through Ribbon panels — here's an easier way to choose from a list of all available ZOOM options: Click the Zoom button on the status bar and then right-click in the drawing area to see the right-click menu, as shown in Figure 12-5.

5. **Zoom and pan by using any of the techniques described in this chapter.**

 Zooming and panning change the appearance of the title block, as shown in Figure 12-6. The effect is similar to moving a plotted sheet in and out and all around in front of your face.

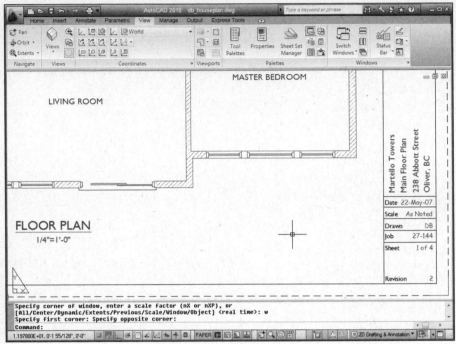

Figure 12-6:
Zooming
in paper
space.

6. **Return to a zoomed-all view using any of these techniques; or type** Z **and press Enter, then type** A **and press Enter.**

 AutoCAD displays the entire layout again.

7. **Type** MSPACE **(or MS) and press Enter.**

 Alternatively, you can double-click with the crosshairs over a viewport.

 You should see the model space UCS icon at the lower-left corner of the display (refer to Step 3 if you don't see an icon). The crosshairs are now in model space, inside the viewport, so zooming and panning change only the display of the objects that are visible in the viewport. The display of the title block doesn't change.

8. **Zoom and pan using any of the techniques described in this chapter.**

 Zooming and panning don't change the appearance of the title block, as shown in Figure 12-7. The result looks as if you're moving a picture of the model space geometry in and out and all around behind a frame.

 In real drawings, you usually shouldn't zoom and pan inside viewports after they've been set up (see Chapter 5). Doing so changes the scale of the viewport, which messes up plotting. I'm asking you to do it here to illustrate the difference between zooming in paper space and zooming in a model space viewport.

Figure 12-7:
Showing
nothing
but the
kitchen sink
in a model
space
viewport.

If the title block changes when you zoom and pan, someone has locked the viewport to prevent the kind of mischief that I warn against in the previous paragraph. (You also see the command prompt `Viewport is view-locked. Switching to Paper space.`) Refer to Chapter 5 for information on locking and unlocking viewports.

9. **Choose Zoom Previous using your favorite ZOOM technique one or more times until you've restored the original view.**

10. **Type** PS **and press Enter.**

 Always leave the crosshairs in paper space when you're ready to call a drawing finished.

11. **Click the Close window control in the upper-right corner of the drawing area. Click No to close the drawing without saving changes.**

 In this example, I have you close the drawing without saving changes just in case you did mess up the viewport zoom scale.

In most cases, you set up a paper space layout once, as described in Chapter 5, and then just return to it to plot. You shouldn't be spending a lot of time zooming and panning in paper space layouts. You zoom and pan to get a

better view of what you're drawing and editing, and that's what full-screen model space is for. But if you do want to zoom in paper space — to get a better look at part of your title block, for example — make sure that you're doing it with the triangular paper space UCS icon on display at the lower-left corner of the drawing area.

The VPMAX and VPMIN commands allow you to maximize and minimize a viewport in the current layout. These commands provide an alternative to switching between the Model and Layout buttons without the potential problems of zooming inside of paper space viewports. The easiest way to run VPMAX or VPMIN is to click the Maximize Viewport/Minimize Viewport button located on the status bar, to the right of the Model and Layout buttons.

Degenerating and Regenerating

As you zoom and pan around your drawing, you may wonder how the image that you see on-screen is related to the DWG file that AutoCAD saves on the hard disk. Well, maybe you don't wonder about that, but I'm going to tell you anyway!

When you draw and edit objects, AutoCAD stores all their geometrical properties (that is, location and size) in a highly precise form — technically, *double floating-point precision*. The program always maintains that precision when you save the DWG file. For computer performance reasons, however, AutoCAD does *not* use that high-precision form of the data to display your drawing on-screen. Instead, AutoCAD converts the highly precise numbers in the DWG file into slightly less precise *integers* in order to create the view that you see on-screen.

The happy consequence of this conversion is that zooming, panning, and other display changes are a lot faster than they would be otherwise. The unhappy consequence is that the conversion, which is a *regeneration* (or *regen* for short), occasionally leaves you with some on-screen debris to deal with.

In most cases, AutoCAD performs regenerations automatically when it needs to. You will sometimes see command line messages like Regenerating model or Regenerating layout, which indicate that AutoCAD is taking care of regens for you.

If, on the other hand, you see the command line message Regen queued, AutoCAD is warning you that it's *not* performing a regeneration, even though one might be advisable now. In addition, you might see a warning dialog box with the message About to regen -- proceed? These messages are

AutoCAD's way of saying, "What your drawing looks like on the screen at the moment may not exactly match the real version of the drawing database that gets stored when you save the drawing. I'll update the display version at the next regeneration." You can control whether regenerations happen automatically with the REGENMODE system variable — see the online help for more information on this variable and refer to Chapter 23 for more information on system variables in general.

Don't confuse the REGEN (RE) command with the REDRAW (R) command. REGEN (command line only) *forces* the synchronization process described in this section. Redraw (also command line only) simply refreshes the screen, without attempting to synchronize the screen with the drawing database. The REDRAW command was useful in the days of very slow computers and older versions of AutoCAD, which didn't handle the display as effectively, but it's essentially a useless command now.

The REGENALL (REA) command (once again, command line only) regenerates all viewports in a paper space layout. If you run the REGENALL command in model space, it has the same effect as the ordinary REGEN command.

Part III

If Drawings Could Talk

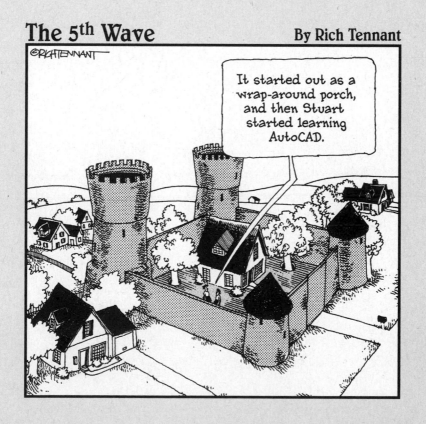

The 5th Wave By Rich Tennant

"It started out as a wrap-around porch, and then Stuart started learning AutoCAD."

In this part . . .

Text, dimensions, and hatching have long been important clarifying elements in drafting. In AutoCAD, these elements are flexible almost to a fault, and you can edit and update them quickly as you change the geometry beneath them. The text, dimension, and hatching annotations that you add "speak" about the geometry so that others can understand exactly what, how big, and how far.

After you've made some drawings that talk, you'll probably send the message around by printing — or as CAD users call it, *plotting* — them. Chapter 16 is your guidebook to navigating the plot process, understanding how the legacy of AutoCAD plotting influences current practice, and most of all, getting a good-looking, properly scaled plot onto paper.

Chapter 13

Text with Character

1t used to be said that "a picture is worth a thousand words." (What with inflation and cost of living increases, a picture is now actually worth 3,780 words!) The opposite is often true as well: Adding a few words to your drawing can save you from having to draw thousands of lines and arcs. It's a lot easier to write `Simpson A35 framing clip` next to a simple, schematic representation of a clip than to draw one in microscopic detail and hope that the contractor can figure out what it is!

Most CAD drawings include some text in the form of explanatory notes, object labels, and titles. This chapter shows you how to add general drawing text and *leaders* (descriptive notes with arrows that point to specific drawing objects) to your drawings. I show you how to take advantage of AutoCAD's annotative text objects and text styles, as well as how to find specific text and check your drawing for spelling errors. Chapter 14 covers text that's connected with dimensions.

In most cases, adding text, dimensions, and other descriptive symbols is something that you should do later in the drafting process, after you've drawn at least some of the geometry. In CAD drawings, text and other annotations are usually intended to complement the geometry, not to stand alone. Thus,

you generally need to have the geometry in place before you annotate it. Many drafters find that it's most efficient to first draw as much geometry as possible and then to add text annotations and dimensions to all the geometry at the same time. In this way, you develop a rhythm with the text and dimensioning commands instead of bouncing back and forth between drawing geometry and adding annotations.

As I mention in Chapter 4, AutoCAD's *annotative objects* present a stream-lined way of adding notes, dimensions, and other annotations to your drawings. This chapter introduces annotative text, and subsequent chapters cover annotative dimensions and hatches. See the "Annotatively yours" sidebar, later in this chapter, for some background.

Getting Ready to Write

In AutoCAD, adding text to a drawing is only slightly more complicated than adding it to a word processing document. Here are the basic steps, which I explain in more detail in the following sections:

1. **Select an existing AutoCAD text style, or create a new style, that includes the font and other text characteristics you want to use.**

 Just like a word processor, AutoCAD uses *styles* — collections of formatting properties — to control the appearance of drawing text. I explain text styles in the next section.

2. **Make an appropriate layer current.**

 To make your AutoCAD drawing efficient and easy to edit for both you and others, create text on its own layer. Most drafting offices already have a set of CAD standards that establish specific layers for text and other object types.

3. **Run *one* of these commands to draw text:**

 • MTEXT draws paragraph (also called multiline) text.

 • DTEXT draws single-line text.

4. **Specify the text alignment points, justification, and (if necessary) height.**

5. **Type the text.**

6. **(Optional) For annotative text, assign annotation scales to the text you just typed.**

You're probably familiar with most of these steps already — especially if you've ever used a word processor. In the next few sections of this chapter, I review the particularities of AutoCAD text styles, the two kinds of AutoCAD text, and ways of controlling height and justification.

Annotatively yours

One of the great things about AutoCAD is that it offers multiple ways of accomplishing your drafting tasks. The drawback, of course, is that it's much more complicated to learn. You could master one of the ways and then find yourself working in an office where you're expected to use a different way, one that you've never tried. The solution — one that this book tries to provide — is to give you at least a taste of the most common methods.

AutoCAD 2010 supports three different methods for adding annotations to your drawings:

✓ **Add text and dimensions in model space, multiplying the drawing scale factor (see Chapter 4 for details) times the desired plotted text height.** For example, assume that someone has drawn a floor plan at a scale of 1/4" = 1'–0" (corresponding to a drawing scale factor of 48), and you want your notes to appear 1/8" high when the drawing is plotted to scale. You need to create text that's 48 times 1/8", or 6", high. And that works fine — until you need to plot your drawing at a different scale.

✓ **Add text and dimensions in layouts in paper space.** Because paper space is plotted at 1:1, you create annotations at their actual plotted size. The scale calculations are simple ("What's 1/8" times 1, boss?"), but sometimes it's beneficial to have drawing annotations in the same space as the drawing geometry, and you may have to duplicate notes in each layout.

✓ **Add text and dimensions in model space using annotative text and dimension styles.** Create your annotations at their actual plotted size — referred to as *paper text height* by AutoCAD — and then assign *annotation scales* for all your desired plot scales. Changing the annotation scale on the status bar automatically changes the visible annotation scale in the drawing.

Using annotative objects makes the most sense to me, as they can cover all plot scales. Also, because they're in model space, they don't have to be duplicated on multiple layouts. As you're learning AutoCAD, one of the more difficult concepts to grasp is the necessity of scaling text and dimensions to apparently ludicrous sizes (6" high drawing text, for example) so that they plot correctly. Annotative objects allow you to keep your annotations in model space and specify the paper size; AutoCAD does the scale calculations for you.

Annotative object types include both single-line and multiline text (covered in this chapter), leaders (this chapter), dimensions (covered in Chapter 14), hatches (see Chapter 15), and blocks and attributes (refer to Chapter 17). By default, only annotative objects at the current annotation scale as set on the application or drawing status bar are displayed, but a handy toggle beside the Annotation Scale list lets you view annotative objects at all scales if you need to.

The annotative workflow does require an additional step compared with the other two methods listed previously. Instead of just creating your text (or other annotative object), you create it as usual and then add annotation scales to the objects. I describe the process in detail in the steps in this chapter and in the following chapters.

Simply stylish text

AutoCAD assigns text properties to individual lines or paragraphs of text based on *text styles*. These text styles are similar to the paragraph styles in a word processor; they contain font and other settings that determine the look and feel of text. An AutoCAD text style includes

- ✔ The font
- ✔ A text height, which you can set or leave at 0 for later flexibility
- ✔ Special effects (where available), such as italic
- ✔ *Really* special effects, such as vertical and upside down, which almost nobody uses

Before you add text to a drawing, use the Text Style dialog box to select an existing style or create a new one with settings that are appropriate to your purpose.

You can assign the annotative property to text styles in old drawings by opening the Text Style dialog box in the drawing, selecting the individual text style you want to update, selecting the Annotative check box, and then saving the drawing in AutoCAD 2010.

Most drawings require very few text styles. You can create one style for all notes, object labels, and annotations and another text style for special titles. You may also want to create a unique text style for your dimensions (refer to Chapter 14 for more on dimension text). A title block may require one or two additional fonts, especially if you want to mimic the font used in a company logo or project logo.

As with layers, your office may have its own text style standards. If so, you'll make everyone happy by following those standards. One of the best ways to make your use of text styles efficient and consistent is to create them in a template drawing that you use to start new drawings. (If your office is well organized, it may already have a template drawing with the company-approved styles defined in it.) See Chapter 4 for information about creating and using templates. Another handy technique is to copy existing text styles from one drawing to another by using the DesignCenter palette. See Chapter 6 for instructions.

Font follies

When you create a text style in AutoCAD, you have a choice of a huge number of fonts. AutoCAD can use two different kinds of fonts: native AutoCAD SHX (compiled shape) fonts and Windows TrueType fonts:

✔ **SHX:** In the Text Style dialog box, SHX font names appear with a drafting compass to the left of the name and display the .shx file extension. SHX fonts usually provide better performance because they're optimized for AutoCAD's use.

✔ **TrueType:** In the Text Style dialog box, TrueType font names appear with a TT symbol to the left of name and no file extension. TrueType fonts give you more and fancier font options, but they can slow down AutoCAD when you zoom, pan, and select and snap to objects. TrueType fonts also can cause greater complications when you exchange drawings with other AutoCAD users.

It's okay to use a TrueType font sparingly for something like a title block logo, but in general, you should stick with standard AutoCAD SHX fonts whenever possible.

The most popular AutoCAD font is Romans.shx (Roman Simplex). (You may also run into Simplex.shx, an older version of Roman Simplex.) Romans. shx is a good, general-purpose font for drafting in AutoCAD. Avoid complicated, thick fonts. They can slow down AutoCAD, and they're usually more difficult to read than the simpler fonts. Remember, you're doing CAD here, not fancy graphic design or reproductions of medieval manuscripts!

Whenever possible, avoid *custom fonts,* which are font files that don't come with AutoCAD or AutoCAD LT (both programs come with the same fonts). AutoCAD installs its standard SHX fonts in the C:\Program Files\AutoCAD 2010\Fonts folder; as long as you haven't added any custom fonts to that folder, you can refer to it for a list of standard fonts. AutoCAD doesn't embed font files in drawings; instead, it must refer to the font files installed locally under either AutoCAD (for SHX fonts) or Windows (for TrueType fonts). If you use a custom font of either type, exchanging your drawings with other people will be more complicated. If you must use a custom font, make a note of it and remember either to send it whenever you send the DWG file (assuming that the font isn't copyrighted, which many custom fonts are) or to warn the recipients that the text will appear different on their systems. It's far less hassle to avoid custom fonts altogether. See Chapter 20 for additional information about how to deal with fonts when you send and receive drawings.

Get in style

The following steps describe how to select an existing text style or create a new one before you enter text into a drawing. If you want to experiment with an existing drawing that contains a variety of text styles, you can download the AutoCAD 2010 sample drawings from www.autodesk.com/autocad-samples. Look for architectural_-_annotation_scaling_and_multileaders.dwg.

1. **On the Ribbon's Home tab, click the Annotation panel's label to open the slideout and then click Text Style.**

 The Text Style dialog box appears, as shown in Figure 13-1.

2. **In the Styles list, select each style in turn to examine the properties of the text styles that have been created in this drawing.**

 Note the font name and look at the Preview panel in the lower-left corner of the dialog box to get a feel for what the different fonts look like.

3. **If you find a suitable text style, select it in the Styles list, click Set Current, and then skip to Step 9.**

 What makes a text style suitable depends on industry practices, office standards, and personal preferences about how the text should look. The information in preceding sections may help you decide. If not, ask an experienced drafter in your office or look at some printed drawings and try to match the text on those. If you're starting from scratch, I highly recommend that you use annotative styles — look for the triangular symbol beside the style name.

4. **If you don't find a suitable text style or if you prefer to create your own text style, click New.**

 Pay attention to the style that's current when you click New. If it's an annotative style, your new style will automatically be annotative; if it's not annotative, it won't. It's easy enough to select or deselect the Annotative check box, but you may overlook this action at first.

 The New Text Style dialog box appears, with a text box for you to type a name.

5. **Type a name for your new text style and then click OK.**

 Your new text style is added to the Styles list and becomes the current style.

Figure 13-1:
Text —
with style.

6. **Choose a font from the Font Name list.**

 `Romans.shx` is the best all-purpose font for most drafting work. If you want to use a different font, review the font suggestions and warnings in the previous section.

 The font that you choose becomes the font that's assigned to your new text style.

7. **To create an annotative text style, select the Annotative check box. Clear the check box for non-annotative text.**

 Click the *i* icon next to the Annotative label to open AutoCAD's online help and find out more.

8. **Adjust the remaining text style settings.**

 The text style shown in Figure 13-1 has the following setup:

 - **Paper Text Height** (just Height for non-annotative styles) = 0.0
 - **Width Factor** = 1.0
 - **Oblique Angle** = 0
 - All check boxes other than Annotative are deselected.

 A text style height of 0.0 makes the style *variable height,* which means that you can specify the height separately for each text object. Assigning a *fixed* (that is, nonzero) height to a text style forces all text using the style to be the same height. Variable height styles are more flexible, but fixed height styles usually make it easier to draw text of consistent height. The decision to use variable height versus fixed height styles is another aspect of text that depends on office practice, so if you work with other AutoCAD users, ask around.

 Dimensions use text styles to format the appearance of the dimension text. When you create a text style that you think you might use for your dimensions, you *must* set a height of 0. Otherwise, the setting that controls the dimension text will not work, and your dimension text is likely to be either enormous or microscopic. This one should be a double warning because it's one of the most common mistakes made by new AutoCAD drafters!

9. **Click Apply and then click Close.**

 The Text Style dialog box closes, and the text style that you selected or created is now the current style for new text objects.

Taking your text to new heights

On the off chance that you're choosing not to use annotative text styles, this section shows you why you might want to change your mind.

In Chapter 4, I describe the importance of choosing an appropriate drawing scale when you set up a drawing. I warn you that you need to know the drawing scale factor for tasks described in other chapters of this book. This is one of those chapters, and I'm about to explain one of those tasks! And when I'm done, remember — you can avoid all the arithmetic by using annotative text — it's just a check box away!

Drawing scale is the traditional way of describing a scale with an equal sign or colon — for example 1/4" = 1'–0", 1:20, or 2:1. The *drawing scale factor* represents the same relationship with a single number, such as 48, 20, or 0.5. The drawing scale factor is the multiplier that converts the first number in the drawing scale into the second number. Make it a point to determine the drawing scale factor of a drawing before you add non-annotative text to it.

Plotted text height

Most industries have plotted text height standards (AutoCAD 2010 refers to *paper* text height, which means the same thing). A plotted text height of 1/8" or 3 mm is common for notes. Some companies use slightly smaller heights (for example, 3/32" or 2.5 mm) to squeeze more text into small spaces.

Calculating non-annotative AutoCAD text height

To calculate non-annotative text height, you need to know the drawing scale factor, the desired plotted text height, and the location of the multiplication button on your calculator. Use the following steps to figure out text height:

1. **Determine the drawing scale factor.**

 If you set up the drawing, you should know its drawing scale, as described in Chapter 4. If someone else set up the drawing, and they're still around, ask them!

 Other methods of figuring out a drawing's scale factor include searching the drawing for a bar scale or a text note that indicates the drawing scale, or if a printout is available, measuring dimensioned distances on the hard copy with an architectural or engineering scale. Finally, if the drawing dimensions are in model space, you can check the value of the DIMSCALE variable (the system variable that controls dimension scale), as described in Chapter 14.

2. **Determine the height that your notes should appear when you plot the drawing to scale.**

 See the preceding "Plotted text height" section for suggestions.

3. **Multiply the numbers that you figured out in Steps 1 and 2.**

 After you know the AutoCAD text height, you can use it to define the height of a text style or of an individual text object.

If you assign a nonzero height to a text style (Step 8 in the "Get in style" section, earlier in this chapter), all text that you create with that style will use the fixed height. If you leave the text style's height set to 0, AutoCAD asks you for the text height when you draw single-line text objects.

This discussion of text height assumes that you're adding non-annotative text in model space. In addition to annotative text in model space, there's a third alternative. You can add annotative or non-annotative text to a paper space layout — for example, when you draw text in a title block or add a set of sheet notes that doesn't directly relate to the model space geometry. When you create text in paper space, you specify the actual, plotted paper height instead of the scaled-up height.

One line or two?

For historical reasons (namely, because the AutoCAD text capabilities used to be much more primitive than they are now), AutoCAD offers two different kinds of text objects and two corresponding text-drawing commands. Table 13-1 explains the two commands, with their aliases shown in parentheses.

Table 13-1	The Two Kinds of AutoCAD Text		
Text Object	*Command (With Alias)*	*Button Icon*	*Comments*
Paragraph text	MTEXT (T)	A	Designed for multiple lines, with word-wrapping. AutoCAD keeps the multiple lines together as a single object. Other special formatting, such as numbered or bulleted lists and columns, is possible.
Single-line text	DTEXT (DT)	A	Designed for creating single lines. Although you can press Enter to create more than one line of text, each line becomes a separate text object.

Although you may be inclined to ignore the older single-line text option, it's worth knowing how to use both kinds of text. The DTEXT command is quite a bit simpler than the MTEXT command, and it's still useful for entering short, single-line pieces of text such as object labels and one-line notes. And it's the command of choice for CAD comedians who want to document their one-liners!

Your text will be justified

Both the DTEXT and MTEXT commands offer a bewildering array of text *justification* options — in other words, which way the text flows from the point or points that you pick in the drawing to locate it. For most purposes, the default Left justification for single-line text or Top Left justification for paragraph text works fine. Occasionally, you may want to use a different justification, such as Center for labels or titles. Both commands provide options for changing text justification. I point out these options when I demonstrate the commands later in this chapter.

Using the Same Old Line

Despite its limitations, the DTEXT command is useful for labels and other short notes for which MTEXT would be overkill. The following procedure shows you how to add text to your drawing by using AutoCAD's DTEXT command.

You *can* use DTEXT for multiple lines of text: Just keep pressing Enter after you type each line of text, and DTEXT puts the new line below the previous one. The problem with this approach is that DTEXT creates each line of text as a separate object. If you later want to add or remove words in the multiple lines, AutoCAD can't do any word-wrapping for you; you have to edit each line separately, cutting words from one line and adding them to the adjacent line.

The DTEXT command doesn't use a dialog box or a fancy formatting toolbar like the MTEXT command's In-Place Text Editor. You set options by typing them into the command line or the dynamic input tooltip.

Here's how you add text with the DTEXT command:

1. **Set an appropriate text style current, as described in the section "Simply stylish text," earlier in this chapter.**

 It's possible to set an already-created text style current at the DTEXT command prompt, but it's usually more straightforward to set the style before starting the command.

 An alternative to opening the Text Style dialog box to make an existing style current is to click the text style drop-down list and choose the style there. Look for the text style drop-down list on the Annotation panel's slideout (Home tab) or the Text panel of the Annotate tab.

2. **(Optional) Use the OSNAP button on the status bar to enable or disable running object snap mode.**

 You may or may not want to snap text to existing objects. For example, you'd want to use a Center object snap to locate a letter or number precisely at the center of a circle.

3. **On the Home tab's Annotation panel, click the lower part of the big button labeled Multiline Text and then choose Single Line from the flyout to start the DTEXT command.**

 Don't click the upper part of the Multiline Text button — that starts the multiline text command, MTEXT, which I cover in the next section.

 If this is the first annotative object you're creating in this drawing session, AutoCAD displays a Select Annotation Scale dialog box advising you that you are indeed creating an annotative object and asking you to set the scale at which you want the annotation to appear; click OK to continue.

 AutoCAD tells you the current text style and height settings and prompts you to select a starting point for the text or to choose an option for changing the text justification or current text style first:

   ```
   Current text style: ìStandardî Text height: 0.2000
           Annotative: Yes
   Specify start point of text or [Justify/Style]:
   ```

 If the text style is annotative, the text height displayed in the prompt is the model space height, not the ultimate plotted text height. For example, if the text style is created with a fixed paper text height of 0.2000, and the annotation scale is set to 1:2, the AutoCAD prompt will read Text height: 0.4000.

4. **If you want a different justification from the default (Left), type J, press Enter, and choose one of the other justification options.**

 Look up *single-line text, aligning* in the online help system index if you need help with the justification options.

5. **Specify the insertion point for the first text character.**

 You can enter the point's coordinates from the keyboard, use the mouse to click a point on-screen, or press Enter to locate new text immediately below the most recent single-line text object that you created.

 AutoCAD prompts you for the text height (or the paper height if the text style is annotative):

   ```
   Specify height <0.2000>:
   ```

6. **Specify the height for the text.**

 This prompt doesn't appear if you're using a text style with a fixed (that is, nonzero) height. See the "Simply stylish text" section, earlier in this chapter, for information about fixed versus variable text heights.

 AutoCAD prompts you for the text rotation angle:

   ```
   Specify rotation angle of text <0>:
   ```

7. **Specify the text rotation angle by typing the rotation angle and pressing Enter or by rotating the line on-screen with the mouse.**

 AutoCAD prompts you to type the text.

 8. **Type the first line of text and press Enter.**

 9. **Type additional lines of text, pressing Enter at the end of each line.**

 Figure 13-2 shows text appearing on-screen as you type it (or it would if this book had animated pages).

 10. **To stop entering text and return to the command prompt, press Enter at the start of a blank line.**

 AutoCAD adds the new single-line text object — or objects, if you typed more than one line — to the drawing.

To align lines of text exactly, make sure that you type all the lines in one instance of the DTEXT command, pressing Enter after each line to make the next line appear just after it. Otherwise, aligning different lines of text precisely is harder to do (unless you set your snap just right or use a complicated combination of object snaps and point filters). To edit single-line text after you've created it, select the text, right-click, and choose Edit (or double-click the text) to open the In-Place Text Editor. (*In-place* simply means that you edit text at its exact size and location in the drawing.) I tell you more about in-place text editing later in this chapter.

An in-place editing box highlights the selected text object, enabling you to edit the contents of the text string. If you want to edit other text properties, such as text height, select the text, right-click, and choose Properties to display the Properties palette. Use the Properties palette to change parameters as needed.

Figure 13-2:
Single-line text appears letter by letter.

If the Quick Properties button on your application status bar is enabled, clicking a single-line text object opens the Quick Properties panel, allowing you to change some (but not all) of the same properties as the Properties palette.

Turning On Your Annotative Objects

As I describe in the "Annotatively yours" sidebar, earlier in the chapter, you have a couple of extra steps in the workflow in order to take advantage of single-line or multiline text you create using annotative styles. You have to assign the scales you're likely to use in your drawing to the text objects and then set the annotation scale accordingly. The following steps explain how to assign annotation scales to text that has been created using an annotative text style:

1. **Make sure the text *is* annotative by hovering the crosshairs over it.**

 Text created with an annotative style but that has not had any annotation scales applied to it displays a single triangular symbol beside the crosshairs. (The symbol represents the end view of a triangular engineering scale.) If there's no symbol, the text isn't annotative.

 If Quick Properties is enabled at the status bar, you can make individual text objects annotative even if they've been created using a non-annotative style by selecting the text and changing the Annotative property from No to Yes in the Quick Properties palette; you can do the same in the Properties palette by selecting the text and pressing Ctrl+1. There may be times when you would want to do this, but they're probably few and far between. Until you become very familiar with annotative objects and decide how you want to use them in both new and old drawings, I recommend that you stick to creating your annotative text by using annotative text styles rather than assigning the annotative property on individual text objects created with non-annotative styles.

2. **Click a text object to select it, then right-click and choose Annotative Object Scale⇨Add/Delete Scales.**

 The Annotation Object Scale dialog box appears and shows a list of all annotative scales assigned to the selected object. In the case of a new text or other annotative object, the only scale listed will be whatever annotation scale is set current on the status bar.

3. **In the Annotation Object Scale dialog box, click Add.**

 The Add Scales to Object dialog box appears, displaying a list of all drawing scale values stored in the drawing.

4. **Select the desired scales from the list, holding down the Ctrl key to select more than one, and then click OK.**

The Annotation Object Scale dialog box reappears, with the scales you added displayed in the list box.

AutoCAD will happily let you select all the scales in the box, but your drawings will be easier to manage if you select only the scales you're likely to use — you can always go back and add another scale later.

Most of the time, for most people, there are way too many scales listed in the Add Scales to Object dialog box. AutoCAD has a handy dandy Edit Scale List dialog box that lets you remove those imperial scales if you never work in feet and inches. And vice versa, for the metrically challenged. To run through your scales, choose Scale List on the Annotation Scaling panel of the Ribbon's Annotate tab. If you make a mistake, the Reset button will restore all the default scales.

5. **Click OK.**

After you assign annotative scales to text (or any annotative object), you'll see a pair of triangular annotative object symbols. Don't worry — although you *are* seeing double, you've done it right!

6. **Open the Annotation Scale list on the application or drawing status bar and select one of the scales you added to the object.**

The annotative objects (text in this case) will change their size as you change the annotation scale. If you select a scale from the list that you did not assign to the object in Step 3, the annotative objects disappear unless you turn on the Annotation Visibility toggle on the status bar. There are a lot of options, a mess of settings, and a slew of system variables in this complex feature. To find out more about annotative objects, refer to the New Features Workshop: Select AutoCAD 2008 (the version in which annotative objects were introduced) from the drop-down list and then choose Scale Annotations.

You can display the drawing status bar (shown in Figures 13-2 and 13-3) by clicking the down arrow near the right end of the application status bar to open the application status bar menu, and then choosing Drawing Status Bar.

Figure 13-3 shows two versions of the same drawing, with the same text objects (the bulleted notes and windows sizes) and wall hatching displaying at the different annotation scales specified in the two status bars. The non-annotative text (the room label) remains unchanged. (I cover hatching your drawings in Chapter 15.)

Figure 13-3:
Annotative
objects
resize auto-
matically as
the annota-
tion scale
changes.

Saying More in Multiline Text

When you just can't shoehorn your creative genius into one or more one-line pieces of text, AutoCAD's multiline text object gives you room to go on and on and on. The following procedure shows you how to create multiline text with the MTEXT command.

Making it with Mtext

The first part of the MTEXT command prompts you for various points and options. The order is a bit confusing, so read these steps and the prompts carefully.

Here's how you use the MTEXT command:

1. **Set an appropriate text style current and (optionally) turn off running object snap mode, as described in Steps 1 and 2 in the earlier "Using the Same Old Line" section.**

 If you're doing real drafting, you should also set an appropriate layer current.

2. **On the Home tab's Annotation panel, click the upper part of the big button labeled Multiline Text to start the MTEXT command.**

The command line displays the current text style and height settings and prompts you to select the first corner of an imaginary rectangle that will determine the word-wrapping width for the text object:

```
Current text style: ìS-NOTESî Text height: 0.2000
        Annotative: Yes
Specify first corner:
```

3. **Pick a point in the drawing.**

The command line prompts you for the opposite corner of the text rectangle that will determine the word-wrapping width and gives you the option of changing settings first:

```
Specify opposite corner or [Height/Justify/Line
        spacing/Rotation/Style/Width/Columns]:
```

4. **Type H and press Enter to change the default text height.**

The command line prompts you for a new default text height:

```
Specify height <0.2000>:
```

5. **Type an appropriate text height.**

See the "Taking your text to new heights" section, earlier in this chapter, for information. If you're adding text in model space, I highly recommend that you use annotative text.

The prompt for the opposite corner of the Mtext rectangle reappears. The command line shows

```
Specify opposite corner or [Height/Justify/Line
        spacing/Rotation/Style/Width/Columns]:
```

6. **If you want a different justification from the default (top left), type J, press Enter, and choose one of the other justification options.**

Look up *multiline text, aligning, Justify Multiline Text* in the index of the online help system if you want an explanation of the other justification options.

7. **Pick another point in the drawing.**

Don't worry about the *height* of the rectangle that you create by choosing the second point; the width of the rectangle is all that matters. AutoCAD adjusts the height of the text rectangle to accommodate the number of lines of word-wrapped text. Don't worry too much about the width, either; you can adjust it later.

The In-Place Text Editor frameless window appears with the tab and indent ruler above it, and a previously hidden Text Editor tab appears on the Ribbon, as shown in Figure 13-4.

Multiline Text Ribbon Tab and indent ruler

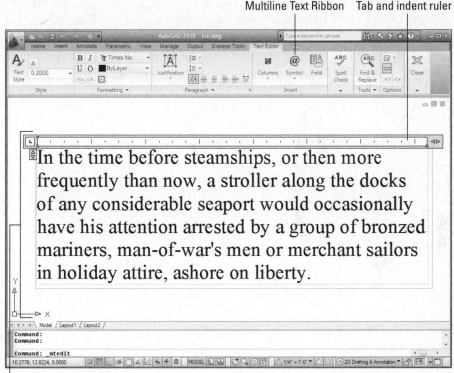

Figure 13-4:
Adding
immortal
multiline
text.

In-Place Text Editor frameless window

New isn't *always* better, and I for one still prefer the classic Text Formatting toolbar over the Ribbon's Text Editor tab. If you want to give the classic version a test drive, change the value of the system variable MTEXTTOOLBAR. The default value (2) displays the Text Editor tab only; setting it to 1 displays both the tab and the toolbar. I don't recommend setting this variable to 0 — that gives you neither option. For more about system variables, see Chapter 23.

8. Verify the text font and height.

The text font and height should be right if you correctly performed Steps 1, 4, and 5. If not, you can change these settings in the Font drop-down list and the Text Height text box on the Text Editor tab (or the classic Text Formatting toolbar).

9. Type text into the text area of the In-Place Text Editor.

AutoCAD word-wraps multiline text automatically. If you want to force a line break at a particular location, press Enter.

10. **If you want other formatting options, select text, right-click, and make an appropriate choice from the menu (as shown in Figure 13-5).**

By convention in most industries, text in drawings is always uppercase. How many times have you forgotten to press the Caps Lock key before entering drawing text? How many times have you forgotten to turn Caps Lock off again when it's time to type your e-mail? To save yourself some agony, right-click in the In-Place Text Editor and choose AutoCAPS from the menu.

11. **Click Close Text Editor (or OK in the classic Text Formatting toolbar).**

The In-Place Text Editor window closes, and AutoCAD adds your text to the drawing.

12. **Add annotation scales to the new multiline text object.**

The steps are the same for multiline text as for single-line text. Refer to the "Turning On Your Annotative Objects" section, earlier in this chapter, if you need a refresher.

As you can tell by looking at the Text Editor tab (or the Text Formatting toolbar) and multiline text right-click menu, the MTEXT command gives you plenty of other options. You can show or hide the toolbar, the ruler, or the Options buttons, and you can give the In-Place Text Editor an opaque background. Other tool buttons give you access to columns and numbered or bulleted lists (both are covered later in the chapter) and right-clicking presents a shortcut to the online help entry on multiline text (choose Learn about MTEXT, then Help).

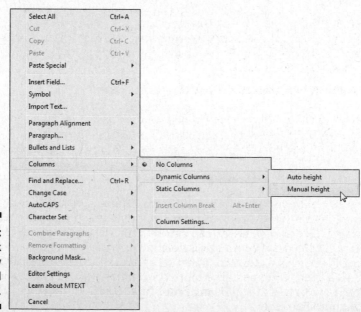

Figure 13-5:
Right-click
your way
to textual
excellence.

Between them, the Text Editor tab and the right-click menu also include a Stack/Unstack feature for fractions, a Find and Replace utility, tools for changing between lowercase and uppercase, options for applying background masks and inserting fields, a special Symbol submenu, and an Import Text option for importing text from a TXT (ASCII text) file or RTF (Rich Text Format) file. I discuss background masks and fields in the next section. If you think you may have a use for any of these other features, choose Contents➪Command Reference➪Commands➪M Commands➪ MTEXT in AutoCAD's online help to find out more about them.

It slices, it dices . . .

Two more useful options on the multiline text right-click menu are Background Mask and Insert Field.

Mtext dons a mask

When you turn on background masking, AutoCAD hides the portions of any objects that lie underneath the multiline text. Use these steps to turn on and control this feature:

1. **Right-click in the In-Place Text Editor and choose Background Mask from the menu.**

 The Background Mask dialog box appears.

2. **Click the Use Background Mask check box so that this option is turned on.**

3. **Either click Use Drawing Background Color (to make the mask the same color as the drawing area's background color) or choose a color from the drop-down list (to make the text appear in a solid rectangle of the specified color).**

4. **Click OK to return to the In-Place Text Editor.**

If you've turned on background masking but it isn't having the desired effect, use the DRAWORDER command to move the text on top of other objects. You can find DRAWORDER on the Home tab's Modify panel.

Mtext plays the field

The Insert Field option on the In-Line Text Editor's right-click menu creates a *text field* that updates automatically every time you open, save, plot, or regenerate the drawing. Fields can contain data such as the date, filename, or author. Fields draw information from the operating system settings, Drawing Properties dialog box, sheet sets feature (not in AutoCAD LT), and AutoCAD system variables. (For more information about system variables, see Chapter 23.) Use the following procedure to add a field while you're creating multiline text:

1. **Right-click in the In-Place Text Editor and choose Insert Field from the menu.**

 The Field dialog box appears.

2. **Choose a Field Name in the left column.**

3. **Choose a Format in the right column, or for date fields, type a format in the Date Format box.**

4. **Click OK.**

 AutoCAD adds the field to the Mtext object that you're creating or editing.

Doing a number on your Mtext lists

Mtext supports bulleted and numbered lists. This feature is especially useful for creating general drawing notes, as shown in Figure 13-6. AutoCAD automates the process of creating numbered lists almost completely. Here's how:

1. **Follow Steps 1 through 8 in the earlier section, "Making it with Mtext," to open the In-Place Text Editor.**

2. **Type a title — for example,** DESIGN CRITERIA.

 If you want your title underlined, click Underline on the Formatting panel (or the Text Formatting toolbar) before you type the title; click Underline again to turn it off. Press Enter to go to the next line and press Enter again to leave a little more space.

3. **On the Paragraph panel of the Text Editor tab, click the Bullets and Numbering flyout button; verify that Allow Auto-List, Use Tab Delimiter Only, and Allow Bullets and Lists are selected; and then click Numbered, as shown in Figure 13-6.**

 The number 1 followed by a period appears on the current line, and the cursor jumps to the tab stop visible in the ruler at the top of the In-Place Text Editor window.

 Enabling *Numbered* places numerals followed by periods in front of items in a list. (*Bulleted* places bullet characters in front of items in a list.) *Auto-list* enables automatic numbering — each time you press Enter to move to a new line, AutoCAD increments the number.

4. **Type the text corresponding to the current number or bullet.**

 As AutoCAD wraps the text, the second and subsequent lines align with the tab stop, and the text is automatically indented.

Indentation of first line

Indentation of second and subsequent lines

Tab

Figure 13-6:
Tabs,
indents, and
automatic
numbering
set to create
numbered
lists.

In-Place Text Editor right-click

5. Press Enter at the end of the paragraph to move to the next line.

Just like creating numbered lists in your favorite word processor,
AutoCAD automatically inserts the next number at the beginning of the
new paragraph, with everything perfectly aligned.

To create nested numbered or bulleted items as shown in Figure 13-6,
simply press Tab at the start of the line. If you change your mind, you
can bump a nested text item up a level by selecting the item in the
In-Place Text Editor and pressing Shift+Tab.

6. Repeat Steps 4 and 5 for each subsequent numbered or bulleted item.

For legibility, you sometimes want to add spaces between the notes. If
you press Enter twice to give yourself a blank line, AutoCAD — like
every good word processor — thinks you're finished with your list
and turns numbering off. AutoCAD is smart, so you need to be smarter.
If you put the cursor at the end of the first note and press Enter, you
get a blank line. The problem is, the blank line is now numbered, and
your intended Note 2 is now Note 3. Just press the Backspace key.
The number on the blank line disappears, and Note 2 is back to being
Note 2 again. When you delete a numbered item, the remaining numbers
automatically adjust.

If you don't like the horizontal spacing of the numbers or the alignment
of subsequent lines, you can adjust them easily by manipulating the tab
and indent markers in the In-Place Text Editor's ruler.

7. **In the ruler, drag the upper slider (the triangle pointing down) to the right a short distance. Drag the lower slider (the triangle pointing up) to the right a slightly greater distance.**

 The upper slider controls the indentation of the first line in each paragraph. The lower slider controls the indentation of the second and subsequent lines. An indent of one to two of the short, vertical tick marks usually works well for the first line. An indent of two to four tick marks works well for the second and subsequent lines.

8. **Click in the ruler just above the lower slider.**

 A small triangle (pointing right) appears above the lower slider. This triangle shows the tab stop.

 Make sure that the corner of the tab stop (right-pointing) triangle aligns horizontally with the point of the lower slider triangle. If not, click and drag the tab stop until it aligns.

If you prefer to type tab and indent distances, not adjust them with the cursor, open the Paragraph dialog box by either

✔ Clicking the little arrow at the right end of the Paragraph panel label (in AutoCADese, it's called a Panel Dialog Box Launcher).

✔ Right-clicking inside the In-Place Text Editor and choosing Paragraph.

Whichever way you do it, if you select text first, the tab and indent changes apply to the selected text. If you don't select text first, the changes apply to new text from that point in the multiline text object forward.

Line up in columns — Now!

AutoCAD is getting more word processor–like with every release! A few versions back, it was simple indents, then came numbered and bulleted lists. The latest addition is columns in multiline text.

Columns come in two flavors: *static* and *dynamic*.

✔ With **static columns**, you specify the number of columns into which to flow your text. Columns are always the same height, and text is allowed to overflow the final column if there's too much of it.

✔ **Dynamic columns,** as you might expect, are friendlier, more flexible, and the life of any party. Column heights can be individually adjusted, and new columns are added automatically to accommodate the text.

Selecting either column type also offers you a Column Settings dialog box where you can specify values numerically instead of by dragging grips.

Figure 13-7 shows a block of multiline text imported as an RTF file from a word processor and then formatted in dynamic columns with the Manual Height option.

Setting up columns is pretty straightforward — the following steps explain how:

1. **Open a drawing that contains a large multiline text object or create a large multitext object in a new drawing.**

 If you already have drawing specifications or general notes in a word processor document, or even a text file, you can right-click inside the MTEXT command's In-Place Text Editor and choose Import Text. The Select File dialog box opens, giving you the choice of Rich Text Format (RTF) or ASCII text (TXT) files.

2. **If the In-Place Text Editor is not already open, double-click the text, or select it, then right-click and choose Mtext Edit.**

Figure 13-7:
Dynamically columnizing your text.

3. **Click Columns in the Insert panel and choose either Dynamic Columns or Static Columns.**

 If you choose Dynamic Columns, select either Auto Height or Manual Height. Selecting Manual Height puts grips on each column so you can adjust their height individually (refer to Figure 13-7). Auto height displays a single grip, so the heights of all columns remain the same, but new columns are still added as required by the amount of text.

 If you choose Static Columns, select the number of columns you want from the menu. Clicking 2, for example, creates two columns regardless of the length of your text — you may end up with overflowing text or empty columns.

4. **Click Close Text Editor (or OK in the Text Formatting toolbar) when you're satisfied with the column arrangement.**

 You can revert to a non-columnar arrangement by clicking the Columns button in the Insert panel and choosing No Columns.

Modifying Mtext

After you create a multiline text object, you can edit it in the same ways as a single-line text object: Select the object, right-click, and choose Mtext Edit or Properties.

- ✔ The **Mtext Edit option** opens the In-Place Text Editor window so that you can change the text contents and formatting.
- ✔ The **Properties option** opens the Properties palette, where you can change overall properties for the text object.
- ✔ If **Quick Properties** is enabled on the status bar, simply selecting a multiline text object opens the Quick Properties palette in which you can modify a subset of the Mtext object's properties.

The easiest way to change the word-wrapping width of a paragraph text object is to *grip edit* it. Select the text object, click one of the corner grips, release the mouse button, move the crosshairs, and click again. Chapter 10 describes grip editing in detail.

 Just like any good word processor or text editor, AutoCAD includes both a spell checker and a find-and-replace tool for text or dimensions. To check the spelling of selected objects or the entire drawing, click the Annotate tab on the Ribbon and choose Check Spelling from the Text panel to display the Check Spelling dialog box. On the same panel, clicking Find Text, or typing FIND and pressing Enter displays the Find and Replace dialog box. Handily,

Find and Replace and Spell Check are both also accessible from the Text Editor tab's Spell Check and Tools panels — in case you just want to replace text or check spelling within a single multiline text object. Look up *SPELL* or *FIND* in the online help index if you need more information on either command.

Gather Round the Tables

You don't know the meaning of the word *tedious* unless you've tried to create a column-and-row data table in older versions of AutoCAD using the LINE and DTEXT commands. AutoCAD's table object and the TABLESTYLE and TABLE commands for creating it make the job almost fun.

Table objects in AutoCAD 2010 are *not* annotative, so you have just two methods of adding them to drawings. You can create them in model space, scaling them up by the drawing scale factor (see Chapter 4 for a refresher), or — and this seems more sensible to me — you can create them in a layout, in paper space, defining them by their actual plotted (paper) dimensions.

Tables have style, too

You control the appearance of tables — both the text and the gridlines — with *table styles* (just as you control the appearance of standalone text with text styles). Use the TABLESTYLE command to create and modify table styles. Follow these steps to create a table:

1. **On the Home tab, click the Annotation panel's label to open its slideout and then choose Table Style.**

 The Table Style dialog box appears.

2. **In the Styles list, select the existing table style whose settings you want to use as the starting point for the settings of your new style.**

 For example, select the default table style named Standard.

3. **Click the New button to create a new table style that's a copy of the existing style.**

 The Create New Table Style dialog box appears.

4. **Enter a New Style Name and click Continue.**

 The New Table Style dialog box appears, as shown in Figure 13-8.

Figure 13-8:
Setting the table.

5. **In the Cell Styles area, with Data showing in the list box, specify settings for the data alignment, margins, text, and borders.**

The settings you're likely to want to change are Text Style, Text Height, and perhaps either Text Color (all three are on the Text tab) or Grid Color (on the Borders tab). If you leave colors set to ByBlock, the text and grid lines will inherit the color that's current when you create the table. That color will be the current layer's color, if you follow my advice in Chapter 6.

6. **In the Cell Styles area, open the drop-down list and repeat Step 5 for the Headers (that is, the column headings) and the Title.**

7. **Click OK to close the New Table Style dialog box.**

The Table Style dialog box reappears.

8. **Click Close.**

Your new table style becomes the current table style that AutoCAD uses for future tables in this drawing, and the Table Style dialog box closes. Now you're ready to create a table, as described in the next section.

You can access the Manage Cell Styles dialog box directly from the Title, Column Head, or Data pages of the New Table Style dialog box. The Table Cell Format dialog box provides a number of additional options for formatting cells by data type.

AutoCAD stores table styles in the DWG file, so a style that you create in one drawing isn't immediately available in others. You can copy a table style from one drawing to another with DesignCenter. (Use the procedure for copying layers between drawings outlined in Chapter 6, but substitute Table Styles for Layers.)

Creating and editing tables

After you create a suitable table style, adding a table to your drawing is easy with the TABLE command. Here's how:

1. **Set an appropriate layer current.**

 Assuming that you leave the current color, linetype, and lineweight set to ByLayer, as I recommend in Chapter 6, the current layer's properties will control the properties of any parts of the table that you left set to ByBlock when you defined the table style. (See Step 5 in the preceding section, "Tables have style, too.")

2. **On the Home tab's Annotation panel, choose Table.**

 The Insert Table dialog box appears.

3. **Choose a table style from the Table Style Name drop-down list.**

4. **Choose an Insertion Behavior:**

 • **Specify Insertion Point** is the easiest method and means that you pick the location of the table's upper-left corner (or lower-left corner if you set Table Direction to Up in the table style). With this method, you specify the default column width and number of rows in the Insert Table dialog box.

 • **Specify Window** means that you pick the upper-left corner and then the lower-right corner. With this method, AutoCAD automatically scales the column widths and determines how many rows to include.

5. **Specify Column & Row Settings.**

 If you chose Specify Window in Step 4, AutoCAD sets the Column Width and number of Data Rows to Auto, which means that AutoCAD will figure them out based on the overall size of the table that you specify in Steps 7 and 8.

6. **Click OK.**

 AutoCAD prompts you to specify the insertion point of the table.

7. **Click a point or type coordinates.**

 If you chose Specify Insertion Point in Step 4, AutoCAD draws the table grid lines, places the cursor in the title cell, and displays the Text Editor tab on the Ribbon.

8. **If you chose Specify Window in Step 4, specify the diagonally opposite corner of the table.**

 AutoCAD draws the table. Based on the table size that you indicated, AutoCAD chooses the column width and number of rows.

9. **Type a title for the table.**

10. **Type values in each cell, using the arrow keys or Tab key to move among cells.**

 The cell right-click menu offers many other options, including copying contents from one cell to another, merging cells, inserting rows and columns, changing formatting, and inserting a *block* (that is, a graphical symbol — see Chapter 17 for information about blocks).

 The fields feature described earlier in this chapter works for table text, too — you can insert a field into a table cell. For example, you might use this feature to create part of a title block, with fields serving as the "date" and "drawn by" data.

11. **Click Close Text Editor on the Ribbon (or click OK on the Text Formatting toolbar).**

 Figure 13-9 shows a completed table, along with the Insert Table dialog box.

You can edit cell values later simply by double-clicking in a cell. To change column width or row height, click the table grid and then click and move the blue grips. (To change the width of one column without altering the overall width of the table, hold down the Ctrl key while you move the grip.) If you want to change other aspects of a table or individual cells in it, select the table or cell and use the Quick Properties palette or the Properties palette to make changes.

Figure 13-9: The Insert Table dialog box and one result of using it.

You can import tables from Microsoft Excel instead of using the Insert Table dialog box. To import Excel data, in Excel, select the desired cells and choose Edit⇨Copy. Then in AutoCAD, choose Paste Special from the Home tab's Clipboard panel and then choose AutoCAD Entities in the Paste Special dialog box. AutoCAD attempts to copy the Excel spreadsheet's formatting along with the cell data, but you'll probably have to adjust column widths and perform other cleanup on the imported table.

You can go the other direction — from AutoCAD to Excel or another program — via a CSV (Comma Separated Value) file. Look up *TABLEEXPORT command* in AutoCAD's online help index.

You can extract attribute data to tables. See Chapter 17 for information about blocks and attributes. You can also perform simple calculations in tables by using predefined functions or your own arithmetical expressions. Look up *Use Formulas in Table Cells* in AutoCAD's online help Search page.

Bring Out Your Inner Leader

Don't worry; I'm not going to make you walk across a bed of red hot coals or give you a sales pitch about office politics or personal growth opportunities! No, I'm talking about those notes with arrows that point to drawing objects that you need to embellish with some verbiage.

Multileaders — *mleaders* for short — are a vast improvement over old-style leaders available prior to AutoCAD 2008. In fact, they're so good, they should be running the United Nations! Mleaders, unlike the old-style leaders, are single objects. They are also able to point in multiple directions at once (just don't ask them which way is the bus station). Finally, multileaders — just like text, dimensions, hatching, and other objects you use to document your drawing — can be annotative.

Multileaders seem to grow in flexibility with each release. In AutoCAD 2010, you can use grips to manipulate a multileader's individual components, just as if it were several objects instead of a single object. Hold down the Ctrl key and click a multileader to select different pieces. You can even use grips to adjust the width of multileader text as if it were a plain everyday Mtext object.

There are two older style leaders stored in AutoCAD's attic (Autodesk hates to throw anything away). These semi-retired leaders are no longer accessible on menus or toolbars, but they're still lurking up there waiting to . . . er, lead you astray. If you've become attached to typing commands, you may be inclined to type either **LEADER** or **LE** to create those pointy-headed thingies. If you do, be aware that LEADER runs the positively ancient command for creating notes-with-arrows. There are no options, so only straight leader lines and infinitely long text strings are what you get. LE (the alias for the QLEADER command) runs the merely elderly command for creating notes-with-arrows;

this one has a Settings dialog box where you can set some options, and it does ask you to specify a width for your Mtext note. However, unlike multileaders, both LEADER and LE create the leader lines and the text as two separate objects.

Electing a leader

You can draw multileader objects that consist of leader lines and multiline text at the same time by using the MLEADER command, as described in the following steps:

1. **Set a multileader style — one that's appropriate for your needs — current.**

 Choose an existing multileader style from the Selects a Multileader Style drop-down list on the Home tab's Annotation panel slideout, or create a new style by choosing Multileader Style from the Annotation slideout. Visit the online help for tips on creating new multileader styles.

2. **Choose Multileader from the Annotation panel.**

 The command line prompts you to select the location for the pointy end of the leader arrowhead:

   ```
   Specify leader arrowhead location or [leader Landing
   first/Content first/Options] <Options>:
   ```

 The initial default method is to locate the arrowhead followed by the leader landing (that is, the short horizontal line between the leader line and the text), at which point AutoCAD displays the In-Place Text Editor, and you enter the text of your note. If you'd rather place the leader landing first, type **L** and press Enter. If you'd rather type the content first, type **C** and press Enter.

 If you want to draw spline-curved rather than straight leader lines, specify the number of pick points for the leader lines and press Enter to display multileader options at the command line or the dynamic input tooltip. Refer to the online help for more information on the command options.

3. **Pick a location in the drawing that you want the leader to point to.**

 If you use an object snap mode, such as Nearest or Midpoint, to pick a point on an object, AutoCAD associates the leader with the object. If you later move the object, AutoCAD updates the leader so that it points to the new location.

 The command line prompts you for the next point.

4. **Pick a second point.**

 AutoCAD draws a shaft from the arrowhead to this point.

If you pick a second point that's too close to the arrowhead point and AutoCAD doesn't have enough room to draw the arrowhead, it omits the arrowhead.

By default, AutoCAD lets you pick two points for the leader line: the first point locates the arrowhead, and the second point locates the start of the short horizontal leader landing. If you need more points than that, restart the command and choose Options, Maxpoints and set a new value.

After you pick the point for the leader landing, AutoCAD opens the In-Place Text Editor.

5. **Enter your comment.**

 You're now in the same In-Place Text Editor I describe earlier in this chapter, with the same Text Editor tab and options.

6. **Click Close.**

 The In-Place Text Editor window closes and adds your comment to the drawing, next to the leader.

Figure 13-10 shows several different leaders with notes.

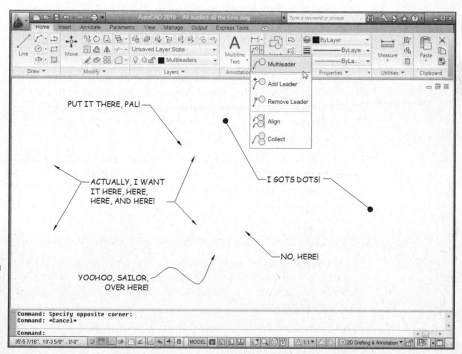

Figure 13-10:
No loss
for (multi)
leaders.

Multi options for multileaders

In addition to the MLEADER command itself, which I walk you through in the preceding steps, multileaders come with a slew of formatting, drawing, and editing commands:

✔ **MLEADEREDIT:** Use this command to add or remove leader lines from multileader objects. You'll find each of those functions on the Multileader drop-down list (refer to Figure 13-10).

✔ **MLEADERSTYLE:** Multileaders, like text, tables, and dimensions, are formatted according to named styles. To display the Multileader Style Manager dialog box (which looks a lot like a simplified version of the Dimension Style Manager) click Multileader Style on the Home tab's Annotation slideout.

✔ **MLEADERALIGN:** A tedious chore in earlier AutoCAD versions was getting all the leaders to line up; it usually involved drawing a construction line and then using object snaps to move common points on the leaders to the construction line. To line up mleaders, choose Align from the Multileader drop-down list.

✔ **MLEADERCOLLECT:** Multileaders can contain blocks as well as text (I cover blocks in Chapter 17). Choose Collect from the Multileader drop-down list to gather a group of leaders containing blocks; they'll rearrange themselves as a single multileader containing the multiple blocks.

For more information on any of these commands, look them up by name in the Command Reference section of the online help.

Multileaders and multileader styles can be annotative or non-annotative. Making them annotative and assigning appropriate annotation scales is a huge time saver for detail views that you might want to plot at different scales.

Chapter 14

Entering New Dimensions

*I*n drafting — either CAD or manual drafting — *dimensions* are special text labels with attached lines that together clearly indicate the size of something. Although it's theoretically possible to draw all the pieces of each dimension by using AutoCAD commands, such as LINE and MTEXT, dimensioning is so common a drafting task that AutoCAD provides special commands for doing the job more efficiently. These dimensioning commands group the parts of each dimension into a convenient, easy-to-edit package. Even better, as you edit an object — by stretching it, for example — AutoCAD automatically updates the measurement displayed in the dimension text label to indicate the object's new size, as shown in Figure 14-1. And perhaps best of all, AutoCAD 2010's annotative dimensions automatically change their size as you change the annotation scale on the model tab or the viewport scale in a layout. I explain the general principles of annotative objects in Chapter 13; in this chapter, I take a closer look at annotative dimensions.

AutoCAD controls the look of dimensions by means of *dimension styles,* just as it controls the look of text with text styles, and tables with table styles. (AutoCAD also uses text styles to control the appearance of the text in dimensions.) But dimension styles are much more complicated than text styles because dimensions have so many more pieces that you need to control. After you find or create an appropriate dimension style, you use one of several dimensioning commands to draw dimensions that point to the important points on an object (the two endpoints of a line, for example).

Why dimensions in CAD?

You may think that CAD would have rendered text dimensions obsolete. After all, you comply with all my suggestions about using AutoCAD precision techniques when you draw and edit, and you're careful to draw each object at its true size, right? The contractor or machinist can just use AutoCAD to query distances and angles in the DWG file, right? Sorry, but no (to the last question, anyway). Here are a few reasons why the traditional dimensioning that CAD drafting has inherited from manual drafting is likely to be around for a while:

✔ **Some people need to or want to use paper drawings when they build something.** We're still some time away from the day when contractors haul computers around on their tool belts (never mind mousing around a drawing while hanging from scaffolding).

✔ **In many industries, paper drawings still rule legally.** Your company may supply both plotted drawings and DWG files to clients, but your contracts probably specify that the plotted drawings govern in the case of any discrepancy. The contracts probably also warn against relying on any distances that the recipient of the drawings measures — using measuring commands in the electronic drawing file or a scale on the plotted drawing. The text dimensions are supposed to supply all the dimensional information that's needed to construct the object.

✔ **Dimensions sometimes carry additional information besides the basic length or angle.** For example, dimension text can indicate the allowable manufacturing tolerances or show that a particular distance is typical of similar situations elsewhere on the drawing.

AutoCAD dimensioning is a big, complicated subject. (It's so complicated, in fact, that Autodesk has an especially wise person in charge of dimensioning in AutoCAD — this person is called the *dimwit*.) Every industry has its own dimensioning conventions, habits, and quirks. As usual, AutoCAD tries to support them all and, in so doing, makes things a bit convoluted for everyone. This chapter covers the essential concepts and commands that you need to know to start drawing dimensions. Be prepared to spend some additional time studying how to create any specialized types of dimensions that your industry uses. Who knows — if you work very hard and practice every day, you too could become an AutoCAD dimwit!

You add dimensions to a drawing *after* you've drawn at least some of the geometry; otherwise, you won't have much to dimension! Your dimensioning and overall drafting efficiency improve if you add dimensions in batches, rather than draw a line, draw a dimension, draw another line, draw another dimension. . . .

Original dimension

Figure 14-1:
Changing objects auto-matically updates dimensions.

Dimension updates when you change the object

Current annotation scale

Discovering New Dimensions

Before digging into the techniques that you use to create dimension styles and dimensions, here's some AutoCAD dimensioning terminology that you need to understand. If you're already familiar with CAD dimensioning lingo, just skim this section and look at the figures in it. Otherwise, read on.

Anatomy of a dimension

AutoCAD uses the names shown in Figure 14-2 and described in the following list to refer to the parts of each dimension:

✔ **Dimension text:** *Dimension text* is the numeric value that indicates the true distance or angle between points or lines. Dimension text can also include other information in addition to or instead of the number. For example, you can add a suffix, such as TYP., to indicate that a dimension is typical of several similar configurations. AutoCAD's default dimension style settings center the dimension text vertically and horizontally on the dimension lines, as shown in Figure 14-2, but you can change those settings to cause the text to appear in a different location — sitting over an unbroken dimension line, as shown previously in Figure 14-1, for example. See the section, "Adjusting style settings," later in this chapter for instructions.

Arrowhead Dimension line

Ø4.00

Figure 14-2:
The parts of
a dimension.

12.00

Extension line Dimension text Dimension text

Dimension line Defpoint

Arrowhead

✔ **Dimension lines:** In linear dimensions, the *dimension lines* indicate the true distance between points. Linear dimension lines can be horizontal, vertical, rotated at a specific angle, or aligned with the object being dimensioned. Angular dimensions have curved dimension lines with the center of the curve at the vertex point of the objects being dimensioned. For radius and diameter dimensions, the dimension line simply points at the object being dimensioned (see Figure 14-3 for examples of these dimension types).

✔ **Arrowheads:** The dimension's *arrowheads* appear at the end or ends of the dimension lines and emphasize the extent of the dimensioned length. AutoCAD's default arrowhead style is the closed, filled type shown in Figure 14-2, but you can choose other symbols, such as dots or tick marks, to indicate the ends of the dimension lines. (Don't get ticked off, but AutoCAD calls the line ending an *arrowhead* even when, as in the case of a tick mark, it doesn't look like an arrow.)

✔ **Extension lines:** *Extension lines* extend outward from the definition points (also known as *defpoints*) that you select (usually by snapping to points on an object) to the dimension lines. By drafting convention, a small gap usually exists between the defpoints and the beginning of the extension lines. Also by convention, the extension lines usually extend just past the dimension lines — see Figures 14-2 and 14-3 for examples. You can make a set of dimensions look tidier by assigning fixed lengths for the extension lines. And if you need to dimension to circles or center-lines, you can assign dash-dot linetypes to either or both extension lines.

Figure 14-3:
Common types of dimensions.

Aligned dimension

Radius dimension

Horizontal linear dimension

Diameter dimension

Angular dimension

Vertical linear dimension

✔ **Defpoints:** When you create any kind of dimension, AutoCAD places one or more definition points (universally known as *defpoints*) on a special layer named (what else?) Defpoints, which the program creates the first time a dimension command is issued. These points are usually invisible because the objects being dimensioned are on top of them, but you can see where they sit by selecting a dimension to turn on its grips. The grips on the objects being dimensioned are on the dimension's definition points. Because you wouldn't want these points to appear when you plot your drawings, the Defpoints layer has a special property: Nothing created on the Defpoints layer will print.

Because of the Defpoints layer's non-printing property, experienced users for many years have been using it for sketches, guidelines, and important notes (for example, "Don't forget to buy bread on the way home!"). I don't endorse this practice because of a convoluted relationship between the Defpoints layer and Layer 0 — it can be very hard to tell what's on which layer, and that can make the drawing harder to edit. If you want a "scratch" layer for those important notes, create one named Scratch and set it to NoPlot in the Layer Properties Manager palette. (For more about layers and the Layer Properties Manager see Chapter 6.)

A field guide to dimensions

AutoCAD provides several types of dimensions and commands for drawing them. Figure 14-3, earlier in this chapter, shows the most common types, and the following list describes them:

- **Linear dimensions:** A *linear* dimension indicates the linear extent of an object or the linear distance between objects. Most linear dimensions are either horizontal or vertical, but you can draw dimensions that are rotated to other angles, too.

- **Aligned dimensions:** An *aligned* dimension is similar to a linear dimension, but the dimension line tilts to the same angle as a line drawn through the origin points of its extension lines.

- **Radial dimensions:** A *radius* dimension shows the radius of a circle or an arc, and a *diameter* dimension calls out the diameter of a circle or an arc. You can position the dimension text inside or outside the curve, as shown in Figure 14-3. If you position the text outside the curve, AutoCAD (by default) draws a little cross at the center of the circle or arc. As shown in Figures 14-2 and 14-3, AutoCAD automatically adds the diameter and radius symbols to the appropriate dimension type.

 If you're wondering when you should use which, because radius and diameter dimensions seem to do the same thing, the convention in most drafting disciplines is to use diameter dimensions for whole circles (for example, a hole) and radius dimensions for part circles or arcs (for example, a fillet).

- **Angular dimensions:** An *angular* dimension indicates the angular measurement between two lines, the two endpoints of an arc, or two points on a circle. The dimension line appears as an arc that indicates the sweep of the measured angle.

Other types of dimensions and dimension-like annotations you can add to AutoCAD objects include arc length and ordinate dimensions, tolerances, inspection dimensions, and center marks. Look up *dimensions, creating* on the Index tab in the AutoCAD online help system for more information about other less frequently used kinds of dimensions.

Dimension associativity

By default, AutoCAD groups all the parts of each dimension — the extension lines, dimension lines, arrowheads, and text — into a special *associative dimension* object. *Associative* means two things:

- **The different parts of the dimension function as a single object.** When you click any part of the dimension, AutoCAD selects all its parts.

- **The dimension is connected to the points on the object that you specified when you drew the dimension.** If you change the size of the object (for example, stretch a line), the dimension updates appropriately — the lines and arrows move, and the text changes to reflect the line's new size.

The associative dimensions I'm talking about here first appeared in AutoCAD 2002. Before that, AutoCAD had a more primitive kind of dimensioning. Dimensions were single objects, and they did update if you stretched an object as long as you were very careful to include the dimension itself in the crossing selection for the STRETCH command. Here's where things can get a bit confusing: AutoCAD used to call these old-style, single-object dimensions *associative* but now calls them *non-associative,* and what used to be called non-associative dimensions before AutoCAD 2002 are now called *exploded* dimensions. For more information about how to determine which kind of dimension AutoCAD draws, see the "Controlling and editing dimension associativity" section, later in this chapter.

Finding your dimension tools

Both the Annotation panel on the Ribbon's Home tab and the Dimensions panel on the Annotate tab provide access to AutoCAD's most frequently used basic dimensioning commands. (If you're an AutoCAD Classic workspace user, you'll find them on the classic Dimension menu and Dimension toolbar.)

As much as I like the 2D Drafting & Annotation workspace and the Ribbon, one task where the classic interface just might be more efficient is in dimensioning. The classic Dimension toolbar provides access to more dimension tools than the Ribbon, and it does so while maintaining consistent one-click access to each command. With the Ribbon, you may find it takes a couple of clicks to get to the command you want, and some dimension commands aren't even there.

Here's how to turn on the Dimension toolbar in a Ribbon-based workspace (warm up your fingers — you're going to do some typing!):

1. **Type –TOOLBAR and press Enter.**

 Don't omit the hyphen; simply typing **TOOLBAR** brings up the Customize User Interface dialog box with no indication of what you should do next.

2. **At the Enter Toolbar Name prompt, type DIMENSION and press Enter.**

 AutoCAD prompts:

   ```
   Enter an option [Show/Hide/Left/Right/Top/Bottom/
         Float] <Show>:
   ```

3. **Type S and press Enter.**

 The classic Dimension toolbar appears either floating or docked on an edge of the drawing area.

All dimensioning commands have long command names (such as DIMARC, DIMLINEAR, and DIMRADIUS) and corresponding command aliases (such as DAR, DLI, and DRA, respectively — do you see a pattern?) that you can type at the command prompt. If you do lots of dimensioning and don't want to toggle the Dimension toolbar on and off repeatedly, memorize the abbreviated forms of the dimension commands that you use frequently. You can find a list of the long command names on the Contents tab in the AutoCAD online help system. Choose Command Reference⇨Commands⇨D Commands.

Doing Dimensions with Style (s)

Creating a usable dimension style that gives you the dimension look you want is the biggest challenge in using AutoCAD's dimensioning features. Each drawing contains its own dimension styles, so changes you make to a dimension style in one drawing affect only that drawing. However, after you get the dimension styles right in a drawing, you can use it as a template or starting point for later drawings.

A *dimension style* (or *dimstyle* for short) is a collection of drawing settings called *dimension variables,* which are a special class of the *system variables* that I describe in Chapter 23.

You can create dimension styles with the *annotative* property — the steps to creating both annotative and non-annotative dimension styles are spelled out in the following sections. Although it's possible to change individual non-annotative dimensions to annotative in the Quick Properties panel or the Properties palette, it's far more efficient to assign the annotative property to a dimension style so that all dimensions created in that style will be annotative.

Borrowing existing dimension styles

If you're lucky enough to work in an office where someone has set up dimension styles that are appropriate for your industry and project, you can skip the pain and strain of creating your own dimension styles. Bear in mind, however, that since annotative objects were introduced in AutoCAD 2008, dimension styles copied from pre-AutoCAD 2008 drawings are not going to be annotative. If the ready-made dimension style that you need lives in another drawing, you can use the DesignCenter palette to copy it into your drawing. For a refresher on using DesignCenter, see the sections "Using AutoCAD DesignCenter" and "Copying layers between drawings" in Chapter 6 — just substitute "*dimension styles.*"

Creating and managing dimension styles

If you *do* need to create your own dimension styles or you want to tweak ones that you copied from another drawing, use the Dimension Style Manager dialog box, as shown in Figure 14-4.

Figure 14-4:
Yet another manager, this one for dimension styles.

Every drawing comes with a default dimension style named Standard (for imperial [feet and inches] drawings) or ISO-25 (for metric drawings). Although you can use and modify the Standard or ISO-25 style, I suggest that you leave them as-is and create your own dimension style(s) for the settings that are appropriate to your work. This approach ensures that you can use the default style as a reference. More important, it avoids a potential naming conflict that can change the way your dimensions look if the current drawing gets inserted into another drawing. (Chapter 17 describes this potential conflict.)

New drawings created in AutoCAD 2010 or AutoCAD LT 2010 using either the imperial template (`acad.dwt` or `acadlt.dwt` in AutoCAD LT) or the metric template (`acadiso.dwt` or `acadltiso.dwt` in LT) contain *two* dimension styles. As noted previously, imperial drawings have a style named Standard, and metric drawings sport a style named ISO-25 — what's new is that both have a new style called *Annotative.* The Annotative style is a clone of Standard or ISO-25 with the single difference being the values of the overall scale factor (also known as the DIMSCALE system variable).

The following steps describe how to create your own dimension style(s):

1. **On the Ribbon's Home tab, click the label of the Annotation panel to open the panel slideout and then click the Dimension Style button.**

 The Dimension Style Manager dialog box appears.

2. **In the Styles list, select the existing dimension style whose settings you want to use as the starting point for the settings of your new style.**

 For example, select the default dimension style named Standard or ISO-25.

3. **Click the New button to create a new dimension style that's a copy of the existing style.**

 The Create New Dimension Style dialog box appears.

4. **Enter a New Style Name and select or deselect the Annotative check box. Click Continue.**

 Select the Annotative check box to create an annotative dimension style, or deselect it for a non-annotative style. Refer to Chapter 13 for more about annotative objects.

 The New Dimension Style dialog box appears. (This dialog box is virtually identical to the Modify Dimension Style dialog box shown in Figure 14-5 in the following section.)

5. **Modify dimension settings on any of the seven tabs in the New Dimension Style dialog box.**

 See the descriptions of these settings in the next section of this chapter.

6. **Click OK to close the New Dimension Style dialog box.**

 The Dimension Style Manager dialog box reappears.

7. **Click Close.**

 The Dimension Style Manager dialog box closes, and your new dimension style becomes the current dimension style that AutoCAD uses for future dimensions in this drawing.

8. **Draw some dimensions to test your new dimension style.**

Avoid changing existing dimension styles that you didn't create unless you know for sure what they're used for. When you change a dimension style setting, *all* dimensions that use that style change to reflect the revised setting. Thus, one small dimension variable setting change can affect a large number of existing dimensions! To play it safe, instead of modifying an existing dimension style, create a new style by copying the existing one and modifying the new one.

A further variation on the already convoluted dimension style picture is that you can create dimension *substyles* (also called *style families*) — variations of a main style that affect only a particular type of dimension, such as radial or angular. If you open the Dimension Style Manager dialog box and see names of dimension types indented beneath the main dimension style names, be aware that you're dealing with substyles.

Adjusting style settings

After you click New or Modify in the Dimension Style Manager dialog box, AutoCAD displays a tabbed New Dimension Style or Modify Dimension Style dialog box (the two dialog boxes are identical except for the title bar) with a mind-boggling — and potentially drawing-boggling if you're not careful — array of settings. Figure 14-5 shows the settings on the Lines tab, which I've modified from the AutoCAD defaults to conform to one office's drafting standards.

Figure 14-5:
Modifying extension line settings on the Lines tab.

Fortunately, the dimension preview that appears on all tabs — as well as on the main Dimension Style Manager dialog box — immediately shows the results of most setting changes. With the dimension preview and some trial-and-error changing of settings, you can usually home in on an acceptable group of settings. For more information, use the dialog box help feature: Just hover your mouse pointer over the setting that you want to know more about.

Before you start messing with dimension style settings, it's important to know what you want your dimensions to look like when they're plotted. If you're not sure how it's done in your industry, ask others in your office or profession, or look at a plotted drawing that someone in the know represents as being a good example.

The following sections introduce you to the more important tabs in the New/Modify Dimension Style dialog boxes and highlight useful settings. Note that whenever you specify a distance or length setting, you should enter the desired *plotted* size. For dimensions created with annotative styles, these are the actual paper (plotted) sizes. For dimensions with non-annotative styles, AutoCAD scales all these numbers by the overall scale factor that you enter on the Fit tab.

Following lines and arrows

The settings on the Lines tab and the Symbols and Arrows tab control the basic look and feel of all parts of your dimensions except text. Use these tabs to change the type and size of arrowheads or the display characteristics of the dimension and extension lines.

Tabbing to text

Use the Text tab to control how your dimension text looks — the text style and height to use (see Chapter 13) and where to place the text with respect to the dimension and extension lines. You may want to change the Text Style setting from the default Arial TrueType font to the more traditional Romans. shx font. The default Text Height is too large for most situations — set it to 1/8", 3 mm, or another height that makes sense. Figure 14-6 shows one company's standard text settings.

Figure 14-6: Whip your dimension text into shape.

If you're not opposed to defacing books, get out a bright red marker and put a circle around this warning (unless you borrowed the book from the library, of course). Here goes: You *must* define the text style that you specify for a dimension style with a height of 0 in the Text Style dialog box. (See Chapter 13 for more information about variable-height and fixed-height text styles.) If you specify a fixed-height text style for a dimension style, the text style's height will override the Text Height setting in the New/Modify Dimension Style dialog boxes. Use a zero-height style to avoid the problem — and bear in mind that using nonzero-height text styles in dimensions is one of the most common mistakes made by new AutoCAD users.

Industry or company standards usually dictate the size of dimension text. (For example, 1/8" or 3 mm is common in the architectural industry.) In any case, make sure you pick a height that's not too small to read on your smallest check plot.

The Text tab in the New/Modify Dimension Style dialog box sports a new option: View Direction. When set to Left-to-Right, horizontal dimension text reads right way up, and vertical text reads from the right side of the drawing. This is nearly always what you want, but occasionally you might need to rotate an entire drawing view by 90 degrees so it fits your drawing sheet (maybe you draw elevator shafts?), and at such times, some of your dimension text may read the wrong way around. You can create a whole AutoCAD 2010 dimension style for this, and you can also modify the view direction of individual dimensions in the Properties palette (see Chapter 6 for more on object properties).

Getting fit

The Fit tab includes a bunch of confusing options that control when and where AutoCAD shoves the dimension text if it doesn't quite fit between the dimension lines. The default settings leave AutoCAD in "maximum attempt at being helpful" mode — that is, AutoCAD moves the text, dimension lines, and arrows around automatically so that things don't overlap. If these guesses seem less than satisfactory to you, try the modified settings shown in Figure 14-7: Select the Over Dimension Line, Without Leader radio button under Text Placement and the Draw Dim Line between Ext Lines check box under Fine Tuning. (You can always move the text yourself by grip editing it, as I describe later in this chapter.)

Even at its most helpful, AutoCAD sometimes makes a bad first guess about how you want your dimension text and arrows arranged. If you're having problems getting the look you want, don't flip your wig — flip your arrows to the other side of the dimension lines by selecting the dimension, right-clicking, and choosing Flip Arrow from the menu.

Most important, the Fit tab includes the Annotative check box, as shown in Figure 14-7. Using annotative dimensions, as I recommend in this chapter, will make your dimensioning go a lot more smoothly!

Figure 14-7:
Keep Fit
and don't
forget the
Annotative
setting.

Annotative check box

Just as with text, as I explain in Chapter 13, you can choose between three different methods for dimensioning your drawings:

✔ **You can dimension in model space using annotative dimensions.**
Assign annotation scales to the dimensions, and they change size as you change Annotation scales on the status bar. I think this system has the most to offer both new and experienced users.

✔ **You can dimension in model space with non-annotative dimensions.** If your drawing includes areas of different scales, you can create multiple dimension styles, one for each scale. This is probably the least convenient — although the longest established — method, especially in a drawing with multiple scale views.

✔ **You can dimension in paper space using either annotative or non-annotative dimensions.** Select the Scale Dimensions to Layout radio button on the Dimension Style Manager's Fit tab and draw dimensions in a paper space layout.

I recommend that you get comfortable with annotative dimensioning in model space first. If you later want to try dimensioning in paper space, look in the AutoCAD online help system; choose User's Guide⇨Annotate Drawings⇨Dimensions and Tolerances⇨Use Dimension Styles⇨Set the Scale for Dimensions. As for old-style (that is, non-annotative) dimensioning, it's still part of the program, and many offices will probably keep doing it that way for a while to come.

The Use Overall Scale Of setting corresponds to the DIMSCALE system variable, and you'll hear AutoCAD drafters refer to it as such. When either Scale Dimensions to Layout (for paper space layout dimensioning) or Annotative (for rescalable model space dimensioning) is selected, DIMSCALE is automatically set to 0. For more information about additional dimension scale options, look up the *DIMSCALE* system variable in the AutoCAD online help system.

Using primary units

The Primary Units tab gives you highly detailed control over how AutoCAD formats the characters in the dimension text string. You usually want to set the Unit format and Precision and maybe specify a suffix for unitless numbers if it's not clear from your drawing what units you're using. You may also change the Zero Suppression settings, depending on whether you want dimension text to read 0.5000, .5000, or 0.5. ("Zero Suppression!" also makes a great rallying cry for organizing your fellow AutoCAD drafters.)

AutoCAD 2010 introduces an interesting tweak to dimension text in dimension *subunits*. If the main unit of measure on your drawing is meters, rather than have a bunch of smaller distances dimensioned as, say, 0.450, you could create a centimeter subunit so that any dimension less than 1 meter would be shown in centimeters. So in this example, such a dimension would read as 45 cm rather than 0.45. Now (personal opinion alert), that's pretty clever programming, but in every office I've ever worked in, there's a very strict drafting standard that says that all dimensions on a drawing must be in the same units — in other words, in a drawing with meters as the dimension unit, 0.45 would be correct, and 45 cm would be incorrect. Check your own office standards before you incorporate this new feature, which you can find on the Primary Units tab of the New/Modify Dimension Style dialog box.

Other style settings

If your work requires that you show dimensions in two different systems of measure (such as inches and millimeters), use the Alternate Units tab to turn on and control alternate units. If your work requires listing construction tolerances (for example, 3.5 +/-0.01), use the Tolerances tab to configure the tolerance format that you want. Unlike subunits (described in the preceding paragraph), alternate units display both dimensions at once; subunits replaces one unit (say, meters), with another unit (say, centimeters).

The New/Modify Dimension Style dialog box Tolerances tab settings are for adding manufacturing tolerances (for example, +0.2 or -0.1) to the text of ordinary dimensions — the kind of dimensions I cover in this chapter. AutoCAD also includes a separate TOLERANCE *command* that draws special symbols called *geometric tolerances*. If you need these symbols, you probably know it; if you've never heard of them, just ignore them. Look up *Geometric Tolerance dialog box* on the Index tab in the AutoCAD online help system for more information.

Drawing Dimensions

Whew! The hard part is getting it to look right. After you've copied or created a suitable dimension style, you're ready to dimension. Fortunately, adding dimensions to a drawing with existing dimension styles is usually pretty straightforward.

When you want to dimension something in AutoCAD, you can either select the object, such as a line or polyline segment, or select *points* on that object, such as the endpoints of the line or polyline segment. If you select an object, AutoCAD finds the most obvious points on it to dimension, such as the endpoints of a line. If you choose to select individual points instead, use object snaps (see Chapter 7). When you change the size of the object (for example, by stretching it), AutoCAD automatically moves the dimension's origin points and updates the dimension text to show the new length.

If you don't use object snaps or another AutoCAD precision technique to choose dimension points, the dimension text probably won't reflect the precise measurement of the object. This lack of precision can cause serious problems. When in doubt, OSNAP to it!

When you set up a new drawing and you want to use annotative dimensions, make sure the Annotative box is selected on the Fit tab in the New/Modify Dimension Style dialog box (refer to Figure 14-7). For a new drawing with non-annotative dimensions, change the Use Overall Scale Of setting on the Fit tab so that it matches the drawing scale factor. Before you draw any dimensions in a drawing that you didn't set up, check this setting to make sure it's correct.

The AutoCAD dimensioning commands prompt you with useful information at the command line or dynamic input prompts. Read the prompts during every step of the command, especially when you're trying a dimensioning command for the first time.

Lining up some linear dimensions

Linear dimensions are the most common type of dimensions, and horizontal and vertical are the most common of those. The following example demonstrates all the important techniques for creating horizontal and vertical linear dimensions, as well as aligned dimensions (which are similar to linear dimensions):

 1. **Use the LINE command to draw a *non-orthogonal* line — that is, a line segment that's not horizontal or vertical.**

 An angle of about 30 degrees works well for this example.

If you want to apply dimensioning to an object other than a line, use these steps as a general guideline, filling in the appropriate commands and data as applicable to your drawing.

2. **Set a layer that's appropriate for dimensions as current.**

 Just as with text, it's a good idea to have a dedicated layer for dimensions in every drawing. See Chapter 6 for details on setting a layer as current.

3. **Set a dimension style that's appropriate for your needs as current.**

 Choose an existing dimension style from the Dimension Style drop-down list on the Annotate panel slideout on the Ribbon's Home tab, or create a new style by using the procedure in the section "Creating and managing dimension styles," earlier in this chapter.

4. **On the Annotate tab's Dimensions panel, click the lower half of the big Dimension button and choose Linear, or type DLI and press Enter.**

 AutoCAD prompts you:

   ```
   Specify first extension line origin or <select
          object>:
   ```

5. **To specify the origin of the first extension line, snap to the lower-left endpoint of the line by using endpoint object snap.**

 If you don't have endpoint as one of your current running object snaps, specify a single endpoint object snap by holding down the Shift key, right-clicking, and choosing Endpoint from the menu. (See Chapter 7 for more about object snaps.)

 AutoCAD prompts you:

   ```
   Specify second extension line origin:
   ```

6. **To specify the origin of the second extension line, snap to the other endpoint of the line by using endpoint object snap again.**

 AutoCAD draws a *horizontal* dimension — the length of the displacement in the left-to-right direction — if you move the crosshairs above or below the line. It draws a *vertical* dimension — the length of the displacement in the up-and-down direction — if you move the crosshairs to the left or right of the line.

 AutoCAD prompts you:

   ```
   Specify dimension line location or
   [Mtext/Text/Angle/Horizontal/Vertical/Rotated]:
   ```

7. **Move the mouse to generate the type of dimension you want, horizontal or vertical, and then click wherever you want to place the dimension line.**

 AutoCAD draws the dimension.

 When you're specifying the dimension line location, you usually *don't* want to object snap to existing objects — you want the dimension line and text to sit in a relatively empty part of the drawing rather than bump into existing objects. If necessary, temporarily turn off running object snap (for example, click the OSNAP button on the status bar) in order to avoid snapping the dimension line to an existing object.

 If you want to be able to align subsequent dimension lines easily, turn on snap and set a suitable snap spacing — more easily done than said! — before you pick the point that determines the location of the dimension line. See Chapter 4 for more information about snap.

8. **Repeat Steps 4 through 7 to create another linear dimension of the opposite orientation (vertical or horizontal).**

9. **On the Annotate tab's Dimensions panel, click the lower half of the big Dimension tool button and choose Aligned from the flyout menu, or type DAL and press Enter.**

 The prompt includes an option to select an object instead of picking two points (you can use this technique with the Linear Dimension command, too):

   ```
   Specify first extension line origin or <select
          object>:
   ```

10. **Press Enter to choose the Select Object option.**

 AutoCAD prompts you:

    ```
    Select object to dimension:
    ```

11. **Select the line or other object that you want to dimension.**

 AutoCAD automatically finds the endpoints of the line and uses them as the extension line origin points (that is, the *defpoints*), as shown in Figure 14-8. (The broken extension line is created with the DIMBREAK command, which is described later in the chapter.)

 AutoCAD prompts you:

    ```
    Specify dimension line location or
    [Mtext/Text/Angle]:
    ```

12. **Click wherever you want to place the dimension line.**

 AutoCAD draws the dimension.

Figure 14-8: Drawing an aligned dimension by selecting an object.

Making dimensions annotative

If you've created your dimensions using an annotative style, you can set them up so that they change to the appropriate plotted (paper) size when you change the drawing's annotation scale. The process is the same for dimensions as it is for text (covered in Chapter 13) or for hatching (covered in Chapter 15). Refer to Chapter 13 for details.

Drawing other kinds of dimensions

After you have the hang of ordinary linear dimensions, you should be able to master other common dimension types quickly. Draw some lines, arcs, and circles and try the other dimension commands on the Home tab's Annotation panel or the fuller set on the Annotate tab's Dimensions panel. You'll find more dimension commands on the Dimension toolbar (see "Finding your dimension tools" earlier in the chapter for instructions on loading it).

If you want to be super-efficient, learn the three-letter aliases for the dimension commands you use the most.

To draw a series of side-by-side dimensions whose dimension lines are perfectly aligned, use the DIMCONTINUE command. To draw an overall dimension above one or more smaller dimensions, use DIMBASELINE. To draw a dimension that does not show the actual measured distance that's indicated by the dimension value, use DIMJOGLINE. See Figure 14-9 for examples of these and other dimension types.

Figure 14-9:
Examples of
additional
dimen-
sioning
commands.

The QDIM (Quick DIMension) command provides a quick way to draw lots of
dimensions that, when necessary, can automatically format themselves into
continued and baseline dimensions in one fell swoop. You can find QDIM on
the Annotate tab's Dimensions panel — but wouldn't you know it — QDIM is
not included in AutoCAD LT.

Editing Dimensions

After you draw dimensions, you can edit the position of the various parts
of each dimension and change the contents of the dimension text. AutoCAD
groups all the parts of a dimension into a single object.

Editing dimension geometry

The easiest way to change the location of dimension parts is to use grip edit-
ing, which I describe in Chapter 10. Just click a dimension, click one of its
grips, and maneuver away. You'll discover that certain grips control certain
directions of movement. In general, selecting a dimension displays grips at
the text, the ends of the dimension lines, and the defpoints. Experiment for a
few minutes to see how they work.

If you want to change the look of a component of a specific, individual dimension (for example, substitute a different arrowhead or suppress an extension line), use the Properties palette. (See Chapter 11 for more on the Properties palette.) All the dimension settings in the New/Modify Dimension Style dialog boxes (see "Adjusting style settings," earlier in this chapter) are available in the Properties palette when you select one or more dimensions.

More fine tweaking

In manual drafting, it's considered bad form to cross object lines (that is, real geometry) with dimension lines or extension lines. Dimension Break (DIMBREAK) prompts you to select a dimension and then an object to break it. In Figure 14-8, earlier in this chapter, the right extension line of the 3.50 horizontal dimension is broken by the lower extension line of the 1.50 vertical dimension.

The Dimension Space (DIMSPACE) command applies a specified separation between existing linear or angular dimensions. Spacing dimensions equally — other than by using the DIMBASELINE command as they're created — requires tedious manipulation with Snap and MOVE.

If you select one or more dimensions and right-click, the menu displays a number of useful options for overriding dimension settings or assigning a different style.

When you change a setting in the Properties palette, you're *overriding* the default style setting for that dimension. If you need to make the same change to a bunch of dimensions, it's usually better to create a new dimension style and assign that style to them. You can use the Properties palette or the right-click menu to change the dimension style that's assigned to one or more dimensions.

You can use the Properties palette to turn on AutoCAD's background mask feature, described in Chapter 13, for the text of individual dimensions: Select the dimensions, display the Text area in the Properties palette, and find the Fill Color item. Click in the list box, scroll down, and select Background to use the drawing background color (which usually gives the best results). To ensure that dimension text lies on top of other objects, use the DRAWORDER or TEXTTOFRONT command — see Chapter 13 for more information.

The AutoCAD EXPLODE command on the Home tab's Modify panel will blow a dimension to smithereens — or at least into a bunch of line and multiline text objects. Don't do it! Exploding a dimension makes it much harder to edit cleanly and eliminates AutoCAD's ability to update the dimension text measurement automatically.

Editing dimension text

In most cases, you shouldn't have to edit dimension text. Assuming that you draw your geometry accurately and pick the dimension points precisely, AutoCAD displays the right measurement. If you change the size of the associated object, AutoCAD updates the dimension and its measurement. However, you may occasionally want to *override* the dimension text (that is, replace it with a different measurement) or *add* a prefix or a suffix to the true measurement.

AutoCAD creates dimension text as a multiline text (Mtext) object, so dimension text has the same editing options as ordinary text. Unfortunately, the right-click menu for dimension objects doesn't include a Text Edit option. You can use the Text Override field in the Properties palette or type **ED** (the keyboard shortcut for the DDEDIT command) to edit dimension text in the In-Place Text Editor.

AutoCAD displays the true dimension length as text in the actual dimension (and keeps the text up to date if you change the size or location of the object). You can override the true length by typing a specific length or other text string. You can preserve the true length but add a prefix or suffix by inserting <> (that is, the left and right angled bracket characters) as a placeholder for the dimension value. For example, if you enter **<> Max.**, and the actual distance is 12.00, AutoCAD displays 12.00 Max. for the dimension text. If you later stretch the object so that the actual distance changes to 14.50, AutoCAD automatically changes the dimension text to read 14.50 Max. Now you can appreciate the importance of drawing and editing geometry precisely!

Avoid the temptation to override the default dimension text by replacing the angled brackets with a numeric value. Doing so eliminates AutoCAD's ability to keep dimension measurements current, but even worse, you get no visual cue that the default distance has been overridden (unless you edit the dimension text). If you're overriding dimension text a lot, it's probably a sign that the creator of the drawing didn't pay enough attention to using precision techniques when drawing and editing. I'm not going to point any fingers, but you probably know whom to talk to.

Controlling and editing dimension associativity

When you add dimensions by selecting objects or picking points on the objects by using object snap modes, AutoCAD normally creates associative dimensions, which are connected to the objects and move with them. This is the case in new drawings that were originally created in any version of AutoCAD starting with 2002.

If you have to work on drawings created or last edited in versions older than AutoCAD 2002, you must set the DIMASSOC system variable to 2 before AutoCAD 2010 will create associative dimensions. An easy way to make this change for the current drawing is to open the Options dialog box (click the Application button and choose Options from the bottom of the Application Menu), click the User Preferences tab, and turn on the Make New Dimensions Associative setting. Be aware that this setting affects only new dimensions that you draw from now on — to make existing non-associative dimensions associative, use the DIMREASSOCIATE command described in the following list. Look up *DIMASSOC system variable* in the AutoCAD online help system for more information.

You aren't likely to need any of these three commands very often, but if you do, look up the command name in the online help system:

- **DIMREASSOCIATE:** If you have dimensions that aren't currently associative (probably because they were created in older versions of AutoCAD) or are associated with the wrong objects, you can use the DIMREASSOCIATE command to associate them with points on the objects of your choice. DIMREASSOCIATE can be found on the Annotate tab's Dimensions panel slideout, or you can just type **DRE** and press Enter.

- **DIMDISASSOCIATE:** You can use the DIMDISASSOCIATE (DDA) command to sever the connection between a dimension and its associated object.

- **DIMREGEN:** In a few special circumstances, AutoCAD doesn't automatically update geometry-driven associative dimensions. (Maybe Autodesk should call them "usually fully awake but occasionally asleep at the wheel associative dimensions.") In those cases, the DIMREGEN (no command alias) command will fix things.

Chapter 15

Down the Hatch

*I*f you were hoping to hatch a plot (or plot a hatch), see Chapter 16 instead. If you want to hatch an egg, look for *Raising Chickens For Dummies.* If you need to fill in closed areas of your drawings with special patterns of lines or solid fills (known as *hatching*), this is your chapter.

Drafters often use hatching to represent the type of material that makes up an object, such as insulation, metal, concrete, and so on. In other cases, hatching helps emphasize or clarify the extent of a particular element in the drawing — for example, showing the location of walls in a building plan or highlighting a swampy area on a map so you know where to avoid building a road. Figure 15-1 shows an example of hatching in a structural detail.

As I mention in Chapter 13, hatching is another component of AutoCAD's annotative objects. Hatch patterns have a scale factor (as I explain in the "Getting it right: Hatch angle and scale" section, later in this chapter) and can be created so that the hatch scale updates as the annotation scale changes.

An AutoCAD *hatch* is a separate object that fills a space, has an appearance dictated by the hatch pattern assigned to it, and is associated with the objects that bound the space, such as lines, polylines, or arcs. If you move or stretch the boundaries, AutoCAD normally updates the hatching to fill the resized area.

Figure 15-1:
A big batch
o' hatch.

Don't go overboard with hatching. The purpose of hatching is to clarify, not overwhelm, the other geometry in the drawing. If your plots look like a patchwork quilt of hatch patterns, it's time to simplify.

Hatching is another kind of annotation of your geometry, similar in purpose to text and dimensions. As I describe at the beginning of Chapter 13, you'll usually be more efficient if you save annotation for later in the drafting process. Draw as much geometry as possible first and *then* hatch the parts that require it. In other words, batch your hatch.

Hatch . . . Hatch . . . Hatchoo

This section outlines the steps you use to add hatching to a drawing with the Hatch and Gradient dialog box, as shown in Figure 15-2. (AutoCAD LT doesn't do gradients, so the dialog box is simply labeled Hatch.) You can use this information to get started quickly with hatching. When you need more information about any part of the process, jump to the relevant sections of "Pushing the Boundary (of) Hatch," later in this chapter.

By default, the right third of the Hatch and Gradient dialog box is hidden; to see the additional hatch options at the right side of the dialog box, as shown in Figure 15-2, click the More Options arrow beside the Help button.

Figure 15-2:
The Hatch
tab of the
expanded
Hatch and
Gradient
dialog box.

The following steps show you how to hatch an enclosed area by using the "pick points" method of selecting the hatch area:

1. **Open a drawing containing geometry that forms fully closed boundaries, or draw some boundaries by using the drawing commands described in Chapters 8 and 9.**

 The areas you want to hatch should be completely enclosed. The CIRCLE, POLYGON, and RECTANG commands, and the LINE and PLINE commands with the Close option, make great hatch boundaries (see Chapters 8 and 9 for details).

2. **Set an appropriate layer current, as described in Chapter 6.**

 It's usually best to put hatching on its own layer.

3. **Start the HATCH command by typing H and pressing Enter. Alternatively, click the Hatch button on the Draw panel of the Ribbon's Home tab.**

 The Hatch and Gradient dialog box (or the Hatch dialog box in AutoCAD LT) appears.

4. **Choose Predefined, User Defined, or Custom from the Type drop-down list.**

 Predefined works best for most purposes. See the "Hatch from scratch" section later in this chapter for details.

5. **If you chose Predefined or Custom in the previous step, select any predefined or custom hatch pattern from the Pattern drop-down list or the Pattern button just to the right of it.**

 If you chose User Defined, you don't need to choose a pattern.

6. **Specify an Angle and Scale for the hatch pattern. (Or, if you chose User Defined in Step 4, specify Angle and Spacing.)**

 See the section, "Getting it right: Hatch angle and scale," later in this chapter, for more information.

7. **Select hatch options as required.**

 For this example, leave the Annotative check box deselected. Try it the old-fashioned way first and then have a look at the "Hatching for the 21st century" section later in the chapter.

 Don't confuse Annotative with Associative, even though both are poly-syllabic words that start with *A* and are right next to one another in the dialog box. *Annotative* hatch objects rescale themselves when you change the annotation scale in model space or in a viewport. *Associative* hatch objects (enabled by default) will update to the new area when you change the hatch boundary.

 By default, when you select a number of closed areas and then click OK, the hatched areas will be created as a single object; select the Create Separate Hatches check box if you want to be able to modify each hatched area individually. Set the Draw Order drop-down list to specify whether the hatch objects are in front of or behind the hatch boundary or other drawing objects.

8. **Click the Add: Pick Points button.**

 The Hatch and Gradient dialog box (temporarily) disappears, and your drawing reappears with the following prompt at the command line:

   ```
   Pick internal point or [Select objects/remove
           Boundaries]:
   ```

9. **Pick a point inside the boundary of the area you want to hatch.**

 AutoCAD analyzes the drawing and decides which boundaries to use. In a complex drawing, this analysis can take several seconds. AutoCAD highlights the boundary that it finds.

 If AutoCAD highlights the wrong boundary, right-click, choose Clear All from the menu, and try again.

10. **Right-click anywhere in the drawing area and choose Enter from the menu to indicate that you're finished selecting points.**

 The Hatch and Gradient dialog box reappears.

11. **Click the Preview button to preview the hatch.**

 The Hatch and Gradient dialog box (temporarily) disappears again, and AutoCAD shows you what the hatch will look like:

    ```
    Pick or press Esc to return to dialog or <Right-click
            to accept hatch>:
    ```

12. **Click anywhere in the drawing area to return to the Hatch and Gradient dialog box.**

13. **Adjust any settings and preview again until you're satisfied with the hatch.**

14. **Click OK.**

 AutoCAD hatches the area inside the boundary.

Occasionally, AutoCAD gets confused and doesn't resize a hatch after you resize the boundary. If that happens, erase and then re-create the hatch in the resized area.

AutoCAD is still reluctant to hatch supposedly closed areas where even a speck of daylight gets through, but AutoCAD 2010 at least shows you where you need to fix a leaky boundary. The Hatch routine displays one or more red circles at gaps in the not-quite-enclosed area you want to hatch. Even it if won't fix the gaps, it does show you where *you* should fix them.

Pushing the Boundary (of) Hatch

The remainder of this chapter shows you how to refine the techniques presented in the preceding section. I describe how to copy existing hatching, take advantage of the various options in the Hatch and Gradient dialog box (including annotative hatches), and choose more complicated hatching boundaries.

Catch a hatch: Copying hatch properties

One slick way to hatch is by using the Inherit Properties button in the Hatch and Gradient dialog box to copy hatch properties from an existing hatch object. Think of it as point-and-shoot hatching. If someone — such as you — added some hatching in the past that's just like what you want to use now, click the Inherit Properties button and pick the existing hatching.

Inherit Properties updates the hatch pattern settings in the Hatch and Gradient dialog box to make them the same as the existing hatch pattern object that you picked. You can use the cloned hatch pattern specifications as they are or modify them by making changes in the Hatch and Gradient dialog box.

Consistency is a good thing in drafting, especially in computer-aided drafting, in which some or all your drawing may be used for a long time. Thus, it's good to use the same hatch patterns, scales, and angles for the same purposes in all your drawings. Find out whether your project, office, company, or profession has hatching standards that apply to your work.

Hatch from scratch

You can use predefined, user-defined, or custom hatch patterns. Most of the time, you'll choose either predefined or user-defined hatch patterns, unless some generous soul gives you a custom pattern.

Pick a pattern, any pattern: Predefined hatch patterns

To use AutoCAD's *predefined* hatch patterns, select Predefined from the Type drop-down list at the top of the Hatch tab in the Hatch and Gradient dialog box. This selection sets the stage for choosing the hatch pattern.

You specify a predefined hatch pattern in one of two ways:

✔ **Pattern drop-down list:** If you know the name of the hatch pattern, select it from the Pattern drop-down list. The list is alphabetical, except that SOLID (that is, a solid fill) is at the very beginning.

✔ **Pattern button:** If you don't know the pattern's name or if you prefer the visual approach, click the Pattern button (the tiny button with the ellipsis [three dots] to the right of the Pattern drop-down list and pattern name) to display the Hatch Pattern Palette with pattern previews and names.

AutoCAD has 72 predefined hatch patterns from which to choose. The list includes ANSI (American National Standards Institute) and ISO (International Organization for Standardization) standard hatch patterns. Figure 15-3 shows the some of the Other Predefined hatch patterns, which cover everything from Earth to Escher to Stars.

Hatch patterns whose names begin with *AR-* are intended for architectural and related industries and use different scaling factors than the non-AR patterns.

After you've selected a pattern, specify angle and scale, as I describe in the section, "Getting it right: Hatch angle and scale," later in this chapter.

Although you may not guess it, AutoCAD treats filling an area with a solid color as a type of hatching. Simply choose SOLID from the top of the Pattern drop-down list.

Like any other object, a solid hatch takes on the current object color — or the current layer's color if you leave color set to ByLayer. Therefore, check whether the current object layer and color are set appropriately before you use the Solid hatching option (see Chapter 6 for details).

Figure 15-3:
Plenty
of hatch
patterns.

It's up to you: User-defined hatches

A *user-defined* hatch pattern makes a hatch pattern out of parallel lines. Use this option to create a simple pattern and specify the space between the lines in paper units for annotative hatches or drawing units for non-annotative hatches. For example, you can hatch a wall in a building plan with an annotative user-defined pattern and specify that the hatch lines be 1/8" apart.

After you choose User Defined from the Type drop-down list in the Hatch and Gradient dialog box, you specify the angle and spacing of the lines. You can select the Double check box to achieve a *crosshatching effect* (two perpendicular sets of hatching lines). User-defined patterns require that you enter an angle and spacing, not angle and scale.

Getting it right: Hatch angle and scale

Predefined and custom hatch patterns require that you enter the angle and scale for AutoCAD to generate the hatching. Usually, you won't have any trouble deciding on an appropriate angle, but a suitable scale can be tricky. Because (with a few exceptions) AutoCAD's hatch patterns don't represent real objects, you don't have to be that precise about scaling them — you can just make them look good. But where do you start?

The answer to that question depends on whether you're using AutoCAD annotative hatching or the old-style, non-annotative hatching. If you're an up-to-the-minute CAD gal or guy, check out the next section, "Hatching for the 21st century." For non-annotative hatching, you need to calculate the

hatch scale based on the drawing scale factor, as described in Chapter 4. As a general rule, hatch patterns look best at somewhere between one-half and three-quarters of the drawing scale factor. For example, the EARTH pattern (in the Other Predefined tab of the Hatch Pattern Palette, as shown in Figure 15-3 and as used in an actual drawing back in Figure 15-1) looks pretty good in a full-scale (1 = 1) drawing with a hatch scale of 0.75. If you're adding EARTH pattern hatching to a 1" = 1'–0" detail (drawing scale factor equals 12), try using a hatch scale of 0.75×12, or 9.0. Using a consistent multiplier like 0.5 or 0.75 applied to the drawing scale factor ensures that hatching looks consistent (that the spaces between the lines are the same) at all scales when you plot.

Autodesk created the hatch patterns whose names begin with *AR-* particularly for use in architectural drawings, and unlike the non-AR patterns, they *do* represent real objects. The AR-patterns were designed with a final hatch scale of 1.0 in mind, but in some cases, you'll have to adjust up or down in order to achieve a suitable scale.

Hatching for the 21st century

With annotative hatching, you start with the paper scale (because that's where all your fancy CAD geometry is going to end up) of 1:1. Once again, most patterns look better at between half and three-quarters of the paper scale, so try setting the hatch scale to, say, 0.75. The following steps explain how to create annotative hatching:

1. **Follow Steps 1 to 6 in the "Hatch . . . Hatch . . . Hatchoo" section earlier in the chapter.**

 In those steps, you open the Hatch and Gradient (just plain Hatch in AutoCAD LT) dialog box and choose a pattern, angle, and scale.

2. **In the Options area of the dialog box, select the Annotative check box.**

 This time, you're going to create annotative hatch objects.

3. **Continue following Steps 8 to 11 in the "Hatch . . . Hatch . . . Hatchoo" section.**

 The Hatch and Gradient dialog box appears and disappears as you adjust settings and preview the pattern. When you're in preview mode, AutoCAD prompts:

   ```
   Pick or press Esc to return to dialog or <Right-click
              to accept hatch>:
   ```

4. **When your hatch looks good, right-click to place the hatch and end the command.**

 AutoCAD hatches the area inside the boundary. If you've correctly created an annotative hatch object, you see the annotative object symbol (the end of a triangular drawing scale) beside the crosshairs if you move your crosshairs over the hatch.

5. **Select the hatch object; then right-click and choose Annotative Object Scale⇨Add/Delete Scales to assign annotative scales to the hatch object.**

 The Annotation Object Scale dialog box appears and shows a list of all annotative scales assigned to the selected object. In the case of a new hatch object, the only scale listed will be the current annotation scale; if you're doing this in a new drawing that will probably be 1:1, the default value.

6. **In the Annotation Object Scale dialog box, click Add.**

 The Add Scales to Object dialog box appears, displaying a list of all drawing scale values stored in the drawing.

7. **Select the desired scales from the list, holding down the Ctrl key to select more than one, and then click OK.**

 The Annotation Object Scale dialog box reappears, with the scales you added displayed in the list box.

 Don't go overboard and select every scale in the list — select only the scales you're likely to use.

8. **Click OK.**

 After you've assigned annotative scales to a hatch (or any annotative) object, you see a pair of triangular annotative object symbols. Don't worry — although you *are* seeing double, you've done it right!

9. **Open the Annotation Scale drop-down list on the application or drawing status bar and select one of the scales you added to the object.**

 The annotative hatch objects will change their spacing as you change the annotation scale. If you select a scale from the list that you didn't assign to the object in Step 7, the hatch reverts to the default 1:1 scale.

Figure 15-4 shows two versions of the same drawing, dressed up with annotative and non-annotative hatch patterns. As the annotation scales displayed on the drawing status bars show, the annotative hatches change their scale while the non-annotative hatches remain unchanged. Before annotative hatching first appeared in AutoCAD 2008, the only way to get the effect in these two views was to create two separate layers, one for each hatch scale, and hatch the object twice.

Figure 15-4:
Hatches
annotative
(and not).

Do fence me in: Defining hatch boundaries

After you specify the hatch pattern, angle, and scale you want to use, you define the boundary (or boundaries) into which you want to pour that hatch pattern in one of two ways:

✔ Picking points within the area(s) you want hatched

✔ Selecting objects that surround those areas

The actual operation involved in using either of these options is confusing to most people. You'll probably need a little practice before you get used to it.

The idea behind either definition option is simple when applied to simple areas — that is, closed areas with no additional objects inside them. To define the hatch boundary for a simple area, do one of these two things:

✔ Click the Add: Pick Points button in the Hatch and Gradient dialog box and then click a point *inside* the boundary.

✔ Click the Add: Select Objects button and select one or more objects that form a fully closed boundary.

This simple hatching gets more complicated if you have one closed object inside another, as in Figure 15-5. The AutoCAD hatch preview and a bit of experimentation will clarify all these potentially puzzling permutations.

As I warn earlier in this chapter, boundaries should be *completely* closed before AutoCAD will hatch them. That's one of the reasons you should employ the precision techniques from this book whenever you draw or edit objects. If the lines surrounding your boundary don't either meet *exactly* or cross, AutoCAD scolds you with a `Valid boundary not found` error message.

The `Valid boundary not found` error message means that you need to repair lines or other objects so they're a fully closed boundary. Sometimes you can use the FILLET command with a zero fillet radius to force two lines to meet exactly. Another possibility is to use grip editing to align one endpoint precisely with another. Chapter 10 discusses these two editing techniques.

Have palette, will hatch

With tool palettes, described in Chapter 2, you can create click-and-drag hatch palettes. With a hatch palette, you click a tool (a swatch) and drag into an enclosed boundary to hatch the area. If your hatching needs are simple, you can create a tool palette for the patterns and scales you often use. See *hatches, adding to tool palettes* in AutoCAD's online help for more information.

Figure 15-5: Get picky about your hatching. (X indicates a pick point.)

Editing Hatch Objects

Editing an existing hatch pattern is simple after you're familiar with the Hatch and Gradient dialog box. Follow these steps:

1. **Double-click the hatch object.**

 AutoCAD opens the Hatch Edit dialog box and displays the hatch object's current settings.

2. **Make any desired changes, use the Preview button to look them over, and click OK to keep the changes.**

Alternatively, you can use the Properties palette (described in Chapter 6) to make most existing hatch pattern changes. The Properties palette is especially good for changing several hatches at once. And in AutoCAD 2010, you can use the Quick Properties panel to do the same thing even more efficiently.

To make one hatch look like another, use the Match Properties button on Clipboard panel of the Ribbon's Home tab.

The multitude of options in the Hatch and Gradient and Hatch Edit dialog boxes let you tweak your hatch patterns in all sorts of useful and semi-useful ways. You can easily set a new origin point for hatch objects, you can hatch areas that are not fully visible on-screen, and you can optionally hatch multiple boundaries at one go and have the hatches treated as individual objects.

You can find the area of any hatch object by simply selecting the hatch object and then opening the Properties palette. The area is listed in the Geometry section, near the bottom of the palette.

Chapter 16

The Plot Thickens

Despite the infinitesimally small number of offices without a computer (or two) on every desk, many people still want or need to work with either easily readable electronic drawings (can you spell PDF?) or actual, dead-tree paper drawings. You may need to give hard-copy prints or PDFs to your less savvy colleagues who don't have AutoCAD. You may want to make some quick paper prints to pore over during your bus ride home. You may even find that checking drawings the old-fashioned way — with a hard-copy print and a red pencil — turns up errors that managed to remain hidden on the computer screen.

Whatever the reason, you'll want to print drawings at some point — probably sooner rather than later. Depending on where you are in a project, plotting is the pop quiz, mid-term, or final exam of your drawing-making semester. This chapter helps you ace the test.

You Say Printing, I Say Plotting

Plotting originally meant creating hard-copy output on a device that was capable of printing on larger sheets, such as D size or E size (or A1 or A0 for the metrically inclined), that measure several feet (or a meter or more) on a side.

(See Chapter 4 for information about drafting paper sizes.) These plotters often used pens to draw, robot-fashion, on large sheets of vellum or drafting film. The sheets could then be run through *diazo blueline machines* — copying machines that create blueline prints — in order to create less-expensive copies. *Printing* meant creating hard-copy output on ordinary printers that used ordinary-sized paper, such as A size (letter size, 8-1/2 x 11 inches) or B size (tabloid or ledger size, 11 x 17 inches) — that's A4 or A3 for you metric folk.

Nowadays, AutoCAD and most CAD users make no distinction between plotting and printing. AutoCAD veterans usually say "plotting," so if you want to be cool, you can do so, too.

Whatever you call it, plotting an AutoCAD drawing is considerably more complicated than printing a word processing document or a spreadsheet. CAD has a larger range of different plotters and printers, drawing types, and output procedures than other computer applications. AutoCAD tries to help you tame the vast jungle of plotting permutations, but you'll probably find that you have to take some time to get the lay of the land and clear a path to your desired hard-copy output.

Get with the system

One of the complications you face in your attempts to create a hard copy is that AutoCAD has two distinct ways of communicating with your plotters and printers. Operating systems, and the programs that run on them, use a special piece of software — a *printer driver* — to format data for printing and then send it to the printer or plotter. When you configure Windows to recognize a new printer connected to your computer or your network, you're actually installing the printer's driver. ("Bring the Rolls around front, James. And bring me a gin and tonic and a D-size plot while you're at it.") AutoCAD, like other Windows programs, works with the printers you've configured in Windows. AutoCAD calls these *system printers* because they're part of the Windows operating system.

But AutoCAD, unlike other Windows programs, can't leave well enough alone. Some output devices, especially some larger plotters, aren't controlled very efficiently by Windows system printer drivers. For that reason, AutoCAD comes with specialized *non-system drivers* (that is, drivers that are not installed as part of the Windows system) for plotters from companies such as Hewlett-Packard, Xerox, and Océ. These drivers ignore the tidy rules for communicating with Windows printers in order to get things done a bit more quickly and flexibly.

Using already-configured Windows system printer drivers usually is easiest, and they work well with many devices — especially devices such as laser and inkjet printers that print on smaller paper. However, if you have a large format plotter, you *may* be able to get faster plotting, better plot quality, or more plot features by installing a non-system driver. To find out more, choose Contents⇨Driver and Peripheral Guide⇨Use Plotters and Printers in the AutoCAD online help system.

Configure it out

For now, you should simply make sure that AutoCAD recognizes the devices that you want to use for plotting. The following steps show you how:

1. **Launch AutoCAD and open an existing drawing or start a new, blank drawing.**

2. **Choose Options on the Application Menu, or type** OP **and press Enter, to open the Options dialog box; then click the Plot and Publish tab.**

3. **Click the drop-down arrow to view the list just below the Use as Default Output Device option, as shown in Figure 16-1.**

 The list includes two kinds of device configurations, designated by two tiny, difficult-to-distinguish icons to the left of the device names:

 • A little printer icon with a sheet of white paper coming out the top indicates a Windows system printer configuration.

 • A little plotter-with-legs icon with a piece of paper coming out the front indicates a non-system (that is, AutoCAD-specific) configuration.

 The non-system configuration names always end in .pc3 because they're stored in special AutoCAD Plotter Configuration version 3 files. So, if you can't tell the difference between the icons, look for the .pc3 at the end of the name.

4. **Verify that the list includes the printers and plotters that you want to have available in AutoCAD.**

 If not, how you add one depends on your operating system. In Windows XP, choose Start⇨Printers and Faxes and click the Add a Printer link under Printer Tasks on the left side of the window. In Windows Vista, choose Start⇨Control Panel⇨Hardware and Sound⇨Printers⇨Add a Printer and then click Add a Local Printer. If your printer isn't in the default Windows list, cancel the wizard and hunt down a driver disk that came with your printer, or better yet, download the current driver from the printer manufacturer's Web site.

System printers List of devices

Figure 16-1:
System and
non-system
printer con-
figurations.

Non-system printers

5. **Choose the output device that you want to make the default for new drawings.**

6. **Click OK to close the dialog box and retain any changes that you made in the previous step.**

You use the AutoCAD Plotter Manager's Add-a-Plotter Wizard to create non-system driver configurations. (Choose Plotter Manager on the Plot panel of the Ribbon's Output tab to display an Explorer window containing a shortcut to the wizard.) This wizard is similar to the Windows Add Printer Wizard; if you can handle adding an ordinary printer in Windows, you can probably handle adding a non-system plotter configuration to AutoCAD. When you complete the wizard steps, AutoCAD saves the information in a *PC3* (Plotter Configuration version 3) file. If you add an HP Designjet printer or certain Océ wide format printers, you will be advised by the Add-a-Plotter Wizard to exit and instead install the device as a Windows system printer (see the online help for more information). Many people find that the standard drivers work fine, but as I mention later in this chapter, custom drivers may include additional paper sizes as well as other handy settings.

A Simple Plot

Okay, so you believe me. You know that you're not going to master AutoCAD plotting in five minutes. That doesn't change the fact that your boss, employee, wife, husband, construction foreman, or 11-year-old daughter wants a quick check plot of your drawing.

Plotting success in 16 steps

Here's the quick, cut-to-the-chase procedure for plotting a simple drawing — a mere 16 steps! This procedure assumes that you plot in model space — that is, that clicking the Model button on the status bar shows you the drawing in a way that you want to plot. (I cover plotting paper space layout tabs in the section "Plotting the Layout of the Land," later in this chapter.) This procedure doesn't deal with controlling plotted lineweights — see the "Plotting Lineweights and Colors" section later in this chapter for those details. It should, however, result in a piece of paper that bears some resemblance to what AutoCAD displays on your computer monitor.

Follow these steps to make a simple, not-to-scale, monochrome (black-and-white) plot of a drawing:

1. **Open the drawing in AutoCAD.**

2. **Click Model (not the MODEL/PAPER button) on the status bar to ensure that you're plotting the model space contents. If you have the model and layout tabs displayed, rather than the status bar buttons, click the Model tab.**

 I explain model space and paper space in Chapters 4 and 5, and how to plot paper space layouts later in this chapter.

3. **Zoom to the drawing's current extents; click the Zoom button on the status bar and then right-click and choose Extents. Or, type Z, press Enter, and then type E and press Enter again.**

 The extents of a drawing consist of a rectangular area just large enough to include all the objects in the drawing.

4. **To display the Plot dialog box, click the Plot button on the Quick Access toolbar.**

 The Plot dialog box appears, as shown in Figure 16-2.

5. **In the Printer/Plotter area, select a device from the Name drop-down list.**

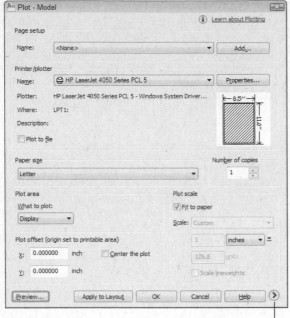

Figure 16-2:
The Plot
dialog box.

More Options button

6. **In the Paper Size area, select a paper size that's loaded in your printer or plotter.**

 Make sure that the paper size is large enough to fit the drawing at the scale at which you want to plot it. For example, if you want to plot a D-size drawing, but you have only a B-size printer, you're out of luck — unless you resort to multiple pieces of paper and lots of tape.

7. **In the Plot Area area (sponsored by the Department of Redundancy Department), select Extents from the What to Plot drop-down list.**

 If you set your drawing limits as I suggest in Chapter 4, you can select Limits instead to plot the drawing area that you defined. The Window option — that is, plot a window whose corners you pick — is useful when you want to plot just a portion of your drawing.

8. **In the Plot Offset (Origin Set to Printable Area) area, select the Center the Plot check box.**

 Alternatively, you can specify offsets of zero or other amounts in order to position the plot at a specific location on the paper.

9. **In the Plot Scale area, either select the Fit to Paper check box or deselect Fit to Paper and specify a scale (by choosing from the drop-down list or typing into the two text boxes).**

For most real plotting, you'll plot to a specific scale, but feel free to select the Fit to Paper check box for now. If you do want to plot to a specific scale, see the "Instead of fit, scale it" section later in this chapter for guidance.

10. **Click the More Options button (at the bottom-right corner of the dialog box, next to the Help button).**

 The Plot dialog box reveals additional settings, as shown in Figure 16-3.

Figure 16-3:
The
expanded
Plot dialog
box.

11. **In the Plot Style Table (Pen Assignments) area, choose monochrome. ctb or monochrome.stb from the drop-down list.**

 AutoCAD may ask you if you want to "Assign this plot style table to all layouts?" Answer Yes to make `monochrome.ctb` (or `monochrome.stb`) the default plot style table for the paper space layout tabs as well as the Model tab, or answer No to make the change apply only to the current tab.

 The "Plotting with style" section, later in this chapter, describes plot style tables.

12. **In the Plot Options area, make sure that the Plot with Plot Styles check box is selected and that the Save Changes to Layout check box is deselected, as shown in Figure 16-3.**

 Leaving the Save Changes to Layout check box deselected tells AutoCAD to use any plot settings changes that you make only for this plot — AutoCAD will revert to the original plot settings the next time you plot the drawing.

TIP

After you become confident with plotting, you may want to select this check box so that AutoCAD *does* save your plotting settings changes as the default. Alternatively, click the Apply to Layout button to make the current plot settings the default for future plotting of this tab (that is, the Model tab) in this drawing.

13. **In the Drawing Orientation area, choose Portrait or Landscape.**

 The icon (the letter *A* on a sheet) in the lower-right corner may help you decide on the right orientation. If not, the full preview in the next step will tell you for sure.

14. **Click the Preview button and check that the drawing displays on the paper at the correct orientation and size, as shown in Figure 16-4; then right-click and choose Exit to return to the Plot dialog box.**

15. **If you found any problems in the preview, adjust the plot settings (for example, Plot Area, Plot Scale, or Drawing Orientation) and repeat the preview until the plot looks right.**

16. **Click OK to create the plot.**

 When AutoCAD finishes generating and sending the plot, it displays a Plot and Publish Job Complete balloon notification from the status bar. If you decide that you don't want to see these notifications, right-click the Plot/Publish Details Report Available icon near the right end of the status bar and deselect Enable Balloon Notification.

EAST ELEVATION

Figure 16-4:
A preview of coming plot-tractions.

There — 16 steps, as promised. If for some reason your plot didn't work, well, I warned you that AutoCAD plotting was complicated and temperamental! Read the rest of this chapter for all the details about the numerous other plotting options that can cause plotting to go awry. If you're in a big hurry, turn directly to the troubleshooting section, "Troubles with Plotting," at the end of this chapter.

Preview one, two

One of the keys to efficient plotting is liberal use of AutoCAD's preview feature. (To maintain political balance, I recommend conservative use of some other AutoCAD options elsewhere in the book.)

The postage stamp–sized partial preview in the middle of the Plot dialog box is a quick reality check to make sure your plot fits on the paper and is turned in the right direction. If the plot area at the current scale is too large for the paper, AutoCAD displays thick red warning lines along the side(s) of the sheet where the drawing will be truncated.

Click the Preview button to see a full preview in a separate window. You see exactly how your drawing lays out on the paper and how the various lineweights, colors, and other object plot properties will appear. You can zoom and pan around the preview by using the right-click menu. (Any zooming or panning that you do won't affect what area of the drawing gets plotted — zooming and panning is just a way to get a better look at different areas of the plot preview.)

Instead of fit, scale it

In most real plotting situations, you want to plot to a specific scale rather than let AutoCAD choose an oddball scale that just happens to maximize the drawing on the paper. And if you're going to plot the Model tab of a drawing to scale, you need to know its drawing scale factor. Chapter 4 describes setup concepts, and Chapter 13 provides some tips for determining the scale factor of a drawing that someone else created.

If your drawing was created at a standard scale, such as 1:50 or 1/4"=1'-0", then you simply choose the scale from the handy Scale drop-down list in the Plot dialog box. If your scale isn't in the list, type the ratio between plotted distance and AutoCAD drawing distance into the two text boxes below the Scale drop-down list, as shown in Figure 16-5. The easiest way to express the ratio usually is to type **1** in the upper box and the drawing scale factor in the lower box. (See Chapter 4 for more information.)

Your CAD manager may have added uncommon scales or removed scales from the Scale drop-down list that your company never uses. If you're designing espresso machines in Milano, for example, you'll probably never need to plot your drawings at 1/128"=1'–0".

Creating half-size plots for some purposes is common in some industries. To plot model space half-size, double the drawing scale factor. For example, a 1/8"=1'–0" drawing has a drawing scale factor of 96, which is equivalent to a plot scale of 1=96. To make a half-size model space plot of it, specify a plot scale of 1=192 (or choose 1/16"=1'–0" from the Scale drop-down list).

Even if you work with drawings that are created to be plotted at a specific scale, plotting with a Fit to Paper scale may be the most efficient way to make a reduced-size check plot. For example, drafters in your office might create drawings that get plotted on D-size sheets (24 x 36 inches), whereas you have access to a laser printer with a B-size (11 x 17 inches) paper tray. By plotting the D-size drawings scaled to fit on B-size paper, you end up with check plots that are slightly smaller than half size. You won't be able to measure distances on the check plots with a scale, but you *can* probably check them visually for overall correctness.

Figure 16-5:
Lots of ways
to scale.

Type a ratio Or choose a predefined scale

Plotting the Layout of the Land

In the previous section, I show you how to plot the model space representation of your drawing by making sure that the Model tab is active when you open the Plot dialog box. However, paper space gives you many additional options for controlling the look of your output without having to modify the underlying geometry. So in some drawings, you may want to plot a paper space layout instead.

Paper space is the environment that's specifically designed for outputting hard copy of your drawings. If you need a refresher on paper space or layouts, have another look (or a first look!) at Chapter 5.

The path to paper space layout plotting success

As I explain in Chapter 5, AutoCAD gives you two alternative ways of switching between full-screen model space and the paper space layouts stored in the drawing. If you choose to display the model and layout tabs, you simply click the appropriate tab to select the one you want. If instead you hide the model and layout tabs, you use the model and layout buttons plus Quick View Layouts on the status bar. For the complete lowdown on using Quick View Layouts, refer to Chapter 5. In this section, I explain using this feature to print your paper space layouts.

Plotting a paper space layout is pretty much like plotting model space except that you need to find the appropriate layout first and make sure that its tab is selected before you open the Plot dialog box, as follows:

1. **Click Quick View Layouts on the status bar and scroll through the image panel.**

 The Quick View image panel opens in the lower part of the drawing area and displays a preview panel of model space and each layout stored in the drawing.

2. **Move your mouse pointer across the images in the Quick View panel and pause over the image of the layout you want to plot.**

 As you move your mouse over each image, icons appear: Publish at the upper-right corner and Plot at the upper left. I describe the PUBLISH command briefly in Chapter 20. In this chapter, I'm sticking with PLOT.

3. **Click the Plot button in the upper-left corner of the image panel of the layout you want to plot.**

 The Plot dialog box appears with the name of the layout to be plotted displayed in the title bar. (In Figure 16-6, I'm plotting a layout named "D-Size Layout.")

 If no one has set up a layout yet, AutoCAD creates a default layout. (If the Show Page Setup Manager for New Layouts setting on the Display tab of the Options dialog box is turned on, you'll see the Page Setup Manager dialog box first — just click the Close button.) The default layout probably won't be useful for real projects, but you can use it to find out about the layout plotting procedure. Refer to Chapter 5 for instructions on creating a real layout.

4. **Specify a Printer/Plotter Name and a Paper Size.**

 If you don't have a printer capable of outputting larger than letter- or tabloid-sized sheets, you can still experiment by selecting a device that outputs to file, such as DWF6 ePlot.pc3.

5. **In the What to Plot drop-down list, choose Layout, as shown in Figure 16-6.**

 The Layout option is available only when plotting a layout tab; Limits is available only when plotting the Model tab.

6. **Specify the Plot Offset (such as 0 in both the X and Y directions).**

 Specifying the Plot Offset as 0 in both X and Y directions places the lower-left corner of the plotted drawing at the lower-left corner of the printable area.

7. **In the Plot Scale area, select 1:1 from the Scale drop-down list, as shown in Figure 16-6.**

 One of the big advantages of layouts is that you don't need to know anything about drawing scale in order to plot the drawing — hence the name *paper* space. Figure 16-6 shows the proper settings for plotting a layout.

 To create a half-size plot of a layout, select 1:2 from the Scale drop-down list. In addition, select the Scale Lineweights check box in order to reduce lineweights proportionally. (I cover plotting lineweights in the next section.)

 If you find that the layout is too big for your plotter's largest paper size at a plot scale of 1:1, you can select Extents from the What to Plot drop-down list and then select the Fit to Paper check box in the Plot Scale area. Alternatively, you can close the Plot dialog box and fix the problem if you want to have a paper space layout that permanently reflects a new paper size. Use the Page Setup dialog box to modify the layout settings, or copy the layout and modify the new copy.

8. **Click the More Options button and change any additional plot options that you want to.**

 Refer to Steps 11 through 13 in the earlier section, "Plotting success in 16 steps."

9. **Click the Preview button, ensure that the drawing displays on the paper at the correct orientation and size, and then right-click and choose Exit to return to the Plot dialog box.**

 If you found any problems in the preview, change your plot settings and preview again until it looks right.

10. **Click OK to create the plot.**

Plotting Lineweights and Colors

In previous sections of this chapter, I help you gain some plotting confidence. Those sections show you how to create scaled, monochrome plots with uniform lineweights in model space or paper space. Those skills may be all you need, but if you care about controlling plotted lineweights and colors or adding special effects such as *screening* (plotting shades of gray), read on.

Plotting with style

Plot styles provide a way to override object properties with alternative plot properties. (See Chapter 6 for information about object properties.) The properties include plotted lineweight, plotted color, and screening (plotting shades of gray). Figure 16-7 shows the full range of options. Plot styles come in two exciting flavors:

- Color-dependent plot styles
- Named plot styles

Color-dependent plot styles are based on the standard way of plotting in earlier versions of AutoCAD (before AutoCAD 2000), whereas named plot styles provide a newer way.

Figure 16-7:
Editing
a color-
dependent
plot style
table.

It's remotely possible that you won't need to bother with plot styles. If the drawings you want to plot have layer and object properties (especially lineweight) that reflect how you want objects to plot, you can dispense with plot styles. But most people and most drawings use plot styles, so you should at least be familiar with them.

A couple of common reasons for using plot styles are to

- ✔ **Map screen colors to plotted lineweights.** If this idea seems completely loony to you, try to suspend judgment until you've read the "Plotting through thick and thin" section, a bit later in this chapter.

- ✔ **Create screened lines on monochrome plots.** Lines that are screened display in various shades of gray, not black. Drafters sometimes use screened lines to de-emphasize secondary objects that otherwise would overwhelm the main objects in the drawing. Screening is expressed as a percentage, with 100 percent being completely black and 0 percent being invisible.

Using plot styles

If you want objects in your drawing to plot with properties that differ from their display properties, you need plot styles. For example, you can plot with different lineweights or colors from the ones you're using for display purposes. Or, as I mention in the preceding section, you may need to map display colors to plotted lineweights. AutoCAD groups plot styles into plot style tables, each of which is stored in a separate file.

Color-based plot styles live in *color-dependent plot style table* (CTB) files, and they map the 255 AutoCAD display colors to 255 plot styles. AutoCAD automatically attaches the color-dependent plot styles to every object, based on — you guessed it — the object's color. (Are those AutoCAD programmers brilliant, or what?) Color-dependent plot style tables mimic the old color-mapped-to-lineweight plotting approach of AutoCAD R14 and earlier releases; this remains the most common method in most companies.

Named plot styles were introduced in AutoCAD 2000, and are object properties, just like color, linetype, and lineweight. Named plot styles live in (wouldn't you know it?) *named plot style table* (STB) files. After you've created a named plot style table, you create one or more plot styles and give them any names you like. Then you can assign the named plot styles to layers or to individual objects. (See Chapter 6 for more information about object and layer properties.)

To use the plot styles in a plot style table (whether they're color-dependent or named), you must attach the plot style table to model space or a paper space layout. The attached plot style table affects plotting only for that layout or for model space. This approach lets you plot the same drawing in different ways by attaching different plot styles to different tabs.

You can attach a plot style to model space or a paper space layout by selecting its image in the Quick View Layouts panel and opening the Plot dialog box, or by right-clicking over an image and choosing Page Setup Manager. Choose the plot style table name in the Plot Style Table (Pen Assignments) area of the expanded Page Setup or Plot dialog box. See the section "Controlling plotted lineweights with screen colors," later in this chapter, for an example.

When you start a new drawing in the usual way — that is, by using a template drawing (see Chapter 4) — the template drawing's plot style behavior determines whether you can choose CTB or STB files. If you want to change from color-dependent plot styles to named plot styles (or vice versa) in a particular drawing, use the CONVERTPSTYLES command.

Creating plot styles

If you're really lucky, you won't need to use plot styles. If you're somewhat lucky, you'll need to use plot styles, but someone will provide the plot style table files for you. If that's the case, you must put the CTB or STB files in your Plot Styles folder in order for AutoCAD to recognize them. (To find the location of your Plot Styles folder, open the Options dialog box, choose the Files tab, and look for the Printer Support File Path⇨Plot Style Table Search Path setting.)

If you're not lucky at all, you'll need to be smart — that is, you'll want to know how to create your own plot style table files. Here's how:

1. **Click the Application button to open the Application Menu, choose Print, and then choose Manage Plot Styles.**

 The Plot Styles folder opens in a separate Explorer window.

2. **Double-click the Add-a-Plot Style Table Wizard program shortcut.**

3. **Read the opening screen and then click Next.**

4. **On the Add Plot Style Table - Begin page, choose the Start from Scratch option or one of the other three options if you want to start with settings from another file. Then click Next.**

 The remaining steps in this procedure assume that you chose Start from Scratch. If you chose another option, simply follow the wizard's prompts.

If the creator of a drawing provides you with an AutoCAD R14/AutoCAD LT 98 PC2 (version 2) or AutoCAD R12/AutoCAD LT 95 PCP (version 1) file, choose the Use a PCP or PC2 File option. With this option, the wizard imports color-to-plotted-lineweight settings automatically.

5. **On the Add Plot Style Table - Pick Plot Style Table page, choose whether you want to create a color-dependent plot style table (CTB file) or a named plot style table (STB file). Then click Next.**

 Choose Color-Dependent Plot Style Table in order to map screen colors to plotted lineweights. Choose Named Plot Style Table in order to create named plot styles that you can apply to layers or objects.

6. **On the Add Plot Style Table - File Name page, type a name for the new CTB or STB file and then click Next.**

7. **Click the Plot Style Table Editor button on the Add Plot Style Table - Finish page.**

 The Plot Style Table Editor dialog box opens to the Form View tab if you're creating a color-dependent plot style table (refer to Figure 16-7), or to the Table View tab if you create a named plot style table.

 If you choose a named plot style in Step 5, the Plot Style Table Editor dialog box opens in *Table View,* with one plot style named Normal in the first data column, a blank column to its right, and Add Style and Delete Style buttons at the bottom. New named plot styles that you create continue to be added in columns to the right of the previous column. For more information, click the Help button in the Plot Style Table Editor.

8. **If you created a color-dependent plot style table, assign Lineweight, Screening, or other plot properties to each color that's used in the drawing. If you created a named plot style table, click the Add Style button and then assign plot properties to each of the named styles that you create.**

 To determine which colors are used in a drawing, switch to the AutoCAD window and open the Layer Properties Manager palette by clicking the Layer Properties button located on the Layers panel of the Home Ribbon.

 To change a setting for all colors or named styles, select them all first by clicking the first color or named style, holding down the Shift key, scrolling to the end of the list, and then clicking the last color or named style. Any subsequent changes you make get applied to all the selected colors or named styles.

9. **Click the Save & Close button to close the Plot Style Table Editor dialog box. Then click Finish to complete the steps for the wizard.**

 The Plot Styles folder now displays your new CTB or STB file.

10. **Close the Plot Styles folder by clicking the X in its title bar.**

Creating your first plot style table can be a harrowing experience because you have so many options. Just remember that your most likely reason for creating one is to map screen colors to plotted lineweights (as I describe in greater detail in the next section). Also remember that you may be able to minimize your effort by getting a CTB or STB file from the person who created the drawing that you want to plot.

In Chapter 6, I recommend that you limit yourself to the first nine Standard AutoCAD Colors when defining layers, and not a patchwork of the 255 colors that AutoCAD makes available. If you follow my advice, your work to create a color-dependent plot style table will be much reduced because you'll have to assign plot properties for only 9 colors, rather than worrying about 255 of them.

For systematic testing of your CTB files, you can download the file named `plot_screening_and_fill_patterns.dwg` from www.autodesk.com/autocad-samples (LT users, feel free to help yourselves to this file too — it's not included with the downloads at www.autodesk.com/autocadlt-samples). This drawing shows an array of color swatches for all 255 AutoCAD colors. The layouts (such as Grayscale and Screening 25%) demonstrate how different CTB files attached to the same layout produce radically different results. And sorry, AutoCAD LT users — even though you can use CTB files in exactly the same way as the full version of AutoCAD, you don't get this test file to experiment with.

Named plot styles hold a lot of promise, but there are at least a couple of places — dimensions and tables — where they don't work as well as traditional color-based plotting. Dimension properties allow you to assign different colors to dimension lines, extension lines, and text. The purpose for this is to allow different parts of a dimension object to print with different lineweights; for example, you can have your dimension text print with a medium lineweight, the same as your annotation text, while keeping extension and dimension lines to a fine lineweight. But because named plot styles are based on objects or layers, you don't have that lineweight control over individual dimension components. The same limitation applies to tables, where you can set your text to be one color and your grid lines to be another.

If you *really* get carried away and decide to take advantage of the 16 million-odd colors in AutoCAD's True Color or Color Book modes, you're not going to be controlling lineweights with color-dependent plot styles. CTB plot styles affect the lineweights only of objects that use the traditional 255 colors of the AutoCAD Color Index set. If you want true color or Color Book colors, use object lineweights or named plot styles to control plotted lineweight.

Plotting through thick and thin

Long ago, manual drafters developed the practice of drawing lines of different thicknesses, or *lineweights,* in order to distinguish different kinds of objects. Manual drafters did it with different technical ink pen nib diameters or with different hardnesses of pencil lead and varying degrees of pressure on the pencil. Because a computer mouse usually doesn't come with different diameters of mouse balls, the AutoCAD developers had to figure out how to let users indicate lineweights on-screen and on a plot. They came up with two different ways to indicate lineweight:

- ✔ Mapping on-screen colors to plotted lineweights. I describe this common approach in Chapter 6.

- ✔ Displaying lineweights on-screen to match what the user can expect to see on the plot. This approach first appeared in AutoCAD 2000.

Plotting with plodders

Color-as-color and lineweight-as-lineweight seem like great ideas, but Autodesk knew when it added object lineweights back in 1999 that longtime users of AutoCAD weren't going to abandon the old colors-mapped-to-lineweights approach overnight. Thus, you can still control plotted lineweight by display color in AutoCAD.

AutoCAD veterans, by and large, have chosen to stick with the Old Way for now. They've done so for a variety of reasons, including inertia, plotting procedures and drawings built around the Old Way, third-party applications that don't fully support the newer methods, and the need to exchange drawings with clients and subcontractors who haven't upgraded. In summary, the ripple effect of those who need to or want to continue using colors-mapped-to-lineweights is lasting a long time. Don't be surprised if you find yourself going with the flow for a while.

The default setting in AutoCAD 2010 is to plot object lineweights, so that's the easiest method if you don't have to consider the historical practices or predilections of other people with whom you exchange drawings. Mapping screen colors to lineweights requires some initial work on your part, but after you've set up the mapping scheme, the additional effort is minimal.

Controlling plotted lineweights with object lineweights

Plotting object lineweights is trivial, assuming that the person who created the drawing first took the trouble to assign a lineweight property to layers or objects (see Chapter 6 for details). Just make sure that the Plot Object Lineweights check box in the expanded Plot dialog box is selected. You may also want to *deselect* the Plot with Plot Styles check box because plot styles can override the object lineweights with different plotted lineweights. You can also make these settings in the Page Setup dialog box for the appropriate layout or Model tab. To access the Page Setup Manager, right-click the Quick View Layouts button on the status bar and choose Page Setup Manager.

If you want object lineweights to control plotted lineweights, make sure that the Plot Object Lineweights check box is selected in the Plot Options area of the Plot or Page Setup dialog box. If you *don't* want to plot the lineweights assigned to objects, you must deselect both the Plot Object Lineweights and Plot with Plot Styles check boxes in the Plot or Page Setup dialog box. Selecting Plot with Plot Styles selects Plot Object Lineweights as well.

Controlling plotted lineweights with screen colors

To map screen colors to plotted lineweights, you need a color-dependent plot style table (CTB file), as I describe in the section "Plotting with style," earlier in this chapter. If you're plotting a drawing created by someone else, that someone else may be able to supply you with the appropriate CTB file or, at least, with a PCP or PC2 file from which you can create the CTB file

quickly. At the very least, the creator of the drawing should be able to give you a printed chart showing which plotted lineweight to assign to each AutoCAD screen color. Use the instructions in the "Plotting with style" section to copy or create the required CTB file.

Unfortunately, no industry-wide standards exist for mapping screen colors to plotted lineweights. Different offices do it differently. That's why it's so useful to receive a CTB, PCP, or PC2 file with drawings that someone sends you.

After you have the appropriate CTB file stored in your Plot Styles folder, follow these steps to use it:

1. **Click the Quick View Layouts button on the status bar to open the Quick View Layouts panel. Move the mouse pointer to the image of model space or the layout that you want to plot.**

 As you move the pointer over each image panel, icons for the PLOT and PUBLISH commands appear at the upper corners.

2. **Click the Plot button in the upper-left corner of the selected image.**

 The Plot dialog box opens. Click the More Options button if the dialog box doesn't open in expanded mode, as shown in Figure 16-8.

3. **In the Plot Style Table (Pen Assignments) area on the Plot dialog box, select the CTB file from the drop-down list, as shown in Figure 16-8.**

 This action attaches the plot style table (CTB file) to the layout or model tab that you clicked in Step 1.

Figure 16-8: Selecting a plot style table that maps screen colors to plotted lineweights.

4. **Click the Apply to Layout button.**

 AutoCAD records the plot setting change with the current layout's configuration information. Assuming that you save the drawing, AutoCAD uses the CTB that you selected as the default plot style when you (or other people) plot that layout in the future.

5. **Continue with the plotting procedures described earlier in this chapter.**

If your drawing uses a named plot style table instead of a color-dependent plot style table, you follow the same procedure, except that you select an STB file instead of a CTB file in Step 3.

You can tell whether the current drawing was set up to use color-dependent plot styles or named plot styles by looking at the Properties panel on the Ribbon's Home tab. If the lower right drop-down list is grayed out, shows ByColor, and doesn't display a tooltip, the drawing uses color-dependent plot styles. If this list isn't grayed out and displays the `Plot style` tooltip, the drawing uses named plot styles.

Plotting in color

Plotting the colors that you see on-screen requires no special tricks. In the absence of a plot style table (that is, if you selected None from the drop-down list in the Plot Style Table [Pen Assignments] area in the Plot or Page Setup dialog box), AutoCAD sends color information as it appears on-screen to the plotter. As long as your output device can plot in color, what you see should be what you get.

If you attach a plot style table to the layout that you're plotting (as described in the previous section), you can — if you really want to — map screen colors to different plotted colors. In most cases, you don't want that kind of confusion. Instead, leave the Color property in the plot style table set to Use Object Color.

If your goal is *not* to plot color, make sure that you set the Color property for all plot styles to Black. If you try to plot colors on a monochrome device, you may find that objects appear in various shades of gray, with lighter colors mapped to lighter shades of gray and darker colors to darker shades of gray. This process of mapping colors to shades of gray is called *dithering,* and it usually is *not* what you want in a CAD drawing. To override it, use the Plot Style Table Editor, as described in the section "Creating plot styles," earlier in this chapter, to set the Color option for all colors to Black. (The default setting is Use Object Color.) If you don't already have a plot style table that you want to use, select `monochrome.ctb` for color-based plot styles or select `mono-chrome.stb` for named plot styles — both of which come with AutoCAD — from the drop-down list in the Plot Style Table (Pen Assignments) area of the Plot dialog box.

When in doubt, send it out

Whether you plot to scale or not, with different lineweights or not, in color or not, consider using a service bureau for some of your plotting. In-house plotting on your office's output devices is great for small check plots on faster laser or inkjet printers. Large-format plotting, on the other hand, can be slow and time consuming. If you need to plot lots of drawings, you may find yourself spending an afternoon loading paper, replenishing ink cartridges, and trimming sheets.

Good plotting service bureaus have big, fast, expensive plotters that you can only dream about owning. Also, *they're* responsible for babysitting those fancy devices, feeding them, and fixing them. As a bonus, service bureaus can make blueline prints from your plots if you need to distribute hard-copy sets to other people.

The only downside is that you need to coordinate with a service bureau to make sure it gets what it needs from you and can deliver the kinds of plots you need. Some service bureaus

plot directly from your DWG files, while others ask you to make PLT (plot) files. Some service bureaus specialize in color plotting, while others are more comfortable with monochrome plotting and making blueline copies.

When you're choosing a service bureau, look for one that traditionally has served drafters, architects, and engineers. These service bureaus tend to be more knowledgeable about AutoCAD, and they should have more plotting expertise than the desktop publishing, printing, and copying shops.

Whomever you choose, do some test plots well before the day that important set of drawings is due. Talk to the plotting people and get a copy of their plotting instructions. Have the service bureau create some plots of a couple of your typical drawings and make sure they look the way you want them to.

If you do lots of plotting with a service bureau, look into whether you can charge it to your clients as an expense (just like bluelines or copying).

To see the full range of AutoCAD colors available on your plotter, or to see how a particular plot style table affects plotting, open and then plot the sample file plot_screening_and_fill_patterns.dwg which you can download from www.autodesk.com/autocad-samples. The Screening 100% layout in this drawing contains color swatches for all 255 AutoCAD colors (and again, sorry LT users — you don't get this file).

It's a (Page) Setup!

Page setups specify the plotter, paper size, and other plot settings that you use to plot a particular layout or the model space of a drawing. AutoCAD maintains separate page setups for model space and for each paper space layout. When you click the Apply to Layout button in the Plot dialog box (or select the Save Changes to Layout check box and then click OK to plot), AutoCAD stores the current plot settings as the page setup for the current layout.

You can also give page setups names and save them. The advantage of doing so is that you can switch quickly between different plot settings and copy plot settings from one drawing layout to another. Named page setups are stored with each drawing, but you can copy them from another drawing into the current one with the Page Setup Manager dialog box (described later in this section).

If you want to get fancier, you can create named page setups in order to plot the same layout (or model space) in different ways, or to copy plot settings from one layout to another or one drawing to another. Click the Add button in the Page Setup area of the Plot dialog box to create a named page setup from the current plot settings. After you create a named page setup, you can restore its plot settings by choosing it from the Page Setup Name drop-down list.

For even greater control, right-click Quick View Layouts on the status bar and choose Page Setup Manager to create, change, and copy page setups. In the Page Setup Manager dialog box, as shown in Figure 16-9, you can create new page setups and modify existing ones. Click the Modify button to open the Page Setup dialog box, which is almost identical to the Plot dialog box. The primary difference is that you're changing plot settings rather than actually plotting. The Set Current button copies the page setup that you've selected on the Page Setups list to the current layout tab. With the Import button, you can copy a layout from another drawing or drawing template (DWT) file.

Figure 16-9:
The Page
Setup
Manager
dialog box.

Continuing the Plot Dialog

In previous sections of this chapter, I cover most of the important options in the Plot dialog box. This section reveals a few more fine points that will make your plotting life easier. I don't cover every minute, obscure, useful-only-at-cocktail-party-discussions detail. (And if this sounds like your kind of cocktail party, remind me that I'm busy that night!) I do point out some occasionally useful options that will increase your vocabulary when you're communicating with the Plot dialog box.

Use the Plot dialog box's tooltips to find out more about any part of the dialog box:

1. Hover your mouse pointer over the part of the dialog box that you want to know more about.

2. Press F1 or click the Help button at the bottom of the dialog box if the pop-up help isn't enough.

3. For a more conceptual take on plotting, click the Learn about Plotting link to view the Quick Start to Plotting section of the online help.

The following list explains most of the remaining controls, check boxes, and lists in the Plot dialog box:

✔ **Printer/Plotter:** As I describe in the section "Configure it out," earlier in this chapter, you use the Name drop-down list to select the Windows system printer or non-system driver configuration that you want to use for plotting.

Clicking the Properties button opens the Plotter Configuration Editor dialog box, with which you can change media (type of paper) and other properties that are unique to the currently selected plotter or printer. In particular, you can define custom paper sizes.

As if AutoCAD's Plot dialog box settings weren't overwhelming enough, depending on your plot device, you may also have to deal with the Plotter Configuration Editor dialog box. Some plotter drivers hide important settings in this dialog box. To access them, you typically click the Custom Properties button near the bottom of the Plotter Configuration Editor dialog box. For example, if you're using the enhanced Windows system driver for HP plotters, available at www.designjet.hp.com, you can click the Custom Properties button and then the More Sizes button to specify which paper sizes are available to you on the Paper Size drop-down list of the main Plot dialog box.

To make matters even *more* confusing, if you make any changes in the Plotter Configuration Editor dialog box, AutoCAD prompts you to save the changes to a separate PC3 file. You should choose Save Changes to the Following File (that is, create a new AutoCAD-specific configuration that includes the revised settings) and type a configuration name that you'll recognize later. When you want to plot with custom settings, remember to choose the AutoCAD-specific PC3 configuration near the end of the Printer/Plotter Name drop-down list, and not the original Windows system printer configuration near the beginning of the list.

✔ **Plot to File:** If you need to plot to a file rather than directly to your plotter or network printer queue, select the Plot to File option. When you click OK to plot, AutoCAD asks you for a plot filename and location.

This option is especially useful when you want to use the ePlot feature to publish a DWF file on a Web site. You also may need to use this option to create files to send to a plotting service bureau.

AutoCAD 2009 added DWFx to its ePlot options. DWFx is a flavored version of DWF that conforms to Microsoft's XPS page description language. For most people, the handiest thing about this format is that if you plot to DWFx, the resulting file can be displayed — in Windows Vista only — in Windows Explorer.

Plotting to the `DWG to PDF.pc3` file creates versions of your drawing files that can be opened and viewed in the free and widely available Adobe Reader software.

✔ **Plot Stamp On:** Use this option to turn on and off and configure the contents of a text string that AutoCAD adds automatically to the corner of each plot. The plot stamp can include useful information, such as the drawing filename and plot date and time.

✔ **Plot Area:** Specify the area of the drawing to plot. Your choices include Display, Extents, and Window, regardless of whether you're plotting a paper space layout or model space. If you defined named views in the drawing, AutoCAD adds a View option. The additional choice is Layout for a paper space layout or Limits for model space.

• **Display** means the drawing as it's currently displayed in the drawing window (including any empty space around the drawing objects).

• **Extents** means the rectangular area containing all the objects in the drawing.

• **Limits** (full-screen model space only) means the model space area that you specified (you did tell your drawing its limits, didn't you?) when you set up the drawing. (See Chapter 4 for details.)

• **Layout** (Layouts only) means the paper space area you defined when you set up the layout.

• **Window** means a rectangular area that you specify.

- **View** means a named view which you select from a drop-down list. (Chapter 12 describes named views and how to create them.)

Usually, you'll choose to plot Layout in paper space. For model space, the choice depends on whether the drawing was set up properly and what you want to plot. If you set limits properly, as I describe in Chapter 4, plot Limits in order to get the whole drawing area. If you're trying to plot a drawing in which the limits weren't set properly, try Extents instead. Use Window or View if you want to plot just a portion of model space.

✔ **Plot Offset:** A plot offset of X=0 and Y=0 positions the plot at the lower-left corner of the plottable area. If you want to move the plot from this default position on the paper, enter non-zero numbers or select the Center the Plot check box. (The Center the Plot check box is not available if you select Layout from the What to Plot drop-down list.)

✔ **Shaded Viewport Options:** If your drawing includes viewports showing shaded or rendered 3D models, use this area to control the plotted appearance.

✔ **Plot Options:** The Plot Object Lineweights and the Plot with Plot Styles check boxes control whether AutoCAD uses the features described in the "Plotting with style" and "Plotting through thick and thin" sections, earlier in this chapter.

The Hide Paperspace Objects check box controls whether AutoCAD hides objects that are behind other objects when a 3D model is displayed in a viewport. If your drawing is entirely 2D, this option doesn't matter. If your drawing includes 3D objects, selecting this setting is like applying the 3DORBIT command's Hidden option to the plot. Look up *3DORBIT command* on the Index tab in the AutoCAD online help system for more information.

✔ **Plot Upside-Down:** Select this check box if you want to rotate the plot 180 degrees on the paper. (It's a handy option for plotting in the southern hemisphere or for avoiding having to cock your head at an uncomfortable angle as you watch plots come out of the plotter.)

AutoCAD normally generates plots in the foreground — that is, the plotting process takes over the program for the entire time that the program is creating the plot. AutoCAD 2010 includes a background plotting feature that returns control of the program to you more quickly. If you have a reasonably fast computer with adequate memory, turn on this feature in the Options dialog box: Type **OPTIONS** (**OP**) and press Enter, click the Plot and Publish tab, and in the Background Processing Options area, select Plotting.

If you want to automate plotting for a batch of drawings, check out AutoCAD's *sheet sets* feature. One of the tasks that sheet sets are designed to accomplish is the publishing of a set of drawing sheets at one fell swoop. If this sounds like your ticket to plotting bliss, go to the online help system and look in Contents⇨Choose a Work Process Before You Begin⇨Work with Sheets in a Sheet Set.

Troubles with Plotting

No matter how many times you read this chapter or how carefully you study the AutoCAD documentation, you'll occasionally run into plotting problems. You're especially likely to encounter problems when trying to plot other people's drawings because you don't always know what plotting conventions they had in mind. (*Plotting conventions* aren't where spies meet; they're a standardized approach to plotting issues.) Table 16-1 describes some of the more common plotting problems and solutions.

Table 16-1	Plotting Problems and Solutions
Problem	*Possible Solution*
Nothing comes out of the plotter (system printer driver).	Check whether you can print to the device from other Windows applications. If not, it's not an AutoCAD problem. Try the Windows Print Troubleshooter (**Windows XP:** Start⇨Help and Support⇨Printing and Faxing⇨Fixing a Printing Problem⇨Printing Troubleshooter; **Windows Vista:** Start⇨ Help and Support, type **printing troubleshooting** in the Search box and press Enter, then click Troubleshoot Printer Problems).
Nothing comes out of the plotter (non-system printer driver).	Choose Plotter Manager on the Output Ribbon's Plot panel, double-click the plotter configuration, and check the settings.
Objects don't plot the way they appear on-screen.	Check for a plot style table with weird settings or try plotting without a plot style table.
Objects appear ghosted or with washed-out colors.	In the plot style table, set Color to Black for all colors.
Scaled to Fit doesn't work right in paper space.	Change the What to Plot drop-down list from Layout to Extents.
The HP-enhanced Windows system driver that you downloaded from HP's Web site doesn't have the right paper sizes (for example, no architectural paper sizes).	In the Plot dialog box's Printer/Plotter area, click the Properties button to display the Plotter Configuration Editor dialog box, click the Custom Properties button (near the bottom), and then click the More Sizes button to specify the standard and custom paper sizes.
Something else is wrong.	Check the plot log: Click the Plot/Publish Details Report Available icon near the right end of the status bar and look for error messages.

Part IV
Advancing with AutoCAD

The 5th Wave By Rich Tennant

GUS & LILY'S DOG GROOMING
NOW USING CAD SOFTWARE

In this part . . .

After you get the lines and text right, you may be justified in thinking that your work in AutoCAD is done. But AutoCAD enables you to do so much more! Blocks and external references help you manage data within drawings, between drawings, and across a network. Parametric drawing lets you maintain the intent of your designs. If you plan to share drawings (whether among your own projects, with people in your office, or with folks in other companies), you need to think about consistency in presentation and drawing organization.

The Internet is the biggest ongoing swap meet in human history, and AutoCAD offers some unique trading possibilities — and potential pitfalls — via e-mail and the Web. With the information in this part, you'll be teaching AutoCAD how to give and receive in no time.

Chapter 17

The ABCs of Blocks

In This Chapter

▶ Introducing blocks

▶ Creating block definitions

▶ Inserting blocks

▶ Using attributes in blocks

▶ Using PURGE to remove unwanted block definitions

Chapter 11 shows you how to copy objects within a drawing or even to another drawing. That's one way to use AutoCAD to improve drafting efficiency. You can copy a DWG file and then modify it to create a similar drawing — an even better productivity booster, as long as you're in the habit of making similar drawings. But all those are baby steps compared to the techniques that I cover in this chapter and Chapter 18: treating drawings, parts of drawings, drawings saved in Web format (*DWF,* or *Design Web Format*), and raster images as reusable and updateable modules. If you want to make drafting production more efficient with AutoCAD, you want to know how to use blocks, xrefs, PDFs, DWFs, and raster files.

A *block* is a collection of objects grouped together to form a single object. You can *insert* this collection more than once in the same drawing, and when you do, all instances of the block remain identical. By redefining the *block definition,* you can automatically change all instances of the block insertion (officially called a *block reference*) at once. Although a block lives within a specific drawing, you can transfer copies of it into other drawings. And you can add fill-in-the-blank text fields, called *attributes,* to blocks.

You can create single line or multiline attributes; in addition to having more than one line, multiline attributes have many of the formatting options of multiline text. And blocks both with and without attributes can be defined as annotative objects to boot. (See Chapter 13 for a rundown on annotative objects.)

In this chapter, I present the ABCs of blocks — basic creation and insertion, adding attributes, and getting rid of block definitions you no longer need or want. In Chapter 18, I show you how to make even more of already-created drawing data, including several flavors of external reference files (including PDFs and MicroStation DGN files) and raster images.

Blocks, along with external references, DWF and PDF underlays, raster images, and DGN files, enable you to reuse your work and the work of others, giving you the potential to save tremendous amounts of time — or to cause tremendous problems if you change a file on which other people's drawings depend. Use these features when you can to save time, but do so in an organized and careful way so as to avoid problems.

How you use blocks and xrefs depends a lot on the profession and office in which you work. Some disciplines and companies use these drawing organization features heavily and in a highly organized way, but others don't. Ask your colleagues what the local customs are and follow them.

Rocking with Blocks

First, a little more block theory and then you can rock right into those blocks. To use a block in a drawing, you need two things: a block *definition* and one or more block *insertions*. AutoCAD doesn't always make the distinction between these two things very clear, but you need to understand the difference to avoid terminal confusion about blocks. (Maybe this syndrome should be called *blockheadedness?*)

A block definition lives in an invisible area of your drawing file called the *block table*. (It's one of those sets of named symbols that I describe in Chapter 6.) The block table is like a book of graphical recipes for making different kinds of blocks. Each block definition is like a recipe for making one kind of block. When you insert a block, as described later in this chapter, AutoCAD creates a special object called a *block reference*. The block reference points to the recipe and tells AutoCAD, "Hey, draw me according to the instructions in this recipe!"

Although a block may look like a collection of objects stored together and given a name, it's really a graphical recipe (the block definition) plus one or more pointers to that recipe (one or more block references). Each time you insert a particular block, you create another pointer to the same recipe.

The advantages of blocks include

- ✓ **Grouping objects together when they belong together logically.** You can draw a screw using lines and arcs and then make a block definition out of all these objects. When you insert the screw block, AutoCAD treats it as a single object for purposes of copying, moving, and so on.

- ✓ **Saving time and reducing errors.** Inserting a block is, of course, much quicker than redrawing the same geometry again. And the less geometry you draw from scratch, the less opportunity there is to make a mistake.

- ✓ **Efficiency of storage when you reuse the same block repeatedly.** If you insert the same screw block 15 times in a drawing, AutoCAD stores the detailed block definition only once. The 15 block references that point to the block definition take up much less disk space than 15 copies of all the lines, polylines, and arcs.

- ✓ **The ability to edit all instances of a symbol in a drawing simply by modifying a single block definition.** If you decide that your design requires a different kind of screw, you simply redefine the screw's block definition. With this new recipe, AutoCAD then replaces all 15 screws automatically. That's a heck of a lot faster than erasing and recopying 15 screws!

- ✓ **Varying the appearance of block references by using dynamic blocks.** If your design requires a different kind of screw, you simply change the view of the screw to the other kind (assuming, of course, you've defined your screw as a dynamic block). Every instance of the screw in the drawing could show a different kind of screw. And *that's* a heck of a lot more efficient than creating 15 different block definitions! For the lowdown on creating, inserting, and manipulating dynamic blocks, open the online help system and choose Contents⇨User's Guide⇨Create and Modify Objects⇨Create and Use Blocks (Symbols)⇨Add Dynamic Behavior to Blocks.

Blocks *aren't* as great for drawing elements used in multiple drawings, however, especially if several people are working on and sharing parts of drawings with one another. That's because blocks, after they get into multiple drawings, stay in each drawing; a later modification to a block definition in one drawing does not automatically modify all the other drawings that use that block. If you use a block with your company's logo in a number of drawings and then you decide to change the logo, you must make the change within each drawing that uses the block.

If all you need to do is group some objects so that you can more easily select them for copying, moving, and so on, use AutoCAD's *group* feature. Type **GROUP** (or the command alias **G**) and press Enter to open the Object Grouping dialog box in AutoCAD or the Group Manager dialog box in AutoCAD LT. Then select some objects, click the New button in AutoCAD or the Create Group button in AutoCAD LT, and type a name for the group. When you're

editing drawings that contain groups, press Ctrl+Shift+A to toggle group-ness on or off. If you've toggled group-ness on, picking any object in a group selects all objects in the group. If you've toggled it off, picking an object selects only that object, even if it happens to be a member of a group. For more information, look up *Groups, about* in the online help.

Creating block definitions

To create a block definition from objects in the current drawing, use the Block Definition dialog box. (The other way to create a block definition is by inserting another drawing file into your current drawing as a block, which I explain in the next section.) The following steps show you how to create a block definition by using the Block Definition dialog box:

1. **On the Ribbon's Home tab, click the Create button on the Block panel.**

 The Block Definition dialog box appears (see Figure 17-1).

 Pay attention to layers when you create the objects that make up a block. As a rule, block geometry created on most layers retains the color, linetype, lineweight and plot style properties of those layers. The exception to the rule is object geometry created on Layer 0. If you create a block using geometry drawn on Layer 0, when you insert the block, it takes on the features of the layer into which it's inserted.

2. **Type the block definition's name in the Name text box.**

 If you type the name of an existing block definition, AutoCAD will warn you when you click OK at the end of the process and ask if you want to replace that block definition with the new objects you select. This process is called *block redefinition*.

Figure 17-1:
The Block
Definition
dialog box.

TIP

To see a list of the names of all the current blocks in your drawing, open the Name drop-down list.

3. **Specify the base point (also known as the insertion point) of the block, using any of the following methods:**

 • Enter the coordinates of the insertion point in the X, Y, and Z text boxes.

 • Click the Pick Point button and then select a point on the screen. (In this case, use an object snap or other precision technique, as described in Chapter 7, to grab a specific point on one of the block's objects.)

 The *base point* is the point on the block by which you insert it later, as I describe in the next section.

 Use an obvious and consistent point on the group of objects for the base point, such as the lower-left corner, so that you know what to expect when you insert the block.

4. **Click the Select Objects button and then select the objects that you want as part of the block.**

 AutoCAD uses the selected objects to create a block definition and displays an icon showing those objects next to the block name. Figure 17-2 shows the base point and group of selected objects during the process of creating a new block definition.

5. **In the Objects area, select one of the radio buttons to tell AutoCAD what to do with the objects used to define the block: retain them in place, convert them into a block instance, or delete them.**

 The default choice, Convert to Block, is usually the best. See Step 9 for a description of what happens with each choice.

Figure 17-2: Building a block.

Base point

6. **Specify the insert units to which the block will be scaled in the Block Unit drop-down list.**

 When you or someone else drags the block from one drawing into another via the DesignCenter palette (see Chapter 6) or Tool Palettes (described later in this chapter), the units you specify here and the units of the drawing you're dragging into will control the default insertion scale factor.

 Three additional features in AutoCAD's Block Definition dialog box give you even more control over what happens to your blocks as they're inserted:

 • If the **Annotative** check box is selected, you can assign multiple plotted drawing scales to the block and then display the inserted block at the different scale representations by choosing one from the Annotation scale list on the status bar. I explain the nuts and bolts of annotative objects in Chapter 13.

 • If the **Scale Uniformly** check box is selected, blocks will be inserted with the same X, Y, or Z scale factors. (Scale Uniformly is automatically selected if Annotative is selected.)

 • If the **Allow Exploding** check box is selected, blocks can be exploded during or after their insertion in a drawing.

7. **Enter a description for the block in the Description text area.**

 You don't have to enter a description to create a block, but it's not a bad idea. Think like a database manager and enter a useful description that will identify the block to yourself and others.

8. **Make sure that the Open in Block Editor check box is deselected.**

 You don't need to use the Edit Block Definition dialog box unless you're going to add dynamic features to the block (visit the online help to find out more about dynamic blocks).

9. **Click OK to complete the block definition process.**

 AutoCAD stores the block definition in the current drawing's block table. The radio buttons you choose from in Step 5 do the following:

 • If you selected the **Convert to Block** radio button (the default) in Step 5, AutoCAD creates a block reference pointing to the new block definition — the objects look the same on-screen, but now they're an instance of the block rather than existing as separate objects. Most of the time, this is your best choice.

 • If you selected the **Retain** radio button, the objects remain in place but aren't converted into a block reference — they stay individual objects with no connection to the new block definition.

- If you selected the **Delete** radio button, the objects disappear (but the block definition still gets created).

When you define a block, you can include a special kind of variable text object called an *attribute definition*. When you insert a block that contains one or more attribute definitions, AutoCAD prompts you to fill in values for the text fields. Attributes are useful for variable title block information (sheet number, sheet title, and so on) and symbols that contain different codes or callouts. I describe how to create and use attribute definitions later in this chapter.

Keep your common symbol drawings in one or more specific folders that you set aside just for that purpose. You may want to use one of the following techniques to develop a library of symbols that you use frequently:

✔ Create a separate DWG file for each block.

✔ Store a bunch of symbols as block definitions in one drawing and use DesignCenter to import block definitions from this drawing when you need them.

Inserting blocks

AutoCAD provides a number of ways to insert a block or a whole drawing file, but the most commonly used and most flexible is the Insert dialog box. Here's the procedure for inserting a block:

1. **Set an appropriate layer current, as described in Chapter 6.**

 It's a good idea to insert each block on a layer that has something to do with the block's geometry or purpose:

 - If all the objects in the block definition reside on one layer, it's usually best to insert the block on that layer.

 - If the block geometry spans several layers, choose one of them to insert the block on.

 If any of the block definition's geometry was created on Layer 0, that geometry will inherit the color, linetype, and other object properties of the layer that you insert the block on. It's like the chameleon changing color to match its surroundings or a politician changing his position to match the day's opinion polls.

2. **On the Ribbon's Home tab click the Insert button on the Block panel.**

 The Insert dialog box appears, as shown in Figure 17-3.

Insert

Name: Plank 2x6 Browse...

Path:

☐ Locate using Geographic Data

Insertion point	Scale	Rotation
☑ Specify On-screen	☐ Specify On-screen	☐ Specify On-screen
X: 0"	X: 1	Angle: 0
Y: 0"	Y: 1	
Z: 0"	Z: 1	Block Unit
	☑ Uniform Scale	Unit: Inches
		Factor: 1

☐ Explode OK Cancel Help

Figure 17-3:
The Insert
dialog box.

3. **Enter the block definition name (or external filename) by using one of the following methods:**

 • Use the Name drop-down list to select from a list of block definitions in the current drawing.

 • Click the Browse button to select an external DWG file and have AutoCAD create a block definition from it.

 You can use an external drawing to replace a block definition in your current drawing. If you click Browse and choose a file whose name matches the name of a block definition that's already in your drawing, AutoCAD asks you to confirm the update and, if you agree, updates the block definition in your drawing with the current contents of the external file. This process is called *block redefinition,* and AutoCAD automatically updates all the block references that point to the block definition.

4. **Enter the insertion point, scale, and rotation angle of the block.**

 You can either select the Specify On-Screen check box in each area to specify the parameters on-screen at the command prompt, or type the values you want in the text boxes in the Insertion Point, Scale, and Rotation areas.

 Select the Uniform Scale check box to constrain the X, Y, and Z scaling parameters to the same value (which is what you want in almost all cases).

5. **If you want AutoCAD to create a copy of the individual objects in the block instead of a block reference that points to the block definition, select the Explode check box and click OK.**

6. **If you selected the Specify On-Screen check box for the insertion point, scale, or rotation angle, answer the prompts on the command line to specify these parameters.**

After you insert a block, all the objects displayed in the block reference behave as a single object. When you select any object in the block reference, AutoCAD highlights all the objects in it.

Another way to insert a block is to drag a DWG file from Windows Explorer and drop it anywhere in the current drawing window. AutoCAD then prompts you to choose an insertion point and optionally change the default scale factor and rotation angle. Similarly, you can drag a block definition from the Blocks section of the DesignCenter palette and drop it into the current drawing window. (Chapter 6 describes DesignCenter.)

AutoCAD provides one additional way of inserting blocks: the Tool Palettes window, which is described in Chapter 2. As is true of using a tool palette for hatching (Chapter 15), you first must create and configure appropriate tools. The easiest method is right-clicking a drawing in DesignCenter and choosing Create Tool Palette. A new tabbed page is added to the Tool Palettes window, containing all the block definitions from the drawing that you right-clicked. Simply click and drag a tool to insert its corresponding block into a drawing. Dragging blocks from a tool palette doesn't give you the chance to specify a different insertion scale, nor can you use all AutoCAD's precision tools to specify the insertion point precisely — you may need to move the block into place after inserting it. I recommend that you first master the other block insertion methods described in this chapter — especially the Insert dialog box and DesignCenter palette. Then if you find yourself inserting the same blocks frequently, consider creating a tool palette containing them. See *tool palettes, adding drawings from* in the AutoCAD online help system for more information.

Although the preceding paragraph refers to the *Tool Palettes window,* palettes in AutoCAD are not like regular windows or dialog boxes. They are *modeless* — they can stay open while you carry on with other tasks outside them. The official programmer-ese term for palettes is *enhanced secondary window,* or ESW for short. (I think I'm sticking with *palettes.)*

Be careful when inserting one drawing into another. If the host (or parent) drawing and the inserted (or child) drawing have different definitions for layers that share the same name, the objects in the inserted drawing take on the layer characteristics of the host drawing. For example, if you insert a drawing with lines on a layer called Walls that's blue and dashed into a drawing with a layer called Walls that's red and continuous, the inserted lines on the wall layer will turn red and continuous after they're inserted. The same rules apply to linetypes, text styles, dimension styles, table styles, multileader styles, and block definitions that are nested inside the drawing you're inserting. As you probably remember from when you were little . . . Parents Rule!

If you need to modify a block definition after you've inserted one or more instances of it, use the Block Editor (BEDIT command); choose Edit on the Home tab's Blocks panel. Look up *BEDIT* in the AutoCAD online help system. BEDIT is available in both AutoCAD and AutoCAD LT.

Locate using Geographic Data is a new option in AutoCAD 2010's Insert dialog box. *Geographic data* refers to specifying locating drawing geometry with reference to specific locations on planet Earth (so far) defined in one of a number of recognized global coordinate systems. This feature promises to be very big in the civil engineering community, or possibly for very large architectural projects, where a ground-based coordinate system is in place. If it sounds like something you need, look in the online help (search on *geographic location* — and visit your local dealer or training center for further direction.

Attributes: Fill-in-the-blank blocks

You may think of attributes as the good (or bad) qualities of your significant other, but in AutoCAD, *attributes* are fill-in-the-blank text fields that you can add to your blocks. When you create a block definition and then insert it several times in a drawing, all the ordinary geometry (lines, circles, regular text strings, and so on) in all the instances are exactly identical. Attributes provide a little more flexibility in the form of text strings that can be different in each block reference.

For example, suppose that you frequently designate parts in your drawings by labeling them with a distinct number or letter in a circle for each part. If you want to create a block for this symbol, you can't simply draw the number or letter as regular text using the MTEXT or DTEXT command. If you create a block definition with a regular text object (for example, the letter *A)*, the text string will be the same in every instance of the block (always the letter *A)*. That's not much help in distinguishing the parts!

Instead, you create an *attribute definition,* which acts as a placeholder for a text string that can vary each time you insert the block. You include the attribute definition when you create the block definition (refer to the "Creating block definitions" section, earlier in this chapter). Then each time you insert the block, AutoCAD prompts you to fill in an *attribute value* for each attribute definition.

When they were first introduced, and for a long time afterward, block attribute values were limited to a single line of variable text with a maximum of 255 characters. AutoCAD 2008 and later support multiline attributes; as well as offering more than one line, multiline attributes have many of the

formatting options of multiline text. For more information on creating and inserting blocks with multiline attributes, look up *attribute definitions, multiline* in the online help system index.

The AutoCAD documentation and dialog boxes often use the term *attribute* to refer indiscriminately to an *attribute definition* or an *attribute value*. I attribute a lot of the confusion about attributes to this sloppiness. Just remember that an attribute *definition* is the text field or placeholder in the block definition, and an attribute *value* is the specific text string that you type when you insert the block.

Attribute definitions

You use the Attribute Definition dialog box to create attribute definitions (clever, eh?). The procedure is similar to creating a text string except that you must supply a little more information. Create attribute definitions with the following steps:

1. **Change to the layer on which you want to create the attribute definition.**

2. **Choose Define Attributes on the Home tab's Blocks panel slideout to run the ATTDEF command.**

 The Attribute Definition dialog box appears, as shown in Figure 17-4.

 You rarely need to use any of the first four Mode settings (Invisible, Constant, Verify, or Preset). Just leave them deselected. If you're curious about what the modes do, hover your mouse pointer over an item and, if that's not enough information, use the dialog box help button to find out more.

Figure 17-4: The Attribute Definition dialog box.

3. **Select or deselect the Lock Position check box.**

 If Lock Position is selected, the attributes can't be relocated within the block reference — the whole thing is treated as a single object. Deselecting Lock Position allows attributes to be moved by dragging their grips, without moving the block reference as a whole.

4. **Select or deselect the Multiple Lines check box.**

 Selecting Multiple Lines in the Mode area disables the "Default" text box and displays a button to open the Multiline Editor. You don't get the whole panoply of formatting options that you get in the MTEXT command's In-Place Text Editor, but you can overscore or underscore text, and a right-click menu lets you import text, assign a background mask, or choose from a number of other options. Refer to the online help system for more information.

5. **In the Attribute area, type values for the tag (the unique identifier for the attribute), the user prompt, and the default value.**

 The name you type into the Tag text box can't contain any spaces. The Prompt and Default text boxes may contain spaces.

 Attribute values can include automatically updating fields, such as date, filename, or system variable setting. Click the Insert Field button to the right of the Default text box to insert a field. See Chapter 13 for more information.

6. **(Optional) If you selected the Multiple Lines check box in Step 4, click the Multiline Editor button (it shows three periods) to enter the multiline default attribute value and add any formatting; then click OK.**

 The value you enter here is the default text stored in the attribute definition, and you can change it when you insert the block.

7. **In the Text Settings area, specify the Justification, Text Style, Text Height, Rotation, and Boundary Width (the last for multiline attributes only).**

 The text properties for attribute definitions are the same as those for text objects — see Chapter 13.

8. **Select Specify On-screen to choose an insertion point for the attribute definition.**

 An attribute definition's insertion point is like a text string's base point. Remember to use snap, object snap, or another precision tool if you want the eventual attribute values to be located at a precise point.

9. **Click OK to create the attribute definition.**

10. **Repeat Steps 1 through 9 for any additional attribute definitions.**

If you need to create a series of attribute definitions in neat rows, create the first one using Steps 1 through 9 and then select the Align below Previous Attribute Definition check box for the subsequent definitions. To make a series of non-adjacent attributes, create the first one using Steps 1 through 9 and then copy the first attribute definition and edit the copy with the Properties palette. You can prevent your attributes from being dragged around the block by selecting the Lock Position check box in the Attribute Definition dialog box.

Block definition containing attribute definitions

After you create one or more attribute definitions — and any other geometry that you want to include in the block — you're ready to create a block definition that contains them. Follow the steps in the section "Creating block definitions," earlier in this chapter.

At Step 4 in the section "Creating block definitions," you can select any attribute definitions before or after you select the other geometry. However, you should select each attribute definition one by one (clicking each attribute definition rather than selecting multiple attributes with a selection window) in the order that you want the attribute value prompts to appear in the Edit Attributes dialog box (see Figure 17-5 in the next section). If you don't select the attributes one by one, your block and attributes will still work, but the order of the attribute prompts in the Edit Attributes dialog box may not be what you want.

You can use the Block Attribute Manager to reorder the attribute definitions in a block definition. Choose Manage Attributes on the Home tab's Blocks panel slideout. You also can use this dialog box to edit other attribute definition settings, such as the prompt, text style, or layer.

Insert a block containing attribute definitions

After you create a block definition that contains attribute definitions, you insert it just like any other block. Follow the steps in the section "Inserting blocks," earlier in this chapter. At the end of the steps, AutoCAD displays the Edit Attributes dialog box, as shown in Figure 17-5. The dialog box contains one row for each of the attribute definitions and has any default values filled in. You simply edit the values and then click OK.

The ATTDIA (ATTribute DIAlog box) system variable controls whether AutoCAD prompts for attribute values in a dialog box (ATTDIA=1) or at the command line (ATTDIA=0). If you insert a block and see command line prompts for each attribute value, type a value and press Enter for each attribute value. When you return to the Command prompt, type **ATTDIA**, press Enter, type **1**, and press Enter again. When you insert blocks with attributes in this drawing in the future, AutoCAD displays the Edit Attributes dialog box instead of prompting you at the command line.

Figure 17-5:
The Edit
Attributes
dialog box.

Edit attribute values

After you insert a block that contains attributes, you can edit the individual attribute values in that block reference with the EATTEDIT command. Click the Edit Attributes flyout on the Home tab's Block panel, choose Single, and click any object in the block reference. AutoCAD displays the Enhanced Attribute Editor dialog box with the current attribute values, as shown in Figure 17-6. The most common attribute editing operation is to edit the text value — that is, the text string that appears in the block reference. You also can change properties of the attributes, such as layer and text style.

Figure 17-6:
The
Enhanced
Attribute
Editor
dialog box.

Many people use attributes in the way I've described so far — as fill-in-the-blank text fields in blocks. But attributes also can serve as data extraction tools. For example, you can export attribute values, such as part numbers and quantities, to a table object in AutoCAD or to a text, spreadsheet, or database file for analysis or reporting.

Extracting Data

 Selecting Extract Data from the Linking & Extraction panel on the Ribbon's Insert tab starts the Data Extraction Wizard. You can find out much more about this specialized function in the online help. Check out User's Guide⇨Share Data between Drawings and Applications⇨Extract Data from Drawings and Spreadsheets. And, LT users, although you don't have this command, you can still extract attribute information to space- or comma-delimited text files by using the Attribute Extraction dialog box. For more information, look up the *ATTEXT* command in the online help.

Exploding blocks

In regular block definitions (not dynamic blocks), the objects in each block reference act like a well-honed marching squadron: If you move or otherwise edit one object in the block reference, all objects move or change in the same way. Usually this cohesion is an advantage, but occasionally you need to break up the squadron in order to modify one object without affecting the others.

 To *explode* a block reference into individual objects, click Explode on the Home tab's Modify panel or type **X** and press Enter, and then select the block reference. When you explode a block reference, AutoCAD replaces it with all the objects — lines, polylines, arcs, and so on — specified in the block definition. You then can edit the objects individually or perhaps use them to make more block definitions.

 If you explode a block that contains attributes, the attribute *values* change back to attribute *definitions.* This usually isn't the sort of change that you want. If you really need to explode the block reference, you'll probably want to erase the attribute definitions and draw regular text strings in their place. If you've installed the AutoCAD Express Tools (not available in AutoCAD LT), you can perform this task automatically with the BURST command. Just type **BURST** and press Enter.

Purging unused block definitions

Each block definition slightly increases the size of your DWG file, as do other named objects such as layers, text styles, and dimension styles. If you delete (or explode) all the block references that point to a particular block definition, that block definition no longer serves any purpose.

You should run the PURGE command periodically in each drawing and purge unused block definitions. Click the Application button to open the Application Menu, choose Drawing Utilities on the left side, and then choose Purge to display the Purge dialog box. Click the Purge All button to purge all unused named objects in the current drawing.

PURGE isn't only for blocks — you can also remove empty layers and unused style definitions. In Figure 17-7, the Purge dialog box shows the unused dimension, multileader, and text styles that can be removed from this drawing with a click of the Purge All button.

AutoCAD 2010 adds two new options to the PURGE command. Neither is strictly related to blocks, but both locate pesky debris that until now has been hard to get rid of — or even know about. PURGE can now remove

✔ Zero-length lines and polylines (linework with the same coordinates for the start and end points)

✔ Blank text strings (text or mtext objects made up of one or more spaces).

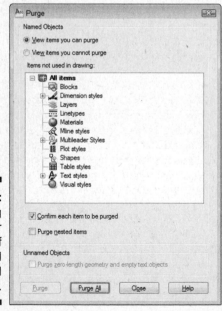

Figure 17-7:
Purging
your
drawing of
unneeded
named
objects.

Chapter 18

Going Dynamic and External

*I*n Chapter 17, I introduce blocks as collections of object geometry that are treated as single entities in AutoCAD. In that chapter, I also describe giving blocks a little more oomph by adding *attributes* — changeable text tags that can differ with each insertion. Other than that kind of slight variation though, the blocks I describe in Chapter 17 tend to be pretty static.

But blocks don't have to be static creations. Instead of having a half-dozen regular blocks for a half-dozen different door sizes, you can create a single *dynamic block* that includes all those sizes. Unlike a regular block, in which every instance of a particular block is geometrically identical, each instance of a dynamic block can display geometric variations. For example, you can insert one furniture block three times and have one instance display as a sofa, one as a loveseat, and one as an armchair. I introduce *block authoring* — the process for creating and editing dynamic blocks — in this chapter.

An *external reference drawing,* or *xref,* is like an industrial-strength block. An xref is a pointer to a separate drawing outside the drawing you're working on. When you attach a reference drawing, it appears on-screen and on plots as part of your drawing, but it continues to live as a separate document on your hard drive or network. If you edit the externally referenced drawing, the appearance of the drawing changes in all drawings that reference it.

A *raster image* file stores a graphical image as a series of dots. Raster files are good for storing photographs, logos, and other images, whereas AutoCAD *vector* files are good for storing geometrical objects such as lines and arcs, along with text and other annotations for describing the geometry. Sometimes it's handy to combine raster images with AutoCAD vector files by attaching them to your drawing files, and the External References palette makes the process straightforward.

Before AutoCAD 2007, *external references* meant AutoCAD drawing files (and only AutoCAD drawing files) that you attached to your current drawing. Images were (and still are) raster graphics files that you attached in a similar way but with a different command. In AutoCAD 2007 and later, *External References* is the name of the palette with which you attach and manage not only externally referenced AutoCAD drawings (xrefs) and 2D MicroStation DGN drawing files, but also image files and DWF or (new in AutoCAD 2010) PDF underlays. (*DWF* stands for Design Web Format; a DWF is a "lightweight" version of a DWG file intended for design review or posting on a Web site.) I discuss attaching DWFs or PDFs as external references at the end of this chapter, and describe the Web functions of DWFs in Chapter 20.

Both AutoCAD 2010 and AutoCAD LT 2010 enable you to attach DGN files to current drawings via the External References palette. *DGN* files are drawing files created by one of AutoCAD's major competitors: MicroStation from Bentley Systems. (You can also import and export DGN drawing data in both AutoCAD and AutoCAD LT.) If you're new to AutoCAD, you're not so likely to encounter DGN files unless you're working for a large company that exchanges a lot of drawings with partners and consultants. For more information on DGN files in AutoCAD 2010, open the Search tab of the online help system and enter *DGN Files*.

As I mention in Chapter 17, blocks, external references, DWF underlays, PDF underlays, raster images, and DGN files enable you to reuse your work and the work of others, giving you the potential to save tremendous amounts of time — or to cause tremendous problems if you change a file on which other people's drawings depend. Use these features when you can to save time, but do so in an organized and careful way so as to avoid problems.

Theme and Variations: Dynamic Blocks

You can add variety to your blocks by making them dynamic. The two most useful applications for dynamic blocks are multiple presentations of similar objects and manipulation of components within individual block inserts.

There's no question that AutoCAD's dynamic blocks feature gives a great deal of flexibility to block creation and insertion. But it's also a very complicated system, with its own set of commands and system variables. I recommend that you become *very* familiar with the regular block creation and insertion techniques I describe in Chapter 17 before you tackle dynamic blocks.

Spend some time planning your dynamic blocks. Sketch out the geometry for each variation in appearance (or *visibility state*) and decide where the common base point should be. Unless you're a lot smarter than I am, you'll probably find that creating dynamic blocks is complex enough without trying to design your blocks as you go.

Now you see it . . .

If your drawing shows six different kinds of windows, one approach is to create six different standard blocks to represent them all. Alternatively, you can create a single dynamic block and define *visibility states* to cover all six different types. The following steps show you how to make your blocks do double (or sextuple?) duty by using the Edit Block Definition dialog box:

1. **Open a drawing that contains some block definitions you want to combine or draw some simple geometry to make some similar types of objects.**

 You can create dynamic blocks from scratch, or you can work with existing standard (that is, non-dynamic) block definitions. Figure 18-1 shows a drawing with three non-dynamic blocks.

2. **On the Block panel of the Home tab, choose Edit to open the Edit Block Definition dialog box.**

3. **In the Block to Create or Edit box, specify a new block name or click <Current Drawing> and then click OK to display the Block Editor window.**

 The Block Editor is a special authoring environment with its own Ribbon tab plus a passel of command-line commands. You also have access to the rest of the Ribbon tabs, so you can draw and edit just like you're in the regular drawing window. The background color is different from the drawing editor's background color to help you remember where you are.

Figure 18-1:
Three blocks to make three seats.

The Block Editor tab's Geometric, Dimensional, and Manage panels (see Figure 18-2) are elements of AutoCAD 2010's new parametric drawing feature. (AutoCAD LT doesn't fully support parametric drawing, so it lacks the Geometric and Dimensional tabs and gets a mini-version of the Manage tab.) In this book, I don't have room to cover parametric constraints in dynamic blocks, but I do cover parametric drafting in Chapter 19. The concepts are pretty similar to adding parametric features to dynamic blocks.

If you enter a new block name, AutoCAD displays an empty block-authoring environment where you draw geometry or insert existing blocks. If you instead select Current Drawing, AutoCAD places all drawing objects inside the block authoring environment.

4. **Create some geometry for the first visibility state. Alternatively, click the Home tab, choose Insert on the Block panel, and select an existing block definition to serve as the first visibility state.**

 When creating geometry from scratch, pay attention to where the common base point should be. Although you use different blocks to assemble a multiple-view block, they should all have the same base point (0,0 is a good one for blocks). You don't want your chairs jumping around between different insertion points!

5. **If you inserted an existing block in Step 4, deselect all three Specify On-Screen check boxes, make sure that the Explode check box is *not* selected, and then click OK.**

6. **Repeat Steps 4 and 5, drawing or inserting all the necessary geometry.**

 At this point, your drawing screen may look pretty strange (see Figure 18-2). Don't worry; you're going to fix it up in the next steps.

7. **Click the Parameters tab of the Block Authoring Palettes and then click Visibility Parameter.**

 If the palettes aren't open, click Authoring Palettes on the Manage panel on the highlighted Block Editor tab of the Ribbon.

 AutoCAD prompts you to specify the parameter location.

8. **Click to place the parameter marker somewhere other than the base point location you chose in Step 4.**

 AutoCAD places a parameter marker at the selected point and returns to the command line. As shown in Figure 18-2, the label *Visibility* appears next to the Visibility Parameter marker, and a yellow Alert symbol indicates that no action has been assigned to the parameter yet. The controls on the Ribbon's Visibility panel become active.

The parameter location you specify will be the spot on the block where the dynamic block option grip will be displayed. It's not crucial where you locate this point, but try to pick a sensible location on the object. If you specify the same point for the parameter location as the base point for the block, you may have a hard time selecting the dynamic option grip.

Visibility Status controls

Figure 18-2:
Three seats
in the Block
Editor.

Block Authoring palettes　　　Visibility Parameter marker　　　Block Editor panels

9. **Click Visibility States on the Visibility panel (or the Block Authoring toolbar). Click Rename and change VisibilityState0 to something more descriptive. Click OK.**

 As is the case with other named objects in AutoCAD, it's good procedure to assign useful, descriptive names rather than accept the default generic labels.

10. **On the Visibility panel, click Make Invisible. At the Select Objects prompt, select the geometry or block inserts that should be invisible in the current visibility state — that is, those that are *not* associated with the current visibility state — and then press Enter.**

 AutoCAD prompts

   ```
   Hide for current state or all visibility states
         [Current/All] <Current>:
   ```

11. **Press Enter to make the selected objects invisible for the current visibility state only, or type** A **and press Enter if you want to hide them for all visibility states.**

 By default, the invisible objects disappear from the screen. You can view them in a faded appearance by clicking Visibility Mode on the Visibility panel.

12. **Click Visibility States again and then click New to create a new visibility state. In the New Visibility State dialog box, enter a descriptive name. Select the Show All Existing Objects in New State radio button and then click OK.**

 All your geometry should reappear.

13. **Repeat Steps 9, 10, and 11 to create additional visibility states associated with the remaining geometry or blocks.**

 The geometry or block insert associated with the last-created visibility state should be visible on-screen.

14. **Click Close Block Editor on the Ribbon. Save the changes to your new block or to <Current Drawing>.**

 AutoCAD displays an alert box asking if you want to save changes to your block. Click Cancel to return to the block editor or Discard the Changes to close the Block Editor without saving your changes. Click Save the Changes to update the block and exit. AutoCAD closes the block authoring environment and returns to the standard drawing editor window.

AutoCAD 2010's Block Editor tab includes a new Test Block tool that lets you see what your finished product will look like without the hassle of closing the editor and inserting or manipulating the block inside the drawing editor. Test Block displays the geometry and lets you try different parameters; then easily return to the Block Editor to tweak your masterpiece.

Lights! Parameters!! Actions!!!

You can modify the appearance of individual instances of the same block by defining *parameters* and *actions* to move, rotate, flip, or align parts of them. You can adjust the block's appearance as you insert it or at any time afterward. The following steps show you how to use the Block Editor to add some action to a block definition:

1. **Open a drawing that contains some block definitions whose appearance you want to spice up a little, or draw some simple geometry that might make a suitably dynamic block.**

 Action parameters are most effective in block definitions that contain groups of related objects — for example, an office desk and chair or a furniture arrangement.

2. **On the Block panel of the Ribbon's Home tab, choose Edit to open the Edit Block Definition dialog box.**

3. **In the Block To Create Or Edit box, type a new block name or click <Current Drawing>, and then click OK.**

4. **Create some geometry or insert some blocks. When you insert blocks, remember to make sure that the Explode check box at the lower-left corner of the Insert dialog box is *not* selected, and then click OK.**

 Draw the geometry or insert the blocks in a group such that you can insert the finished arrangement into your drawings — for example, Figure 18-3 shows the creation of a dynamic block for a coffee shop or cafeteria.

5. **Repeat Step 4 until you've drawn all the needed geometry or inserted all the necessary blocks.**

6. **Click the Parameters tab of the Block Authoring Palettes and then click Rotation Parameter.**

 AutoCAD prompts you to specify the parameter location.

7. **Click to place the parameter marker somewhere on the object geometry other than the base point location.**

 If you specify the same point for the parameter location as the base point for the block, you may have a hard time selecting the dynamic option grip.

8. **AutoCAD places a parameter marker at the selected point and returns to the command line, prompting you to specify the radius of the rotation parameter, the default rotation angle, and finally the parameter label location.**

 The parameter marker's label appears next to the rotation parameter marker.

9. **Click the Actions tab of the Block Authoring Palettes and then click Rotate Action. Select the Rotate Parameter, select the objects that should be modified when the grip is used, and specify a point for the action's label.**

 AutoCAD returns to the command prompt. At this point, it's fine to go with default values and on-screen pick points.

10. **Repeat Steps 6 through 9, trying different parameters and actions.**

 For example, choose a Point Parameter and a Move Action.

 Figure 18-3 shows a set of block components, several of which have action parameters assigned to them. After the block is inserted, you can manipulate the components to which you've added parameters to vary the appearance of the blocks. I explain how a little later in this chapter.

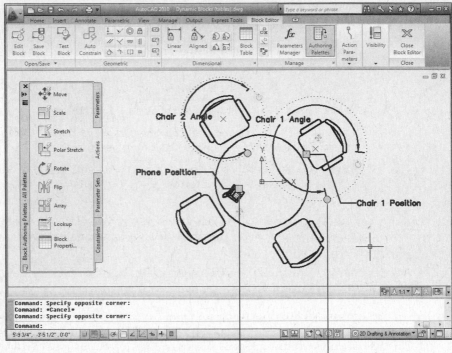

Figure 18-3:
A passel of
parameters
ready for
action.

Point Parameter marker Rotation Parameter marker

11. **Click Close Block Editor on the Ribbon.**

 An AutoCAD alert box asks whether you want to save or discard the changes to your block; click Save to save the changes.

 AutoCAD closes the block-authoring environment and returns to the standard drawing editor window.

Manipulating dynamic blocks

After a dynamic block has been inserted in a drawing, you can select it and modify its display through a special set of *custom grips*. (That's what AutoCAD calls them, so I'm following suit.)

When you select a non-dynamic block, you see a single grip at the insertion point. When you select a dynamic block, you see at least two — and maybe more — custom grips, as well as the insertion point grip. The custom grips usually look different from the regular object grips, but not always, so take care when clicking grips.

The following steps show you how to make your dynamic blocks do the things you just spent all this time teaching them to do:

1. **Insert a few blocks that contain some dynamic parameters, such as visibility or action parameters.**

 If your block inserts don't have any action parameters, go to Step 4.

2. **Select a block that includes some action parameters.**

 The block insert displays a number of grips (see Figure 18-4). If the insert displays only one grip, it isn't a dynamic block.

3. **Click one of the custom grips — for example, clicking a round grip opens the rotation parameter of the object. Rotate the component as required.**

4. **Select a block that includes a visibility parameter and then click the visibility grip. Choose the desired visibility state from the right-click menu.**

 For additional information on manipulating actions and visibility states, refer to the online help system.

Dynamic blocks, as I've suggested more than once, are a powerful — and complicated — feature. Prior to AutoCAD 2010, the Block Authoring Palettes contained 10 selectable parameters, 8 actions, and 20 parameter sets. AutoCAD 2010 adds 12 geometric constraints and 6 dimensional constraints. I'm thinking of writing a new book called *AutoCAD Block Authoring For Dummies* (although, truth be told, it may never happen). Until I do, AutoCAD's online help system is your best resource for more information on all the possibilities of dynamic blocks. The quickest and most direct way to AutoCAD's own help is to type **Dynamic Blocks** into the Search box on the program title bar.

Figure 18-4:
Variations on dynamic blocks (original on the right, and a handy grip tip on a chair at left center).

Going External

In AutoCAD, an *xref,* or external reference, is a reference to another, *external* drawing file — one outside the current drawing — that you can make act as though it's part of your drawing. Technically, a reference is simply a pointer from one file to another. The xref is the actual pointer, but many people call the combination of the pointer and the external file the xref.

In AutoCAD 2010, external drawing files are just one of five different file types you can attach to your current drawing by using the Select Reference File dialog box. You use this dialog box to attach externally referenced AutoCAD drawings (xrefs), raster image files, DWF files, PDF files, and MicroStation DGN drawing files.

Use the Attach button on the Insert tab's Reference panel to open the Select Reference File dialog box. When you attach an external drawing to your current drawing, you become the host of the external file. No need to break out the cocktails and canapés though . . . it's actually your current drawing that's doing the hosting and in AutoCAD, it's called (what else?) the *host drawing.* You can think of the attached xrefs as guests, but most of the time they're pretty well-behaved ones, and like the best of guests, they go away as soon as you want them to.

Xrefs have a big advantage over blocks: If a drawing is inserted as a block into another drawing, its geometry doesn't change if the original drawing is changed in any way — it always looks the way it looks when it's inserted. If that drawing is attached as an xref, however, AutoCAD will automatically update every host drawing to which it's attached when the host drawing is reopened. You can also manually reload the changed xref if you don't want to close and reopen the host drawing.

When you open a drawing that contains xrefs, AutoCAD displays a little symbol (which looks like papers with a binder clip) on the right end of the status bar. This symbol alerts you to the fact that some of the things you see in the drawing are actually parts of other, xrefed drawings. If an xref changes while you have the host drawing open (because you or someone else opens and saves the referenced drawing), the status bar xref symbol displays an `External Reference Files Have Changed` balloon notification. Simply click the Reload link in the balloon notification to show the updated xrefs. (If you want to change how AutoCAD checks for changes, look up *XREFNOTIFY* in the online help.)

There are few things I enjoy more when revising this book than telling LT users they finally have access to useful commands that AutoCAD users have enjoyed for years! AutoCAD LT 2010 includes the XREFNOTIFY system variable, which means LT will now check for changed references and notify you with a balloon message on the status bar. In both AutoCAD and AutoCAD LT, you can use the Reload option on the External References palette to

update the xrefs. See the "Managing xrefs" section, later in this chapter, for details. LT 2010 also includes the REFEDIT, XOPEN, and XCLIP commands, which I describe in more detail later.

Another advantage that xrefs have over blocks is that their contents aren't stored in your drawing even once. The disk storage space taken up by the original drawing (that is, the xref) isn't duplicated, no matter how many host drawings reference it. This characteristic makes xrefs much more efficient than blocks for larger drawings that are reused several times.

You can always buy a larger hard drive, however, so the storage issue isn't crucial. The key benefit of xrefs is that they enable you to organize your drawings so that changes you make to a single drawing file automatically "ripple through" all the host drawings into which it's xrefed. This benefit is even greater on larger projects involving multiple drafters, each of whose work may be incorporated in part or in whole in the work of others.

The automatic update feature of xrefs is a big advantage only if you're organized about how you use xrefs. Suppose that an architect creates a plan drawing showing a building's walls and other major features that are common to the architectural, structural, plumbing, and electrical plan drawings. The architect then tells the structural, plumbing, and electrical drafters to xref this background plan into their drawings so that everyone is working from a consistent and reusable set of common plan elements. If the architect decides to revise the wall locations and updates the xrefed drawing, everyone will see the current wall configuration and be able to change their drawings. But if the architect absentmindedly adds architecture-specific objects, such as toilets and furniture, to the xrefed drawing, or shifts all the objects with respect to 0,0, everyone else will have problems. If different people in your office share xrefs, create a protocol for who is allowed to modify which file when, and what communication needs to take place after a shared xref is modified.

Becoming attached to your xrefs

Attaching an external reference drawing is similar to inserting a block, and almost as easy. Just use the following steps:

1. **Set an appropriate layer current, as described in Chapter 6.**

 It's a good idea to insert xrefs on a separate layer from all other objects. Note that if you freeze the layer an xref is inserted on, the entire xref disappears. (This behavior can be either a handy trick or a nasty surprise.)

2. **If the External References palette isn't already open, click its icon (it looks like a sheaf of papers with a bulldog clip and a silhouetted user) on the Palettes panel of the View tab to open it.**

 The toolbar at the top of the palette lets you attach an external DWG file, a DWF underlay, a PDF underlay, a MicroStation DGN drawing file, or a raster image file. I cover attaching images and DWFs or PDFs later in this chapter. If you need to attach DGN files, visit the online help.

3. **Click Attach DWG. (Click the down arrow if the tooltip offers to attach something else — see Figure 18-5.)**

 The Select Reference File dialog box appears.

4. **Browse to find the file you want to attach, select it, and then click Open.**

 The Attach External Reference dialog box appears.

5. **Specify the parameters for the xref in the dialog box.**

 Parameters include the insertion point, scaling factors, and rotation angle. You can set these parameters in the dialog box or specify them on-screen, just as you can do when inserting a block, as described earlier in this chapter.

List View

Attach DWG Tree View

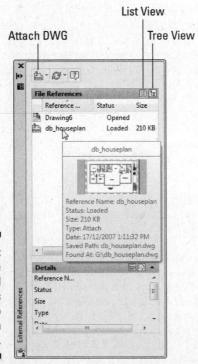

Figure 18-5:
Using the
External
References
palette to
attach an
xref.

You can select the Attachment or Overlay radio button to tell AutoCAD how to handle the xref. The choice matters only if you create a drawing that uses xrefs, and then your drawing is, in turn, used as an xref. Attachment is the default choice, and it means that the xrefed file will always be included with your drawing when someone else uses your drawing as an xref. Overlay, the other choice, means that you see the xrefed drawing, but someone who xrefs your drawing won't see the overlaid file. By choosing Overlay, you can xref a map, for example, to your drawing of a house but not have the map show up when someone else xrefs your house drawing. (That person can xref the map, if need be.) I recommend that you use the default Attachment reference type unless you have a specific reason to do otherwise.

The Path Type drop-down list provides more flexibility in how the xref's path gets stored. See the "Forging an xref path" section, later in this chapter, for more information. For now, I recommend that you choose Relative Path instead of the default Full Path.

6. **Click OK.**

 The externally referenced file appears in your drawing.

Layer-palooza

When you attach or overlay an xref, AutoCAD adds new layers to your current drawing that correspond to the layers in the xrefed DWG file. The new layers are assigned names that combine the drawing name and layer name; for example, if you xref the drawing MYSCREW.DWG, which has the layer names GEOMETRY, TEXT, and so on, the xrefed layers will be named MYSCREW|GEOMETRY, MYSCREW|TEXT, and so on. By creating separate layers corresponding to each layer in the xrefed file, AutoCAD eliminates the potential problem with blocks I warn you about in Chapter 17, when layers have the same name but different color or linetype in the two drawings.

Creating and editing an external reference file

To create a file that you can use as an external reference, just create a drawing and save it. That's it. You can then create or open another drawing and create an external reference to the previous one. The xrefed drawing appears in the host drawing as a single object, like a block insert. In other words, if you click any object in the xref, AutoCAD selects the entire xref. You can measure or object snap to the xrefed geometry, but you can't modify or delete individual objects in the xref — you open the xref drawing in order to edit its geometry.

AutoCAD's XOPEN command (now in AutoCAD LT 2010) provides a quick way to open an xrefed drawing for editing. You just start the command and pick any object in the xref. Alternatively (also now in LT 2010), you can select the xref in the External References palette and then right-click and choose Open to open one or more xrefs for editing. See the "Managing xrefs" section, later in this chapter, for more information.

An alternative to opening the xrefed file when you need to edit it is to use the REFEDIT command (now i5ncluded in AutoCAD LT 2010 and regular AutoCAD). REFEDIT (short for *Reference Edit)* lets you edit the external file from within the host drawing, rather than having to open the reference in its own window. Look up *REFEDIT* in the AutoCAD online help system.

With several xrefs attached to your drawing, it can be difficult to tell which objects belong to the drawing you're currently editing, and which are part of the xref. For several releases it's been possible to fade a reference file while using REFEDIT. In AutoCAD 2010, you can fade your xrefs at all times, not just when you're editing them, as follows:

1. **Open a drawing containing an external reference drawing.**

 Alternatively you can attach a drawing to your current drawing by following the steps in the "Becoming attached to your xrefs" section, earlier in this chapter.

2. **On the Insert tab, click the Reference panel label to open the Reference slideout.**

 The Reference slideout also contains the Reference Edit button which runs the REFEDIT command described in the previous section.

3. **Click the Xref Fading button to toggle reference fading off and on.**

4. **Drag the Xref fading slider to increase or decrease the level of fading in the reference file.**

 The default value is 70; increasing the value towards 90 (the maximum) increases the degree of fading, while lowering it reduces the fade level.

Forging an xref path

When you attach an xref, AutoCAD, by default, stores the xref's full path — that is, the drive letter and sequence of folders and subfolders in which the DWG file resides — along with the filename. This default behavior corresponds to the Full Path setting in the Path Type drop-down list. (Figure 18-6 shows the three xref path options.) Full Path works fine as long as you never move files on your hard drive or network and never send your DWG files to anyone else — which is to say, it almost never works fine!

Figure 18-6:
Follow the
path less
traveled
when you
attach
an xref.

At the other end of the path spectrum, the No Path option causes AutoCAD not to store any path with the xref attachment — only the filename is stored. This is the easiest and best option if the host drawings and the xrefs reside in the same folder. However, if the host and the xref are in different folders, you have to browse to find the reference file every time you open the host drawing.

If you prefer to organize the DWG files for a particular project in more than one folder, you'll appreciate AutoCAD's Relative Path option, as shown in Figure 18-6. This option permits xrefing across more complex folder structures but avoids many of the problems that the Full Path option can cause. For example, you may have a host drawing, `H:\Project-X\Plans\First floor.dwg`, that xrefs `H:\Project-X\Common\Column grid.dwg`. If you choose Relative path, AutoCAD will store the xref path as `..\ Common\ Column grid.dwg` instead of `H:\Project-X\Common\Column grid. dwg`. Now if you decide to move the `\Project-X` folder and its subfolders to a different drive (or send them to someone else who doesn't have an H: drive), AutoCAD can still find the xrefs.

When you use Relative Path, you'll see xref paths that include the special codes . and .. (single and double period). The single period means *this host drawing's folder,* and the double period means *the folder above this host drawing's folder.*

You can report on and change xref paths for a set of drawings with the AutoCAD Reference Manager (not in AutoCAD LT). See Chapter 20 for more information.

If all these path options and periods leave you feeling punchy, you can keep your life simple by always keeping host and xref drawings in the same folder and using the No Path option when you attach xrefs.

Managing xrefs

The External References palette includes many more options for managing xrefs after you attach them. Many of these options are hiding in right-click menus. Important options include

- ✔ **List of external references:** You can change between the List view and Tree view of your drawing's external references just by clicking the appropriate button at the top of the palette (refer to Figure 18-5). You can resize the columns by dragging the column dividers or re-sort the list by clicking the column header names, just as in Windows Explorer.

- ✔ **Unload:** Right-click an xref and choose Unload to make the selected xref disappear from the on-screen display of your drawing and from any plots you do of it, but retain the pointer and attachment information. Right-click again and choose Reload to redisplay an unloaded xref.

- ✔ **Reload:** Right-click an xref and choose Reload to force AutoCAD to reread the selected xrefed DWG file from the disk and update your drawing with its latest contents. This feature is handy when you share xrefs on a network and someone has just made changes to a drawing that you've xrefed.

- ✔ **Detach:** Right-click an xref in the External References palette and choose Detach to completely remove the selected reference to the external file from your drawing.

- ✔ **Bind:** Right-click an xref and choose Bind to bring the selected xref into your drawing and turn it into a block. You might use this function, for example, to roll up a complex set of xrefs into a single archive drawing.

 In many offices, binding xrefs without an acceptable reason for doing so is a crime as heinous as exploding blocks indiscriminately. In both cases, you're eliminating an important data management link. Find out what the policies are in your company. When in doubt, keep yourself out of a bind. And even when you do have a good reason to bind, you generally should do it on a copy of the host drawing.

- ✔ **Open:** Right-click an xref and choose Open to open one or more xref drawings in separate drawing windows. After you edit and save an xref drawing, return to the host drawing and use the Reload option in the External References palette to show the changes.

None of these options (other than opening and editing the xref) affects the xrefed drawing itself; it continues to exist as a separate DWG file. If you need to delete or move the DWG file that the xref refers to, do it in Windows Explorer.

The fact that the xrefed drawing is a separate file is a potential source of problems when you send your drawing to someone else; that someone else needs *all* the files that your drawing depends on, or it will be useless. Make sure to include xrefed files in the package with your drawing. See Chapter 20 for a procedure.

Both AutoCAD 2010 and AutoCAD LT 2010 include an additional xref feature called *xref clipping.* You can clip any kind of externally referenced file or a block insertion so only part of it appears in the host drawing. In addition to the XCLIP (for DWGS) and IMAGECLIP (for raster images) commands in earlier AutoCAD (but not AutoCAD LT) versions, the new releases add PDFCLIP and DGNCLIP. Finally, the new CLIP command bundles all reference types into one command.

Blocks, Xrefs, and Drawing Organization

Blocks and xrefs are useful for organizing sets of drawings to use and update repeated elements. It's not always clear, though, when to use blocks and when to use xrefs. Applications for xrefs include

- The parts of a title block that are the same on all sheets in a project.
- Reference elements that need to appear in multiple drawings (for example, wall outlines, site topography, column grids).
- Assemblies that are repeated in one or more drawings, especially if the assemblies are likely to change together (for example, repeated framing assemblies, bathroom layouts, and modular furniture layouts).
- Pasting up several drawings (for example, details or a couple of plans) onto one plot sheet.
- Temporarily attaching a background drawing for reference or tracing.

On the other hand, blocks remain useful in simpler circumstances. Situations in which you might stick with a block are

- Components that aren't likely to change.
- Small components.
- A simple assembly that's used repeatedly but in only one drawing.
- When you want to include *attributes* (variable text fields) that you can fill in each time you insert a block. Blocks let you include attribute definitions; xrefs don't. Refer to Chapter 17 for the lowdown on attributes.

Everyone in a company or workgroup should aim for consistency as to when and how they use blocks and xrefs. Check whether guidelines exist for using blocks and xrefs in your office. If so, follow them; if not, it would be a good idea to develop some guidelines.

Mastering the Raster

AutoCAD includes four more xref-like features: the ability to attach raster images, DWF files, PDF files, and DGN files to drawings. I cover DWF and PDF files in the next section and refer you to the online help if you should find some DGN files on your hands. The image feature is useful for adding a raster logo to a drawing title block or placing a photographed map or scene behind a drawing. A raster, or *bitmapped,* image is one that's stored as a field of tiny points.

Most AutoCAD drawings are vector files. A *vector* drawing is a graphic file defined by storing geometrical definitions of a bunch of objects. Typical objects include a line, defined by its two endpoints, and a circle, defined by its center point and radius. Vector-based images are typically smaller (in terms of the disk space they occupy) and more flexible than raster images but also are less capable of displaying visually rich images, such as photographs.

Raster images often come from digital cameras or from other programs, such as Photoshop. Raster images also can come into the computer from some kind of scanner that imports a blueline print, photograph, or other image.

Whether you're doing your own scanning or having a service bureau do it for you, you need to know that AutoCAD handles most of the popular image file formats, including: the Windows BMP format; the popular Web graphics formats GIF and JPEG; common print formats like PCX, PNG, and TIFF; and the less popular DIB, FLC, FLI, GP4, MIL, RLE, RST, TGA, and several even more obscure ones.

Here are three scenarios in which you could incorporate raster images in your drawing:

- ✔ **Small stuff:** You can add logos, special symbols, and other small images that you have in raster files.

- ✔ **Photographs and maps:** You can add photographs (such as a future building site) and maps (for example, showing the project location).

✔ **Vectorization:** To convert a raster image into a vector drawing by tracing lines in the raster image, you can attach the raster image in your drawing, trace the needed lines by using AutoCAD commands, and then detach the raster image. (This procedure is okay for a simple raster image; add-on software is available, from Autodesk and others, to support automatic or semiautomatic vectorization of more complex images.)

Using raster images is much like using external references. The raster image isn't stored with your drawing file; a reference to the raster image file is established from within your drawing, like an xref. You can clip the image and control its size, brightness, contrast, fade, and transparency. These controls fine-tune the appearance of the raster image on-screen and on a plot.

When you attach raster images, you have to make sure that you send the raster files along when you send your drawing to someone else.

Attaching an image

Follow these steps to bring a raster image into AutoCAD:

1. **If the External References palette isn't already open, click its icon on the Palettes panel of the View tab to open it.**

 Use the drop-down list on the first toolbar button to attach a drawing, an image, a DWF file, a PDF file, or a DGN file.

2. **Click Attach Image and locate the image file you want to attach.**

 The Select Reference File dialog box appears, as shown in Figure 18-7.

Figure 18-7: The Select Reference File dialog box.

3. **Browse to find the file you want to attach, select it, and then click Open.**

 The Attach Image dialog box appears.

 Click the Show Details button in the Attach Image dialog box to see more information about the resolution and image size of the image you're attaching.

4. **Specify the parameters for the attached image in the dialog box.**

 Parameters include the insertion point, scale factor, and rotation angle. You can set these parameters in the dialog box or specify them on-screen, similar to what you can do with blocks and external references, as described earlier in this chapter.

 The Image dialog box includes the same Full Path, Relative Path, and No Path options as those for attaching xrefs. (See the "Forging an xref path" section, earlier in this chapter.)

5. **Click OK.**

 The image appears in your drawing.

6. **If you need to ensure that the raster image floats behind other objects in the drawing, select the raster image, right-click, choose Draw Order, and then choose Send to Back.**

 The DRAWORDER command provides additional options for which objects appear on top of which other objects. If you need this kind of flexibility, look up *DRAWORDER command* in the AutoCAD online help system.

Maintaining your image

You manage the images in your drawing with the External References palette. You can view a list of image files that appear in the current drawing, detach (remove) image references, and unload and reload images when needed. You can't bind an image to your drawing; it always remains an external file.

You can clip images so that only part of the image is displayed in your drawing. Choose Clip on the Insert tab's Reference panel and follow the prompts to clip the image. You can have multiple overlapping or distinct pieces of any number of images in your drawing, and only the parts you need are loaded into memory when you have your drawing open.

Raster image files often are larger than DWG files of corresponding complexity; raster file size can affect performance within AutoCAD because the raster file loads into memory when you're working on your drawing. Some workarounds speed up operations:

✔ Attach raster images late in the production process.

✔ Create a lower-resolution version of the raster file, just large enough to create the desired effect in your drawing.

✔ Right-click over an image in the External References palette and choose Unload to temporarily hide an image without losing the attachment information.

In addition, raster files can increase the time that AutoCAD takes to generate plots (and the plot file sizes) dramatically. Before you settle on using large raster files in your AutoCAD drawing, do some testing on zooming, editing, and plotting.

A DWF Is Just a DWF

DWF stands for *Design Web Format.* You could think of a DWF as "DWG Lite" because it looks just like a drawing file and contains some of the actual drawing file data. I talk more about the Web side of DWFs in Chapter 20; in this section, I explain how you can use DWFs as reference files in your own drawings. (Some people call DWF files *dwiffs,* but I'm going to hold off on that one until I start hearing DWG files called *dwiggs.*)

You create DWFs from within AutoCAD in one of two ways. Either choose Plot and select a DWF option in the Printer/Plotter name list, or choose Print⇨Batch Plot from the Application Menu and select DWF in the Publish To area of the Publish dialog box. DWFs are compact and secure: You can't edit a DWF in AutoCAD. The DWF format is ideal for two purposes: You can post DWFs on the Web, and you can send your drawings to consultants and clients in a form that they can't mess up. You can attach DWFs to your drawing files in pretty much the same way you attach drawings as external references. DWFs attached to drawing files are referred to as DWF underlays.

AutoCAD 2010 adds the hugely popular PDF format to the list of file types you can attach to your drawings. As with DWF and DGN attachments, you can object snap to entities in the PDF underlay by enabling the Snap to Underlays function in the Reference panel slideout on the Insert tab. Setting PDF parameters is virtually identical to setting DWF parameters, and you can attach a PDF to your drawing using exactly the same steps as the ones that follow.

The previous sections show how to attach a DWG and a raster image. Follow these steps to attach a DWF (or a PDF!) file as an underlay:

1. **If the External References palette isn't already open, click its icon on the Palettes panel of the View tab to open it.**

 The toolbar at the top of the palette lets you attach an external file as an xref, a raster image file, or a DGN or DWF underlay. I cover attaching xrefs and images earlier in this chapter. See the online help for information on attaching DGN files.

2. **Click Attach DWF or Attach PDF and locate the file you want to attach.**

 The Select Reference File dialog box appears.

3. **Browse to find the file you want to attach, select it, and then click Open.**

 The Attach DWF Underlay or Attach PDF Underlay dialog box appears.

4. **Specify the parameters for the DWF or the PDF in the dialog box.**

 Parameters include specifying a sheet, the insertion point, scaling factors, rotation angle, and path type (see Figure 18-8). You can set these parameters in the dialog box or specify them on-screen, just as you can do when inserting a block, attaching an xref, or attaching an image, as described earlier in this chapter.

5. **Click OK.**

 The externally referenced DWF or PDF file appears in your drawing.

DWF files aren't as precise as DWGs — that's why they're a lot smaller. When using object snap to locate points in DWFs, you may see the word *approximate* on the object snap tooltip. If this is a problem, you can increase the precision of your DWF file when you create it.

Figure 18-8:
The Attach PDF Underlay dialog box.

Chapter 19

Call the Parametrics!

I'm planting the New in 2010 icon at the very beginning of this chapter, and you're not going to see it again because *everything* I discuss in this chapter is brand new in this release.

AutoCAD 2010 includes a set of parametric drawing tools and, offhand, I can't think of a more significant new feature in recent years. (Don't worry, I'm going to offer a definition of parametric in just a few more paragraphs.) In fact, if you work primarily in 2D, and especially if you're in the manufacturing business, the addition of parametrics to AutoCAD 2010 is probably the most significant new feature *ever*.

If you know what I'm talking about, you're probably pretty interested in finding out more about what you can do with parametrics. If you know what I'm talking about and you're using an older AutoCAD release, maybe I've already convinced you to think about an upgrade. If, on the other hand, you think parametrics are the folks who show up when you dial 911, the following paragraphs should straighten you out.

Maintaining Design Intent

Parametric (rule-based) drawing is by far the best way of enforcing design intent in 2D drafting. *Design intent* in AutoCAD 2010 (or any other engineering software) means that when drawings are edited — this part made wider, that hole made larger — all the attached or related objects behave in a predictable way that honors the designer's intent when she created the drawing in the first place.

Before AutoCAD 2010, there was simply no way of maintaining the design concepts that went into a drawing. You could use AutoCAD's drawing and editing commands to draw accurate, precise plans, sections, and details, but as far as AutoCAD was concerned, they were just a bunch of lines and circles.

Take, for example, that base plate drawing example in Chapter 3. Maybe the engineer has had a second look and determined that those 1 1/2 inch (38 mm for the metric crowd) bolts aren't quite up to the job — they need to be changed to 1 3/4 inch (44 mm). To revise the drawing using AutoCAD in the traditional way, you draw a new, larger circle for the bolt and erase the old one. Now the nut is too small, and so is the hole in the plate (maybe you can't see it, but you know and I know it's there). There's a whole lot of editing required to fix this drawing.

In AutoCAD 2010, you can add some intelligence to those lines and circles by applying constraints to them. For example, you could apply a *dimensional constraint* to the bolt circle and the hole circle such that the hole circle is always 1/16" (2 mm) bigger than the bolt circle. And while you're at it, you'd probably want to apply a concentric *geometric constraint* between the circles so that whenever the bolt circle moved, the hole circle moved with it.

Now *that* is intelligent design!

Defining terms

As you might have guessed, the adjective *parametric* is derived from the noun *parameter* (and so endeth today's English lesson). If you look up *parameter* in most dictionaries, you'll get an explanation in terms of pure math — and that's *waaaay* deeper than you need to go. For the purposes of making drawings in AutoCAD, think of a parameter as a *rule* — and therefore think of parametric drawing as *rule-based drawing*.

AutoCAD's parametric rules (officially they're *constraints*) fall into two categories:

 ✔ **Dimensional constraints:** Based on dimensioned distances on or between objects or points on objects. For example, you could apply a dimensional constraint to two lines that represent a wall thickness so that regardless of where you moved them or how you rotated them, they would always be 6" apart.

 ✔ **Geometric constraints:** Based on object types and relationships between objects; different object types have different potential constraints. For example, you can apply a concentric constraint to an arc and a circle so that when you move one, it maintains its position in relation to the other.

Both AutoCAD and AutoCAD LT support constraints, but as is usually the case, the feature is limited in LT. If you use the full version, you can create and modify geometric and dimensional constraints, as I describe in the steps in this chapter. If you're using LT, you can't *create* either type of restraint, but you can work with existing constraints in drawings that were created in the full version. Figure 19-1 shows the difference between the AutoCAD and AutoCAD LT Parametric tabs.

If you're using AutoCAD LT, or if you just want to check out some ready-made parametric possibilities, you can download the sample drawing datasets from either www.autodesk.com/autocad-samples or www.autodesk.com/autocadlt-samples. The parametric samples are architectural_example-imperial.dwg, civil_example-imperial.dwg, and mechanical_example-imperial.dwg.

Figure 19-1: Parametric tabs in AutoCAD (above) and AutoCAD LT (below).

Constrain yourself

You can apply dimensional or geometric constraints to new geometry as you create it, or you can assign constraints to existing geometry in old drawings. You can even convert existing associative dimensions to dynamic dimensional constraints. The following sections describe the available constraints in each of the two categories. I start with dimensional constraints, as they're conceptually a little easier to understand, and they nearly all have analogues to regular dimension commands (which I cover in Chapter 14).

Understanding Dimensional Constraints

The normal practice in AutoCAD is to create some geometry — of course, using all the precision techniques I discuss in Chapter 7 — and then apply dimensions as I describe in Chapter 14. Assuming that you're using fully associative dimensions, you can then edit the geometry and watch the dimensions update automatically. The length of the line or the radius of the

circle are in control, and those dimensions are called *driven dimensions* because they change when the object geometry changes.

Dimensional constraints, unlike regular AutoCAD dimensions, are *driving* dimensions, which means that when you change the value of a dynamic dimension on a line, the line changes to match — in other words, the length of the line is being driven by the dimension, not the other way around.

There are only eight dimensional constraint options, but they cover all the bases. Table 19-1 lists them and describes their purposes.

Table 19-1		Dimensional Constraints
Button Icon	**Constraint Name**	**Description**
	Linear	Applies a horizontal or vertical dimensional constraint (similar to DIMLINEAR)
	Horizontal	Applies a dimensional constraint aligned with the x-axis of the coordinate system (similar to DIMLINEAR's Horizontal option)
	Vertical	Applies a dimensional constraint aligned with the y-axis of the coordinate system (similar to DIMLINEAR's Vertical option)
	Aligned	Applies a dimensional constraint aligned with the object or with the points being dimensioned (similar to DIMALIGNED)
	Radial	Applies a set value or formula to the radius of an arc or circle
	Diameter	Applies a set value or formula to the diameter of an arc or circle
	Angular	Applies a set value or formula to the angle between two lines or three points
	Convert	Converts an existing associative dimension object to a dimensional constraint

Practice a little constraint

The objects you add to your drawing from the Dimensional panel are not the same as the dimension objects you add from the Annotate tab. Dimensional constraints are *driving* dimensions — that means when you change the value of one of these dimensions, the geometry changes.

A lot is happening behind the scenes as you apply parametric constraints. You can get a great sense of how these constraints work at keeping your drawing objects in order by trying the STRETCH command on objects after you apply a constraint to them.

The following steps are a simple example of dimensional constraints:

1. **Start a new drawing and make the Ribbon's Parametric tab current.**

 Turn on some appropriate precision drawing aids on the status bar, such as Snap, Ortho, and Osnap.

2. **Draw some reasonable precise geometry using some of those precision techniques I describe in earlier chapters.**

 In the following example, I've used the RECTANG and CIRCLE commands to draw the geometry you see in Figure 19-2. The rectangle is 10 units square, and the 2.5-unit-radius circle is deliberately drawn away from the middle of the square.

Make sure that Show Dynamic Constraints in the Ribbon's Dimensional panel is turned on (see Figure 19-2; the button is blue when it's enabled) — otherwise, your dynamic dimensional constraints will disappear as soon as you place them.

Show Dynamic Constraints

Figure 19-2:
Simple geometry badly in need of constraining.

3. **On the Dimensional panel of the Parametric tab, click Linear.**

 A linear dimension icon appears beside the pickbox.

 Like the DIMLINEAR command, the Linear dimensional constraint tool is inferential — which way you drag the crosshairs controls whether you get a horizontal or vertical dimension. Also, like DIMLINEAR, you can press Enter at the command prompt and select an object to dimension.

4. **Press Enter at the command prompt to confirm you want to select an object and then select the bottom horizontal line segment.**

 If you see red markers at the midpoint and ends of the bottom line, you didn't press Enter; you're in point selection mode, not object selection.

 AutoCAD generates a preview of a dimensional constraint and prompts you for a location.

5. **Click to locate the dimension position.**

 AutoCAD draws a dimensional constraint with a highlighted text field displaying the dimension name (d1 in this example) and the value returned by AutoCAD (see Figure 19-3). You could type a new value in the edit box, but for now, just press Enter to confirm the value and the dimension location.

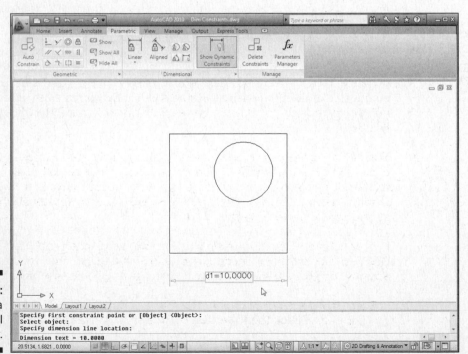

Figure 19-3:
Placing a dimensional constraint.

Dimensional constraints are not regular dimension objects — they're not going to plot, so it doesn't really matter where you put them or what they look like. I show you how to turn dimensional constraints into properly styled, plottable dimensions in the next section.

6. **Repeat Steps 3–5 and add a dimensional constraint to the right vertical edge of the rectangle.**

 AutoCAD draws a second dimensional constraint, this one named d2.

As you mouse over the Linear button, you can see that unlike its Aligned neighbor, it's in two parts. You can force a linear dimensional constraint to be either horizontal or vertical (rather than dependent on the direction in which you drag your crosshairs) by clicking the bottom part of the Linear button and making your choice from the flyout.

Making your drawing even smarter

If this were a traditional mechanical drawing that followed the rules of drafting, those two dimensions would be enough — whoever is reading your drawing understands that if sides are parallel and perpendicular, a dimension on one side applies to the opposite side as well. But in this chapter, I'm talking about *intelligent* drawings that respect design intent, not dumb collections of lines and circles, even if they *do* follow the rules!

If you try stretching the rectangle in various ways, only the bottom and left sides are constrained to 10 units in length. You could add two more linear dimensional constraints to the unconstrained sides, but you'd have to remember to edit both dimensions. Rather than constraining both sides to be 10 units long, the way to maintain design intent is to make both sides equal in length.

You can make the two sides equal using either dimensional or geometric constraints. It's sometimes a good idea to apply some geometric constraints to your drawing so objects are at least a little locked down. In fact, in a real-world workflow, you'd be using both geometric and dimensional constraints as you produce your design.

I cover geometric constraints in a little more detail in the "Understanding Geometric Constraints" section, later in the chapter, but for now, I'm going to apply three geometric constraints so the drawing behaves more predictably.

1. **On the Geometric panel of the Parametric tab, click Fix (the padlock icon) and click the lower-left corner of the rectangle.**

2. **On the Geometric panel, click Horizontal and click the bottom side of the rectangle. Then click Vertical and click the left side.**

 Icons appear near the drawing geometry, showing that those three geometric constraints are active (see Figure 19-6 a few pages ahead).

I explain those icons, and geometric constraints in general, in the next section, but I'm going back to dimensional constraints to finish this drawing.

3. **On the Dimensional panel of the Parametric tab, click Linear and add a dimensional constraint to the top horizontal line.**

4. **Click to locate the dimension, type** d1**, and press Enter when AutoCAD prompts for the dimension text.**

 Instead of having numeric values like the first two linear constraints, this new dimensional constraint displays d3=d1.

5. **Repeat Steps 3 and 4, this time adding a constraint to the vertical line at the left and entering** d2 **as the dimension text.**

 All four dynamic dimensional constraints display their name plus a value or expression.

Dimensional constraints have names as well as values. They can also include expressions or formulas. You can set the default appearance of dynamic dimensional constraints by clicking the dialog-box launcher (the little arrow at the right end of the Dimensional panel label) to open the Constraint Settings dialog box with the Dimensional tab active (see Figure 19-4). The options are

✔ **Name:** The first linear dimension is named d1, the second d2, and so forth. You use the dimension names in expressions.

✔ **Value:** The numeric value that you enter into the dimensional constraint or that AutoCAD enters if you don't override it.

✔ **Name and Expression:** The dimension name shown as equal to an expression. The expression can be a value, as in this example, or it can be a formula.

Figure 19-4:
Format the appearance of dimensional constraints in the Constraint Settings dialog box.

Using the Parameters Manager

Both AutoCAD and AutoCAD LT include the *Parameters Manager* palette, accessible on the Manage panels of their Ribbon's Parametric tab. You can use Parameters Manager to give all those dimensional constraints more sensible names than d1 and d2, but even more usefully, you can enter expressions instead of plain numeric values, as I explain in the following steps.

1. **Click Parameters Manager in the Manage panel.**

 The Parameters Manager palette appears, showing a list of dimensional constraints currently applied in the drawing (see Figure 19-5).

 In Figure 19-5, the Expression column shows the *numeric values* I specified for d1 and d2 and the *expressions* I entered for d3 and d4. The read-only Value column shows the calculated value. You can't change a value in the Value column; you can only edit the cells in the Expression column.

Figure 19-5:
The
Parameters
Manager
palette.

2. **In the d1 row, click in the Expression field to highlight the current value (10 in this example) and type a new value. For example, type** 13 **and press Enter.**

 The rectangle resizes itself in the drawing editor, and because the d3 constraint on the top side was made equal to the d1 constraint on the bottom side, both sides change equally.

 Next, use an equation as an expression.

3. **In the d2 row, click in the Expression field to highlight the current value and then type an expression. For example, type** d1*0.75 **and press Enter.**

The read-only Value column as well as the drawing geometry show that the d1 distance of 10 has been multiplied by 0.75 and is now 9.75 units long (see Figure 19-6).

Finally, constrain the circle so its center is always at dead center of the rectangle, no matter how the rectangle's size changes.

4. **Apply a horizontal dimensional constraint from the upper-left corner of the rectangle to the center of the circle. Locate the dimension and then type** d3/2 **and press Enter.**

 The rectangle is now dimensionally constrained on all four sides, so it doesn't really matter which corner you start from. And you don't have to type the whole expression d5=d3/2. AutoCAD knows what you mean!

5. **Repeat Step 4, this time adding a vertical constraint from one of the corners to the center of the circle. Locate the dimension and then type** d4/2.

 Figure 19-7 shows the object geometry with all constraints added in this section. Who knew that drafting could be such fun?

Figure 19-6: Editing constraints in the Parameters Manager.

Dimensions or constraints — have it both ways!

After all that hard work adding dimensional constraints to your drawings, it would be a downright shame to have to go back and apply regular dimensions, wouldn't it? Well — you don't have to — you can make dimensional constraints look and behave like regular dimensions. You can go the other way too and make your regular dimensions act like dimensional constraints.

Figure 19-7:
All locked
down —
dimension-
ally at least.

Dimensional constraints are available in two flavors:

- **Dynamic constraints:** The default form. Dynamic constraints appear gray with a padlock icon next to them in the drawing area. You can make them appear and disappear by clicking Show Dynamic Constraints in the Dimensional panel. They don't plot, and they resize as you zoom in and out of the drawing so they're always legible.

- **Annotational constraints:** This form is controlled as an object property, so you have to set it in the Properties palette. Annotational constraints do plot, don't resize as you zoom in and out, and don't disappear as you toggle the Show Dynamic Constraints button on and off. Annotational constraints conform to dimension style settings.

The dimension name format of annotational constraints can be set to Name, Value, or Name and Expression, just like dynamic constraints (refer to Figure 19-4 for another look at the Constraint Settings dialog box). If you're going to plot your drawing with annotational constraints, remember to reset the format so it doesn't show the dimension name or the expression.

Here's how to turn dynamic dimensional constraints into annotative constraints:

1. **Open a drawing that contains some geometry with dimensional constraints.**

 You can also start a new drawing, draw some simple geometry, and add a dimensional constraint to two.

2. **Select a dynamic constraint, right-click, and choose Properties.**

 The Properties palette opens with the object properties of the selected dimensional constraint listed in table form.

3. **Click in the Constraint Form field and in the drop-down list, change Dynamic to Annotational (see Figure 19-8).**

 The dynamic constraint becomes annotational and takes on the appearance of the current dimension style. If you change the dimension style in the Properties palette, the annotational constraint updates to the new dimension style format.

 You can go the other way too, from regular dimension objects to dimensional constraints.

4. **Add a linear, radius, diameter, aligned, or angular dimension to your drawing geometry.**

 Nearly every type of dimension object has a parametric analog; the exceptions are arc length, jogged radius, jogged linear, and ordinate dimensions.

5. **Click Convert in the Dimensional panel, select one of the dimension types in Step 4, and press Enter.**

 The dimensional constraint text box displays as soon as you click an associative dimension, and the dimension becomes a dynamic constraint as soon as you press Enter.

The only clue that a dimension is an annotational constraint rather than a regular old associative dimension is the padlock icon that appears next to the dimension value. You can turn off the display of the padlock in the Constraint Settings dialog box, but I recommend you leave it on. It doesn't plot anyway, and you might decide to delete the dimension without realizing it's controlling your object geometry.

Figure 19-8:
Turning dynamic constraints into annotational ones.

Understanding Geometric Constraints

Adding geometric constraints to object geometry may take a little getting used to because it's unlike anything AutoCAD has offered before.

In a few cases, AutoCAD's geometric constraints have equivalent object snaps. There are tangent, parallel, and perpendicular object snaps and tangent, parallel, and perpendicular geometric constraints. The difference between these relations as object snaps and geometric constraints is that constraints are *persistent*.

For example, you can draw a line at any angle, start another line, turn on parallel object snap, and create a second line that's parallel to the first. But then you can easily rotate either line so they're no longer parallel. If, however, you apply a parallel *constraint* to the second line, it will rotate with the first line, always maintaining that parallel relation until you delete the constraint.

There are twelve geometric constraints you can apply to your drawing objects, and the easiest way to apply them is by clicking buttons on the Geometric panel of the Ribbon's Parametric tab. Table 19-2 presents a list of the geometric constraints and explains their function.

Table 19-2		Geometric Constraints
Button Icon	Constraint Name	Description
	Coincident	Forces two or more points, such as endpoints or midpoints, to coincide; can also constrain a point to lie anywhere on an object
	Collinear	Forces two or more lines to lie along an infinitely long projection of the first line selected
	Concentric	Forces the centers of two or more arcs, circles, ellipses, or arc segments of polylines to coincide
	Fix	Locks the location of an object or a point on an object to a specific location in the drawing
	Parallel	Forces two lines to be parallel; the second line selected becomes parallel to the first line
	Perpendicular	Forces two lines to be perpendicular to one another

(continued)

Table 19-2 *(continued)*

Button Icon	Constraint Name	Description
	Horizontal	Forces a line or two points to be horizontal relative to the current coordinate system
	Vertical	Forces a line or two points to be vertical relative to the current coordinate system
	Tangent	Forces an object to be tangent to a selected arc or circle
	Smooth	Joins a selected spline object with another spline, line, arc, or polyline while maintaining curvature (also known as G2) continuity
	Symmetric	Forces two objects, or two points on objects to be symmetrical about an imaginary line
	Equal	Forces two lines or linear polyline segments to be the same length; forces two arcs or circles to have the same radius

Applying a little more constraint

If you're using the full version of AutoCAD (not AutoCAD LT), you can geometrically constrain drawing objects by clicking buttons on the Geometric panel of the Parametric tab. In the following steps, I show you how to get started with geometric constraints.

1. **Start a new drawing. Make the Ribbon's Parametric tab current and turn off Snap, Ortho, Polar, Osnap, and Otrack at the status bar.**

 For real drafting, you probably want to use these precision aids, but for this example, you get a better sense of parametrics with a *really* imprecise drawing.

2. **Draw some linework using the PLINE command and add a couple of circles.**

 Draw something similar to Figure 19-9 if you want to follow closely.

 Every drawing will be tackled differently. It's a good idea to think ahead and figure out the most efficient way to apply the constraints you need so that your design intent is maintained. In this example, I want to end up with two concentric circles in the middle of a square.

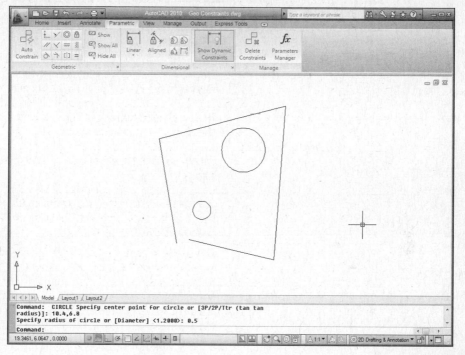

Figure 19-9:
Random
shapes that
badly need
constraining.

As I mention earlier, you'll find it a lot easier to apply constraints if at least one point on the geometry is fixed in space. In many cases, one of the first constraints you should think about applying is Fix, the one that constrains a point to one location in the drawing area.

In this example, I'll lock an endpoint of the polyline into position.

3. Click Fix in the Geometric panel and then click a point you want to fix in space.

A blue padlock icon is displayed beside the pickbox, and the red pick point marker appears when you're over a point you can constrain (see Figure 19-10). In this example, I click one of the endpoints on the polyline. A padlock icon appears in the constraint bar indicating the line segment is fixed in place.

With at least one point on the geometry fixed in place, I start constraining the geometry by closing the gap in the linework.

4. Click Coincident in the Parametric tab's Geometric panel.

You use a coincident constraint to make two points coincide. A blue coincident icon appears near the pickbox and, as you move your crosshairs over an object, a marker appears over relevant points — in the case of lines or polyline segments, at the endpoints and midpoint.

Figure 19-10:
Locking
down an
object in
drawing
space.

 Use appropriate drawing commands based on your design intent. I use a
polyline in this example because the ends of the segments are already
coincident-constrained by being part of a single polyline object. If I draw
this shape with lines, I have to apply individual coincident constraints to
each corner.

**5. Click an endpoint on the first polyline segment you want to connect
and then click an endpoint on the second segment.**

The endpoint of the second polyline segment jumps to the endpoint of
the first line, and a small blue square — the marker for coincident con-
straints — appears at the intersection. (If you don't see the little blue
square, click Show All in the Geometric panel.)

Next, I apply some orthographic parameters so my linework starts to
look a little more like a rectangle.

 **6. Click Horizontal in the Parametric tab's Geometric panel and then click
a line or polyline segment you want to be aligned with the
drawing's x-axis.**

The segment realigns itself horizontally from the endpoint nearest
to where you picked the line, and a horizontal constraint marker —
officially called a *constraint bar* — appears near the object.

 **7. Click Vertical to align a line or polyline segment with the drawing's
y-axis.**

The segment realigns itself at 90 degrees to the horizontal segment,
and a constraint bar showing a vertical constraint appears. With
one horizontally and one vertically constrained line segment, you're
halfway to a geometrically precise rectangle!

Because rectangles have parallel and perpendicular sides, next I apply those constraints to my linework.

8. **Click Parallel in the Parametric tab's Geometric panel, click the vertically constrained line segment, and then click the line segment opposite.**

 Because there's already a vertical constraint applied to one segment, it doesn't matter which line you pick first. If neither line had an existing constraint, the second line you picked would become parallel to the first line.

 Always keep your design intent in mind as you think about which constraints to apply and when to apply them. As a general rule, it's good to start with the most important and drill down to the least important. And, as I remind you above, applying a fix constraint early in the game can prevent your geometry rearranging itself in ways you don't expect.

 To make the final side of the almost-rectangle orthogonal with the other three, I could use another parallel constraint and click the bottom line. However, I don't want to wear out my Parallel button, so I'll use Perpendicular on the final segment.

9. **Click Perpendicular on the Geometric panel, click either of the vertical sides, and then click the non-orthogonal side.**

 Again, because three of the four sides are already constrained to horizontal and vertical, it doesn't matter which segment you pick first.

 To delete a constraint, move the mouse pointer over the constraint marker to display the constraints bar (see Figure 19-11), right-click and choose Delete.

Figure 19-11:
Constraining
to
orthogonal.

From four nonorthogonal, not even closed line segments, applying a handful of constraints yields a perfect rectangle — but I *really* want a square! Here's where the equal constraint comes in.

10. Click Equal on the Geometric panel, click the bottom side, and then click either of the vertical sides.

A perfect square! Now I want to constrain those circles.

My design intent in this example is to have the circles be concentric and to locate their centers in the exact center of the rectangle. First the easy part: Making the circles concentric.

11. Click Concentric in the Geometric panel, click one circle, and then click the other.

The two circles are concentrically constrained (try saying that ten times in a hurry!), and a new constraint bar appears in their vicinity. Try moving one circle by clicking it and watch the other tag along.

As I suggested, concentric was the easy constraint. I'd love to be able to use the Mid Between 2 Points object snap and just click two diagonally opposite corners to locate the circles dead center in the rectangle.

However, you can constrain only objects or points on objects, so I'm going to have to add some construction geometry in order to maintain my design intent.

12. Draw a line between diagonally opposite corners using Endpoint object snaps and then apply coincident constraints between the endpoints of this line and the corners of the rectangle (see Figure 9-12).

Figure 19-12:
Adding some construction geometry.

Draw construction geometry on a separate layer and set that layer to NoPlot in the Layer Properties Manager. If you don't want to even see it, let alone not plot it, you can turn off your construction geometry layer or even freeze it — the geometric constraints will still work.

13. **Click Coincident in the Geometric panel. Click either circle so the parametric marker appears in the center, move the pickbox over the construction line, and click when the parametric marker is over the midpoint of the line.**

You're done (whew!). You can test your design intent by using the STRETCH command on the corner of the rectangle that's diagonally opposite from the one with the little blue square. As you drag the corner, you should see the two circles moving too, always maintaining their position in the middle of the rectangle (see Figure 19-13).

Figure 19-13:
Full-on geometric constraints.

Autoconstrain yourself!

The geometric constraints listed in Table 19-2 are meant to be applied one at a time. It's great to have that flexibility, but it can be pretty darned time-consuming to go around a complex object, trying to figure out what the best constraint option would be and then applying it.

The Auto Constrain button on the Parametric tab's Geometric panel can apply constraints to a selection of objects with a single click — but before you execute that single click, take a look at the many Auto Constrain settings.

Click the dialog box launcher (the arrow at the right end of the Geometric panel label) to open the Constraint Settings dialog box with the AutoConstrain tab active (see Figure 19-14). Choose which constraints you want to apply automatically, and what order you want them in the list so the ones that should take precedence have a higher priority. Auto Constrain works only with geometric constraints, not with dimensional constraints.

The three buttons at the right side of AutoCAD's Geometric panel — and the *only* buttons on AutoCAD LT's Geometric panel — are for controlling the visibility of geometric constraint markers. Show All shows them all, and Hide All (surprise!) hides them all. Use the Show button to display the constraints on selected objects. This last button is a little clunky. It would be nice to be able to hover over an object and have the constraints show, but you actually have to click an object and then press Enter to see any results.

Figure 19-14:
Autocon-
strainable
geometric
relations in
the
Constraint
Settings
dialog box.

Although in this chapter, I present the two varieties of parametric constraints separately, you'll get the most mileage from this feature when you incorporate both geometric and dimensional constraints with all those other precision techniques I tell you about in Chapter 7. In fact, if you start a drawing using Snap, Ortho, Osnap, and other precision techniques before you start adding dimensional and parametric constraints, you'll be well on the way to creating a library of intelligent drawings that maintain your design intent.

Chapter 20

Drawing on the Internet

*U*nless you've been living under a rock for the past 20 years, you know that the Internet is causing major changes in the way people work. Because of the Net, most of us communicate differently, exchange files more rapidly, and phone out for pizza less frequently.

In this chapter, I show you how and when to use AutoCAD's Internet features. I also cover how the Internet features can connect with traditional CAD tasks, such as plotting. The emphasis of this chapter is on useful, no-nonsense ways to take advantage of the Internet in your CAD work.

The Internet and AutoCAD: An Overview

As with all things Webby, the Internet features in AutoCAD are a hodgepodge of the genuinely useful, the interesting but still somewhat immature or difficult to use, and the downright foolish. In this chapter, I steer you toward features and techniques that are reliable and widely used today and away from features that (to put it kindly) might not be ready for prime time. On the other hand, a few of today's questionable features may become the reliable, commonplace ones of tomorrow. I give you enough context to see how everything works and where it may lead. Table 20-1 summarizes AutoCAD's Internet features and tells you where in this book to find more information.

Table 20-1	AutoCAD 2010 Internet Features		
Feature	*Description*	*Comments*	*Where You Can Find More Info*
ETRANSMIT command	Package DWG files for sending via e-mail or FTP or posting on the Web	Useful to most people	The "Send it with ETRANSMIT" section in this chapter
Reference Manager (not in AutoCAD LT)	Report on and modify paths of referenced files	Useful for people who send drawings and use complex, multifolder xref schemes	The "Help from the Reference Manager" section in this chapter
DWF files	A "lightweight" drawing file format for posting drawings on the Web or sharing them with people who don't have AutoCAD	The recipient must have Autodesk Design Review installed; potentially useful for sharing drawings with people who don't have AutoCAD	"Design Web Format — Not Just for the Web" in this chapter
DWFx files	Like DWF files but compliant with Microsoft's XML specification	With Windows Vista, the recipient can view DWFx files with the included XPS viewer	"Design Web Format — Not Just for the Web" in this chapter
PUBLISH command	Create DWF or DWFx files, plot (PLT) files, or paper plots in batches	Can help automate the traditional plotting procedure; if DWF files ever catch on, will streamline their creation	"Making DWFs (or plots) with PUBLISH" in this chapter
Publish to Web	A wizard that builds and publishes a Web page containing drawings	Like most wizards, fairly easy to use but limited; possibly useful as a quick-and-dirty Web publishing approach	*PUBLISHTOWEB* command in the AutoCAD online help system
Insert hyperlink	Add hyperlinks to objects in drawings	Of questionable use, except in specialized applications	"Hyper objects" in this chapter

Feature	Description	Comments	Where You Can Find More Info
Password protection (not in AutoCAD LT)	Requires a password in order to open a drawing	Useful for limiting access to sensitive DWG or DWF files	"The Drawing Protection Racket" in this chapter
Digital signatures	Provide electronic confirmation that someone has approved a particular version of a particular drawing	Requires an account with a digital certificate provider; new technology, so look before you leap — and talk to your attorney first	"The Drawing Protection Racket" in this chapter

Sending Strategies

E-mail and FTP (File Transfer Protocol) have largely replaced blueline prints, overnight delivery, floppies, and higher-capacity disks as the standard means of exchanging drawings. Some companies even use specially designed Web-based services, such as Autodesk's Buzzsaw, as a repository for project drawings from all the companies working on a particular project. Whether you're exchanging drawings in order to reuse CAD objects or simply to make hard-copy plots of someone else's drawings, you need to be comfortable sending and receiving drawings electronically.

Sending and receiving DWG files doesn't differ much from sending and receiving other kinds of files, except for the following:

✔ **DWG files tend to be bigger than word processing documents and spreadsheets.** Consequently, you may need to invest in a faster Internet connection. For instance, if you still rely on dialup modem access to the Internet, you may want to consider upgrading to broadband access, such as DSL or cable.

✔ **You can easily forget to include all the dependent files.** I tell you in the next section how to make sure that you send all the necessary files — and how to pester the people who don't send you all their necessary files.

✔ **It's often not completely obvious how to plot what you receive.** Read Chapter 16 and the "Bad reception?" section later in this chapter to solve plotting puzzles.

Whenever you send DWG files together, follow the Golden Exchange Rule: "Send files unto others as you would have them sent unto you." That means sending all the dependent files along with the main DWG files, sending plotting support files (CTB or STB files — see Chapter 16), and including a description of what you're sending. And ask the recipient to try opening the drawings you sent right away so you both have more time to respond if there's any problem.

Send it with ETRANSMIT

Many people naively assume that an AutoCAD drawing is always contained in a single DWG file, but that's often not the case. Each drawing file created in AutoCAD can contain references to other kinds of files, the most important of which are described in Table 20-2. Thus, before you start exchanging drawings via e-mail or FTP, you need a procedure for assembling the drawings with all their dependent files.

Table 20-2	Other Kinds of Files That DWG Files Commonly Reference		
Description	*File Types*	*Consequences If Missing*	*Explained In*
Custom font files	SHX, TTF	AutoCAD substitutes another font	Chapter 13
Other drawings (xrefs)	DWG, DGN, DWF, DWFx, PDF	Stuff in the main drawing disappears	Chapter 18
Raster graphics files	JPG, PCX, TIF, and so on	Stuff in the drawing disappears	Chapter 18
Plot style tables	CTB, STB	Lineweights and other plotted effects won't look right when you plot the drawing	Chapter 16

As you can see from the table, the consequences of not including a custom font aren't that dire: The recipient will still see your text, but the font will be different. Of course, the new font may look odd or cause text spacing problems within the drawing. If, on the other hand, you forget to send xrefs or raster graphics that are attached to your main drawing, the objects contained on those attached files simply will be gone when the recipient opens your drawing. Not good!

Table 20-2 doesn't exhaust the types of files that your DWG files might refer to. Custom plotter settings (such as custom paper sizes) may reside in PC3 or PMP files. If you use sheet sets, a DST file contains information about the sheet structure. An FMP file controls some aspects of font mapping. Look up *sheet sets* and the *FONTALT* and *FONTMAP system variables* in the AutoCAD online help system for detailed information.

Rapid eTransmit

Fortunately, AutoCAD's ETRANSMIT command pulls together all the files that your main DWG file depends on. Follow these steps to assemble a drawing with all its dependent files by using ETRANSMIT:

1. **Open the drawing that you want to run ETRANSMIT on.**

 If the drawing is already open, save it. ETRANSMIT requires that any changes to the drawing be saved before you proceed.

2. **Click the Application button and choose Send.**

 The Create Transmittal dialog box appears, as shown in Figure 20-1.

Figure 20-1:
Rapid
eTransmit.

3. **On the Files Tree or Files Table tab, remove the check mark next to any file that you want ETRANMSIT *not* to copy with the main drawing.**

 Unless you have assigned custom font mapping, you can omit the Acad. fmp file.

4. **Select a transmittal setup from the list.**

 Transmittal setups contain settings that control how ETRANSMIT processes the drawings and creates the transmittal package. Click the Transmittal Setups button to create new or modify existing setups. The default Standard transmittal setup works fine for many purposes, except that you probably want to turn on the Include Fonts setting, as described in the next paragraph. In any case, you should view the settings (click the Modify button) just to see what options you can change if you need to later.

 If you want AutoCAD to include SHX and TTF font files, including any custom fonts that you're using, you must turn on the Include Fonts setting in the transmittal setup. (Click Transmittal Setups, click Modify, and check the Include Fonts check box.) Note, however, that many SHX and TTF files are custom fonts, which work like licensed software. Sending them to others is just like sharing your AutoCAD program CD with others. No, I don't mean that it's easy and fun; I mean that it's illegal and unethical. Before you send a custom font file to someone else, find out the licensing restrictions on the font and work within them.

5. **Click the View Report button.**

 You see a report listing the files that ETRANSMIT will copy, along with warnings about any files that it can't locate.

6. **Review the report and make sure that ETRANSMIT was able to find all the files.**

7. **Click OK.**

 ETRANMSIT displays a file dialog box so that you can specify the name and location of the transmittal package.

8. **Click Save.**

 ETRANSMIT creates the transmittal package (which is a Zip file by default). Zipping creates a single, tidy package of all your DWG, raster image, plot style table, and font files.

AutoCAD 2010's ETRANSMIT command has a new option hidden away in the Transmittal Setups dialog box that lets you include *unloaded* reference files in the package. As I explain in Chapter 18, you can unload an external reference so you can't see it, which can make editing the drawing easier. However, prior to AutoCAD 2010, you had to reload the external reference, or it would be skipped by eTransmit.

FTP for you and me

FTP, or *File Transfer Protocol,* is a simple but robust protocol for copying files over the Internet. A computer that's connected to the Internet can act as an FTP *server,* which means that part of its hard disk is accessible over the Internet. The person who configures the FTP server can place restrictions so that only people who enter a particular logon name and password can see and download files. FTP overcomes the file size limitations that often occur with e-mail.

Because of all these FTP benefits, it's increasingly common for people at larger companies to place drawing files on their company's FTP site and tell you to go get them. This approach relieves them of having to e-mail you the files, and relieves you of waiting for that 10MB e-mail download when you least expected it.

In most cases, the person making the files available to you via FTP will send you a Uniform Resource Locator (URL) that looks like a Web page address, except that it starts with `ftp://` instead of `http://`. If you open your Web browser and enter the FTP URL into the address field, the browser connects to the FTP site, asks you for a location and name to use for the file when it gets copied to your system, and begins downloading the file. If the FTP site uses password protection, you'll have to enter a logon name and password first.

If you want fancier FTP download options, you can use an FTP utility such as CuteFTP (`www.cuteftp.com`).

Bad reception?

Other sections in this chapter focus on sending files to others. What happens when you're on the receiving end? Not everyone will be as conscientious as you are about following the Golden Exchange Rule. You'll receive drawings with missing dependent files and no information or support files for plotting.

When you receive an e-mail message or FTP download containing drawings (zipped, I hope!), copy the file to a new folder on your hard disk or a network disk and unzip the files.

Check at least a few of the drawings in the package to make sure that all the xrefs, fonts, and raster image files were included. You can perform this check by opening each main drawing in that folder. After you open each file, press the F2 key to view the AutoCAD text window and look for missing font and xref error messages of the following sort:

```
Substituting [simplex.shx] for [helv.shx].
Resolve Xref "GRID": C:\Here\There\Nowhere\grid.dwg
Can't find C:\Here\There\Nowhere\grid.dwg
```

A `Substituting . . .` message indicates that AutoCAD couldn't find a font and is substituting a different font for it. A `Can't find . . .` message indicates that AutoCAD couldn't locate an xref. Any missing raster files appear as rectangular boxes with the names of the image files inside the rectangles. Missing DWFs appear as an error message at the insertion point. Alternatively, you can open the External References palette, which reveals any missing referenced files. (See Chapter 18 for details.)

Write down each missing file and then tell the sender to get on the ball (in a nice way, of course) and send you the missing pieces. While you're at it, tell that person to buy this book and read this chapter! Or buy it for them yourself!

If you receive drawings with custom TrueType font files (files whose extensions are TTF), you must install those files in Windows (not AutoCAD) before Windows and AutoCAD will recognize them. Refer to your Windows version's online help for instructions on installing fonts.

Help from the Reference Manager

In Chapter 18, I warn you about the complications of xref paths and the potential perils of AutoCAD not being able to locate xrefs if you move project folders around or transfer drawings to or from someone else. A similar danger exists for raster image files and DWF, DGN, and (new in AutoCAD 2010) PDF underlays (Chapter 18) and for font files (Chapter 13). The ETRANSMIT command, described earlier in this chapter, does a good job of gathering dependent xrefs, raster files, and font files, but it can't gather what AutoCAD can't locate.

AutoCAD's Reference Manager utility (not available to LT users) is a real life-saver if you find yourself suffering from file path perils — whether they occur in your own company or when sending files to or receiving them from others.

Reference Manager is a separate program, not a command inside AutoCAD. Follow these steps to launch the utility from your Windows desktop:

1. **Choose Start⇨All Programs⇨Autodesk⇨AutoCAD 2010⇨Reference Manager.**

 The Reference Manager program opens, as shown in Figure 20-2.

Figure 20-2:
The
Reference
Manager.

2. **Click the Add Drawings button to add one or more DWG files to the Drawings pane on the left.**

 Navigate to the folder that contains the drawings you want to send, select them, and click Open.

3. **In the Reference Manager - Add Xrefs dialog box, choose Add All Xrefs Automatically Regardless of Nesting Level.**

 The Reference Manager processes the drawings and displays all referenced objects in its right pane.

4. **Click Export Report to create a text report listing all the dependent files and their paths, or click Edit Selected Paths to modify paths of selected reference files.**

 Click the Help button in Reference Manager to find out more about the utility's capabilities.

If you always keep parent and child DWG files in the same folder — the simplest approach to dealing with xref paths — you probably won't need to use the Reference Manager.

Design Web Format — Not Just for the Web

Earlier in this chapter, I explain how you can exchange drawings via e-mail and FTP. That's all the Internet connectivity that many AutoCAD users need, but if you're curious about connecting drawings to the Web or sharing drawings with people who don't have AutoCAD, this section is for you.

The AutoCAD Web features are built on three pieces of technology:

- ✔ A special "lightweight" drawing format called DWF that Autodesk originally developed especially for putting drawings on the Web.

- ✔ An updated, XML-compliant version of the DWF format called DWFx that can be viewed using the Microsoft XPS Viewer that's built into Windows Vista or available as a plug-in for Windows XP.

- ✔ A free program from Autodesk called Autodesk Design Review 2010 that enables anyone to view and print DWF files without having AutoCAD.

All about DWF and DWFx

The AutoCAD DWG format works well for storing drawing information on local and network disks, but the high precision and large number of object properties that AutoCAD uses make for comparatively large files.

To overcome this size problem and encourage people to publish drawings on the Web, Autodesk developed an alternative lightweight vector format for representing AutoCAD drawings: DWF (Design Web Format). A DWF file is a more compact representation of a DWG file. DWF uses less space — and less transfer time over the Web and e-mail — because it's less precise and doesn't have all the information that's in the DWG file.

DWFx is a version of regular DWF that's compliant with Microsoft's XML Paper Specification (or XPS for short — had your fill of alphabet soup yet?). Everything about DWF in this chapter also applies to DWFx. The DWFFORMAT command determines whether the PUBLISH, 3DDWF, and EXPORT commands output to DWF or DWFx. If this sounds like something that might be important in your work, look up *DWFFORMAT* in the online help system. Windows Vista includes an XPS Viewer, and the long and the short of this feature is that drawings plotted to DWFx can be viewed automatically in Windows Vista, without AutoCAD or any special viewing software.

You can create DWF or DWFx files from your drawings and send those files to people who don't have AutoCAD. Your recipients can view and plot the DWF files after they download the free Autodesk Design Review program, which is available on Autodesk's Web site, www.autodesk.com.

DWFs and DWFxs can be used just like external references. Here's one more file type — and one more reason — to use Reference Manager or ETRANSMIT to package up your drawings before you send them out. For more on DWF underlays, see Chapter 18.

ePlot, not replot

A DWF file captures a single, plotted view of your drawing, so, unlike a DWG file, it can provide a clear-cut snapshot of what you want to see on paper. With a DWG file, on the other hand, you have to provide lots of information to other people — drawing view, scale, plot style settings, and so on — in order for them to get the same plotting results that you did.

Potential ePlotting scenarios include the following:

✔ Architects and other consultants on a building project periodically upload DWF files to the project Web site. Architects and engineers with some minimal CAD knowledge can review the drawings on-screen and create their own hard-copy plots, if necessary. Principals and clients who don't want anything to do with CAD, or even with computers, can have their employees create hard-copy plots for them to examine.

✔ When Internet-savvy people need hard-copy prints of your drawings, you e-mail a zipped file containing DWF files, along with the URL for Autodesk DWF Viewer and simple instructions for creating plots from the DWF files. (Be ready to walk them through the process by phone the first time or two to reduce anxiety on everyone's part.)

✔ A CAD plotting service bureau encourages its customers to send DWF files instead of DWG files for plotting. The DWF files are much smaller and require less intervention on the part of the service bureau's employees.

Autodesk hopes to establish ePlot and the DWF/DWFx format as a standard for CAD documents similar to what Adobe's PDF has become for word processing documents. It remains to be seen whether ePlotting will become a popular way to generate hard-copy output (although DWFx will certainly push it that way — at least for Vista users). In particular, many people outside CAD-using companies don't have access to large-format plotters. They're limited to 8-1/2 x 11-inch — or, at best, 11 x 17-inch — reduced-size check plots. Consequently, many people won't be able to plot your DWF files to scale and may not even be able to plot them large enough to read everything.

Don't be afraid to try ePlotting with colleagues inside or outside your company, but don't become too dependent on it until you see whether the rest of the CAD world shares your enthusiasm. Otherwise, you risk becoming the only one who's willing to use your DWF files for plotting — in which case, the next version of the feature will be called mePlot.

Making DWFs with ePlot

As I describe in the preceding section, AutoCAD treats DWF files like electronic plots, or *ePlots*. You create a DWF file from the current drawing just as if you were plotting it to a piece of paper, as I describe in Chapter 16.

The only difference is that, in the Plot dialog box's Printer/Plotter area, you choose one of two plotter configurations: `DWF6 ePlot.pc3` or `DWFx ePlot (XPS Compatible).pc3`, as shown in Figure 20-3. When you do so, AutoCAD automatically turns on the Plot to File setting. Then, when you click OK to generate the ePlot, AutoCAD displays a dialog box in which you specify a filename and location for the DWF file that gets created. The location can be a folder on a hard drive or a Web server.

When you make DWFs with ePlot, pay particular attention to the Scale setting in the Plot Scale area. If you're creating a DWF simply for viewing in a browser, you can select the Fit to Paper check box rather than worry about a specific plot scale. If you want to enable others to plot your DWF file to scale, as described earlier in this chapter, you need to choose the desired plot scale factor. Chapter 16 describes how to choose an appropriate plot scale factor.

Figure 20-3: "Look ma, no paper!" Plotting to a DWF file.

Making DWFs (or plots) with PUBLISH

The ePlot method of creating DWF files described in the previous section works fine for single drawings. But if you want to create DWF files for a lot of drawings or plot a bunch of drawings the good ol' fashioned way (on paper, that is), you can use the Publish dialog box, as shown in Figure 20-4, to speed the process.

AutoCAD 2010 adds PDF output as a PUBLISH output option. You access PUBLISH from the AutoCAD 2010 Application Menu. Click the Application button, choose Print *(not Publish!),* and then Batch Plot.

Figure 20-4:
Hot off the
presses:
AutoCAD's
Publish
dialog box.

Although the Publish dialog box is wired to support DWF, DWFx, and PDF as well as regular (paper) plotting, for now, more people are likely to use it for paper plotting. (An alternative use is creating plot files to send to a plotting service bureau.) But if you do decide to go into large-scale DWF publishing, including multisheet DWF or PDF files, use the Publish dialog box, as shown in the following steps:

1. **Click the Application button, choose Print, and then Batch Plot.**

 The Publish dialog box appears (refer to Figure 20-4). The dialog box lists all tabs (model and paper space layouts) of the current drawing for plotting. The Publish dialog box refers to each tab as a *sheet*.

2. **Click the buttons above the sheet list to preview any sheet, add sheets from other drawings, remove sheets from the to-be-plotted list, or rearrange the plotting order.**

 With the additional buttons, you can save and recall lists of sheets. See Step 4 for more information.

3. **After you select the sheets that you want to plot, specify whether you want to plot them to an actual plotter or plot (PLT) file or to a DWF/ DWFx or PDF file.**

 You can select a specific plotter configuration for each sheet by choosing a Page Setup in the sheet list. See Chapter 16 for more information about page setups.

4. **Click the Publish Options button to display a dialog box containing additional settings.**

 Most of these options are of concern only if you're creating DWF/DWFx or PDF files. The one exception is Default Output Directory, which also applies to creating plot (PLT) files.

5. **If you anticipate having to publish the same group of drawings again, click the Save Sheet List button to save the current drawings and settings list.**

6. **Click the Publish button to start the process.**

Don't confuse the PUBLISH command with the little-used PUBLISHTOWEB command. (Don't worry about starting it accidentally; unless you're working in the AutoCAD Classic workspace, you have to type the whole command name to start this command.) The PUBLISH command creates sets of DWF, DWFx, or PDF files, plot files, or actual plots. The PUBLISHTOWEB Wizard creates a Web page containing images of your drawings. The results of this wizard won't put any Web designers or programmers out of work, but you can use it to create primitive Web page paste-ups of your drawings. See *PUBLISHTOWEB command* in the AutoCAD online help system if you want to give it a whirl.

Hyper objects

No Web file format would be complete without hyperlinks, and DWF has those, too. You can attach a hyperlink to any drawing object in AutoCAD, not just to a text string. As you pass the crosshairs over an object with a hyperlink, the cursor changes from the ordinary pointer to a globe and two links of a chain (as in "World Wide Web" and "link," not "world-wide chain gang"). Right-click the object and select the Hyperlink option from the menu, which opens your browser and navigates to the URL that's attached to the object. If you create a DWF file that includes objects with hyperlinks, Autodesk Design Review 2010 displays them in the DWF file so that you can click to navigate to them.

Hyperlinks on objects are a clever trick, but they're of limited practical value in most DWG and DWF files:

- The drawing images are so small that it's difficult to distinguish the hyperlink on one object from the hyperlink on another object.

- Most people aren't used to associating hyperlinks with individual lines and other objects. The interface is likely to leave them perplexed.

If you want to experiment with hyperlinks on objects, look up *HYPERLINK command, about* in the online help system.

Autodesk Design Review 2010

After you create DWF files, whether with ePlot or PUBLISH, you or the recipient of your DWF files can use Autodesk Design Review to view and print them. (Autodesk Design Review 2010, the current release, is a free viewer from Autodesk.) If you send DWFs to people without AutoCAD, they can download Design Review from Autodesk's Web page, www.autodesk.com.

When you install AutoCAD 2010, the setup program, by default, installs Autodesk Design Review 2010 as well. From your Windows desktop, choose Start⇨All Programs⇨Autodesk⇨Autodesk Design Review 2010 — or simply double-click a DWF file in Windows Explorer to launch the viewer.

The Drawing Protection Racket

Whether you're sending DWG or DWF files, you may be concerned about their misuse (that is, by the wrong people or for the wrong purposes); abuse (for example, modification without your consent); or reuse (on other projects or by other people without due compensation to you). AutoCAD has two features for securing your drawings when you send them to others:

✔ **Password protection** enables you to lock a DWG or DWF file so that only those who type the password that you've specified can open, insert, or xref it (not available in AutoCAD LT).

Add password protection to drawings only when you really need it:

- If you forget the password, *you* can no longer open the drawing. Neither AutoCAD nor Autodesk has any magical way to extract the password or unlock the drawing.

- After you password-protect a drawing, others can't insert the drawing as a block or attach it as an xref.

If you're using a password, you probably should do it on a *copy* of the drawing that you send; keep an *unprotected* version for yourself.

✔ A **digital signature** is a high-tech way to add an electronic marker to a DWG file that verifies that someone approved the drawing. You must first get an account with a digital certificate provider, who serves to authenticate you and your computer. Of course, for this feature to be useful, you need to send drawings to someone who wants to receive digitally authenticated drawings from you (or vice versa) and who has the technological savvy to deal with digital certificates. For more information, see *overview of digital signatures* in the AutoCAD online help system.

To activate either of these options for the current drawing, open the Application Menu, choose Save As, and then choose AutoCAD Drawing to display the Save Drawing As dialog box; then choose Tools⇨Security Options to display the Security Options dialog box before you save the file. If you want to add a digital signature and you have a digital ID from a certificate provider, enter your information on the Digital Signature tab of the Security Options dialog box. If you want to add a password to the current drawing, just type it in the text field on the Password tab of the Security Options dialog box.

After you password-protect and save a DWG file, anyone who tries to open, insert, or xref it will see a dialog box similar to the one shown in Figure 20-5.

To password-protect a DWF file, use the PUBLISH command and click the Publish Options button in the Publish dialog box. In the General DWF options section, click Disabled and choose Specify Password, then type your secret word into the Password field.

Although electronic security features, such as the ones described in this section, can be useful as part of a strategy to protect your work from misuse, they're not a substitute for communicating clearly, preferably in the form of written contracts, what constitutes appropriate use of drawings that you send to or receive from others.

Password	
Enter password to open drawing:	
G:\Top secret baby.dwg	
••••••••	
OK	Cancel

Figure 20-5:
Password,
please.

Part V
The Part of Tens

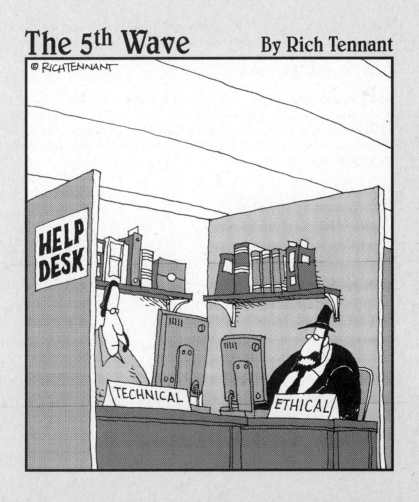

The 5th Wave By Rich Tennant

HELP DESK

TECHNICAL ETHICAL

In this part . . .

*T*ens sounds a lot like *tense,* and *tense* is how AutoCAD may make you feel sometimes. *Tens* also may remind you of the metric system, and if you're not used to it, that may also make you feel tense. But never fear — help is on the way! A Top Ten List is a good way to quickly spot the best — or the worst — of almost anything, AutoCAD included. This Part of Tens features lists that help you understand some of the nuts and bolts that make AutoCAD work, figure out whether you should be using AutoCAD or AutoCAD LT, and hunt for the most valuable AutoCAD resources.

Chapter 21

Ten Great AutoCAD Resources

Much as I want to make a claim to the contrary, you probably *do* need just a teensy bit more than this book and a copy of the software to reach the very highest peaks of AutoCAD mastery! This chapter lists ten likely suspects if you want to find out more about your favorite software program.

Autodesk's My Feedback

Interested in helping shape future versions of AutoCAD? If so, visit Autodesk's My Feedback Portal (http://myfeedback.autodesk.com) and sign up. In return for small — or sometimes considerable — time commitments, you can contribute your ideas to the AutoCAD Futures group or apply to beta test the next release of AutoCAD.

Autodesk's Discussion Groups

Although there are still some independent, newsreader-based discussion groups out there, the majority of the AutoCAD action nowadays happens on Autodesk's own moderated discussion groups. These are user-to-user groups, but even so, you frequently see Autodesk employees jumping in to answer questions in their areas of expertise — sometimes on their own time!

To see what's there, point your browser to www.autodesk.com/discussion. There are product-based discussion groups for AutoCAD and AutoCAD LT.

Autodesk's Own Bloggers

Several of Autodesk's employees run their own blogs through the company's servers, and they're chockablock with tips, techniques, and some occasionally highly entertaining digressions. For a list of all Autodesk's

blogs, go to `www.autodesk.com/blogs`. The AutoCAD-based blogs I highly recommend are Shaan Hurley's Between the Lines, Heidi Hewitt's AutoCAD Insider, and Lynn Allen's blog (that's what it's called, honest!).

The World Wide (CAD) Web

I'm reluctant to list any specific sites; I just went looking for an old favorite, and it's not there any more. Your search engine will be your best friend here. Apart from Autodesk's own Web presence, there are thousands upon thousands of other sites scattered around the world. Search on *AutoCAD tutorials* for online exercises, or try *AutoCAD blogs* for some independent views and opinions as well as tips and tricks for using AutoCAD.

Autodesk University

Autodesk University is an annual event, sponsored by Autodesk, that usually runs for four or five days in the late autumn. For the last few years, the location has alternated between Orlando, Florida, and Las Vegas. The days are filled with educational sessions in a dozen or more different disciplines, and the nights are filled with socializing and taking in the local attractions. Check out `http://au.autodesk.com` to find out how to schmooze like a pro and come home a guru!

Your Local ATC

Autodesk's Authorized Training Centers, or ATCs, are located around the world in both private institutions and public colleges and institutes. At an ATC, you attend scheduled, instructor-led classes where you learn AutoCAD from the ground up. Courses are designed for rank beginners or experienced users who want to learn the latest customization techniques. To find the location of your nearest ATC, browse to `www.autodesk.com/atc`.

Your Local User Group

AutoCAD has had an incredibly loyal following in the quarter-century since its initial release. There are many reasons for this, but one of the main ones was the especially enthusiastic individuals who would arrange to meet up one evening a month and talk about what they'd discovered they could do with AutoCAD. Those folks are still out there — although some are a bit

grayer and more wrinkled than they used to be — and they still love to get together and talk about AutoCAD. And most are especially welcoming to newcomers! My own local group, the Vancouver AutoCAD Users Society (`www.vaus.org`), happens to be the oldest user group in existence, and its newsletter grew and grew until it became *Cadalyst* magazine! To find a nearby group, enter **"AutoCAD user group"** and your city in your browser's search box.

AUGI

AUGI (the acronym for Autodesk User Groups International) is the umbrella organization for the global user group community. You don't even have to belong to a group to participate — individuals can join too, and membership is free. AUGI is probably best known for the annual wish list it presents to Autodesk; the list is compiled from requests from members for changes or new features in AutoCAD. It's often the case that top wish list items find their way into new releases of AutoCAD, so here's another place where you can help to shape future releases. Browse to `www.augi.com` to find out more.

Books

Although I want to fill you in on *all* the wonders of AutoCAD, there's only so much I can do in a 400-page book. As I explain in the introduction, I simply don't have the space to cover things like 3D and customization (not that either of those are of much use to AutoCAD LT users anyway). There are dozens of books on AutoCAD — just go to `www.amazon.com` and search on *AutoCAD* if you don't believe me! For a more comprehensive look at AutoCAD (which a thousand pages allows!), have a gander at Ellen Finkelstein's *AutoCAD 2009 and AutoCAD LT 2009 Bible.* For an introduction to 3D modeling in AutoCAD, pick up Lee Ambrosius's *AutoCAD 2008 3D Modeling Workbook For Dummies.* Both titles are published by Wiley Publishing, Inc.

Magazines

There used to be many more CAD magazines than there are now; in North America, AutoCAD alone had three periodicals devoted to it: *Cadalyst, Cadence,* and *AutoCAD User. Cadalyst* is the last one standing, and it no longer covers AutoCAD exclusively, but it's still worth a look. You can get a taste of the magazine's content and find out how to subscribe at `www.cadalyst.com`.

Chapter 22

Ten Differences between AutoCAD and AutoCAD LT

· ·

 This book is aimed at users of both the full version of AutoCAD and AutoCAD LT. Throughout the text, you can find icons in the margin that highlight places in my descriptions or steps that are significantly different between the two versions.

Rather than make you go through the entire text (not that it wouldn't be a highly rewarding task!) looking for tidbits of information, in this chapter, I gather the ten most significant differences between the two versions.

Price

Most important to many people — especially if you exclusively work in 2D drafting and don't see a need to spend a lot of time learning AutoCAD's customization languages — is the much lower cost of AutoCAD LT. You can buy either version online (visit www.autodesk.com and click Purchase, then Shop Online) and in the first month of 2009, AutoCAD listed at $3,995 and AutoCAD LT at $1,200.

3D Abilities

This may be the most significant difference for some users. If you want to model in 3D, you have no choice but to use the full version. In AutoCAD LT, you can open and view 3D models created in the full version of AutoCAD, but you can't edit them or create new ones. The only 3D construction you can do in AutoCAD LT is to apply a thickness property to linework. (In AutoCAD, thickness means *perpendicular* to the drawing plane; don't confuse it with width, which applies to objects *on* the drawing plane.)

And even if you can open 3D models from the full version in AutoCAD LT, it's not easy to view them. There are only a limited number of preset viewing positions, unlike the full version where you can rotate or orbit around your model to your heart's content.

Finally, because AutoCAD LT is really a 2D drafting program, there are no visualization or presentation capabilities, unlike the full program which has several built-in visual styles like Conceptual and Realistic as well as a humongous materials library for rendering models.

Customization Options

This one is also a biggie for many people. Talk to seasoned AutoCAD users at work or your local user group, and you'll find that the key to happiness is being able to customize AutoCAD so it does what they want with the minimum amount of time or effort. The full version of AutoCAD supports a number of *Application Programming Interfaces, or APIs.* These include AutoCAD's very own programming language — AutoLISP — and its marginally friendlier sibling Visual LISP, ActiveX Automation, Visual Basic for Applications, or VBA, and compiled language programming using ObjectARX or Microsoft's .NET framework.

Although you can do fairly simple customization in AutoCAD LT — for example, creating or modifying toolbars, writing scripts, or using custom hatch patterns or linetypes — none of the higher-level programming described in the preceding paragraph is possible in LT.

Express Tools

The Express Tools are a set of officially unsupported but nevertheless pretty reliable "bonus" commands. The Express Tools are an optional item when you install AutoCAD, but I highly recommend you choose to include them. There are additional drawing and editing commands, a far more elaborate hatch routine than the regular HATCH command, and commands for working with blocks and xrefs, text, dimensions, and layouts.

Because most of the Express Tools are written using the APIs mentioned in the earlier "Customization Options" section, they won't work in AutoCAD LT. On the positive side, sometimes a few of the Express Tools are moved into the core of the AutoCAD executable; because they're not using one of those APIs I mention earlier, they can be made available to AutoCAD LT. For example, AutoCAD LT now includes a number of layer tools that had previously been Express Tools.

Sheet Sets

Sheet sets provide a way of packaging drawing sets for distribution and plotting or publishing. A typical AutoCAD project can include dozens of drawings, scores of sheets, lots of layouts, copious cross-drawing references, and more than a few people working on those components at once. How do you create, manage, update, plot, and generally keep a handle on all that stuff without going crazy? The answer is AutoCAD's sheet sets feature.

Sheet sets allow projects to be managed automatically; drawings get numbered correctly, title-block information is entered correctly, and sheet indexes can be created with the click of a button.

Sheet sets, introduced in AutoCAD 2005, are not included in AutoCAD LT.

Standards Checking

Like sheet sets, standards checking is deemed by Autodesk to fall in the realm of the big players who are far likelier to be using the full version of AutoCAD rather than AutoCAD LT. With standards checking, you configure a DWS file (that is, a DWG file set up with your standard layers, text and dimension styles, layouts, and so forth), and then compare your current drawing, or drawings done by outside consultants, with that DWS file to ensure they conform to your office standards.

External References

As I hypothesize in Chapter 18, Autodesk assumes that AutoCAD LT users typically work on small projects, either in very small teams or on their own. So while being able to reference external drawings is handy at times, that type of user hardly needs the same functionality as drafters in huge corporations working on mega-projects with just-in-time deadlines.

AutoCAD LT users may not have AutoCAD's full suite of external reference tools at their fingertips, but a few more of those external reference tools have made their way into the junior program. AutoCAD LT 2010 users can now open external references directly with the XOPEN command. And they can now use the REFEDIT command to edit the reference file from within the host drawing. Users can also be automatically notified when a drawing they're referencing is modified by someone else.

Data Extraction

As I explain in Chapter 17, attributes are variable text strings that you create as part of a block definition. The data in the attributes can be edited or extracted easily in regular AutoCAD, and nearly as easily in AutoCAD LT (AutoCAD LT lacks the full version's Data Extraction Wizard which extracts information from objects and attributed or non-attributed blocks.) If being able to use *all* the data in your AutoCAD drawings, choosing the full version would be a better bet.

AutoCAD LT 2010 has gained both the Enhanced Attribute Editor (the EATTEDIT command opens this dialog box) and the Block Attribute Manager (the BATTMAN command — insert your own joke here!) from its senior sibling. I explain EATTEDIT in Chapter 17 but refer you to the online help index for BATTMAN.

MLINE versus DLINE

Here's a case where AutoCAD LT beats its big sibling! AutoCAD (full version) includes an extremely unwieldy command called MLINE for drawing multiple lines. You can draw multiple parallel lines in the same way you pick points for the LINE command, but multilines are unintuitive to configure and pretty darned difficult to edit.

AutoCAD LT doesn't have MLINE, but it does have a different command called DLINE. DLINE (as in Double LINE) may not draw more than two parallel lines, and it can't add colored fills, but it's logical to use and much easier to edit. And sorry, AutoCAD users (I've been waiting to write that for the whole book!), but you don't have DLINE.

Reference Manager

Reference Manager is a free-standing program, not part of AutoCAD or AutoCAD LT. If you have the full version installed, you'll find Reference Manager on the Windows Start menu. Reference Manager helps you make sure that any dependent files (for example, font files, images, or xrefs) are included when you ship a set of files anywhere. There's no technical reason why AutoCAD LT shouldn't include the Reference Manager. But it doesn't.

Chapter 23

Ten System Variables to Make Your Life Easier

*S*ystem variables are settings that AutoCAD checks before it decides how to do something. For example, if you set the system variable SAVETIME to 10, AutoCAD automatically saves your drawing file every ten minutes; if you set SAVETIME to 60, the time between automatic saves is one hour. Hundreds of system variables control AutoCAD's operations.

To change the value of a system variable, just type its name at the AutoCAD command prompt and press Enter. AutoCAD displays the current value of the system variable setting and prompts for a new value. Press Enter to confirm the existing setting, or type a value and press Enter to change the setting.

Being able to change system variables by typing their names is a boon to power users and occasionally a necessity for everybody else. The only problem is finding or remembering what the names are. In most cases, you'll be told what system variable name you need to type — by me in this book or by the local AutoCAD guru in your office.

Here are the three kinds of system variables:

- ✓ **Those saved in the Windows Registry:** If you change this kind of system variable, it affects all drawings when you open them on your system, but not necessarily on other computers.

- ✓ **Those saved in the drawing:** If you change this kind of system variable, the change affects only the current drawing, but on any computer.

- ✓ **Those that aren't saved anywhere:** If you change this kind of system variable, the change lasts only for the current drawing session.

The System Variables section of the online help's Command Reference tells you which kind of system variable each one is. There are several hundred system variables, but understanding the ten listed in this chapter will go a long way to making you a happy CADster.

APERTURE

APERTURE controls how close the crosshairs must get to an object before an object snap marker displays (I discuss object snaps in Chapter 7). You can set APERTURE at the command line anywhere from 0 to 50 pixels, or you can set it in the Options dialog box by adjusting a slider to a maximum of 20 pixels. The initial value is 10, but I find 20 pixels is just about right for me. APERTURE is stored in the Windows registry.

DIMASSOC

DIMASSOC controls how AutoCAD's dimension objects are created (see Chapter 14 for dimensioning). When DIMASSOC is 0, AutoCAD creates exploded dimensions of separate lines, 2D solids, and text. You really don't want to work on DIMASSOC=0 drawings. When DIMASSOC=1, dimensions are referred to as *non-associative* — they're single objects, but they usually don't update if you change an object's size. When DIMASSOC=2 (the default), AutoCAD creates fully associative dimensions. You can set this value at the command line or select the Make New Dimensions Associative check box in Options⇨User Preferences. If you work with older drawings, you'll likely find that the DIMASSOC value is 1, which is the best that versions prior to AutoCAD 2002 could manage.

MENUBAR

When MENUBAR is 1, AutoCAD's traditional classic menu bar displays below the program title bar. If MENUBAR is set to 0 (the default) the menu bar doesn't display. MENUBAR is set automatically when you switch between the AutoCAD Classic and 2D Drafting & Annotation workspaces.

If you want training wheels while you get used to the Ribbon, display the classic menu bar. (I describe the differences between the traditional AutoCAD Classic and the newer Ribbon-based workspaces in Chapter 2.)

MIRRTEXT

You'll frequently want to build up a drawing by mirroring already-drawn components of it. That's what the MIRROR command does, but unfortunately, if text or dimensions are included in what you're mirroring, those end up being reversed as well. Using a mirror to read the text on your drawing is counterproductive, so you can invoke MIRRTEXT to fix things. When MIRRTEXT

is 0 (the default), text is mirrored with everything else; setting it to 1 means everything gets mirrored but the text reads the right way around. MIRRTEXT is stored in the drawing.

PICKBOX

The *pickbox* is the little square box that the crosshairs turn into when AutoCAD prompts you to select something. You control pickbox size by setting a value in pixels for the PICKBOX variable. The initial setting of PICKBOX is 3, which is fine for a lower screen resolution like 1024 x 768. But when you start running at higher resolutions — or when your hair is grayer, your face more wrinkled, and your vision not *quite* as acute as it once was, a higher setting might be more useful. My old laptop computer ran at 1600 x 1200 resolution, and I had to set PICKBOX to 5 to be able to use it effectively. My newer desktop runs at 1280 x 1024, and PICKBOX=4 is fine for that. But I've just acquired a new tablet PC that runs at 1400 x 1050, and I'm back to PICKBOX=5 for this one. As they say, your mileage may vary.

REMEMBERFOLDERS

Sometimes you don't want AutoCAD to start in the same Documents folder where every other program stores its files. Maybe you work on a number of projects and want a separate desktop icon for each to start in a particular folder. REMEMBERFOLDERS is your tool. By default, it's set to 1, which means it defaults to storing files in My Documents (just plain Documents in Windows Vista). Set it to 0, and it will open from and save to the folder you specify in your desktop icon when you start, and the last folder you visit as you work. REMEMBERFOLDERS is a permanent setting that's stored in the Windows registry (permanent, until you change it to something else).

ROLLOVERTIPS

ROLLOVERTIPS controls the tooltip-like message boxes you see when you hover the mouse pointer over objects in the drawing editor. If ROLLOVERTIPS is 1, mousing over your drawing displays a temporary panel showing the object type with its layer, color, and linetype.

You can get double-duty from this command. Not only can you key it into AutoCAD, but if you have a dog named Tips, you can use it to teach him a neat pet trick! ROLLOVERTIPS is stored in the Windows registry. (And believe it or not — and I'll bet you won't — there's another system variable called NOMUTT! Could that be AutoCAD-ese for BAD DOG TIPS!?)

TOOLTIPS

Tooltips themselves are the little text boxes that appear by default when you hover your mouse pointer over a toolbar or Ribbon button, or just about anywhere in a dialog box. Tooltips are useful when you're getting to know your way around, but when you have a sense of where things are, they can get in the way. By default, TOOLTIPS is set to 1, which means they display when you hover the pointer over something. Set TOOLTIPS to 0 if you don't want to see them again. The TOOLTIPS setting is stored in the system registry.

VISRETAIN

If you work with xrefs (refer to Chapter 18), you know the potential for competing layer properties. Sometimes you want your xref to look different from your current drawing so you can tell which is which. You can change layer colors of xrefs in the Layer Property Manager, but whether you have to do that every time you open a drawing with an attached xref depends on the setting of the VISRETAIN system variable. When VISRETAIN is set to 0, the layer properties in the xref take precedence, which means you *would* have to make those changes every time you opened the host drawing. When VISRETAIN is set to 1 (the default value), changes to layer properties you make in the host drawing remain intact every time you open that host drawing; however, those changes have no effect on the external file itself. The VISRETAIN value is stored in the current drawing.

VPROTATEASSOC

When working with layouts (see Chapter 5), sometimes it's handy to rotate a viewport so the model space objects inside the viewport fit on the sheet better. For example, maybe you draw elevator shafts, which (in my part of the world anyway) are vertical constructions. But your drawing sheet is probably oriented horizontally (that is, in *landscape* format). Before AutoCAD 2010, rotating a viewport left the model space geometry unrotated. You then had to switch to model space inside the viewport and change the user coordinate system or use the arcane DVIEW command's Twist option. The new VPROTATEASSOC variable lets you automatically rotate the view within the viewport as well as the viewport object itself.

This automatic rotation is the default behavior in AutoCAD 2010. If you want things to work the old way, set VPROTATEASSOC to 0.

Index

• **E** •

• U •

• V •